Researching the Vulnerable

A Guide to Sensitive Research Methods

Pranee Liamputtong

SAGE Publications
London • Thousand Oaks • New Delhi

SAGE Publications Ltd
1 Oliver's Yard
55 City Road
London EC1Y 1SP

SAGE Publications Inc.
2455 Teller Road
Thousand Oaks, California 91320

SAGE Publications India Pvt Ltd
B-42, Panchsheel Enclave
Post Box 4109
New Delhi 110 017

British Library Cataloguing in Publication data

A catalogue record for this book is available from the British Library

ISBN13 978 1 4129 1253 2
ISBN13 978 1 4129 1254 9 (pbk)

Library of Congress Control Number: 2006926739

Typeset by Newgen Imaging Systems (P) Ltd, Chennai, India
Printed in Great Britain by Athenaeum Press, Gateshead
Printed on paper from sustainable resources

To My parents, Yindee and Saeng Liamputtong
and
My sisters and brothers, Prapaporn, Somsri, Uaichai,
Chalita, Areeya, Patanee and Kajornsak,
who once were vulnerable identities in society

Contents

Preface   vi
Childhood Memory   viii

1 The Sensitive Researcher: Introduction to
   Researching Vulnerable People   1

2 Moral and Ethical Issues In Researching
   Vulnerable People   23

3 The Vulnerable Research Participants:
   Procedural Sensibilities   47

4 The Sensitive and Vulnerable Researcher   71

5 Traditional Interviewing Research Methods
   Appropriate for Researching Vulnerable People   95

6 Flexible and Collaborative Investigative Methods   118

7 Innovative and Alternative Research Methods in
   Consideration   140

8 (Re)Presentation of Vulnerable Voices – Writing
   Research Findings   164

   A Closing Word.... For Now   189

   Glossary   191
   References   195
   Index   240

Preface

This book was written partly for my own sake. I was born into a very poor family in Southern Thailand. Mum and Dad were the products of marginalised migrant populations in Thailand. My childhood was plagued with hunger, and discrimination from our neighbours. Very often, we did not have much food to eat. Due to our poverty, whatever I did would be seen as another poor bastard's attempts. Despite the fact that I did very well at schools, our neighbours would still refer me to as the 'bad girl' next door. I had to fight with better-off children in the neighbourhood to protect my younger siblings so that often, again, I was labelled as 'a bad girl'. I moved schools very frequently as my family moved around to find the next shelter to live in. Mum was a great believer in education. She strongly believed that education would be the only means to make her children's lives better and she insisted on me going to school. But I had to skip school very often, particularly on the days that my parents did not have the bus fare to give me. Now I am older and living in Australia. But living here as an immigrant, I again have to deal with certain discriminations. Covert racism and sexism are the things I come to grips with nowadays, not hunger anymore. I dedicate this book to my parents and siblings in acknowledgement of our marginalisation and vulnerability.

Putting aside my personal life, I argue that globally, there are so many vulnerable people out there in most societies. It will be difficult, or even impossible, for researchers to avoid carrying out research regarding vulnerable and marginalised populations within the 'moral discourse' of the postmodern world, as it is likely that these population groups will be confronted with more and more problems in their private and public lives as well as in their health and well-being. Despite the proliferation of qualitative books in the last decade or so, there is not a single book that discusses methodological and practical issues regarding research on vulnerable people. Clearly, there is a great need for a new book that will devote an entire discussion on how best to work with vulnerable and marginalised people in our research endeavours. This book is a response to that need.

In this book, I attempt to bring together salient issues for the conduct of research within vulnerable and marginalised groups of people. The task of undertaking research with the 'vulnerable' presents researchers with unique opportunities, and yet also, with dilemmas. I make no claim to be an expert on this subject matter, but hope that the book will provide some thought-provoking points so that research may proceed relatively well and yet be sensitive and ethical in approach. Although I assume that the readers of this book will have basic knowledge of qualitative research methods, I believe that it is necessary to include details of those methods which are more appropriate for conducting research with vulnerable groups. I intend to make the text more comprehensive and, therefore, both methodology and procedural sensibilities are included in this book.

The subject of the book is the methodology and procedures in researching vulnerable and hard-to-reach participants. The book will carry readers through a series of questions: Who am I researching? How will I find and reach them? How will I negotiate access? How should I conduct research which is sensitive to the needs of the people I am researching? What ethical considerations do I need to observe? What research method should I apply to ensure a successful research process? What is my role as researcher in relation to the researched? And how will I represent their voices?

In each chapter, I integrate the following features: chapter objectives, chapter summaries, case examples from empirical research, tutorial exercises, and sources of further reading. A glossary of terms is provided at the end of the text. Case examples are drawn from a wide selection of extended empirical studies in the United States, the United Kingdom, Australia and other English-speaking and non-English speaking countries.

The book is intended for researchers who are working with vulnerable people. It is also valuable for the training needs of postgraduate students who wish to undertake research with special groups of people, as it provides essential knowledge not only on the methods of data collection but also on salient issues that they need to know about if they wish to succeed in their research endeavours. The book will also be of value to researchers who work with vulnerable and marginalised people in Australia, the United Kingdom, the United States, Canada and other parts of the world.

Like any other publication, this book could not have been possible without assistance from others. First, I wish to express my gratitude to Patrick Brindle, the Senior Acquisition Editor of Sage in London, who believes in the value of this book, and who was so quick in giving me the contract to write it. I was so thrilled when I received an email from him to congratulate me. My utmost thanks go to Rosemary Oakes who endlessly edited the whole manuscript for me. Rosemary's assistance with this task is much appreciated. I thank a few friends who have been supportive of this book: Allan Kellehear, Jan Fook, Roberta Julian, Jan Morse and Lenore Manderson. Finally, I thank my children, Zoe Sanipreeya Rice and Emma Inturatana Rice, for putting up with my busy working time, which to them, is endless.

Pranee Liamputtong
Melbourne

Childhood Memory

Mum and Dad are away
working at the field
far away
to bring food home.

Mum says
'We would be back
before dark.
You
my oldest one
take care of your brothers and sisters.
We will be back
before dark'.

Darkness comes
I look out
for mum and dad
to return.
No sign.
No sound.
No mum and dad.

Darkness becomes darker
Sisters and brothers
start to cry
'We are hungry'.
They say.
'Wait
a bit longer'.
I say.
For there is
no food at home.

Darkness becomes darker and darker.
No sign
of mum and dad.
Shops are closing.
Street is very dark.
I look out
to the road
that leads to home.
No sign.
No sound.
No mum and dad.

Sisters and brothers
cry more.
'We are very hungry'
they say.
My heart
starts to beat louder
and
quicker.
Worry overwhelms me.
Mum and dad
Where are you?

Darkness becomes darker and darker and darker.
I close
the door, but
stand there
at the door.
Crying.

Then
there is
a sound.
A motorbike sound.
I stop breathing
Mum and dad.

I open the door
Mum is standing
out there.
I look up
on
her face.
Mum's face.

I can see
the sorrow
and
horrified thought
on
her face.

I hug mum
Mum hugs me
and
I cry
more
with mum.

Pranee Liamputtong
2006

1

The Sensitive Researcher: Introduction to Researching Vulnerable People

Chapter Objectives 1
Introduction 1
The 'Vulnerable' and Sensitive Research 2
The 'Vulnerable': Who are these Populations? 2
Sensitive Research 5
Qualitative Research: Researching Sensitive Issues 7
Theoretical Framework 9
Feminism and Feminist Research 9
Postmodernism 14
Conclusion 20

Starting research from the standpoint of the oppressed is valid because it is often the lives and experiences of oppressed people that provide significant insight and perspective. Complex human relations can become visible when research is started at the bottom of the social hierarchy.

(Hesse–Biber et al. 2004: 16)

The goal of research is 'that of discerning and uncovering the actual facts of [people's]' lives and experience, facts that have been hidden, inaccessible, suppressed, distorted, misunderstood, ignored'.

(DuBois 1985, cited in Bergen 1993: 200)

Chapter Objectives

In this chapter, readers will be introduced to the following issues:

- An preamble to the text.
- The concepts of the vulnerable population and sensitive research.
- The utilisation of qualitative research in researching vulnerable people.
- A theoretical framework including feminist research and postmodernism.

Introduction

It is almost inevitable in the present climate of our fractured world that sensitive researchers will have to engage with the vulnerable, disadvantaged and marginalised groups as it is likely that these population groups will be confronted with more and more problems to their health and well-being. Despite this, there have been few books that document and provide advice on how to go about performing sensitive research with vulnerable people. This, as Margaret Melrose (2002: 338) contends, may leave us, as sensitive researchers, 'feeling methodologically vulnerable, verging on the distressingly incapable, because of emotional and anxiety challenges, and thus ill equipped to deal with some of the issues that may arise in this context'.

In this book, I attempt to bring together numerous salient points for the conduct of research among vulnerable people. The task of undertaking research with vulnerable people presents researchers with unique opportunities, but also dilemmas (Pyett 2001; Melrose 2002; Dickson-Swift 2005). My discussions are by no means exhaustive, but I include issues pertaining to both the researched and the researcher. I hope that throughout this book, I will be able to provide some thought-provoking points so that our sensitive research may proceed well and that we may still retain ethical values in our approach.

The 'Vulnerable' and Sensitive Research

Social researchers increasingly undertake research on topics which are 'sensitive' as they are concerned with behaviour that is 'intimate, discreditable, or incriminating' (Renzetti and Lee 1993: ix). De Laine (2000: 67) refers to these sensitive areas as 'back regions'. Accordingly, back regions are 'private space, where personal activities take place and only "insiders" participate'. To a researcher, this 'private space' renders 'the need to be sensitive to the confidences and intimacies of others. One who intrudes into private space may pose a threat or risk to actors who fear exposure and sanctions' (see also Lee 1993; Wolcott 1995). De Laine's (2000) position situates neatly within the private space of the 'vulnerable' populations that I am discussing in this book.

The 'Vulnerable': Who are these Populations?

A precise definition of the 'vulnerable' is problematic as the concept is socially constructed (Moore and Miller 1999). Silva (1995: 15) suggests that a vulnerable person is an individual who experiences 'diminished autonomy due to physiological/psychological factors or status inequalities'. Based on Silva's definition, Moore and Miller (1999: 1034) contend that vulnerable individuals are people who 'lack the ability to make personal life choices, to make personal decisions, to maintain independence, and to self-determine'. Therefore, vulnerable individuals may 'experience real or potential harm and require special safeguards to ensure that their welfare and rights are protected'. Vulnerable populations, according to Jacquelyn Flaskerud and Betty Winslow (1998: 69), are 'social groups who have an increased relative risk or susceptibility to adverse health outcomes'. These vulnerable people then will include those who are 'impoverished, disenfranchised, and/or subject to discrimination, intolerance, subordination, and stigma' (Nyamathi 1998: 65). Based on these descriptions, we may include children, the elderly, ethnic communities, immigrants, sex workers, the homeless, gay men and lesbians and women (Nyamathi 1998: 65; Flaskerud and Winslow 1998; Russell 1999; Weston 2004). Adeline Nyamathi (1998: 65) also argues that historically, people suffering from chronic illness, the mentally ill and the caregivers of the chronically ill are also referred to as vulnerable populations.

The term 'vulnerable' is often used interchangeably with such terms as 'sensitive', the 'hard-to-reach', and 'hidden populations' (see Melrose 2002; Benoit et al. 2005). To Wayne Wiebel (1990: 6), the term 'hidden population' points to a group of people 'whose membership is not readily distinguished or enumerated based on existing knowledge and/or sampling capabilities'. Wiebel argues that this definition is particularly applicable to the hidden population in research relating to drug trends and patterns of drug use. We may extend Weber's group to include sex workers, bouncers, gang members and those engaging in so-called 'illegal' activities including burglaries. As Cecilia Benoit and others (2005: 264) suggest, sex workers are likely to be legally and socially labelled as ' "outcast"-the whore stigma typically permeates all aspects of a sex worker's life'. Similar to other stigmatised people (see Goffman 1963; Falk 2001; Melrose 2002), women who sell sex services are discriminised and rejected by other societal members. Due to their social stigma, sex workers tend to be isolated from the community and society. This often weakens any support and social networks they have, and, hence, increases their vulnerability to stress, depression and other ill health (see also Downe 1997; Wojcicki and Malala 2001; Melrose 2002).

Tammie Quest and Catherine Marco (2003: 1297) refer to the 'vulnerable' as people with 'social vulnerability'. They contend that some population groups, including children, the unemployed, the homeless, drug addicts, sex workers and ethnic and religious minority groups, face particular social vulnerability. When these groups of people are involved in research, they need special care from the researchers. According to Howard Stone (2003: 149), the 'vulnerable' are those who are 'likely to be susceptible to coercive or undue influence'. To Stone (2003), the 'vulnerable' include children, pregnant women, mentally disabled persons and those who are 'economically or educationally disadvantaged'. Samantha Punch (2002: 323) suggests that children are marginalised in an adult-dominated society, and as such they 'experience unequal power relations with adults' in their lives. In this sense, children are particularly vulnerable in society, especially when their situation involves abusive behaviour on the part of adults in their lives (see also Melrose 2002). Some groups may be vulnerable due to their so-called 'legal status'. Some immigrants in the United States, for example, are undocumented immigrants (see Birman 2005). Due to their illegal status, they are denied access to health and social services. Most of these groups live in poverty, and most are employed in seasonal cropping industries which are prone to poor health and bad living conditions.

Other vulnerable groups may also experience several factors that diminish their autonomy and marginalise their lives. Their vulnerabilities are then double, hence the terms 'doubly vulnerable persons' (Moore and Miller 1999: 1034), 'multi-faceted vulnerability' (Radley et al. 2005: 274) and 'overlapping marginality' (Madriz 1998: 7) have been coined. For example, these doubly vulnerable populations may include women who are single mothers and who come from ethnic backgrounds and live in poverty. Their social statuses as women, single mothers, ethnic persons and low-class individuals render them doubly vulnerable. This may also apply to low-income black men who sell sex on streets, gay men living with HIV/AIDS, homeless young Asian men living with mental health problems and drug dependents. Men who have sex with men, and intravenous drug users share hidden population characteristics. They, too, may become doubly stigmatised if they also engage in trade in sex (see also Romero-Daza et al. 2003).

In this book, I refer to the 'vulnerable', 'difficult-to-access' and 'hidden populations' of several social groups: homeless people, children and adolescents, older people, people with disabilities, chronically and terminally ill persons, women who have experienced violence such as rape and domestic violence, female and male sex workers, gay men and lesbians, indigenous populations, people from ethnic minority backgrounds, the mentally ill, illicit drug users and dealers, and those who are affected by stigmatised diseases such as mental illness and HIV/AIDS. The list is not exhaustive, but these groups of people are often hard to reach; they are the silent, the hidden, the deviant, the tabooed, the marginalised and hence 'invisible' populations in society (Stone 2003).

The reasons for their invisibility are many and may include their marginality, lack of opportunity to voice their concerns, fear of their identity being disrespected, stigma attached to their social conditions, heavy responsibilities and scepticism about being involved in research (Sieber 1992; Lee 1993; Polit and Hungler 1995; Silva 1995; Scambler and Scambler 1997; Moore and Miller 1999; Anderson and Hatton 2000; Pyett 2001; Dunne et al. 2002; Morse 2002; Wenger 2002; Stone 2003; Weston 2004; Benoit et al. 2005; Birman 2005; Fisher and Ragsdale 2005). Lynn Cannon and her colleagues (1988) state that women from ethnic backgrounds and low socioeconomic backgrounds are less willing and able to participate in research due to their heavy responsibilities and their well-founded scepticism about the value of social research (see also Edwards 1990; Phoenix 1994). Some vulnerable people may face pressing socioeconomic needs that limit their participation in research (Anderson and Hatton 2000). Dina Birman (2005: 197) suggests that most undocumented immigrants in the United States, do not wish to be identified and, hence, will avoid participation in any research, especially if the research reveals their identification to authorities. Refugees may 'feel vulnerable' in taking part in any research due to their past experiences of dealing with authorities (Liamputtong Rice 1996; Birman 2005). For others, like sex workers, as Cecilia Benoit and colleagues (2005: 264) suggest, simply to be identified as belonging to the group can be threatening. Being a part of the sex trade can subject one to hate, scorn and prosecution. These people are, therefore, 'distrustful of non-members, do whatever they can to avoid revealing their identities, and are likely to refuse to cooperate with outsiders or to give unreliable answer to questions about themselves and their networks' (see also Heckathorn 1997).

Sensitive Research

A closely related issue with vulnearable and marginalised people is the concept of 'sensitive research'. Research is deemed as sensitive, Kaye Wellings and colleagues (2000: 256) suggest, 'if it requires disclosure of behaviours or attitudes which would normally be kept private and personal, which might result in offence or lead to social censure or disapproval, and/or which might cause the respondent discomfort to express'. In this sense, research into topics like sexual conduct and preferences (gays or lesbians, children as sex workers, the use of drugs and abuse, illegal activities, illness status (particularly stigmatised disorders, e.g. schizophrenia, bulimia, anexoria and HIV/AIDS), miscarriage and abortion to name a few, may be included within the definition of sensitive research. In her research with mature women and bulimia, Janet Robertson (2000: 531–32) contends that sensitive research may include research which involves the private sphere of an individual. In her research, she is involved with women who 'engage in deep and meaningful conversations about life experiences, many of which have not previously been voiced'. This potentially carries an element of risk to the well-being of the participants and to herself as a researcher. Once the women trusted Robertson, they told her about their isolation and their attempt to keep their bulimia secret. The women told her they felt 'ashamed and disgusted' by their own behaviour. By disclosing their secret to her, these women have a lot to lose.

Socially sensitive research, according to Loan Sieber and Barbara Stanley (1988: 49), encompasses 'studies in which there are potential consequences or implications, either directly for the participants in the research or for the class of individuals represented by the research'. Although one might argue that all research has its consequences and implications, some groups of people may have to deal with the consequences or implications more than others, and hence these groups of individuals are deemed more vulnerable than others. Marina Barnard (2005: 2) refers sensitive research to as those projects dealing with the 'socially-charged and contentious areas of human behaviour', such as the impact of parental drug problems on the well-being of their children. Rebecca Campbell (2002: 33) contends that sensitive topics would be 'often the "difficult" topics – trauma, abuse, death, illness, health problems, violence, crime – that spawn reflection on the role of emotions in research'.

Claire Renzetti and Raymond Lee (1993: ix) suggest that sensitive research includes studies which are 'intimate, discreditable or incriminating'. Lee (1993: 4) too convincingly argues that sensitive research is 'research which potentially poses a substantial threat to those who are or have been involved in it'. And this includes not only the research participants but also the researchers (Jones and Tannock 2000; Robertson 2000; Melrose 2002). In her recent piece of research on undertaking sensitive health research, Virginia Dickson-Swift (2005: 11) contends that sensitive research 'has the potential to impact on all of the people who are involved in it'. She also argues that this definition obliges sensitive researchers 'to examine the potential for harm to the researchers as well as to the research participants'. As I shall show in this book, researchers are caught in emotionally laden research, and they too are vulnerable to harm as much as the participants in their sensitive researches.

Renzetti and Lee (1993: 6) point to some areas that will make research sensitive and pose more threats and create vulnerability of the researched and these include the following:

* Studies which are concerned with deviance and social control.
* Inquiries which exercise coercion or domination.
* Research that intrudes into the private lives or deeply personal experiences of the research participants.
* Research that deals with sacred things.

Raymond Lee (1993: 4) contends that sensitive research poses several threats to the people: intrusive threat, threat of sanction and political threat. Research which intrudes into private lives creates stressful experiences and will pose intrusive threats to the research participants. Threats of sanction encompass researches which result in stigmatisation or incrimination of the researched. Political threats occur when the research involves social conflict and powerful individuals in society. Lee (1993: 3) also suggests that sensitive research stretches beyond the consequences of carrying out the research, but methodological issues are also inherently essential in doing such research. Lee advocates the need to examine this issue from the view of both the researchers and the researched, and this is what I have done in this book.

From the definitions outlined in this section, it is clear that sensitive research encompasses many areas which are deemed to be sensitive. According to Lee (1993) and Renzetti and Lee (1993), sensitive research includes deviance behaviours, drug use and abuse, death, sexual behaviours and any so-called 'taboo topics' including child prostitution. Claire Draucker (1999) and Virginia Dickson-Swift (2005) include issues involving abuse, death and violence as sensitive research. In this book, I would include issues like miscarriage, abortion, exploitation of the marginalised, the critically ill, being old, children who work as prostitutes and so on, as sensitive research.

Whatever definition we may use to best represent the 'vulnerable', it is clear that extreme sensitivity is needed in the conduct of research with these groups. As Barbara Johnson and Jill Clark (2003: 422) suggest, in conducting sensitive research, 'the process of gathering such information necessarily involves direct contact with vulnerable people, with whom sensitive and difficult topics are often raised and sometimes raised within difficult contexts'. Therefore, undertaking research with vulnerable groups can present numerous serious difficulties for the researcher as well as the researched.

Sensitive researchers who are researching vulnerable issues and people must make their judgements on the impact of their research on not only the participants, but also on themselves as researchers. As such, they have to think carefully about the methodology used in collecting their data and the procedures which must be observed as sensitive to vulnerable research participants. These are things I will discuss in this book. I raise several questions here:

- What makes researching these social groups different to researching others?
- How might their vulnerabilities prevent researchers accessing research sites and undertaking their research?
- How would researchers ensure that their research processes will not further marginalise the vulnerable?
- What safety issues do researchers need to carefully plan before embarking on conducting sensitive research?
- What research methods would be more appropriate to research involving vulnerable people?

These issues will be discussed in the chapters that follow.

Qualitative Research: Researching Sensitive Issues

Qualitative investigations are not explorations of concrete, intact frontiers; rather, they are movements through social spaces that are designed and redesigned as we move through them. The research process is fuelled by the raw materials of the physical and social settings and the unique set of personalities, perspectives, and aspirations of those investigating and inhabiting the fluid landscapes being explored.

(Tewksbury and Gagné 2001: 72).

According to Kerry Daly (1992: 3–4), qualitative methods are especially appropriate to the study of vulnerable people. In its original Greek meaning, the word 'method' means 'a route that leads to the goal' (Kvale 1996: 4). This means the researcher 'wanders along with the local inhabitants, asks questions that lead the subjects to tell their stories of the lived world, and converses with them in the original Latin meaning of *conversation* as "wandering together with" ' (Kvale 1996: 4). Clare Warren (2002: 86) contends that qualitative research is more 'open-ended' as 'it is more concerned with being attuned to who is being travelled with, so to speak, than with setting out a precise route for all to follow, as in survey research'.

Qualitative research methods are flexible and fluid, and therefore, are suited to understanding the meanings, interpretations and subjective experiences of vulnerable groups (Wiebel 1990; Lee 1993; Miller 1997; Renzetti 1997; Dunne 2000; Dunne et al. 2002; Hutchinson et al. 2002; Melrose 2002; Liamputtong and Ezzy 2005). Qualitative research methods allow researchers to be able to hear the voices of those who are 'silenced, othered, and marginalized by the dominant social order', as the methods 'ask not only "what is it?" but, more importantly, "explain it to me – how, why, what's the process, what's the significance?" ' (Hesse-Biber and Leavy 2005: 28). The in-depth nature of qualitative methods allows the researched to express their feelings and experiences in their own words (Gregory and McKie 1996). In her study of rape survivors, Rebecca Campbell (2002) argues that qualitative methods provide opportunities to hear survivors' stories in ways quantitative research is unable to match. Campbell (2002: 120) contends: 'if we as researchers provide opportunities for survivors to talk about what has happened to them – either orally in interviews and focus groups .... we can bring their experiences to light'.

Kerry Daly (1992: 4), in his writing about family research, strongly advocates the adoption of qualitative research. Often, it is a challenging task for researchers to step into 'the relatively closed and highly protected boundaries of families' experiences'. Qualitative research, however, provides more opportunity for the researchers to form relationships with participants, which gradually leads to the establishment of trust and rapport. This, in turn, allows the researchers to access ' "backstage" family meanings'. Through its holistic approach, qualitative researchers are able to access the private meanings of families. Additionally, the versatility of qualitative research is particularly useful for researchers to examine the diversity of family structures and experiences. As Daly (1992: 4) puts it, 'qualitative methods give us windows on family processes through which we can observe patterns of interaction and the ongoing negotiation of family roles and relationships'. Similarly, in Wayne Wiebel's study (1990: 5) of substance abusers, he argues that the abuse of illicit substances is a relatively rare and isolated phenomenon. This poses methodological constraints on the scientific inquiry process of the positivist science (quantitative approach). In order to develop meaningful data collection tools for drug-related research, Wiebel (1990: 5) suggests that the researcher needs to obtain 'sufficient a prior familiarity with the topic to frame appropriate, meaningful questions. Such knowledge is the province and product of qualitative methodology'. Clearly, as Wiebel (1990: 5) succinctly puts it in his argument for researching substance abusers,

> Qualitative research is often the only appropriate means available for gathering sensitive and valid data from otherwise elusive populations of substance abusers.

John Bond and Lynne Corner (2001: 113) contend that qualitative approach is 'well suited' to researching people living with dementia. Qualitative research allows researchers 'to examine socially meaningful behaviour, albeit deviant behaviour, holistically, in context and with due attention to the dynamic aspects of social events and interactions'. Qualitative research commits to seeing the world from the research participants' own perspectives, and this is crucial if researchers are serious in their explanations of the personhood of those living with dementia. This commitment necessitates examining the meanings and experiences of people with dementia 'on their own terms' (Bond and Corner (2001: 106).

In her research regarding juvenile prostitution across England and Wales, Margaret Melrose (2002) adopted qualitative research as a way to elicit sensitive information from young people. In discussing the methodology of her research, Melrose (2002: 334) writes as follows:

> Its aims, which were to investigate the phenomenon of prostitution from the point of view of those who had been involved as juveniles, set the project quite squarely within the qualitative/interpretive tradition. It sought to 'learn from' those who were, or had been, involved in prostitution as juveniles in the hope that such qualitative insights would provide an empirical basis from which to inform policy developments and practical solutions for supporting such vulnerable young people.

Deborah Warr (2004: 578) echoes this, suggesting that qualitative research provides 'researchers with an opportunity to listen to people tell their life stories'. The stories offer researchers a clear window into the lived experiences of the participants. Qualitative approach requires the involvement of the researchers and very often it means that they will be out somewhere on the ground. This provides the researchers with rich and complex data that no other means may offer. Warr's fieldwork clearly illustrates her argument. During her fieldwork in a research on the health risks of street sex workers in one of the well-known red-light areas in Australia, she talked with the women on the streets, often very late at night when it was really dark and cold. She also encountered the police and ran the risks of being harassed by troublemakers who often abused the workers. However, these experiences gave her a better understanding about the lives of these sex workers. Warr (2004: 580) tells us,

> The emotions and sensations I experienced on these occasions gave me powerful impressions of how the world feels from the perspective of the women working on the streets. These insights were qualitatively different from those I gained when I interviewed the women. They served, however, to supplement their words, and we understood why the women insisted that the risk of acquiring a sexually transmissible disease was only one kind of harm among many that were presented to them each time they went out to work.

Throughout this book, I too advocate the qualitative research approach in researching sensitive issues with vulnerable people.

Theoretical Framework

In writing about performing research with sensitive topics or with vulnerable populations, I will base my arguments within feminist and postmodern frameworks.

Feminism and Feminist Research

> Feminism is a perspective (a way of seeing), and epistemology (a way of knowing), and an ontology (a way of being in the world).
>
> (Allen and Walker 1992: 201)

Feminist research differs from other types of research by its 'worldview rather than method' (Allen and Walker 1992: 201; see also Nielsen 1990; Hesse-Biber and Leckenby 2004). Within feminist methodology, women and their concerns are the focus of investigation. A clear intention of feminist research is to undertake research which is beneficial for women, not just one about women (see also Campbell and Wasco 2000; Paradis 2000; Hesse-Biber and Leckenby 2005; Hesse-Biber and Leavy 2005). According to Rebecca Campbell and Sharon Wasco (2000: 783), the ultimate aim of feminist research is to 'capture women's lived experiences in a respectful manner that legitimates women's voices as sources of knowledge'. To put it simply, feminist methodology argues that the process of research is as importance as its outcome.

Feminism challenges the 'passivity, subordination and silencing of women' (Maynard 1994: 23). Women are encouraged to tell their stories and their situations. By doing so, women are able to challenge the experts and dominant males who oppress them by limiting their own knowledge and understanding. Within social science research, a feminist construction of reality is 'grounded in the willingness to name oneself "feminist" and to perceive the social construction of women as oppressive' (Allen and Walker 1992: 202). As Stanley (1990: 14) puts it, 'it is the experience of and acting against perceived oppression that gives rise to a distinctive feminist epistemology'.

A commitment to social change has been translated into a need for research methods that consider and witness everyday processes of women's lives, and that would limit the isolation between participants (Fonow and Cook 1991). Undertaking feminist research is to witness resistance. Feminist research opposes research methods which are the products of standard research like those of positivist science (Allen and Walker 1992). As such, feminist research calls for qualitative inquiry which is less structural and more flexible than that of the positivist science. Primarily but not exclusively, feminist methods are qualitative (see Stanley 1990; Allen and Baber 1992; Renzetti 1997). Feminist research contends that due to the standardised nature of positivist science, much of what occurs to individuals and groups involved in the research including the researcher and the researched remains 'unsaid and unanalysed' (Allen and Walker 1992: 201).

The concern of feminism and feminist research, according to Maggie O'Neill (1996: 131), is to construct knowledge that 'writes women into his-story and exploring, challenging, resisting and changing sexual and social inequalities'. In her study with street sex workers, O'Neill (1996: 131) argues that her methodological approach allows the involvement of the women. They are active players in 'the social construction of knowledge, empowerment and social change'. She continues her relationship with some of the women. They have been working together on numerous research projects. She asserts that the emotional nature of her work, especially working on-street, necessitates that she immerses herself in the range of differing experiences of women working as sex workers. Her own concern is that her work must have some practical benefits for this vulnerable group of women. Maggie O'Neill (1996: 131) writes, 'from the onset I was committed to women's voices being heard and listened to, that the research should be action oriented, with knowledge arising out of the study being "knowledge for" as "feminist praxis," facilitating empowerment, resistance and social change'.

Research on sexual abuse of women with learning disabilities in London conducted by Michelle McCarthy (1996) clearly argues for feminist research. She follows many essential elements of feminist research methodology. Her research focuses on the experience of individual women, but it does not pathologise them. She locates the personal experiences of the women within a larger political context. The major goal of her research is to make an attempt to improve the lives of women with learning disabilities. McCarthy (1996: 121) tells us that her work attempts to 'bring the experiences of a highly marginalized and oppressed group of women into mainstream feminist and sociological thinking'. In doing so, she highlights some commonalities, as well as differences, amongst these women.

A consciously feminist methodology must provide a way in which the researchers can include their own experiences, as women and researchers, in both the conduct of their research and a sharing of their subjectivities with their research participants (Moran-Ellis 1996: 177). Within the research domain, there is now recognition of the need to pay more attention to the experience of carrying out research and the impact of that experience on data collection, analysis and presentation. Jo Moran-Ellis (1996: 176) writes, 'the positioning of the researcher as a person who is gendered and has their own particular origins has come to be seen as an important, albeit often invisible, component in the research process' (see also Stanley and Wise 1993; Wilkins 1993). Research, according to Liz Stanley and Sue Wise (1993: 175, original emphasis), 'is a process which occurs through the medium of a person – the researcher is always and inevitably *in* the research. This exists whether openly stated or not'. Within a feminist sociology, Stanley and Wise (1993) strongly argue for incorporating personal and research experience in the data collection and the analysis of the data. This is also crucial in the formation of theories.

Feminist research is 'consciously reflexive' (Allen and Walker 1992: 202), or 'excruciatingly self-conscious' (Stacey 1988: 25). Reflexivity provides insight and crucial scrutiny of the research process (Fonow and Cook 1991). Feminist researchers tend to unashamedly admit that the process of undertaking their research transforms them in some ways (as we shall see in Chapter 3 in this volume; see also the Postmodern section in this chapter). Reflexivity, Elizabeth Stanko (1997: 83) contends, is 'the process of standing outside and gazing back to see what we can from afar'. It is a tool for researchers to become more sensitive to 'silence' in the research process. In her research into sexual violence, Stanko (1997: 83) points out that feminist reflexivity about sexual violence acknowledges the impact of such information on the researchers' lives. Reflexivity provides material that researchers can use to suggest that sexual violence is a vehicle for maintaining inequality. In her writing, Stanko (1997: 75) uses reflexivity to break her silence about her experiences of dealing with anger, fear, pain and frustration during her own research process. Reflexivity was also used to tell readers about her political attempts as an academic activist and her personal (nonetheless very public) struggles for coming to terms between her beliefs and hard facts. Rebecca Campbell and Sharon Wasco (2000: 788) echo this, suggesting that 'the personal is political, therefore, research is both explicitly personal and political'. In feminist scholarship, emotional closeness with research is made public. Feminist research not only involves thinking, but it is also about feeling. Feminist methodologists encourage all social scientists to 'explore the process of research in more depth, to locate all facets of researchers' identities – values, beliefs, and emotions – within the research context'. They strongly advocate that the articulation of the self of researchers must be 'made public' (see also Campbell 2002). This is what I will show in Chapter 3: that researching vulnerable people has emotional costs to sensitive researchers and they should reflect on this – put simply, to make their personal lives public (see C. Wright Mills 1959, 2000). See also Lather (1991), Reinharz (1992), Stanley and Wise (1993), Hertz (1997), Wasserfall (1997), Campbell and Wasco (2000), Cosgrove and McHugh (2000), and Hesse-Biber and Leavy (2005).

Research carried out from a feminist framework, (Sharlene Hesse-Biber and others (2004: 3) suggest pays attention to issues of difference, questions social power, resists scientific oppression, and commits to political action and social reform (see also Byrne and Lentin 2000; Hesse-Biber and Leavy 2005). Essentially, feminist research aims to give voice to the marginalised. A feminist methodology, Marjorie DeVault (1999: 31) contends, aims to construct knowledge which may benefit women and other minority groups. The feminists approach to methodology, say Sharlene Hesse-Biber and Denise Leckenby (2004: 210), 'allows for "new" types of questions about women's lives and those of "other/ed" marginalized groups to be addressed within their respective fields of research'. Research carried out within a feminist perspective encourages the building of new knowledge which often leads to the development of innovative methods, as I shall show in Chapter 7 in this volume. As Hesse-Biber and others (2004: 3) suggest, feminist researchers use a number of strategies to construct knowledge about women and their social worlds which are often invisible within the dominant male society. I say that this is applicable to all groups who lie hidden from mainstream society, and these clearly include the marginalised, the deviant, the silenced and the oppressed populations that I am including in this book.

Essentially, feminist methodology embraces qualitative methods, although contemporary feminist researchers promote both qualitative and quantitative approaches (see Campbell and Salem 1999; Campbell and Wasco 2000; Campbell 2002). More often, feminist methodology utilises familiar methods of data collection in qualitative approach including focus groups, in-depth interviews and oral history (Campbell and Wasco 2000). However, Reinharz (1992) and Campbell and Wasco (2000) suggest that feminist methodology tends to embrace and has created more innovative ways of data collection.

Campbell and Wasco (2000: 787) contend that the ultimate aim of feminist research is to 'identify the ways in which multiple forms of oppression impact women's lives and empower women to tell their stories by providing a respectful and egalitarian research environment'. This goal necessitates the use of multiple methodologies which are more flexible and collaborative like ethnography and participatory action research, and in some circumstances, more innovative methods. But whether adopting traditional methods such as individual inter-viewing, or more unusual techniques, such as collaborative group interviews, feminist researchers strive to 'strengthen connections between researchers and participants'. A unique feature of feminist research is a more caring research environment that is non-hierarchical. I also include innovative ways of data collection in this book (see Chapter 8).

Feminism aims to transform exploitative aspects of positivist science. It focuses on enhancing the interests of marginalised people and proposing the transformation of an oppressive social system (Paradis 2000: 840). To Paradis, research is exploitative if the interests of the researchers alone form every stage of the research process. Paradis (2000: 840) strongly suggests that 'research resembles a colonial economy when researchers enter the world of participants uninvited, extract a resource called data, process this resource into a product called theory, and use the product only toward their own ends'. This is a typical process utilised in positivist research. Feminist researchers tend to avoid this methodology and promote the more interpretive approach belonging to qual-itative research that I am advocating in this book (see earlier section on research methodology in this chapter). In order to guard against exploitation in the research relationship, feminist researchers attempt to create a process which will inherently empower the research participants. This can be achieved through active and direct involvement in the research process. Ideally, a full collaboration between the researchers and the participants or local communities should be undertaken so that power between the researchers and the participants can be shared and this will provide some intrinsic benefit for those who take part in the research.

Claire Renzetti (1997: 134) suggests that feminist research promotes a model of collaboration and rejects the traditional researcher/participants divide. Within the feminist methodological framework, Renzetti (1997: 134) contends, 'researchers are encouraged to "start from their own experience"; to freely share information about themselves, their personal lives, and their opinions with those they are studying; and to adhere to a feminist ethic of care by complying with requests for help and by offering advice and direct assistance when possible' (see also Cook and Fonow 1984; Reinharz 1992). According to the feminist methodology, Renzetti (1997: 134–35) continues, self-disclosure, the establish-ment of reciprocity, rapport and trust between the researchers and the researched, enhances the success of a research process (see also Bergen 1993, 1996; Campbell and Wasco 2000). Feminist methodology commits to giving voice to personal, everyday experiences of individuals, particularly those who are marginalised in a society. This has resulted in the promotion of qualitative inquiries (p. 135; see also Reinharz 1992; Campbell and Wasco 2000). Renzetti (1997: 135) also points out that the attempt to see research as a collaborative endeavour has prompted feminist researchers to call for the use of participatory methods (see Maguire 1996; de Ishtar 2005a,b,c; see also Chapter 6 in this volume).

Renzetti (1997: 143) suggests that the feminist participatory methodology may be seen as biased social science. She contends that it may be so, however, all social science is biased. Renzetti (1997: 143, original emphasis) puts it clearly:

> In my view, what sets this type of research apart is that it is also *good* social science; that is, it seeks to give voice to and to improve the life conditions of the marginalized, and it transforms social scientific inquiry from an academic exercise into an instrument of meaningful social change.

Having elaborated on essential notions of feminist research, I wish to sum it up using the work of Claire Renzetti (1997: 133), who paraphrases the work of Francesca Cancian (1992) and Shulamit Reinharz (1992) in suggesting that feminist methodology has five important elements:

- Feminist research focuses on gender and gender inequality and this implies a strong moral and political commitment to decreasing inequality;
- It aims to give voice to personal and everyday experiences of women and other marginalised individuals and groups;
- It commits to social activism and aims to bring about social transformation which improves the situation and conditions under which women and the marginalised live;
- It promotes reflexivity which critically scrutinises how social structures like gender, ethnicity, social class, and sexual orientation as well as larger social, economic and political conditions of the researchers may impact on the research process; and
- It rejects the traditional imbalanced power relationships between the researcher and the researched and attempts to provide the research participants with more power in the research enterprise.

Postmodernism

> The only constant in today's world is change.
>
> (Braidotti 2000: 1062)

> I think of the postmodern attitude as that of a man who loves a very cultivated woman and knows he cannot say to her, 'I love you madly', because he knows that she knows (and that she knows that he knows), that these words have already been written by Barbara Cartland. Still, there is a solution. He can say, 'As Barbara Cartland would put it, "I love you madly" '. At this point, having avoided false innocence, having said clearly that it is no longer possible to speak innocently, he will nevertheless have said what he wanted to say to the woman: that 'he loves her madly', but he loves her in an age of lost innocence. If the woman goes along with this, she will have received a declaration of love all the same.
>
> (Eco 1984: 67–68)

What Umberto Eco means, to me, is that there are different ways of saying 'I love you madly'. This depends on the situational position of the person. He may not be able to say what other people have said before him, and hence he has to invent his own version of the words. But, in the end, it will mean that he is really in love with the woman.

This is postmodernism. Postmodernism rejects the idea that there is a single reality or truth; rather there are many realities and many truths. People have different stories and different ways of saying and expressing their stories. All stories and ways of expressing them are legitimate. Sandra Harding (1987: 188) suggests that there are 'many stories that different women tell about the different knowledge they have'. We may replace the 'women' with others like men, children, an older person, the mentally ill, the critically ill, sex workers or any vulnerable people, and we can see that many realities and truths occupy the world in which we live. Postmodern researchers attempt to deconstruct the meanings that participants have about their lived experiences and the language they use. Postmodern scholars scrutinise similarities and differences in the meanings that people claim about their lived experiences (Campbell and Wasco 2000: 782–83). This is in line with the qualitative methods that I am advocating in this text. In what follows, I shall point to salient issues concerning the influences of postmodernism on qualitative research and in particular on research concerning vulnerable people.

Postmodernism has a great influence not only on culture, literature, arts, politics, and individuals, but also on research (Grbich 2004). Carol Grbich (2004: 25) poses that the assumptions under the influence of modernity which suggest that reality is 'ordered and completely knowable by observation', and that 'an objective reality exists' which is a common feature of positivist science, have been replaced with a view that reality is 'chaotic and unknowable'. Within postmodernism, 'social construction and questionable discourses are increasingly seen to dominate knowledge, meanings become recognised as individual creations, which require interpretation and negotiation'.

Researchers adopting the postmodern theoretical paradigm reject the grand narratives of positivist science which ignore the differences between individuals and their social contexts. Instead, they attempt to deconstruct the grand narratives in order to remove the established power of objectivist science (Grbich 2004). Andrea Fontana (2002: 162) contends that postmodernism dismisses 'overarching paradigms and theoretical and methodological metasystems'. Postmodernism challenges traditional premises and attempts to deconstruct them. Postmodernism reveals 'the ambiguity and contexuality of meaning'. It aims at theorising society 'not as a monolithic structure but as a series of fragments in continuous flux'. It also invites researchers to focus their attention on the fragments, 'the minute events of everyday life', and to 'understand them in their own right rather than gloss over differences and patch them together into paradigmatic wholes' (see also Silverman 2004).

Postmodernism advocates 'mini-narratives', which offer explanations for small-scale research, situated within specific social and cultural contexts, where 'no pretensions of abstract theory, universality or generalisability are involved' (Grbich 2004: 26; see also Richardson 2002). Within the postmodern paradigm, descriptive explanations of particular processes, instead of the power of grand narratives, are promoted (Grbich 2004). In research, this is a qualitative approach. And in researching sensitive issues, we have seen postmodernist researchers find different ways to obtain their data, different ways to analyse it and different ways to represent the voices of their participants, as I will discuss in the following chapters.

Postmodernism argues that realities are constructed within a specific social and cultural context. Hence, the meanings can only be understood within this particular social and cultural understanding. Postmodernism argues that 'realities are multiple'. Realities are not static but always in flux; they are formed and reformed, constructed and reconstructed. The interpretation of the individual is authoritative. There is no one true reality. Truth and reality are situated with the meanings individuals create according to their perceptions of their everyday lives and their own subjective experiences (Grbich 2004). I contend that in this book this is how we perform qualitative research and represent the voices of our participants.

Under the postmodern framework, the focus of research moves from large to small qualitative research. Postmodernism focuses on phenomenological examination of small, in-depth grounded theory studies and participatory action research. Grbich (2004) argues that under postmodernism, multiple methods are perceived as crucial. I would also suggest that alternative methods, which will allow for a more reflexive and collaborative approach, are also needed in researching vulnerable populations (see Chapter 6 in this volume).

Within postmodernism, all stories and expressions are valid and no one story or expression is privileged over others (Grbich 2004). Subjective experiences are superior. Multiple identities are permitted. There is an assumption that an individual holds multiple subjectivities and these subjectivities can change, shape and reshape in unforeseeable ways. Different identities are created, or become the focus of different people in different contexts and within different situational circumstances. The researcher and the researched are no longer divided. Rather, they 'interweave their constructed meanings in a delicate dance of recognition and interpretation as the same narratives are told and re-told, presented and re-presented for the reader to become involved with' (Grbich 2004: 28).

Norman Denzin's works (1989, 1997, 2002, 2003a) are a main drive for adopting postmodern sensibilities to research inquiry. In his earlier piece, Denzin (1989: 14–15) focuses on the meanings individuals ascribe to themselves and their conditions. His attempt is to allow the participants to 'speak for themselves'. Denzin contends that by doing so, researchers may reach the hidden experiences of people and these hidden experiences can be revealed for others to understand the positions of the research participants. In his later work, Denzin (1997) has become more politically engaged with his research participants. He strongly rejects traditional forms of 'non-involvement and objectivity' research. Instead, Denzin advocates 'partnership' between the researcher and the researched (Fontana 2002: 165).

Within the postmodern theory, Grbich (2004: 28–29) contends, objectivity is replaced by 'reflexive subjectivity and the politics of position'. Self-reflexivity requires an awareness of the self in the process of creating knowledge. It requires researchers to clarify how they construct their beliefs (a process of self-revelation), and how these beliefs influence their data collection in their research endeavours. This is also a practice within feminist framework (see Harding 1991, 1992; Hertz 1997; Fontana 2002; Anderson and Umberson 2004; Errante 2004; Hesse-Biber and Leckenby 2004; Naples 2004 and previous section on feminist research). Reflexively, and sensitively, Antoinette Errante (2004) explores her own role within the research setting. The emotions and personal transformation resulting from self-reflexivity are essential components of her feminist research project. Often, feminist researchers make special attempts in their published works to tell others how they carry out their work. They explain and scrutinise the process of co-constructing knowledge and their experiences of the research setting. The articulation of experience and a willingness to admit to any emerging messy issues when undertaking their methods is a crucial portion of many stories of the research endeavours of feminist researchers (Hesse-Biber and Leckenby 2004; see dé Ishtar 2005a,b in particular).

In postmodern research, there is a strong focus on self-disclosure (Grbich 2004). The researchers are not separable from their backgrounds, recollections and life experiences. Researchers need to be critically aware of their own self and the influence of their lived experiences and knowledge on the research performance (Lee 2002). Echoing Raymond Lee's position (2002), Carol Grbich (2004: 60) contends, 'reinvention and adaptation of self in the uncertain and changed world (of postmodernity) are essential, enabling the emergence and acceptance of multiple selves and fractal identities'. Grbich (2004: 60) also suggests that postmodern researchers do not see themselves as 'a static, centred object'. Rather, their 'self' is seen as 'interlinked with others and undergoing processes of change'. In this process, there are 'several selves – the central, historically-constructed self, the self that is currently undergoing change (bifurcating, doubling) and another self, the reflexive observer of this process'. This aspect of postmodern framework influences the way researchers interact with the research participants in their data collection. I will discuss this issue in detail in Chapter 3.

Similar to feminist research, postmodern researchers are concerned about bringing the 'Other' – the vulnerable and marginalised – into research. Postmodern researchers aim at empowering those who have been discriminated against and oppressed (Denzin and Lincoln 1998). Therefore, postmodern research is a 'transformative endeavour' aiming to 'denaturalize and transform oppressive power–knowledge relations' in order to make the world fairer to vulnerable people (Hesse-Biber et al. 2004: 18; see also Denzin and Lincoln 1998). Specifically, postmodernism uses 'the voice of the "Other" in highly reflexive and politically imbued ways in order to deconstruct "metanarratives" (overreaching stories) used in the domination of some over others' (Hesse-Biber et al. 2004: 18). Reflexive practice is, therefore, adopted for 'the dialectical and reciprocal workings of power' and this includes 'the changing position of the researcher within the research process, the sociohistorical context, and the changing relations of power within which the research participants operate' (Hesse-Biber et al. 2004: 18).

The emergence of postmodern theory, Hesse-Biber and colleagues (2004: 18) suggest, has resulted in the 'emergence of new epistemological and methodological practices'. With the attempt to permit the voices of the research participants to be heard loudly and to be seen as having more credit, both the data collection methods and the components of data have been transformed (Fontana 2002; Grbich 2004). And as this book will show, researchers have developed and utilised many alternative methodological practices in their research with vulnerable and marginalised people – the 'Other' in the postmodern world (Denzin and Lincoln 1998). Arts-based inquiry (Finley 2005) is a good example of various forms of postmodern qualitative research. Susan Finley (2005: 682) puts it well:

> Postmodern foundational shifts brought about new conceptualizations of how research works, how meanings are made, and what social purposes research might serve. Social scientists began to act on their realization that traditional techniques of research were not adequate to handle the many questions that needed to be asked when the frame was shifted to take on new and diverse perspectives.

The emergence of autoethnography is another example of the influence of postmodernism in qualitative tradition. The autoethnographic orientation has become popular among sensitive researches. Autoethnography engages extensive life experiences of the researcher/author within a specific social and cultural location (Grbich 2004). I will discuss this methodology in Chapter 7 in greater details. See Chapters 6 and 7 in this volume for other forms of postmodern-influenced innovative research methods.

Postmodernism has also greatly influenced the ways sensitive researchers write about their research and their findings (Richardson 1992, 1994a,b, 1997, 1999, 2002; Richardson and St. Pierre 2005). Postmodernist researchers/writers have doubts and are impatient with the standard reporting style in qualitative research (Rosenblatt 2002: 901; Richardson and St. Pierre 2005). In their most recent work, Laurel Richardson and Elizabeth St. Pierre (2005: 962) put this clearly:

> Postmodernism claims that writing is always partial, local, and situational and that our selves are always present no matter how hard we try to suppress them—but only partially present because in our writing we repress parts of our selves as well. Working from that premise frees us to write material in a variety of ways—to tell and retell. There is no such thing as 'getting it right', only 'getting it' differently contoured and nuanced.

George Marcus and Michael Fischer (1986) strongly advocate different ways to represent the voices of the powerless research participants. They point to the problems of presentation developed by the authorial position of the researchers, as a data collector and as a writer (see also Fontana 2002). In anthropology, Marcus and Fischer (1986: 69) promote 'postmodern alternatives' which permit different voices to emerge. They suggest that researchers need to adopt a 'dialogue approach', which focuses on the dialogue between researchers and their research participants, as a means to reveal how ethnographic knowledge establishes itself. In Kevin Dwyer's writing in the *Moroccan Dialogues* (1982), he only minimally edited the interview transcripts with the intention of showing the problematic nature of interviewing in his research fieldwork.

Marcus and Fischer (1986: 71) also propose the use of 'polyphony', 'the registering of different points of views in multiple voices' in the representation of voices. Doing it this way, the editorial power of the researcher is minimised. Within polyphonic interviewing, Andrea Fontana and James Frey (2005: 709) suggest, 'the voices of respondents are recorded with minimal influence from the researcher and are not collapsed together and reported as one through the interpretation of the researcher. Instead, the multiple perspectives of the various respondents are reported, and differences and problems encountered are discussed, rather than glossed over'. Susan Krieger's work (1983) concentrates on polyphony by showing the diverse perspectives of her research participants to highlight contradictions and problems rather than reducing them. In Allen Shelton's work (1995) on a study of victimisation, social process and resistance, he utilises the machine and other powerful imageries to communicate his message. To highlight his points, paintings are used as metaphors for mixing sociological data with his past stories. Polyphonic interviewing is not only creative, but also adds 'epiphanies', which Norman Denzin (1989a: 15) refers to as 'those interactional moments that leave marks on people's lives [and] have the potential for creating transformational experiences for the person'. Hence, subjects of investigation are dramatised by focusing on present moments in people's lives. This will produce data which are not only more meaningful but also richer (Fontana and Frey 2005).

In the postmodern text, the researchers/authors are moved to a 'decentred position'. The 'decentring' of the researcher/author permits all parties including the researcher/author, to become performers in the research process (Polkinghorne 1997). The researcher/author, Grbich (2004: 68) puts it, 'becomes the eye of the text – the facilitator of the display or voices, including his/her own, and the illuminator of the text through reflexive/reflective/refractive critique'. In the postmodern text, the 'decentring' of the researcher/author can be done in different ways (Grbich 2004: 29):

* Research stories are presented through the voices and eyes of research participants who directly talk to the audience.
* The stories of research participants are merged with the stories of the researchers/authors who present them through their own angles.
* The privileged third-person voice of the researcher/author is 'replaced by the voices of participants, voices from other texts, or the "I"/"I" voice of the author speaking in her/his own right'.

Andrea Fontana (2002: 162) suggests that 'postmodern sensibilities' have tremendously influenced the methodologies used by sensitive researchers. She maintains that researchers who are influenced by a postmodern paradigm have become extremely sensitive to issues and problems which have formerly been ignored. According to Andrea Fontana (2002: 162–63), there are several points of importance under postmodern influence research:

* The boundaries between the researcher and the researched as well as their roles have become blurred and the traditional relationship between these two parties is no longer seen as natural.
* Researchers have become more concerned about issues of representation, rather than adhering to traditional forms of research report writing.
* The authority of the researcher is challenged. Research participants are no longer seen as 'faceless numbers' who do not have opinions in the research process. The participants' own understandings of realities are the focus of postmodern research.
* There is more recognition and acceptance of new ways to enable previously unarticulated voices to be heard.
* The genres used to represent research findings have been expanded to include those of expression from literature, poetry and drama.
* There is a growing use of online research as a means to access and work with vulnerable people and this includes e-mail, internet chat room and other electronic modes of communication.

Conclusion

In this chapter, I have pointed to salient backgrounds relevant to researching vulnerable people. I have set clearly my position and boundaries in creating this book. By now, readers have learned about the meaning of sensitive research, my definition of vulnerable people, the methodology I propose and the theoretical orientations on which this book is based.

Some research questions can only be answered by vulnerable individuals or groups. This necessitates that sensitive researchers initiate their enquiries with them. Living in a postmodern world, and as responsible researchers, it is our duty to undertake some research on sensitive topics with the vulnerable sections of the society. As Joan Sieber and Barbara Stanley (1988: 55) warn us,

> Sensitive research addresses some of society's most pressing social issues and policy programs . . . Shying away from controversial topics, simply because they are controversial, is an avoidance of responsibility.

Undertaking research with vulnerable persons and particularly those who are doubly vulnerable presents unique and often difficult challenges. Because of these challenges, many researchers deliberately exclude vulnerable people from their research enterprises (Larson 1994; Moore and Miller 1999). There may be reasons for this exclusion and these may include fear that the research may become too difficult to carry out, fear that the research may not be approved by the ethics review board and fear that the researchers may not be able to access the vulnerable groups. Because of these factors, the needs and concerns of vulnerable people are often ignored in the scientific literature (Moore and Miller 1999). I contend that this will make these people even more vulnerable. As sensitive researchers, we need to find ways to bring the voices of these vulnerable people to the fore, and this book intends to help researchers to do so. As readers go through this book, it will become clear that performing research with vulnerable people is achieveable.

As sensitive researchers, we are committed to giving voice to vulnerable people because this will be our first step in empowering them (Cosgrove and McHuge 2000). And this way we may be able to help many vulnerable people to have better opportunities to enhance their lives and well-being. I agree entirely with Moore and Miller (1999: 1040) who assert that 'only when vulnerable groups receive the appropriate research attention will their care and quality of life be enhanced'.

TUTORIAL EXERCISES

1. Suggest some issues that makes your research 'sensitive'.
2. Define the 'vulnerable' and 'marginalised' people who you might encounter in society and discuss what makes them vulnerable and marginalised.
3. Discuss other theories which may be relevant to researching vulnerable people.

SUGGESTED READINGS

DeVault, M.L., 1999, *Liberating Method: Feminism and Social Research*, Philadephia: Temple University Press.
Dickson-Swift, V., 2005, *Undertaking Sensitive Health Research: The Experiences of Researchers*, Unpublished doctoral thesis, Department of Public Health, School of Health and Environment, La Trobe University, Bendigo, Australia.
Fontana, A., 2002, 'Postmodern Trends in Interviewing', pp. 161–75, In *Handbook of Interview Research: Context & Method*, edited by J.F. Gubrium and J.A. Holstein, Thousand Oaks, CA: Sage Publications.
Grbich, C., 2004, *New Approaches in Social Research*, London: Sage Publications.

Hesse-Biber, S.N. and M.L. Yaiser (eds), 2004, *Feminist Perspectives on Social Research*, New York: Oxford University Press.

Lee, R.M., 1995, *Dangerous Fieldwork*, Thousand Oaks, CA: Sage Publications.

Liamputtong, P. and D. Ezzy, 2005, *Qualitative Research Methods*, 2nd edition, Melbourne: Oxford University Press.

Reinharz, S., 1992, *Feminist Methods in Social Research*, New York: Oxford University Press.

Renzetti, C.M. and R.M. Lee (eds), 1993, *Researching Sensitive Topics*, Newbury Park: Sage Publications.

Stanley, L. and S. Wise, 1993, 'Method, Methodology, and Epistemology in Feminist Research Process, pp. 20–60, In *Feminist Praxis: Research, Theory and Epistemology in Feminist Sociology*, edited by L. Stanley, New York: Routledge.

2

Moral and Ethical Issues In Researching Vulnerable People

Chapter Objectives   23
Introduction   24
The Morality of Research   25
Ethical Issues   32
Informed Consent   33
Confidentiality   35
Risk and Harm: Safety Issues of the Participants   37
Strategies to Protect the Research Participants   41
Conclusion   44

Research ethics is often much more about institutional and professional regulations and codes of conduct than it is about the needs, aspirations, or worldviews of 'marginalized and vulnerable' communities.

(Smith 2005: 96)

Ethics is a set of moral principles that aims to prevent researchers from harming those they research . . . Researchers undertaking research on sensitive topics need to be acutely aware of their ethical responsibilities.

(Dickson–Swift 2005: 21)

Research should, as far as possible, be based on freely given informed consent of research subjects who have been provided with adequate information on what is being done to them, the limits to their participation, as well as any potential risks they may incur by taking part in research.

(Sin 2005: 279)

Chapter Objectives

This chapter aims to

- Discuss moral aspects of researching vulnerable people.
- Examine ethical issues including the issue of informed consent and confidentiality.
- Examine risks and harm that may occur to research participants.
- Suggest some safeguards to protect vulnerable research participants.

Introduction

For a long time, ethical issues relating to the conduct of research have been important aspects in medical sciences. Ethical standards in social science research, however, have been a more recent development and this is because, in part, participants in social science research are generally seen as not being exposed to 'acute physical harm' (Sin 2005: 279) like what has happened in the medical sciences (see Coney 1988; Jones 1993; Heintzelman 1996; Gunsalus 2002; Liamputtong and Dwyer 2003). The first international code of ethics which was established to protect the rights of people from research abuse was The Nuremberg Code in 1949. There are also other codes of agreement including the World Medical Association Declaration of Helsinki Agreement in 1964 and the Belmont Report in 1979. In addition, the Council for International Organization of Medical Sciences (CIOMS) was established for researchers working in developing countries (Beyrer and Kass 2002). Nowadays, there are committees referred to as Institutional Review Boards (in the United States) or Ethics Committees (in Australia and the United Kingdom) established in most institutions worldwide that aim to protect research participants. The new codes were developed so that potential partici-pants in any research project would have the rights to know what is required of them. They would also need to know the actual consequences of their par-ticipation in a research. Under the new codes, potential research participants must formally agree to their own participation.

Recently, there have been more discussions of ethics in qualitative research (see Baez 2002; Mauthner et al. 2002; Van Den Hoonaard 2002; Fluehr-Lobban 2003). Ethical issues regarding researching vulnerable and disadvantaged people have also been noted by several researchers (see McIsaac 1995; Morrow and Richards 1996; Usher and Holmes 1997; Sachs 1998; Stalker 1998; James and Platzer 1999; Humphries and Martin 2000; Loff and Black 2000; Lawton 2001; McCosker et al. 2001; Gilhooly 2002; Huber and Clandinin 2002; Fluehr-Lobban 2003; Dyregrov 2004; Grinyer 2004). Additionally, there are now more discussions about making ethical issues an essential part of research. I argue that this is partic-ularly important in research with vulnerable people, where we do not want to cause any harm to our research participants (such as in the case of the Tuskegee Syphilis Study in the United States and the 'Unfortunate Experiment' in New Zealand). As Hesse-Biber and Leavy (2005: 86) put it, 'ethical discussions usually remain detached or marginalized from discussions of research projects. In fact, some researchers consider this aspect of research an afterthought'. Ethics 'is not a kind of "bolt-on" which is only considered when one is engaging in doing research, and then only at certain points' (Humphries and Martin 2000: 69). Ethical issues need to be considered throughout the research process and continued afterwards, as one may have a lasting effect on research participants. As Tina Miller and Linda Bell (2002) contend, ethical considerations need to be an ongoing part of research: they should take part before, during and after research.

In this chapter, I will discuss several salient issues relating to moral and ethical issues in research involving vulnerable people. As sensitive researchers, we are obliged to consider the safety and well-being of our research participants. Ethically sensitive approaches are, however, complicated. I shall point to some basic understanding and assumptions in this chapter.

The Morality of Research

> As researchers (and human beings) we act as 'morally responsible selves' . . . – we need to be flexible and reactive, but above all, accountable for our actions.
>
> (Hallowell et al. 2005: 149)

There are some debates about moral issues regarding research with vulnerable people. Should researchers carry out investigative work with some extremely vulnerable populations such as frail or elderly people, people suffering from mental illness or those who experience extreme loss, grief, or on the homeless or the terminally ill? These people are already vulnerable in many ways (see Lewis Fravel and Boss 1992; De Raeve, 1994; Beaver et al. 1999; Rowling, 1999; Russell 1999; Paradis 2000; Sque 2000; Beauchamp et al. 2002; Dyregrov 2004; Grinyer 2004; Hallowell et al. 2005). Cherry Russell (1999: 404) attempted to research social isolation with older people in Sydney, Australia. In order to be responsive to the vulnerable participants, she and her co-researchers had amended many aspects of their research, but throughout the research process they encountered 'a sense of unease about the ethicality (or even morality) of some aspects of their research'. They asked themselves, for example, 'should we be "mining the minds" of these disempowered people for our own research purposes?' Kim Usher and Colin Holmes (1997) argue that people with mental illnesses are seen as vulnerable research participants. They tend to be seen as incapable or less capable to make informed decisions about their participation in research studies. However, research has shown that this is not always the case (see Stanley et al. 1981; Usher and Holmes 1997). In fact, people with mental illness may wish to take part in a research project despite the paternalistic view of their caregivers, advocates, guardians or family members (Usher and Holmes 1997). As Stanley and others (1981) argue, labelling the mentally ill as such may compromise the autonomy of the whole group and people with mental illness may therefore miss out on some important research projects that may improve their health and well-being. Tom Beauchamp and colleagues (2002: 560) argue similarly with homeless people, that it is not immoral or exploitative to include them in research if it is done ethically. Indeed, they contend, 'it would be unfair to exclude homeless persons categorically as a group from . . . research merely on grounds that they are homeless'.

Morally speaking, many sensitive researchers strongly believe that the benefits of undertaking the research need to be measured against the risks of being involved in the research (Flaskerud and Winslow, 1998; Beaver et al. 1999; Cutcliffe and Ramcharan 2002; Hall and Kulig 2004; see above discussion). As Flaskerud and Winslow (1998: 10) strongly argue, 'findings of studies of vulnerable groups should be directed first toward benefiting the group to be served'. But, as Dickson–Swift (2005: 26) contends, this can be problematic because some issues 'surrounding sensitive research are not always apparent at the outset of the research'. Glesne and Peshkin (1992: 112) remark,

> Questions of exploitation, or 'using' others tend to arise as you become immersed in research and begin to rejoice in the richness of what you are learning. You are thankful, but instead of simply appreciating the gift, you may feel guilty for how much you are receiving and how little you are giving in return.

Magi Sque (2000: 25), in her work with bereaved relatives of organ donors, remarks that only for the sake of research, painful memories of the participants are brought up. When researchers delve into the private lives of vulnerable people, they have 'the potential to invade, distort or destroy this private world'. This is what Erving Goffman (1973) refers to as a 'mortification of self, that is, "a person is changed or remade by invasive exposure because embodiments of self have been violated"' (Sque 2000: 25).

Maggie O'Neill (1996), for example, contends that conducting research with women working on the street has moral ramifications for the women themselves. The time the women have to spend in our research can have a negative impact on their contacts with their clients. O'Neill (1996: 132) writes

> 'Taking from women' may be perceived by the women themselves as another form of pimping, particularly given the way the media has portrayed female prostitutes. Most documentaries open with a seedy depiction of the deserted, dark street with the 'hooker' in stilettos, fishnets and miniskirt. The message is clear and the stereotype upheld of the dirty, disease ridden prostitute, irresponsible, immoral and probably feeding a drug habit – the whore stigma in operation. Given this level of stereotyping and the concomitant whore stigma it underpins, it is no wonder female street prostitutes are wary of researchers and research 'on' her.

In some cases, it may also result in problems with pimps. Morally speaking too, O'Neill (1996: 132) suggests that researchers can be perceived as similar to pimps:

> Coming into the field to take, then returning to the campus, institution or suburb where they write up the data, publish and build careers – on the backs of those they took data from.

The moral issue of questions that researchers ask in their study with vulnerable people has been raised by sensitive researchers. Emily Paradis (2000: 844), for example, contends that 'certain questions could produce results that would be harmful to the community as a whole'. Morally, sensitive researchers should not ask questions which may contribute to the stigmatisation of their research participants. In research with homeless women that she was involved with, for example, Paradis (2000: 844–45) puts it clearly that 'data were available whether the victim or assailant had been using drugs or alcohol at the time of assault, but I believed that to study this area using only categorical data would erase the nuance and complexity of homeless women's experiences of substance use, and risk perpetuating both stereotypes about homeless women and victim-blaming myths about sexual assault'. Paradis (2000) makes a strong case advocating for asking research questions which would reflect better on the marginalised lives of these women. This essentially renders the use of qualitative research questions, rather than hypothesis testing as positivist science.

Paradis (2000: 854) also argues that morally and ethically, researchers 'must begin with consideration of the personal, interpersonal, community, and political ramifications of research' on their research participants. In a study involving homeless women, for example, researchers must recognise that 'homeless women are very vulnerable to harm as individuals, and as a community because of the extreme victimization, stigmatization and marginalization they endure'. The moral challenges for researchers is then to develop their inquiries in ways that do not make the individual participants suffer further. It is also imperative that researchers be cautious and aware that their studies have the potential to reinforce stereotypes and contribute to discrimination against homeless women as a whole.

In their case study of parents of missing children, Deborah Lewis Fravel and Pauline Boss (1992: 130) argue that researching parents whose children have disappeared, within normal circumstances, may raise serious moral and ethical questions. Many researchers, including themselves, would see that it is exploitative to conduct research with families in these tragic circumstances. They extensively discussed if their research 'would cause the family to feel compelled to talk of issues they did not want to share, or whether the study might in some way bring them undesired publicity and thus violate their privacy'. However, the family they intended to interview had discussed their situation/the issue with the media and agreed to appear on a television show to talk about their missing children. This allowed Lewis Fravel and Boss to conclude that their attempt to interview the family, with their consent, would be morally acceptable.

Sensitive researchers have raised the issue of self-disclosure of the research participants (Etherington 1996; France et al. 2000; Melrose 2002; Dickson-Swift 2005). Unanticipated disclosure or 'intimate knowledge', terms by James Henslin (2001: 25), may occur in research with vulnerable people. Through the process of talking in depth, people might disclose more about their lived experiences than they thought they would do (Daly 1992; Lupton 1998; Henslin 2001; Seymour et al. 2002; Meadows et al. 2003). Kerry Daly (1992: 10) suggests that the informal atmosphere of qualitative research, particularly when it occurs in the home, may lead the participants to disclose more than what they had originally planned. When researching a family, it involves more than one family member and a disclosure of one family member may violate the privacy of others. Daly also suggests that the inherent power imbalance between researchers and research participants may result in disclosure, as some participants may feel obligated to respond to questions they would not otherwise answer. Although sometimes it is beyond our control, researchers should actively encourage their participants not to talk about others in the interview by reminding them of privacy issues or asking the participants to withdraw segments of data from the record so that the privacy of other people may not be breached. This type of situation can be problematic for both the researcher and the participants. Researchers must develop their own strategies for handling these types of difficulties (Henslin 2001).

In their research on midlife with Aboriginal women, Lynn Meadows and colleagues (2003) point out that once the women were more comfortable talking with the researchers, they disclosed extremely sensitive details about not only themselves, but also about their families and communities. Often, women spoke about issues which were sensitive at a community level, such as the band council politics that prevented them obtaining employment, and the incompetence of the native police officer which again prevented them from reporting domestic violence. In their focus group research on end-of-life care with older people in Sheffield, England, Jane Seymour and colleagues (2002: 523) tell us that one participant recounted that 18 years ago she had engaged in euthanasia without any guidance when she was left with morphine syrup to give her mother who was dying from cancer. What would you do in this case? Seymour and colleagues responded to this occasion by getting the group to discuss the meaning of euthanasia and the differences between intention to kill and the delivering of relief to suffering.

Barry Hall and Judith Kulig (2004: 365), in their research with Kanadier Mennonites in Canada, confronted an ethical issue that left them with an uneasy answer. During the research process, it became known that Kanadier mothers drove, to take their children to a health clinic, without a driving licence. This placed the researchers in a dilemma as to whether they should report these activities, knowing that if the mother could not drive her child would be denied health care. They admit that there are no easy answers to these circumstances. The nature of qualitative research as well as human nature, Hall and Kulig suggest, may lead to some unanticipated events such as the one they had encountered in their research.

In their study on the health beliefs of children and young people, Alan France and colleagues (2000) had to consider a possibility that the children may disclose their experiences of sexual and physical abuse and risk-taking behaviours. Not only are researchers legally required to report sexual abuse to the appropriate authority, but it is also their moral obligation that something has to be done to help the children who are at risk or in danger. But this would override the confidentiality and anonymity that the researchers have promised the children. As such, they decided that the children must know about this before agreeing to take part in the research. France and colleagues (2000: 161) elaborate:

> In our introduction, we therefore announced that we offered complete confidentiality although if any disclosure of sexual abuse is made then we had an obligation to take appropriate action. Our rationale for this statement was that those who may have considered disclosure would be clearly informed of what our ultimate response would be, therefore, allowing them to make an informed decision about disclosure themselves.

France and others contend that they did not intend to discourage disclosure, but to give young people sufficient information so that they could make their own decision. This strategy was also employed by Melrose (2002) in her research with juvenile prostitutes in England and Wales.

However, Tim and Wendy Booth (1994a) provide an example which I think can protect the researcher working with vulnerable people. In their study with parents with learning difficulties, very often, the participants revealed experiences such as rape, incest, child abuse, rejection and attempted suicide. Booth and Booth (1994a: 40) contend that such disclosures can create ethical dilemmas for the researchers, particularly 'when the principle of confidentiality comes into conflict with wider moral and legal responsibilities'. They take a position that 'confidentiality must be upheld although interviewers should not be expected to carry the moral burden of their knowledge alone'. As such, in their research, they established a reference group comprising a priest, workers from an advocacy group (one had learning difficulties), a social worker who has been working with people with learning difficulties, and a researcher in the learning difficulties area. The reference group enables them to 'share ethically sensitive or traumatic information which is presented anonymously so that their traumas and difficulties can be eased'.

It is, however, not all as negative as it sounds. The research participants may find that by taking part in a research project, they are able to talk about matters which they might not have otherwise had a chance to talk about in every day life or to anyone (Dunlap et al. 1990; Morse and Field 1995; Morse 2000; Cutcliffe and Ramcharan 2002; Gair 2002; Dyregrov 2004; Grinyer 2004; Hall and Kulig 2004; Hess 2006). The confidential nature of research may permit these people to open up and reveal their concerns. Additionally for some, participating in research provides them with a therapeutic experience (Munhall 1991; Norris 1991; Morse and Field 1995; Usher and Holmes 1997; Cutcliffe 2002; Cutcliffe and Ramcharan 2002; Parnis et al. 2005; Hess 2006), and in some cases it is empowering (Campbell 2002; Rickard 2003). People feel that at last someone is listening to their vulnerable stories and for many, this gives them a chance to 'put it all together' (Morse and Field 1995; Gair 2002; Dyregrov 2004; Grinyer 2004; Baker et al. 2005). The participants in Sue Gair's study on adoptive parents (2002: 134) told her that they had been waiting for someone who would be interested in their stories. One woman, Madge, put it this way:

> I couldn't believe it when I saw your article in the paper. I said to Geoff, look at this, this is exactly what we've been waiting for, someone interested in us ... I've always felt there wasn't anything done, they've neglected the parents. Thank you for bothering to listen.

In a study on child rape in South Africa and Namibia (Jewkes et al. 2005), the children and parents who participated in the study remarked that they looked forward to seeing a researcher again as they felt that they could talk about their experiences and the way they managed to work through their trauma. Norris (1991), during her interviews with mothers who give their consent to their daughters' terminations of pregnancy, found that the mothers became distressed when confronted for the first time, but by the time they finished the interviews, they would be engaging in small talk, joking and laughing. Norris (1991) remarks that the interviews were therapeutic opportunities which allowed the mothers to talk about these highly sensitive issues, and hence they could relieve their distress in ways that they had not been able to do earlier, even with their husbands. As Cutcliffe and Ramcharan (2002: 1003) contend, although participation in research can bring up some painful feelings, 'it is also possible that telling their story can be therapeutic for the participants and thus could be regarded as producing a positive outcome for them, that is, a beneficent act'.

Eloise Dunlap and colleagues, in their research on crack users in New York City (1990: 133), paid the participants some incentives for their time in the study. Although the incentive was the reason for their initial agreement to be interviewed, many participants remarked that having an opportunity to tell the stories of their addiction and criminal acts in a safe environment offered more important rewards than monetary payments. Many were happy to have the opportunity to talk and to have someone listen to the accounts of their problematic lives. Dyregrov (2004: 392) contends that researchers have opposed carrying out research with vulnerable people such as bereaved parents who have lost their children through death. But these parents may in fact benefit from participating in research as it is an indication that they are 'the focus of interest, concern, and caring attention', and that they are being taken seriously. The value of being able to tell their stories by participating in research can be seen from the account of Denise, a participant in Anne Grinyer's study (2004: 1341) of parents whose children died of cancer. She puts it succinctly:

> I can now value Alexander's death with the same equal measure as his life, for its profound effect on shaping our future lives and the whole experience being used for the future benefit of others. It has given added meaning to our loss. It will continue to reinforce my newer need to work helping children and adolescents with cancer and their families.

In her research with women who had experienced domestic violence, Emma Williamson (in Hallowell et al. 2005: 16) tries to justify the morality of her research. She puts it this way:

> Even before I began interviews with the women, I was well aware that I would be asking them to recall very personal and traumatic experiences. Consequently, I spent a long time justifying to myself the need to put them in potentially difficult and distressing situations. The only way I felt able to do this was to ensure that the research would be 'useful' to people other than myself.

Although Williamson was concerned that she was not a professional counsellor, she felt that, occasionally, the interview process was therapeutic to her research participants.

Another important study that deserves mentioning is that of Wendy Booth and her husband (see Booth and Booth 1994a,b, 1998; Booth 1998) who carried out research with parents with learning difficulties. At first, it was unclear whether the research participants would be able to articulate their views in the research, and hence an unstructured approach for data collection was adopted.

Their study was carried out with the highest ethical standards and produced first-hand information for health and social services to support people with learning difficulties and their parenting roles.

Here, I wish to point to another angle of the debate on the morality of research. Within some highly sensitive and vulnerable groups, such as people with terminal illnesses and injuries, there is a debate regarding the moral imperative of involving them in research. Why should researchers intrude into the lives of these people at the times during which they are extremely vulnerable? Many may agree with this, but not Jan Morse (2000: 545) who puts it bluntly that 'it is immoral not to conduct research with the critically ill or dying; they are the most disenfranchised members of our society and most in need of understanding. Qualitative research can provide insights into their experiences, their discomforts, and their needs and show how care can be improved and their needs met'. Morse argues that conducting research with extremely vulnerable people 'is good – good in the moral sense'. Kinta Beaver and colleagues (1999) too argue that it is important to gain knowledge about people with terminal illnesses if we aim to achieve a service provision with high quality that meet their needs.

Another moral issue concerns the degree of involvement of the researcher with the participants (Fontana and Frey 2005). Laud Humphrey's research on Tearoom Trade (1970, 1975) is a good example here. In Tearoom Trade, Humphrey examined homosexual encounters in public toilets in parks, which he called 'tearooms', by volunteering to act as a 'watch queen' (to lookout for them). As Humphrey could not reveal his true identity to the men in the tearoom, he kept the record plate numbers of their cars and this allowed him to find their addresses later on (with the help of police files). He then interviewed many of these men in their homes without them knowing that he had been their watch queen. Humphrey's attempt to secure his research participants certainly has been condemned by many sensitive researchers. Would this be morally right or wrong for sensitive researchers?

Another interesting and important example of moral issues in research involving sexuality that I wish to point out is that of Joseph Carrier (1999). Carrier, who is gay, carried out a participant observation of male homosexuality in Mexico. Carrier argues that a study on male homosexuality conducted by a gay man should not be seen as different from a study on heterosexuality or bisexuality conducted by a heterosexual or a bisexual man. However, as he (1999: 208) puts, participant observation of male homosexuality carried out by a gay man is 'generally given special scrutiny and viewed with suspicion'. The moral concern, and also a main fear, is that 'the gay male researcher may be diverted by uncontrollable urge and target male respondents as sexual partners during the field investigation'.

The work of Erich Goode, with the fat civil rights organisations (2002), is another moral issue that has been controversial in academia. Goode (2002) admitted that he had sexual intimacies with some of the research participants. In fact, one of the persons he met at research meetings became pregnant and had a child with him. In his publication (2002), Goode talked about the problems of sexual relationships between researchers and the respondents. He also suggested that researching with these organisations was a waste of time. His attitudes and behaviours were criticised by many sensitive researchers (see Bell 2002; Manning 2002; Sagui 2002; Williams 2002). And Williams (2002: 560) has this to say, 'I would hope and expect that sociologists and their audiences could understand public discrimination without sleeping with their victims'. Again, is it morally acceptable for Goode to behave the way he did?

Ethical Issues

Conducting research on vulnerable people raises numerous ethical issues and these require careful consideration. As Kong and colleagues (2002: 252) contend, 'forming an ethical strategy is as much art as science and figures as much in personally sensitive research of any kind'. Within the research agenda of sensitive topics, Lee-Treweek and Linkogle (2000b: 15) argue that researchers need to protect their research participants. Discussions around the ethics of bringing people through painful experiences are essentially necessary. Sensitive researchers must carefully manage the emotions of the participants and ensure that by participating in their studies, the vulnerable research participants are not left with painful experiences. As Lee (1993) and Flaskerud and Winslow (1998) suggest, in carrying out our research with vulnerable people, we need to be more ethically responsible for their lives and well-being and see that we do not make them more vulnerable. Although ethical issues are important for all research, sensitive researchers must be more cautious about the confidentiality, privacy and anonymity of their participants (Dickson-Swift, 2005). As Flaskerud and Winslow (1998: 10) clearly put it:

> Research with vulnerable populations challenges us to consider once again ethical principles basic to research. Issues of providing informed consent, maintaining confidentiality and privacy, weighing the risks and benefits of a study, and paying attention to issues of fairness are all especially important when working with groups who are vulnerable.

In their research with people living with HIV infection, Flaskerud and Winslow (1998: 10) investigated risk behaviours of their participants. When it came to the time to present their findings, they had to be extremely careful about their writing. They had to ensure that what they wrote would not stigmatise their participants further, as this might make it even more difficult for this vulnerable group to receive appropriate health care, obtain a job and participate in the larger community. (See also Brown and Thompson (1997), Soskolne (1997), McCarthy (1998), Stalker (1998), Booth (1999), Seymour and Ingleton (1999), Ramcharan and Cutcliffe (2001), Cutcliffe and Ramcharan (2002).)

Clifford Christians (2005: 144–45) suggests that codes of ethics comprise informed consent, deception, privacy and confidentiality and accuracy. In this chapter, I will focus on three issues: informed consent, confidentiality and issues concerning risk and harm.

Informed Consent

Informed consent, according to Emanuel and others (2000: 2703), is defined as 'the provision of information to participants, about purpose of the research, its procedures, potential risks, benefits, and alternatives, so that the individual understands this information and can make a voluntary decision whether to enrol and continue to participate'. Although obtaining informed consent from participants is required in conducting any research (see Cassell and Young 2002; Christians 2005; Hoeyer et al. 2005; Sin 2005), gaining the consent from certain groups of vulnerable people requires special sensitivity (see Brown and Thompson 1997; Usher and Holmes 1997; Brigham 1998; McCarthy 1998; Stalker 1998; Seymour and Ingleton 1999; Whittell and Ramcharan 1999; Knox et al. 2000; Crigger et al. 2001; Bosk 2002; Melrose 2002). Charles Bosk (2002: 5–65) points out that morally valid consent comprises four criteria: disclosure, understanding, voluntariness and competence. Researchers are required to provide sufficient information (disclosure) so that the research participants 'will have the understanding necessary to provide a voluntary and competent informed consent'. Some vulnerable groups, such as older people living in institutions, often feel disempowered and because of their vulnerability, may unthinkingly agree to participate in research (Fisk and Wigley 2000). Hence, researchers need to ensure that they are not knowingly coerced to take part in their research.

Virginia Dickson-Swift (2005: 23) contends that 'researchers seeking to gain informed consent from participants need to ensure that the participants fully understand what it means for them to participate in the study and that they have really consented to do so' (see also Warren 2002; Christians 2005; Sin 2005). Sue Booth (1999: 78) suggests that obtaining informed (and conscious) consent from individuals who are under the influence of medication or drugs, who are mentally ill, intoxicated or under-aged necessitates clear and simple language so that these people thoroughly understand what they have agreed to do. It may also be appropriate that researchers read the consent to the participants, as some may not be able to read properly, or fear some negative consequences on signing the consent form (Warren 2002). Similarly, Jan Morse (2000) suggests that when obtaining informed consent from critically ill people, sensitive researchers need to make sure that they are fully aware of what is happening around them. Researchers need to choose the moment when they are not at the anxious, fatigued or extremely ill stage for their consent, as these conditions will affect their understanding and rational judgement. Sensitive researchers also need to be aware that often, there are language and cultural factors which may affect people's understanding of what participation in a research project means (Dickson-Swift 2005). This is particularly so when researchers wish to conduct sensitive research with vulnerable groups from different cultures.

Sensitive researchers need to ensure that vulnerable research participants are able to give a full informed consent. In order to do so, the researchers need to 'provide a full disclosure of the nature of the research that will take place, including a warning about any potentially sensitive or emotional topics that will be covered' (Dickson-Swift 2005: 24). People need to know that they have the right to refuse to participate and withdraw from the research anytime (see also Corti et al. 2000; Christians 2005; Sin 2005). Again this is particularly essential when conducting research with vulnerable people from a cross-cultural background (such as with ethnic minority groups) as there are often issues of language involved, and children or people with learning disabilities, and it is likely that they do not really understand what they are consenting to (Booth and Booth 1994a,b; Swain et al. 1998; Bagley 2000; Costley 2000; Detheridge 2000; France et al. 2000). People with a profound level of disability may not be able to give consent at all, and in this case, parents or family members may be asked to provide consent (Detheridge 2000; France et al. 2000). This is also applicable to young children who legally cannot give their own consent. In these cases, researchers have to secure informed consent through adult gatekeepers such as parents and guardians (Punch 2002).

Michelle McCarthy (1996), for example, conducted research in England on sexual experiences and sexual abuse of women with learning disabilities. McCarthy (1996: 119–120) elaborates on her attempt to gain informed consent in this study:

> Because people with learning disabilities can often find it difficult to understand what is being put to them and can find it difficult to make choices, careful attention needs to be paid to seeking *informed* consent to participate in this kind of process. With regards to the women's consent to come to my sessions in the first place, I would explain what it might entail, then they were simply asked if they wanted to come. Almost all said yes. As a member of staff and therefore in a position of authority, it would clearly have been difficult for them to have said no to me. Because of the power imbalance that exists between service providers and service users with learning disabilities, there was little I could do at this stage to decrease this acceptance other than make it explicit that they did not have to see me if they did not want to.

McCarthy (1996: 120) also tells us that it was not easy to obtain informed consent from the women, as the words and concepts of 'research' or 'methods' or 'policy' did not have much meaning to them. She then uses a very simple explanation: 'I'm talking to women about sex, so I can learn more about it and to try to make sure women get the help they need. I might want to talk to other people and write about what I learnt, but I won't tell them anything personal about you or use your name'. With this attempt, many women with learning disabilities agreed to take part in McCarthy's research and all allowed her to tape-record their interviews.

Informed consent can be problematic in qualitative research involving families (Daly 1992). This happens when the participants discuss issues regarding family life, where they may refer to other family members, friends, colleagues or neighbours. The researchers, as Daly (1992: 10) suggests, need to encourage the participants to 'draw their own boundaries of privacy and emphasise participants' prerogative to withdraw materials from the study at any time'.

In research with critically ill, injured and dying people, Jan Morse (2000: 542) points to some problems in obtaining informed consent from these vulnerable participants. These people are often very ill, fatigued and in pain, and they might not be able to talk because they are attached to a respirator. They might not be fully conscious, or they may be in a confused state. Because of these conditions, it may become impossible to obtain informed consent at the time of the data collection. This may stop researchers from asking questions of these extremely vulnerable people simply because informed consent cannot be obtained. According to Morse (2000), it is immoral to do so. She contends that 'what is immoral is avoiding or neglecting to do research with this population simply because it is impossible to obtain consent in the usual way. Such an attitude denies this group the possibility of any improvement in care that might result from our work'. In a case like this, Morse (2000: 542) suggests, researchers need to think about another way of securing informed consent. They may secure permission from family members, and then wait for the data collection to take place when the conditions of the participants improve and they can give their own consent.

Marina Barnard (2005: 14–15) too suggests that the issue of informed consent needs to be more emphasised in researching vulnerable people and sensitive issues because 'it is much more elusive'. When researchers invite potential participants to take part in their study, the researchers guarantee their participants that the interview information will be treated as confidential, and that they will be protected from being personally identified by others. In her research, Barnard (2005: 15) tells us that she told the participants that they will be protected from individual harm occurring from what they would be telling her as a researcher. But researchers cannot really promise participants that they would not be harmed as a community group. This is what Sieber and Stanley (1988) refer to as 'socially sensitive', because the research findings can have great ramifications for the group of people who are represented in the research (see also Johnson and Clarke 2003). In Barnard's study, she tells us, one mother with a drug problem made a comment during the interview: 'you'd sell your wean for a tenner bag' (£10 bag of heroin). Mothers in her study tended to make comments about the burden of having children, their irritations and drug use habit. If taken out of context, these types of comments confirm public stereotyping images of all problem drug users and their parenting roles. This is an ethical dilemma that many sensitive researchers have to deal with.

Confidentiality

Confidentiality aims to conceal the true identity of the participants (Christians 2005). Therefore, it is essentially important in research with the vulnerable groups. Sometimes, confidentiality is violated, not by the researchers but by other sources, and the researchers are blamed (Demi and Warren 1995: 196; Baez 2002). As Deborah Lupton (1998) points out (and I have discussed this in an earlier section too), the flexible nature of qualitative research may provide the vulnerable a chance to speak about their secret affairs – the secrets that they find difficult to tell people outside the research sphere – due to the promise of confidentiality. In conducting research with groups who are engaged in illicit behaviours or illegal activities, this will pose some ethical hurdles. As Sue Booth (1999: 78) asks, if during the course of our research, a participant discloses his or her involvement in criminal activity, what do we, as researchers do? Do we have ethical obligations to report such activities to relevant authorities? My position is that this illegal activity is disclosed in the course of our research. Prior to participating in our research, the participant has signed a consent form which will ensure confidentiality regarding his or her life. We are acting as researchers, and we are bound to the ethical commitment that we have promised our participants. Then, our discovery must be confidential. This standpoint may not be agreed upon by some researchers who argue that researchers must be responsible for the social well-being of the participants. If researchers are under pressure to report on this issue, they then 'have an obligation to inform the participants "up front" ' (Booth 1999: 78; Melrose 2002). In her research with juvenile prostitutes in England and Wales, Margaret Melrose (2002: 342) contends that due to the extremely sensitive nature of the research, it was essential for the research team to promise confidentiality to the participants. They also anticipated that there may be some circumstances, where confidentiality could not be guaranteed, particularly where there was an urgent risk to the safety or life of their participants. The participants were, therefore, informed up front about the conditions on which confidentiality might be breached. As Clifford Christians (2005: 145) puts this clearly, 'no one deserves harm or embarrassment as a result of insensitive research practices'. The most disturbing and unethical harm in research is when the participants are damaged by the disclosure of their private world. This is precisely the point I wish to make here.

Confidentiality is extremely important with some vulnerable groups, particularly those who are marginalised and stigmatised in society. Researching the complex nature of gay men and lesbians, for example, as Kong and colleagues (2002: 252) strongly put it, necessitates the researcher to take 'a pragmatic ethical strategy'. Most gay men, lesbians, and bisexual and transgendered people will not talk about their personal experiences unless they feel safe. More importantly, Kong et al. (2002: 251) caution us that to ask gay men to speak about their lived experiences is equivalent to asking them to 'go through another form of coming out'. Hence, to me, confidentiality must be ensured and researchers must make every effort to maintain this.

Confidentiality is also important when sensitive researchers present the voices of their participants. Most often, qualitative research relating to vulnerable people or sensitive topics have very small numbers of people or contain very specific groups, such as members of small ethnic minority groups or of particular geographical areas, which can make the process of maintaining anonymity difficult. Sensitive researchers must ensure that these people or their community will not be easily identified by the research findings (Dickson-Swift 2005). In reporting their findings about the 'vulnerable', researchers may adopt different ways to protect the true identity of their search participants. For example, the research sites where researchers conducted their research can be made anonymous by giving a fictitious name (Melrose 2002). When presenting the participants' verbatim explanations, their pseudonyms are used rather than their real names (Dickson-Swift 2005; Hess 2006). This is what I have done in my writing, and many other qualitative researchers also do the same.

Risk and Harm: Safety Issues of the Participants

> For most, if not all of us, harm is the very last thing we want to happen, particularly where those we research are already socially excluded.
>
> (Barnard 2005: 13)

Safety issues and risk to the participants have largely been silenced within the social science domain (see Paterson et al. 1999; McCosker et al. 2001; Barnard 2005; Dowling 2005). This is probably because researchers have conformed to issues of informed consent and promises of anonymity and confidentiality of the participants (Morse 2001), and this is seen as sufficient to protect them from harm. But as Chih Hoong Sin (2005: 279) suggests, we as sensitive researchers have our responsibility to ensure the physical, emotional, and social well-being of our research participants. We must ensure that they will not be adversely affected by participating in our research. Margaret Melrose (2002: 343) too contends that 'researchers have a duty to ensure that no harm comes to their subjects, whatever their ages, as a result of their agreement to partici-pate in research. If we cannot guarantee that such participation may improve their lives, we must ensure, at least, that our scrutiny of them does not leave them worse off'. Like Raymond Lee (1995), I suggest that safety issues need to be more visible in discussions of qualitative research methodology due to the extent and depth of involvement of the participants, not just as individuals taking part in our research, who can be harmed by our research findings. For example, if our research points to negative images of homeless people and drug users, the whole community of homeless people and drug users will be stigmatised, and it may have great influence on health and welfare services provided for these groups of vulnerable people (see Paradis 2000 for example).

Conducting research with vulnerable populations may lead to unintentional danger to the participants (de Laine 2000; Melrose 2002; Sin 2005). Hence, special attention needs to be paid to risks to the participants throughout the research processes (Melrose 2002). By taking part in our research, some participants may have to deal with the consequences of our research actions as well as with the disclosure and publishing of our research findings (Lee 1993; Tunnell 1998; Carrier 1999; de Laine 2000; Langford 2000; Paradis 2000;

Ellsberg et al. 2001; Williamson and Prosser 2002; Farquhar and Wing 2003; Barnard 2005; Sin 2005).

Some, like women who are subjected to domestic violence, may be vulnerable to threats from their partners if they participate in a research project (Bergen 1993, 1996; Langford 2000). David Langford (2000: 135) cautions us that abusive men tend to be suspicious, jealous and controlling. They often search through their partner's handbags or other belongings. If such a man learns that his partner is taking part in a research project, by discovering a signed consent form for example, this could put the woman at high risk due to the man's retaliatory violence.

In a research with pulmonary TB patients in northern Thailand conducted by Ngamvithayapong-Yanai and colleagues (2005), one potential participant refused to take part in the research as she was afraid that she would lose her employment at a restaurant if her TB became known to her employer through research publication or any other means. Tunnell (1998: 208) contends that the research may be known to legal authorities and they may want to access research data. In many cases, participants were subjected to scrutiny as a result of taking part in research. In his study in Brazil, Peritore (1990) interviewed members of the Communist party and found that his participants were subsequently re-interviewed by security forces. Shahidian (2001: 59), in his study of Iranian underground political activists in exile, contends that his study was sensitive as 'it reveals information that could be potentially harmful to (former) activists'. In the course of undertaking his study, Shahidian was concerned about 'the danger potentially caused by revealing sensitive information'. During the interviews, the participants revealed 'information regarding networking in prison, preparation for smuggling out of and into countries, and mechanisms that refugees have developed to deal with various institutions in host countries such as immigration or welfare offices'. Shahidian realised that by the time he published his work, the data would be too old to cause any threat to the participants. However, he argues, 'there was no guarantee that all people involved would be out of danger before publication. Political prisoners were particularly concerned'. Therefore, Shahidian omitted many details or kept them to an absolute minimum to protect his participants. This is what sensitive researchers have advocated: that we make sure that what we find in our study will not further marginalise our participants, as I have suggested earlier (see also Dickson-Swift 2005).

Participants who take part in some areas of research may reveal personal and intimate details about their lives and these people can be vulnerable in many ways (Brannen 1988; Renzetti and Lee 1993; Demi and Warren 1995; Carrier 1999; James and Platzer 1999; Johnson 2002; Seymour et al. 2002, 2004; Sin 2005). John Johnson (2002) points out that in the process of talking in great depth with the participants, the discussions may include information concerning their illegal or deviant activities, which could have grave consequences for the lives and reputations of these people if it becomes known publicly. As Joseph Carrier (1999: 207) contends, the risk to the social well-being of the participants is 'heightened' when the research involves 'highly private, sensitive and sanctioned human behaviours such as sexual relations', particularly when it concerns male homosexuality which is still stigmatised in many societies and in some, is still 'illegal' to a certain extent.

Psychological and emotional distress is also common (Kavanaugh and Ayers 1998; Paradis 2000; Barnard 2005; Sin 2005; Hess 2006; see also Chapter 3 in this volume). As Dickson-Swift (2005: 26) points out, the participants may be 'vulnerable to their own emotions being stirred by taking part in the research'. Sin (2005: 279) too contends that 'the experience of participating in research may cause some participants to feel disturbed and anxious. It may also give rise to uncalled for self-knowledge with adverse psychological implications'. In her study with bereaved relatives of organ donors, Sque (2000) remarked that painful memories of the participants were being dragged up in the process of interview. Doing this type of inquiry, researchers delve into the private worlds of the participants and it is likely that their private worlds will be invaded, and this may distort their lives, emotionally and physically. In Sin's study (2005) on social network and social support amongst older ethnic groups in Britain, one woman disclosed that her son was in jail and her daughters had suffered mental illnesses. She talked about her sense of guilt, hopelessness and depression and blamed herself for the problems that her children had. During the interview, she broke down many times and shed tears.

Due to the extreme vulnerability of their study with parents of missing children, Deborah Lewis Fravel and Boss (1992) made extra attempts to protect the family they interviewed. To be sure that the family clearly understood their participation and rights in participating in this research, the researcher read the informed consent form to the family before the interview took place. The family members were also given a lot of opportunities to ask questions before they signed the consent form, which they were also given a copy of to keep. Even though the family members wanted their story made public (as an attempt in finding their missing children), they were given a choice of remaining anonymous. More importantly, Lewis Fravel and Boss (1992: 130) remark that it was very likely that emotional issues, which the family was not prepared for, or even able to address, would be brought out in the interview. Pauline Boss is an experienced therapist who has been working with families under stress for many years. They believed that Boss's experience would assist her to detect and manage any stressful issue that might emerge in the interviews. Boss was asked to initiate and guide the interview.

I wish to cite a good example of ethical research undertaken by Marina Barnard (2005) in her research with parents who have drug-use problems. Barnard (2005: 1) strongly argues that 'research on socially-sensitive areas of human experience is particularly prone to raising thorny issues over the legitimacy and social consequences of the sociological gaze'. Particularly, in drugs research, the effect of drug use by parents on the safety and well-being of their children is a sensitive issue. She argues that the findings of her study will inevitably suggest an opposition between the parents' dependent drug use and their ability to take care of their children. This would mean that her findings have the capacity to harm those who took part in her research. Barnard (2005: 2) remarks,

> In the public mind problem drug use is incompatible with effective parenting and is a key component of the stigma that accrues, particularly to women with drug problems. Such terrain is tricky for research. Morality is not neutral but value laden and most researchers are uncomfortable with the notion that they might implicitly or explicitly stand in judgement of people, particularly where they are already socially excluded.

Bamard's findings strongly suggested that the children of parents with drug problems have to deal with poor development and neglect. She asserts that she 'had to steer a course between prejudice and whitewash' (2005: 5) (see also Huby 1997; Bostock 2002). She confronted dilemmas about when to probe if there were contradictory but extremely sensitive stories. She felt strongly about the sensitivity of what she had to ask the parents and their children, particularly when there were issues of stigma, shame and denial involved in the narratives. In the course of the study, Barnard (2005: 13–14) suggests that it was very likely that some participants would become distressed when they were asked about their parenting issues. The interviews may prompt the participants to confront a part of their lives that they might have tried to conceal, and hence, they may not like to be asked about it and may become upset. In such a highly sensitive area, Barnard (2005: 14) warns us, researchers must 'balance the interests of the research with those of the respondents in deciding when and when not to push for a fuller or less inconsistent account'.

Ethically speaking, how far can researchers probe their participants? This has not been discussed in research manuals. But Barnard contends that this is clearly an essentially important area because it has impact on the information that we may obtain. She contends that if the participant is willing to disclose events that were painful, it is likely that the researcher would continue to probe and ask for more details. She argues that there is a limit with researching a sensitive issue. Would it be ethical and moral that we should delve into a more distressing experience when our research participants have already been so distressed about their story? In her research, there were a few occasions when both she and her colleague deliberately avoided asking more in-depth details. One woman lost her eldest son through a suicide. Although this tragic incident may or may not be related to the experience of having parents with a drug problem, it was too unethical to probe the woman further. Barnard (2005: 14) says, although from a research perspective, it might have been better to obtain more information on this, it was ethically and morally wrong to do so. Hence, she and other researchers did not go deeper into this issue.

Clearly, Barnard felt strongly about asking the parents in her study to elaborate on the impact of their drug problem on their children. She (2005: 14) tells us,

> The mother I was interviewing started to talk about her daughter having been sexually abused when she was too enmeshed by her drug problem to supervise her adequately. She

began to cry and despite saying that she would continue to talk it through, I made the decision to stop the tape recorder and not to ask any further questions. By the close of the data collection period, however, the focus had shifted to a much greater concern with understanding the overall dynamics of the problem.

In her study, Barnard made special attempts to balance the interests of her research question with the interests and sensitivities of the research participants. It was an ongoing issue that she had to encounter throughout the life of her research project.

Strategies to Protect the Research Participants

Researchers need to consider some strategies to protect the research participants from harm arising out of their participation in the research. David Langford (2000: 136), for example, advocates a safe approach for contacting participants and argues that this is an essential part in conducting research with vulnerable groups of women who have experienced domestic violence. In his study, Langford asked the potential participants to leave a telephone number and time when it would be safe to ring. When returning the woman's telephone call, Langford also asked each participant if it was safe for her to talk. The women were asked to provide him with guidelines for leaving messages on answering machines where anyone could access the telephone. And for each contact he had with the women, a protocol of how to safely contact them was updated because the requirement for safety for some women might be changed due to the likely violence of their partners. This was also the way Hess (2006) adopted in her study on post-abortion experiences.

A similar approach was adopted by Eloise Dunlap and colleagues (1990) in their study with crack users in New York City. To create a safe environment for their participants, Dunlap and others were particularly cautious about the place for conducting their interviews. After serious consideration, a one-room office situated in an office building was selected. The building was easily accessed by public transportation and had other agencies serving many low-income people. Crack users would look just like other individuals who sought assistance from any of the agencies in the building. This reduced the participants' fears of entering unfamiliar buildings where they would be more likely to stand out.

Langford (2000: 138) particularly emphasised ensuring safety for his participants in his sensitive research. He tells us that 'interviews were held in the Health Sciences Library of a university and medical centre located within a dense urban area. Initially, public libraries or nearby churches closer to the women's neighbourhood had been considered as interview sties. However, the isolation of these locations made them undesirable'. As Lee (1995) suggests, in planning a safe interview location, the ability to obtain assistance or leave the site must be considered. In Langford's study, the health sciences library where he conducted his interviews was in close proximity to the campus police and it was located in the area where women could come and go without being too easily noticeable. Langford went to the extent of remaining in the library for at least 5 minutes after the woman he was interviewing left. This was to ensure that his participant would not be seen leaving with him.

In her research with juvenile prostitutes in England and Wales, Margaret Melrose (2002: 342–43) adopted a safety strategy to protect her research participants. She conducted interviews in the safety environment of agency buildings as much as possible. If this was not possible, the interviews would be carried out at other premises, but she would be accompanied by a worker from the agency who had organised the interview for her. Being in a familiar place or having someone they knew, Melrose points out, created a safe atmosphere for the participants.

As I have pointed out earlier, the research participant may become emo- tionally distressed or disturbed by participating in the research (Barnard 2005), and the researchers have their ethical responsibility to find ways to minimise this emotional experience. Alty and Rodham (1998: 280) recommend a debrief session after the interview in order to assist the participants to have an oppor- tunity to talk about the situations or feelings that trigger their emotions. They contend that without this debriefing, researchers fail to fulfil their obligations to their research participants and it is a breach of their ethical responsibility. But Emily Paradis (2000: 847) contends that debriefing may not suffice to protect vulnerable participants. They need to have access to other types of support services, including counselling, once debriefing is done. These support services must also be made appropriate to vulnerable people and this may include access hours, location and the model of services to be accessible and culturally appropriate to research participants.

In their study on child rape in South Africa and Namibia, Rachel Jewkes and colleagues (2005: 1811) were particularly cautious about ethical issues in their study with children. They strictly observed the WHO Guidelines for Ethical Research on Violence Against Women and held discussions with other researchers of child rape before embarking on, and during, the fieldwork period. They sought ethical approval from the University of the Witwatersrand Ethics Committee in Namibia, and from the Ministry of Health and Social Services. The University Ethics Committee was concerned about how to ensure the confidentiality of abused children, and to avoid the possibility that the children would be further victimised. The Committee also required that some referral systems must be pre- pared in case there was a disclosure of child rape. These serious concerns were incorporated into the design and the conduct of their study. All the potential participants were also informed that their participation was totally voluntary. They did not have to agree if they did not wish to, and they would not be adversely affected if they did so. Jewkes and his colleagues opted for a verbal con- sent rather than a written one as this was seen as less intrusive for the vulnerable children. Children were only asked to participate after their parents had agreed.

An innovative ethical attempt which aims to protect the vulnerable participants is the 'ethics-as-process' approach, theorised by Paul Ramcharan and John Cutcliffe (see Ramcharan and Cutcliffe 2001; Cutcliffe and Ramcharan 2002;

Parnis et al. 2005). This approach proposes a different way of obtaining informed consent, but sits neatly within the flexible nature of qualitative methodology. The 'ethics-as-process' approach necessitates 'viewing research as a process with its ongoing and negotiated ethical dimensions'. It allows researchers to be informed about any ethical issue that may occur at any stage during the research process. Put simply, the 'ethics-as-process' approach includes the following (Cutcliffe and Ramcharan 2002: 1006):

> An initial attempt to gain consent, where the purpose and procedure of the research are described to the participant. The potential risks and benefits, as they are known at that point in time, are also explained, and the emergent nature of the design is made clear, which is an important component of informed consent. With this, the possibility of unforseen risks and benefits emerging during the course of the research is highlighted. Along with such explanation is the reassurance that matters of consent will be raised again during the research process, particularly as hitherto unknown risks or benefits become clear or, indeed, whenever the participant feels the need to raise matters of consent. Finally, the consent to represent a person in a particular way might be handled through member checks; this would provide the final vindication of the researcher's work from the interviewee's point of view.

This innovative approach has been referred to as 'process consent' by Munhall (1991), who suggests that the approach would encourage mutual participation and affirmation between the research participants and researchers. When working with some vulnerable groups, this process provides an opportunity for the researchers and participants to be able to re-negotiate and re-arrange some forms of consent during the research life if needs arise due to unforseen situations. The approach sits neatly within the major ethical principles of research set out by the Department of Health in the United Kingdom (2001: 8): 'dignity, rights, safety and well-being'. And it sits neatly within the feminist standpoint that argues for pursuing research 'as a collegial activity... which subject-participants and researcher-participants collectively negotiate the terms of participation and the goals of the activity' (Baylis et al. 1998: 246).

A good example of the 'ethics-as-process' approach is that of Cutcliffe and Ramcharan (2002: 1006) in their unpublished research examining potential reasons for suicide. In this study, they interviewed the family and friends of 70 suicide victims. They elaborate:

> The manner of death and the proximity of the interview to the day of the person's death indicate that the families of these victims might well have felt threatened, lonely, and/or vulnerable. With the ethics-as-process approach in mind, we did not view the research interview as a solitary, isolated, or 'one off' event. During many of the interviews, which usually lasted more than 2 hours, a rapport was established and a tentative relationship or qualitative nexus formed. At the conclusion of the initial interview, the families were informed that should they wish to discuss anything further about the suicide or the research process, they were welcome to make contact with any of us. Furthermore, we offered the families the opportunity to view the transcripts of the interviews and copies of the research reports as they were produced and to attend any of the presentation seminars as the results were disseminated.

Many families took up these offers and many continued to make contacts long after the research had ended. The research team was able to manage these contacts and ensured that its departure was conducted sensibly. The participants' feedback indicated that they did not experience a 'hit-and-run' event and that the research team dealt with these 'potentially emotive matters with sensitivity', and because of this, they 'experienced a gradual withdrawal from the research' (Cutcliffe and Ramcharan 2002: 1006).

Taking the 'ethics-as-process' approach as a framework, Cutcliffe and Ramcharan (2002: 1002) suggest that ethical considerations need to include the following so that the research participants can be protected:

- Trust must be developed with the participants and is essentially required throughout the research process; not just as a one-off event at the beginning of the research.
- Ensure that informed consent is obtained prior to the commencement of the research, and re-established during the research process.
- Make sure that the participants are clearly informed that they have their rights to withdraw from the research at any point of time.
- Ensure that the participants are respected and that their dignity remains intact throughout the research process.
- Terminating the research process and withdrawal from the field must be dealt with tactfully and sensitively.
- Inform the participants that they have the right to check how they are represented in transcripts and writing.
- Be cautious about potential harm to the research participants, and prepare the necessary 'safety net' of support if needed.

Here, and before I end this chapter, I wish to make reference to a valuable ethical attempt that Hannah Cooper and colleagues (2005) have undertaken to protect their research participants. As their study was about drug injectors and the interference of police for their harm reduction practice, illegal behaviours were often elicited in their interviews. They obtained a Federal Certificate of Confidentiality from the National Institutes of Mental Health to prevent their data being subpoenaed by any authorities. In addition, oral consent, rather than written consent was sought and granted by the Harvard School of Public Health Human Subjects Committee, in order to totally protect the anonymities of their research participants. This is an example of an excellent effort that sensitive researchers may be able to emulate, so that vulnerable participants can be really protected from harm.

Conclusion

The ethical choices we make as researchers are motivated by an underlying morality (for example, a desire to: respect and care for others; promote justice and equality; protect others' freedom and avoiding harming others), which guide our behaviour, not just during the course of our research, but in all of our social interactions.

(Hallowell et al. 2005: 149)

Taking part in sensitive research may create a stressful situation for the researched who are also vulnerable due to their social or life situations. Also, by participating in research, many vulnerable people may have to deal with stigma or discrimination if a private and hidden part of their lives is publicly known. In planning sensitive research, it is essential for sensitive researchers to balance the risks against the benefits by thinking carefully about whether the research is morally justified, or if it is ethical to carry out the research, and whether the research results will further discriminate, marginalise or stigmatise the group of people (Flaskerud and Winslow, 1998: Dickson-Swift, 2005). Clearly, there are moral and ethical issues that sensitive researchers must consider before embarking on research with vulnerable people. I think we need to remember, as Sharlene Hesse–Biber and Patricia Leavy (2005: 97) remind us, that in conducting research,

Bear in mind that it is you, the researcher, who has initiated this process and involved others (your subjects). Consider this carefully as you contemplate your ethical obligations to your research participants, but as you think through these issues, do so with your own 'humanness' in mind – be realistic and fair to all involved.

TUTORIAL EXERCISES

1. You are asked to conduct research with chronically ill people. As a sensitive researcher, how would you deal with moral obligations? How would you go about obtaining an informed consent?
2. You are planning to carry out your research with a group of young people who have been involved in criminal acts. If the participants, during the process of fieldwork, disclose to you their 'illegal' activities or some socially disapproved matters, how would you deal with this?

SUGGESTED READINGS

Baez, B., 2002, 'Confidentiality in Qualitative Research: Reflections on Secrets, Power and Agency', *Qualitative Research*, 2(1): 35–58.
Coney, S., 1988, *The Unfortunate Experiment*. Auckland, Penguin Books.
Heintzelman, C., 1996, 'Human Subjects and Informed Consent: The Legacy of the Tuskegee Syphilis Study', *Scholars: Research, Teaching and Public Service*, Fall: 23–29.
Huber, J. and D. Clandinin, 2002, 'Ethical Dilemmas in Relational Narrative Inquiry With Children', *Qualitative Inquiry*, 8(6): 785–803.

Jones, J.H., 1993, *Bad Blood: The Tuskegee Syphilis Experiment*, New York: Free Press.

Liamputtong, P. and J. Dwyer, 2003, 'Women and Health: An Ongoing Agenda', pp. 119–140, In *Health, Social Change & Communities*, edited by P. Liamputtong and H. Gardner, Melbourne: Oxford University Press.

Mauthner, M., M. Birch, J. Jessop and T. Miller (eds), 2002, *Ethics in Qualitative Research*, Thousand Oaks, CA: Sage Publications.

Ramcharan, P. and J.R. Cutcliffe, 2001, 'Judging the Ethics of Qualitative Research: The "Ethics-As-Process" Model', *Health and Social Care*, 9(6): 358–67.

Sieber, J.E., 1992, *Planning Ethically Responsible Research: A Guide for Students and Internal Review Boards*, Newbury Park: Sage Publications.

Van Den Hoonaard, W.C. (ed.), 2002, *Walking the Tightrope: Ethical Issues for Qualitative Researchers*, Toronto: University of Toronto Press.

3

The Vulnerable Research Participants: Procedural Sensibilities

Chapter Objectives   47
Procedural Sensibiltiies: Introduction   47
Gaining Entrée and Recruiting the Potential Participants   48
Trust Building and Rapport   56
Reciprocity and Respect for the Participants   59
Compensation and Incentive: Inducement or Respect?   62
Sensitivity to the Needs and Lives of the Participants   66
Conclusion   69

It is particularly important when we conduct research with marginalised and disenfranchised social groups that we recognise that we may need to compromise some of the specific requirements of scientific methods. Not only do we have to ensure that our actual research process do not cause harm to the groups we are researching, but also that the research is not used to further marginalise these already vulnerable people.

(Pyett 2001: 109)

Chapter Objectives

This chapter aims to discuss salient issues pertaining to vulnerable research participants. In particular, it will

- Provide some discussions on how to access research participants who are vulnerable and difficult to access.
- Discuss the importance of building trust and rapport, the need for respect for the participants, and issues of reciprocity, incentive and compensation.
- Point to the importance of sensitivity to the lives and needs of vulnerable research participants.

Procedural Sensibiltiies: Introduction

In any qualitative research, researchers need to consider certain processes in order to ensure the success of their research. However, when the research deals with vulnerable and hard-to-reach research participants, it is important that sensitive researchers need to be more vigilant about the procedures. To borrow Christopher Dunbar's words (Dunbar et al. 2002: 290), I will discuss 'procedural sensibilities' that sensitive researchers need to bear in mind when conducting research with vulnerable groups. There are numerous issues involved in carrying out research with most vulnerable and hard-to-reach research participants. In this chapter, I will refer to the following issues: accessing research participants, the importance of trust building and rapport, the need to have respect for the participants, issues of reciprocity, incentive and compensation, and the importance of being sensitive to the needs and lives of vulnerable research participants.

Gaining Entrée and Recruiting the Potential Participants

How do we gain access to difficult-to-reach individuals and learn about their lives which are usually kept hidden and secret? How do we make contact with these individuals, particularly if they do not wish to be found? Locating these populations is a challenging task and too often problematic (see Griffiths et al. 1993; Lee 1993; Faugier and Sargeant 1997; Alty and Rodham 1998; Flaskerud and Winslow 1998; Groger et al. 1999; Moore and Miller 1999; Anderson and Hatton 2000; Jamieson 2000; Atkinson and Flint 2001; Miller and Tewksbury 2001; Wright et al. 2001; Melrose 2002; Barnard 2005; Dickson-Swift 2005). The general level of distrust keeps many people in hard-to-reach or transient populations from interacting with the researcher (Booth 1999). Accessing potential participants becomes more difficult when the research issues are more sensitive or threatening since these people have greater need to hide their identities and involvement (Renzetti and Lee 1993; Miller and Tewksbury 2001; Melrose 2002; Dickson-Swift 2005). According to Virginia Dickson-Swift (2005: 20), the vulnerable people we need in our research are 'marginal, hidden or unwilling to speak about their experiences'. Very often, vulnerable families are reluctant to enter the research field, as they do not 'trust the researchers, and have higher priority concerns such as fear of legal repercussions for use of illegal drugs or fear of exposure of their secret status' (Demi and Warren 1995: 192). Some vulnerable groups such as Hispanic Americans have high mobility rates due to their employment and other issues, and hence locating these groups can be a great challenge to researchers (Lange 2002). Due to this, recruiting these people can be a formidable task for researchers carrying out research in sensitive areas.

Social science researchers, however, have successfully gained access to their potential participants. The snowball sampling method has been extensively adopted in researching the 'vulnerable' or difficult-to-reach populations (see Biernacki and Waldorf 1981; Lee 1993; Renzetti and Lee 1993; Gagné 1996; Lichtenstein and Nansel 2000; Atkinson and Flint 2001; Wright et al. 2001; Dawson and Gifford 2003; Roberts et al. 2004; Weston 2004; Barnard 2005; Benoit et al. 2005; Cooper et al. 2005; van Kesteren et al. 2005). Lee (1993: 66) contends that 'snowball sampling is ubiquitous in the study of deviant populations because it often represents the only way of gathering a sample'. Biernacki and Waldorf's study (1981), for example, relied heavily on snowball sampling and the chain referral method in order to seek untreated ex-heroin addicts for an interview. This study is a classic example of undertaking sensitive research as it demonstrates an attempt to 'study illegal, widely condemned behaviours among members of a hidden, difficult-to-define population' (Martin and Dean 1993: 84). Atkinson and Flint (2001) too advocate the use of snowball sampling technique to locate hard-to-reach populations. They (2001: 2) argue that 'the use of snowball strategies provides a means of accessing vulnerable and more impenetrable social groupings'. It is common for members of such populations to be involved in deviant activities (such as taking drugs or selling sex). This makes them reluctant to take part in research. Accessing these hidden groups can only be done by referrals from their acquaintances or peers rather than other more formal methods of identification such as the use of existing lists or screening. In Vance's study of older homeless people (1995), he attempted to reach this group by firstly establishing a rapport with a few older homeless people. They later on introduced him to others. Umaña-Taylor and Bámaca (2004: 267) and Madriz (1998) refer to this approach as the 'word-of-mouth' technique in their study with Latinos in the United States. They assert that this approach is extremely useful in focus group research with ethnic minorities as the potential participants are more likely to take part if someone they know is also participating.

In their study on cervical cancer and Pap test with Appalachian women who were rarely or never screened, Nancy Schoenberg and colleagues (2005) had to rely heavily on the snowball method to recruit the women. They tell us,

> Since identifying women who are rarely or never screened is not a straightforward process (such individuals are often described as a 'hard to reach populations'), we relied on the trustworthiness and reputations of the local interviewers, all of whom had lived in their communities for their entire lives. These interviewers recruited the women through a snowball sampling approach, wherein one locates key informants and asks if they would know others who are likely candidates to participate and by posting themselves in locations, including a community college cafeteria, a low income housing project, and a senior citizen center, where they might encounter a wide range of women.

But, how do we locate the initial contact for a snowball sampling technique? This is the most difficult part of using this method. Placing advertisements in local newspapers and magazines or shopfronts have been adopted by some researchers (see for example, Todorova and Kotzeva 2003; Wuest et al. 2003; Stephens et al. 2004; Weaver et al. 2005). An interesting strategy was employed by Patricia Gagné (1996), who carried out in-depth interviews with battered women who had been charged of killing or assaulting abusive partners or stepfathers, and who had been granted clemency for their crimes. She utilised a snowball in accessing these women. Her initial recruitment was, however, done through the assistance of Ohio's First Lady, Dagmar Celeste and through snowball technique, she managed to interview 12 of the 26 women who had received clemency.

Richard Wright and his colleagues (2001) also adopted the snowball sampling technique in their research with burglars in St. Louise, Missouri. They located and interviewed 105 active burglars and this was done by a snowball method. Their initial access was done through employing an ex-offender who 'had few arrests and no felony conviction' although he had committed many serious crimes. He also had a high status among black street criminals in the area. At the time he was invited to take part in the research, he had retired from crime and earned a bachelor's degree. He continued to live in his old neigh-bourhood and remained friendly with local criminals. This ex-offender approached his former criminal associates, some of whom were still 'hustling' (actively involved in crimes) but others were only involved peripherally or had retired from crime. A number of 'street-wise law-abiding friends' and a youth worker were also contacted. These initial contacts were informed about the nature of the research, ensured confidentiality including an assurance that the police were not involved, and that the research participants would be paid $25 for their time. These contacts were then asked to put the ex-offender in touch with active residential burglars. In their study with drug injectors in New York City, Hannah Cooper and colleagues (2005: 676) started their snowball sampling through individuals who were identified by a local council member and community board staff. Once Cooper managed to locate parks, soup kitchens and others where the users tended to congregate, she started to have some informal conversations with them. This attempt generated new snowballs for the study.

Hanging out at services or sites commonly used by the hidden people for a period of time is a useful way of gaining access to these populations (Wiebel 1990; Rosenthal 1991; Reid et al. 1998; Wright et al. 2001; Melrose 2002; Sterk et al. 2004; Weston 2004). In his study with substance abusers, Wayne Wiebel (1990: 8) suggests that researchers should gain access through 'known and trusted confidants' as much as possible. However, if it is possible, hanging out at public places where these people tend to congregate should be done, but it should also be done 'in a friendly yet nonintrusive manner'. Wiebel (1990) also recommends that to make the presence of the researcher legitimised, it is essential that the researcher finds something to do, for example, playing pool at a pool hall or having a meal at a restaurant. Rob Rosenthal (1991) employed the 'hanging out' strategy and subsequently recruited more informants through snowballing. Rosenthal (1991: 110) contends that 'in most cases I was intro-duced to a group by someone I had previously met and such introduction in itself provided entry to the group. Through the process of snowballing, my circle of acquaintances and knowledge of places to go was constantly enlarged'. Rosenthal argues that this strategy led him to a far more diverse group of homeless participants than shelters or street surveys.

David Seal and colleagues (2000), in their current ethnographic study of young men who have sex with men (YMSM), point out that an important task of their research is to locate the hidden segment of the YMSM population who are at high risk for HIV infection, but have limited access to prevention and treatment services. Initially, the researchers spend extensive time visiting public places frequently used by YMSM including bars, parks and coffee shops. They passively observed YMSM's social–sexual interactions in these settings. As the researchers spent more time in these places, they established formal relationships with key gatekeepers including bartenders, doormen and waiters. These key gatekeepers eventually became key informants who provided their 'insights into the social–sexual interactions of YMSM' (Seal et al. 2000: 13).

With some vulnerable groups, particularly highly closed groups, having 'a visible and respected individual who holds a position of authority, high respect, or leadership' (Tewksbury and Gagné 2001: 78) to introduce researchers to the group is extremely essential (see van Maanen 1982; Calhoun 1992; Leinen 1993; Gagné 1996; Whyte 1996; Hopper and Moore 2001; Tewksbury and Gagné 2001; Wright et al. 2001). Richard Tewksbury and Patricia Gagné (2001: 78) point out that this person in authority will act 'as a bridge to link into a new social world, as a guide who points out what occurs and how culturally different actions are locally meaningful, or as a patron who helps to secure the trust of community members'. This not only helps researchers with their success in gaining access to their research participants but also to have an in-depth understanding of the researched. The study of battered women who had received clemency by Patricia Gagné (1996) is a good example of this introduction. Initially, Gagne relied on the assistance of the former first lady of Ohio, Dagmar Celeste. In her initial interview with Celeste, she provided Gagné with the history of the battered women's movement and its relevance to the clemency decisions. Dagmar Celeste gave Gagné permission to use her name. This provided Gagné a good chance to enter the world of activism. To be able to obtain access to the women granted clemency, Gagné needed a trusted insider to help her. In most cases, the first lady's name proved to be very effective.

Gatekeepers have been utilised to gain access to the participants (Sieber 1992; Booth and Booth 1994a; Liamputtong Rice 1996, 2000; Moor and Miller 1999; MacDougall and Fudge 2001; Umaña-Taylor and Bámaca 2004). Linda Moore and Margaret Miller (1999: 1038) propose the use of gatekeepers like families and guardians as an entry point to access the potential participants. But families and guardians may also be vigilant protectors and hence present the biggest obstacles to accessing vulnerable participants. Very often, the families or guardians believe that these vulnerable people have suffered many times and they do not deserve another disruption in their vulnerable lives (McNeely and Clements 1994; Moor and Miller 1999). Moore and Miller (1999: 1038) suggest some strategies which help to overcome this obstacle including 'carefully outlining who will conduct the study, the possible risks, how the participant will be involved, who will fund the research, and what will happen with the data'. This may 'encourage families to more willingly grant access to their vulnerable loved ones'. A helpful tactic is to highlight the benefits for the participants and ensure confidentiality and ethical approval from the researcher's reputable institution.

'Gatekeeping agencies' may also be used as a point of gaining access to the vulnerable. Health and social care agencies and others such agencies tend to act as gatekeepers for vulnerable people (McNeely and Clement 1994; Moor and Miller 1999; MacDougall and Fudge 2001; Melrose 2002; Goodman 2004; Umaña-Taylor and Bámaca 2004; Parnis et al. 2005; Takahashi and Kai 2005). In their study of adolescents with severe burns, Moor and Miller (1999) worked with a tertiary care institution specialised in paediatric burns. Miyako Takahashi and Ichiro Kai (2005) recruited Japanese women who survived breast cancer through the assistance of surgeons in breast surgery clinics in the Tokyo metropolitan area. Janice Goodman (2004) recruited Sudanese refugee youths from the resettlement agency who held legal guardianship of the youth.

But as Virginia Dickson-Swift (2005: 21) argues, these gatekeeping agencies 'can also assist the community in keeping the researcher out'. The power of gatekeepers to deny access to vulnerable people has been evidenced (Thomas 1990; Mirza 1995; Fisk and Wigley 2000; MacDougall and Fudge 2001; Sin 2005). Researchers have also experienced some difficulties in not only accessing research participants but also making progress with their research when working with gatekeeping agencies (see Parnis et al. 2005).

Peer leader researchers have also been used to access some difficult-to-reach groups. Orthodox strategies of recruiting the vulnerable, for example, placing advertisements through newspaper or health care sites may not affect some highly vulnerable groups because they have had prior negative experiences with exploitation by research projects (Flaskerud and Winslow 1998). Researchers need to work with members of the targeted group to invite potential participants and to retain them. Peer leaders, they contend (1998: 9), are 'a source of advice that is accepted by the target audience because they are people who have "walked in the shoes" of the targeted group'. Reaching out to vulnerable individuals through persons who are trusted by the potential participants is one of the most effective ways of accessing them (Gueldner and Hanner 1989; Moor and Miller 1999). Such persons, often termed 'informal gate-keepers', have great ability to recruit others to become research participants (McNeely and Clements 1994). Informal gatekeepers include key members of a group or an informal network of individuals who have similar vulnerabilities. When Adriana Umaña-Taylor and Mayra Bámaca (2004: 267) attempted to recruit Latina mothers, they placed flyers in grocery shops, restaurants, churches and schools, but they had little success. They sent letters to 900 parents of the children who went to a middle school that had 94 per cent Latino students, but only one phone call was received. Umaña-Taylor and Bámaca (2004) suggest that with Latino populations, a more personal strategy (such as by word-of-mouth from informal gatekeepers) may be more successful than using traditional methods of recruitment. In her research with Latino women, Esther Madriz (1998) applied a more personal approach including using personal net-works such as students, community leaders, and friends of friends who worked in community organisations to recruit the women and this proved to be a successful endeavour because the women were asked to participate in research by someone they knew. (See also MacDougal and Fudge 2001 for a similar argument regarding this issue.)

Richard Wright and colleagues (2001) made use of an ex-offender to initially recruit active burglars in their study in St. Louise. This ex-offender, after retiring from crime, studied for and earned a bachelor's degree. He continued to reside in his old neighbourhood and remained friends with many local burglars. Wright and colleagues met him when he attended a colloquium and expressed his (more correct) opinions about street criminals. The same strategy was employed by Dunlap and others (1990) in their study with crack users and their criminal careers in New York City, and it proved to be effective in recruiting these hard-to-reach participants. Terry Williams (1996), in his study on the cocaine culture, accessed his potential participants through ex-inmates to whom he became known through his teaching in the satellite programme. Williams (1996: 28) tells us that

> Upon their release, three of them called me and offered to take me out on the town. They showed me the night life of New York City as I had never seen it before. In the small, intimate clubs known as after-hours spots, I was introduced to a bewildering variety of people – musicians, drug dealers, punk rockers, transvestites, secretaries, doctors, dancers, gamblers, actors, policemen, prostitutes – all of whom were there to share in a lifestyle based on the enjoyment of cocaine and the pleasure and excitement brought on by the intensity of their interaction.

Most often, researchers working with the vulnerable groups employ a combination of methods in gaining access to these hard-to-reach people (MacDougall and Fudge 2001). Judith Wuest and colleagues (2003), in their study with single mothers who left their abusive partners in New Brunswick and Ontario, Canada, recruited their participants by placing advertisements in local newspapers, posters in grocery stories, community sites and libraries, contacting agencies and through their personal contacts. Similar recruitment strategies were employed by Kathryn Weaver and colleagues (2005) in their research with women who were recovering from Anorexia Nervosa in New Brunswick.

In her study with young men and crime in Scotland, Janet Jamieson (2000) utilised a number of strategies to recruit her research participants. The recruitment of young-age group participants was relatively easy as it was done through local schools. However, with the older group, it was not as simple as with the younger one. At the beginning, Jamieson utilised the electoral register to recruit 18-year-old people as she believed this would give her a sufficient base for snowballing more participants. But this method alone was not sufficient to complete her targeted sample. She then put an advertisement in the local paper in one of the study areas, which included flyers in the weekly newspaper that were distributed free of charge to all homes, and made contact with a number of local organisations and businesses in two study areas. But again, each of these means produced insufficient responses. In the end, Jamieson (2000: 66–67) tells us that her most successful attempt of recruitment

> [i]nvolved leafleting homes, local organisations and community groups and offering young people a modest financial incentive to participate in the study. We had found it particularly difficult to identify young men in the categories of desister and persister. However, when we were able to offer payment for interviews clients of a local probation project and drugs centre become more willing to participate in the research.

In her study on rape, Rebecca Campbell (2002: 2) employed what she calls 'non-invasive sampling strategies'. Campbell printed posters and fliers about her project and distributed them throughout Chicago. To access women in the communities, Campbell approached nail salons, was beauty parlours, gyms and laundry shops, among many other places. Recruiting through nail salons, I think, was an interesting and successful strategy for Campbell. Regardless of their races, ethnicities and social classes, many women are likely to use nail salons and so they would be ideal recruitment sites. In one salon, the owner placed the flyers on the drying table where women sit to wait for their nails to dry. This of course caught women's attention. Through this innovative recruitment strategy (although she admitted it was strange), Campbell was able to recruit many women for her study.

Andrea Shelton and Nahid Rianon (2004) provide an interesting recruitment strategy in their research on spousal abuse with Bangladeshi immigrants living in Houston. Following MacDougall and Fudge's (2001) strategy for recruiting the participants for focus groups and in-depth interviews, Shelton and Rianon conducted the three stages of preparation, contacting and following up in their attempt to recruit Bangladeshi women to take part in their study. Shelton and Rianon contend that a moderation of the recruitment strategies suggested by MacDougall and Fudge (2001) 'proved helpful in the recognition of cultural diversity, intercultural differences, and social differentiation with the Bangladeshi community'. Initially, the researchers were not able to obtain any participation from the women despite the attempts that were made to meet their needs and despite the fact that Rianon is a Bangladeshi woman who speaks the same language and shares the cultural background of the women. But through the outreach efforts of the first two stages, they decided that recruitment had to be done at a large social gathering where the whole family would attend. They suggested that the interviews conducted in this setting were about the Bangladeshi women's immigrant experiences, the quality of life, physical and mental distress, and suffering. After these, information about spousal abuse might be volunteered. Most women suggested that 'there would be less attention given to them individually and that they would feel less intimidated at a social outing with their husbands and peers in the midst of a large group of people engaged in the same activities (eating, watching a band, listening to music)'. In the end, 29 women were recruited during 3 cultural events held in January and February 2000 with the approval of the Bangladeshi Association. More women were invited to take part in the study, but most declined as their husbands did not approve. It took the researchers a year of repeated efforts to engage the women in their research.

Interesting recruitment strategies adopted by Beverly Leipert and Linda Reutter (2005) deserve our attention here. In their study exploring how women in geographically isolated settings in Northern Canada maintain their health, because of logical constraints caused by distance, terrain and weather, Leipert and Reutter recruited the women by television and radio interviews. They also placed advertisements about the research in local newspapers, and posters were displayed in tack-and-feed stores and auction markets. And they used word of mouth to recruit the participants. With these efforts, more than 100 women from across the north responded in order to participate in the study.

Cecilia Benoit and others (2005: 265) provide interesting strategies in accessing the participants in their research with people selling sex services in Canada. They contend that the difficulty of accessing hard-to-reach research participants have led them to work as team with community partner organisations (CPOs) 'whose local knowledge of and access to members of the hidden population are indispensable'. They refer to this method as the 'community–academic collaboration' approach (see also Ebata 1996; Small 1996; Denner et al. 1999; Warr and Pyett 1999; Lewis and Maticka-Tyndale 2000). Benoit et al. (2005: 267) tell us that 'we conducted the project in partnership with a nonprofit community partner organization (CPO) located in the study site that is largely staffed by ex-sex workers who offer street outreach services, public education, counselling, and job skills training to women, men, and, more recently, female and male youths wanting to exit the sex trade as well as those currently working in the trade'. The researcher, in working closely with the local CPO, applied for a research grant, which was approved. An advisory committee was set up and this committee included representatives from different government agencies who have had experience on the health and legal issues of sex workers and from members of outreach agencies who take care of marginalised women. Beniot and others (2005: 267) tell us that the 'multifaceted research team' played an essential part in making their research project into a 'community–academic partnership'.

Advertising for a number of research assistants (RAs) to conduct interviews, data entry and transcription was made, and several former sex workers applied for the advertised positions. Ten RAs were eventually trained to carry out different aspects of the research process. All RAs had experience working in a different area while still in the trade and these included escort agencies, massage parlours, strip clubs, bars, homes and on streets. This means that RAs and the research participants in their study had common work experience, language used in the trade and a good understanding of the working conditions in the sex trade during the life of the research. Additionally, the RAs 'had access to overlapping sex workers' networks, which they could tap to help recruit respondents otherwise hidden not only from the academics but, to some extent, also from our CPO itself' (p. 267). Due to this strategy, they were able to list potential participants who were active in the sex trade and who agreed to take part in their research. In the end, Beniot and colleagues (2005: 268) recruited their

research participants through several means including the following: personal
networks; advertisements in a local weekly magazine, the local newspaper,
and college and university student newspapers; announcements on public
bulletin boards, in shops and in clubs and through the CPO's programmes.
Many who were still active in the street sex trade during their research period
were recruited through 'a local emergency shelter for hard-to-house women'
(p. 268). In their conclusion, Benoit et al. (2005: 279) argue that

> In any event, it is highly unlikely that academic researchers without sex trade experience
> would have gained access to the worlds of adult sex workers in the first instance, or, even
> if they had, respondents would have opened up to them to the extent that took place in
> this project without the ongoing cooperation of the community partner organization and
> involvement of [local] research assistants.

Richard Tewksbury (2001: 9) suggests that researching sensitive and hard-to-
reach people requires special knowledge and skills of the researchers. He asserts,
researching 'highly stigmatized, secretive settings (such as an adult bookstore or
a sexualized public park) may present researchers with initially seeming, anom-
alous encounters'. He also warns us that 'when entering a hidden, sexual setting
it may be necessary to enter and find your way as opportunities present themselves. This trial-and-error approach can be highly stressful, and, if not successfully navigated, it can set the investigator up for embarrassment, ostracization,
and, in extreme cases, deal a fatal blow to the research'. I think this warning is
indeed legitimate in researching any hard-to-reach research participants.

Trust Building and Rapport

> Becoming trusted and seen as someone with whom research participants are comfortable
> spending time, talking, and sharing their lives is called 'establishing rapport'. In order for
> a researcher to truly understand the world from the perspectives of those being studied
> and to see how persons being studied think about their world it is critically important for
> rapport to be established.
>
> (Miller and Tewksbury 2001: 55)

As Mitchell Miller and Richard Tewksbury suggest above, building trust and
rapport are extremely necessary ingredients for conducting sensitive research
with the 'vulnerable' and hard-to-reach populations (see also Lee 1993; Booth
and Booth 1994a,b; Campbell and Wasco 2000; Harden et al. 2000; Robertson
2000; Tewksbury and Gagné 2001; Reinharz and Chase 2002; Corbin and
Morse 2003; Goodwin et al. 2003; Dickson-Swift 2005; Fontana and Frey
2005; Hesse-Biber and Leavy 2005; Irwin and Johnson 2005). A critical aspect
of research success is a researcher's ability to establish rapport and a trusting
relationship with the participants (Booth and Booth 1994a,b; Seymour 2001;
Fontana and Frey 2005). Andrea Fontana and James Frey (2005: 708) say that
'it is paramount to establish rapport with respondents; that is, the researcher
must be able to take the role of the respondents and attempt to see the situation
form their viewpoint rather than superimpose his or her world of academia

and preconceptions on them'. And 'a close rapport with the respondents opens the doors to more informed research'. Researchers need to develop rapport with their participants. Although this is important for qualitative inquiry, it is essential for sensitive research with vulnerable people because they are asked to talk about 'intimate aspects of their lives' (Dickson-Swift 2005: 99). Miller and Tewksbury (2001: 55) too suggest that rapport is much more important for researchers who deal with extreme groups.

> When persons are engaged in highly deviant activities, or believe they are stigmatized by society, or suspect that they may be arrested, harassed, fired, or shunned for their activities or lifestyles, they tend to be suspicious of 'researchers'.

Sue Booth (1999: 77) suggests that when conducting research with vulnerable and hard-to-reach populations, it is important to avoid what Yoland Wadsworth (1984) refers to as a 'data raid', where researchers do a 'smash and grab', meaning getting in, getting the data and getting out, as this raises the question of whether the researcher has any real interest in the participants. Tim Booth and Wendy Booth (1994a: 26) call this the 'hit and run' approach. And this is what Shulamit Reinharz (1983: 80) refers to as the 'rape' model of research. It is important to take the time to build trust and get to know the participants as this will provide researchers with a better understanding of their situations. It is likely that the vulnerable participants will share their lived experiences, which they have never shared with anyone, with the researchers if they feel that they have a good relationship with them and they can trust the researchers (Dickson-Swift 2005). In her study on coping with trauma and hardship among unaccompanied refugee youths from Sudan, Janice Goodman (2004) did volunteer work with the resettlement of Sudanese refugees and facilitated a support group for the youth. This volunteer work, she claimed, contributed to the young people trusting her and this led to their enthusiasm in participating in the study.

In researching the effects of AIDS on family members responsible for care of persons with AIDS (PWAs), Linda Matocha (1992) tells us that before family members agreed to take part in her study, they invited her to have dinner with them and the PWA. The dinner was served by the PWA or the caregiver and their dishes were used. Trust developed from this simple act. As Matocha agreed to this simple gesture, trust developed and continued from then on, even until the finish of her research.

Diana Russell (1990) particularly emphasised rapport in her study on sexual assault against women. She made sure that an interview schedule was designed to encourage good rapport with the participants. The selection of her research interviewers was based on their interviewing skills and their sensitivity to sexual violence. Additionally, she ensured that the research interviewers and participants shared a similar ethnic background and provided extensive training on rape and sexual abuse as well as the desensitisation of sexual language used in the interviews for her researchers. Russell (1990) believes strongly that all these tasks were essential in building good rapport with the women in her study and this ensured the success of her research.

In conducting research with older people, Clare Wenger (2002: 265) also cautions us about the importance of putting the participants at ease. This can be done by being friendly with the potential participants and showing them that their contributions are valued by the researcher. This often creates trust and rapport among older people. Once this rapport has been established, older people's reluctance to participate will be reduced and perhaps they will agree to participate in the project. Wenger (2002: 265) also strongly suggests that 'it is never appropriate for the interviewer to push too hard. Discussion and negotiation are acceptable, but "no" must mean "no" in the final analysis'.

Lori Irwin and Joy Johnson (2005: 823), in their research related to health needs and experiences of young children, suggest that it takes time to build rapport with children. Researchers should not expect that suitable rapport can be established at the first meeting with a child. This is particularly so when the researcher is a stranger, as children are nowadays taught to be cautious of strangers. Building rapport might also be promoted through allowing the children to choose the location of the interview; in their research, it was most often in the front or back garden. Irwin and Johnson also used play such as drawing, role-playing and using props, to make the children feel at ease. Irwin and Johnson (2005: 824), however, suggest several strategies which may enhance building rapport with young children, and these include the following:

- Getting to know the child before commencing the research by meeting with the child a few times.
- Talking with parents to learn about the child.
- Making use of multiple interviews in order to respect the needs of the child. Some children might find a long interview more difficult to cope with than two or three shorter ones (see also Deatrick and Ledlie 2000; Harden et al. 2000; Punch 2002).

Claire Renzetti and Raymond Lee (1993: 101) suggest that developing trustful relations is not an easy task. Very often, researchers have to deal with hostility and even danger. They contend that 'it is not unusual for the powerless or the disadvantaged to treat the researcher with scepticism, fearing that cooperation will bring in its wake only their further exploitation'. This can be clearly seen in Ilse Pauw and Loren Brener's study (2003) with female street sex workers in Cape Town. Their initial fieldwork was undertaken prior to data collection using in-depth interviews and focus groups. The researchers argue that this 'initial fieldwork allowed the research team to gain access to the population, established legitimacy for the project and initiate relationships with key informants'. The initial fieldwork took 9 months. Pauw and Brener (2003: 467) tell us that sex workers were initially suspicious of the researchers. Their suspicions were formed by their negative past experiences with the police, church groups, reporters or even health and welfare agencies. But after regular visits, the researcher became known and accepted. The researchers shared a similar race and spoke the same language as the sex workers, and this helped to increase the establishment of rapport and trust. When trust had been developed, sex workers in fact looked for the researchers and had longer conversations with them. Sex workers also asked the researchers for advice and counselling in addition to seeking help with arrests, court appearances and bail applications. The fact that sex workers perceived the researchers as 'wise' assisted the establishment of trust and provided the researchers with great opportunities 'to gain insight into the otherwise hidden worlds of the sex worker. The role of confidant and counsellor alerted researchers to the range of issues faced by sex workers in their working and private lives'. In Adler's study (1990) with drug users, she was seen and accepted as a 'wise' person and this 'wise status' allowed her to interact with, and enabled her to observe, people who saw her as an 'outsider'.

Richard Berk and Joseph Adams (2001: 61), in their study with heroin addicts and juvenile delinquents in Baltimore's inner city, suggest that developing and maintaining rapport with the participants are essential. This can be difficult in any situation, but 'when the groups in question are unusually suspicious, the necessary task of gaining ongoing rapport may be an extremely troublesome obstacle'. They suggest several strategies for researchers to over-come this. First, the researchers need to 'demonstrate consistent commitment to the goals of the investigation'. If the participants are clear that the researchers are 'sincerely involved in gathering' their data, the participants' 'trustworthiness increases'. Second, the researchers must show the participants that they are responsible individuals and are 'not motivated by morbid curiosity'. Hence, the researchers must be sincere and honest with the participants. They need to work outside the working hours, including nights and weekends. When they say they will do something, they must follow it through. It is important that the researchers need to explain the reasons for their research in as 'flattering terms' as possible. In talking with the vulnerable groups, researchers should not reinforce their 'deviant' identity or make it sounds like the groups are 'social problems' of the society. Researchers need to convince them that they possess certain knowledge and skills that the researchers do not have. Berk and Adams (2001: 63) used the following introduction in their research with heroin addicts: 'I'm just trying to find out what it is like to live around here. I don't know anything about this neighbourhood, and I thought that may be you guys could help me to find out'. Berk and Adams (2001: 63) contend that:

> Many groups are increasingly extremely sensitive to the reasons why they are being studied: and unless the researcher can justify in non-demeaning and non-threatening terms why he wants to do the research, rapport will be difficult to achieve.

Reciprocity and Respect for the Participants

Working with vulnerable and marginalised people, the process of reciprocity and respect is essential (Corbin and Morse 2003). Donna Eder and Laura

Fingerson (2002: 185) argue that ethical responsibility towards the 'vulnerable' groups such as young children needs to go beyond the protection of children's rights. Indeed, it needs to include 'a greater emphasis on reciprocity'. The reciprocity may also mean that the participants can gain from the research experience. By giving something in return for receiving information, researchers can reduce the power inequality between themselves and the researched (see Shakespeare, cited in Hallowell et al. 2005: 138–40; see also Chapter 3 in this volume). Deborah Warr (2004: 586) advocates this reciprocity in her provocative discussion on researching the 'vulnerable', such as the disadvantaged and disenfranchised, that, as researchers, 'we must make every effort to ensure that the research we undertake among the disadvantaged and disenfranchised makes a positive difference in the lives of those it touches'.

Reciprocity can also take the form of giving something back to the community in which the study takes place (Gair 2002; Dickson-Swift 2005). In the study on drugs and prostitution in Hartford, Connecticut conducted by Romero-Daza et al. (2003), the women were given educational material on HIV/AIDS and referrals to health and social services, and drug treatment was arranged if there was a need. In Pauw and Brener's study (2003) with female street sex workers in Cape Town, the participants were provided with AIDS education as well as HIV/STD educational material after their participation in in-depth or focus group interviews. In their study in Melbourne, Australia, Warr and Pyett (1999) too provided access where needed to relevant support services for female street sex workers.

Tom Shakespeare (cited in Hallowell et al. 2005: 138–40), in his research on sexuality and disability, recounts the interesting reciprocity that he has experienced. Shakespeare invited Eddie, a working-class man with spina bifida and also an artist, to take part in his interviews. Eddie said he would do so only if Shakespeare agreed to be painted during the interview. Shakespeare, as a person with restricted growth, was anxious about exposing himself to painting, but also delighted by this symbolic gesture. He tells us (cited in Hallowell et al. 2005: 139),

> It seemed to be a way of making the interview process more equal. He would be putting himself on the line by revealing his hopes and fears, and his rather chequered past. But I was also exposing myself, by allowing him to represent me in a portrait. As a person with restricted growth, I have not always been comfortable about seeing the way I look. Sometimes, I have found it hard to look in a mirror, or to see myself in visual representations.

As a sensitive researcher, Shakespeare wanted to give something back to his research participants. For him, researchers needed to have a commitment to those who kindly agree to take part in their research, and at a very simple level, reciprocity is something we all can do. This will reduce the power imbalance between the researcher and the researched. To me, Shakespeare's experience is a wonderful example of what sensitive researchers may do when working with vulnerable people. Shakespeare (cited in Hallowell et al. 2005: 140) concludes as follows:

> Eddie painting my picture was one of the times when the balance seemed most obvious. I think he was relaxed, concentrating on blending colours and planes to capture my unusual physicality, and answering questions almost as an afterthought. It made it slightly difficult to read my aide-memoire, and the tape of that interview has more pauses. After all, we were trying to do a number of different things at once: pose, question, paint and answer. We were both presenting our selves to the other. And, perhaps, this is what this form of social research is all about.

Reciprocity may include some form of social action or social changes as part of the project. This can be seen in my own research with the Hmong ethnic community in Melbourne. One Hmong woman believed strongly that her ill health after her last delivery was due to the loss of one of her souls resulting from having a caesarean operation. During the course of my research, I took her back to a maternity hospital to conduct a soul-calling ritual to regain her health (see Liamputtong Rice et al. 1994). Michelle Fine, in her work with high school dropouts (1994), represented 'the voices of African American and Hispanic adolescents in courts and public policy debates as well as in academic scholarship'. Angela Valenzuela (1999) assisted an English teacher in the high school where she was conducting her research. This teacher was dealing with problems in controlling the classroom. Valenzuela was asked to talk to the class. Through her research, Valenzuela was able to explain to the teacher the roots of the difficult classroom dynamic and the situation was solved. After completing her research on gender, status and peer culture, Donna Eder (in Eder and Fingerson 2002: 187), used knowledge about peer culture from her research for the development of a conflict intervention programme for the schools in the community.

Providing feedback or results to the participants after researchers have finished their research is one way to show respect to the participants. It is a common practice in feminist research that the participants will have an opportunity to read their interview transcript prior to the analysis and publication of their voices (Reinharz 1992). In research with children, researchers need to provide a report of their findings for the children to check the accuracy of their interpretations. The children can then hear what the researchers say about their lives and be able to respond directly to any misinterpretations of the researchers (Mayall 1999). If researchers wish to avoid treating the participants as 'objects of knowledge', we may use an interactive interviewing approach such as a focus group to provide the participants with an opportunity to express their voices during the production of data (Cook and Fonow 1984).

Reciprocity may mean that the participants asked for some form of help or assistance from the researchers. Traditional methodology texts advise against offering assistance to the participants. But the moral implications of withholding needed information has been challenged by feminist researchers

(Cook and Fonow 1984; Ribbens 1989; Stanley 1990; Cotterill 1992; Reinharz 1992; Stanley and Wise 1993; Dickson-Swift 2005). Raquel Bergen (1993), like other feminist researchers, believes that rejection of requested help has the potential for harm to the 'vulnerable' participants. She advocates adherence to a feminist ethic by offering her participants assistance, which in her study involves emotional support, counselling and referral.

In research regarding family, Kerry Daly (1992: 7) asserts that as sensitive researchers, we often 'ask questions about the intimate sphere, observe family struggles, and provide openings for family members to discuss their "personal troubles" as a way of gaining insight into families' day-to-day reality'. When these families have difficulties, they may expect some opinions of the researcher as part of the research exchange. Should we, as researchers, give advice, information or counselling? Daly suggests that there are many issues to consider. However, we need to remember that by inviting individuals to take part in the research, the researcher and participants have developed a relationship based on a fair exchange. Due to this, we should expect some requests for information and advice or some responses to the intimate disclosure of our participants (see also Matocha 1992; Liamputtong Rice et al. 1994). It is wise that researchers need to anticipate these requests. They should be prepared to provide the information the participants need or to direct them to other relevant resources including reading materials or referrals to qualified professionals.

In their study with street burglars, Wright and colleagues (2001) provided various forms of assistance to their participants as long as those requests were legal. They accompanied the respondents to job interviews or work, assisted with school enrolments and provided advice on legal issues. On one occasion, they arranged an emergency surgery for one young offender who was injured when trying to run away from the police.

Compensation and Incentive: Inducement or Respect?

Compensation or payment for participating in a research project is a controversial issue. Some argue that payment is not appropriate as the participants may 'skew responses' (Booth 1999: 78). As Wendy Hollway and Tony Jefferson (2000: 84) comment, 'payment can be seen as a means of inducement which undermines the free choice of a person to participate in research'. Payment can also be seen as 'coercion' if researchers work with extremely poor people (Brody 1998; Crigger et al. 2001), the homeless (Paradis 2000), or drug users who need money to buy drugs (Dunlap et al. 1990). Nancy Crigger and others (2001: 464), for example, point out that potential participants from poor countries are indeed vulnerable to coercion. The income level (if there is any) is very low compared to the Western standard. Ten US dollars may be equivalent to a week's income for a worker in the Honduras. Hence, these vulnerable poor people may try to be included in research and this is seen as coercion. Some researchers view this as unethical (Paradis 2000). But others assert that researchers need to 'value the contribution, knowledge and skills' of the participants and payment should be provided to them, particularly if they have no or little money (Booth 1999: 78), such as homeless and poor people (Rosenthal 1991; Beauchamp et al. 2002; Umaña-Taylor and Bámaca 2004). Hollway and Jefferson (2000: 84) contend that payment for their time should be seen as 'equalising the relationship (our money for their time) or as having the material power that the financial relation afforded us'. As such, compensation for their time is crucial. It is also a symbol of the researchers' respect for the participation of these people. This stance is applicable to researching the 'vulnerable', as most of these groups such as ethnic women, homeless persons and the mentally ill tend to be poor and money may assist them with their daily living (Madriz 1998; Umaña-Taylor and Bámaca 2004). Tom Beauchamp and colleagues (2002: 550) for example, point out that compensation from participating in a research study 'provides an opportunity for the homeless to earn relatively significant amounts of money for short term and unskilled effort. These funds can be used in several ways that stand to improve the life circumstances of the volunteer'. Besides, we have asked the research participants to sacrifice their time to participate in our research. Some feminist researchers have argued that money given to research participants should be perceived as the compensation for being research partners in the research project (Landrine et al. 1995; Paradis 2000). Like Beauchamp and colleagues (2002), I advocate that some compensation is essentially appropriate with vulnerable groups.

Valerie Martinez-Ebers (1997) argues that compensation or monetary incentives are essential in securing hard-to-reach populations. In her study of the analysis of the effects of monetary incentives on the response rate and composition of respondents from Latino groups, Martinez-Ebers (1997: 80) found that 'monetary incentives clearly play a vital role in securing the cooperation of the targeted population' and 'monetary incentives do not encourage panel respondents to provide more favourable answers to subjective questions'. In their study on the connection of religion and health among African-American church members, Cheryl Holt and Stephanie McClure (2006) gave the participants US$20 at the end of the interview. The participants were not informed about these incentives when they were recruited. Two participants did not wish to take the money, and one actually returned it to the researchers whereas the other one donated it to the church. Holt and McClure (2006: 271) contend that their participants were 'intrinsically interested in participation', and not because of its incentive.

Wayne Wiebel (1990: 10) advocates compensation for the participants in his study of active intravenous drug users and their sex partners in the community setting. He argues that

> The payment of subject fees is a near-imperative prerequisite to obtaining cooperation and meaningful data from community-based research samples. Payment of subject fees both indicates the value of the data being collected, and acknowledges the worth of the time subjects are expected to dedicate in cooperating with the research protocol.

He was convinced that payment provided for his participants has helped him reach 80 per cent in follow up rates (see also Dunlap et al. 1990).

In recent times, more and more sensitive researchers provide compensation to their research participants. In Pyett's work with street female sex workers (2001), the researchers working on the research team paid the participants AU$10 for coffee and cigarettes on top of the AU$50 as compensation for their time in taking part in the sensitive research. Beardwood and colleagues (2005) provided Cdn $25 and travel costs to the injured workers who participated in their participatory action research project. Romero-Daza et al. (2003: 240) paid US$10 as incentive and tokens for transportation to the Hispanic Health Council to poor Hispanic women who took part in their study of violence, drugs and street-level prostitution in Hartford, Connecticut. In their studies with drug users, Cooper et al. (2005) and Ware et al. (2005) paid US$20 and US$21 as compensation for the time and effort of their participants. Van Kesteren and others (2005) gave 50 Dutch guilders to their participants in their research on sexual risk behaviour in HIV-positive men who have sex with men and Varas-Diaz and colleagues (2005) paid US$50 to their Puerto Ricans living with HIV/AIDS.

Nevertheless, David Langford (2000: 139) contends that when giving an honorarium to the participants, cash should be provided and the respondents should not be required to sign a form, as this signed document can be traced and therefore the participants' confidentiality will be breached. He argues that this is essential in a study involving sensitive issues and vulnerable populations, such as a domestic violence study. He suggests that researchers and their institutions should pay their participants with petty cash for the participants' parking fees and honorarium. The participants in his study were paid cash from a petty cash account so that there would be no record which linked them with the study, medical centre or university. Lynn Meadows and others (2003) contend that the requirement of an ethic committee to obtain a signature for receipt of compensation can compromise the confidentiality of the research participants. This has to be discussed carefully in researching vulnerable groups like Aboriginal people. Adriana Umaña-Taylor and Mayra Bámaca (2004: 265) assert that obtaining personal information for payment such as a Social Security number from Latinos in the US may cause the feeling of vulnerability amongst these groups as most of them are undocumented immigrants. This could discourage them from participating in the research. Dina Birman (2005) gives a similar warning to researchers who work in cross-cultural research. In her inquiry with former Soviet immigrants, the respondents were given some cash and the university required not only signed receipts from these people but also their Social Security numbers. The participants were very uncomfortable with this process. They felt that it completely undermined the assurances of confidentiality of the researchers. Because this was attempted, the participants became suspicious that their Social Security number was used by the researcher to obtain private information on them for the state office of refugee resettlement.

Incentive or compensation may not need to be in cash. Umaña-Taylor and Bámaca (2004: 265) suggest that if personal information is needed for compensation, researchers may provide other means of incentives such as gift vouchers. They supplied the participants with $20 gift vouchers from a local general store. In their study on breast cancer screening among African-American women, Husaini and others (2001) gave all the women grocery gift certificates worth US$30. In Shelton and Rianon's study about spousal abuse within the Bangladeshi community in Houston (2004: 377), the participants were given a gift bag that included sample products and coupon vouchers donated by local shops. Takahashi and Kai (2005) gave a pre-paid, public telephone card worth 1000 yen (US$9) as a thank you gift to the participants. In their study, Deborah Bender and colleagues (2001) gave a gender and language-neutral baby toy to Latina immigrant women as a way to thank them for their participation. Romero-Daza and colleagues (2003) provided educational material on HIV/AIDS and referrals to drug treatment, health and social services for the women in their study. As Kathleen Ragsdale and her co-resercher (in Fisher and Ragsdale 2005: 16) had a limited budget in their research with sex workers in Belize, monetary incentive was not provided to the women. Through the process of learning from the research participants, nail polish was suggested as a culturally appropriate token of appreciation for the participants. Nail polish was perceived as 'extras' by these young women as they did not have easy access to it. The women received a few bottles of nail polish and they were allowed to choose their own colours. However, this can be assessed on an individual case. Lynn Meadows and colleagues (2003) intended to buy traditional offerings of tobacco for the Aboriginal women in their study, but were informed by their Aboriginal assistant that the women preferred cash as they had more needs of cash than tobacco.

However, Janet Jamieson (2000: 67) provides an interesting response to this incentive affair. Payment can result in snowballing. When she arrived at a participant's home, she found two or three young male friends of the respondent waiting to be interviewed because they learned that they would be paid for their participation. This made her feel uncomfortable about being in a room with a group of young men she did not know and who had track records of criminal offences. Not only that, Jamieson felt that payment might even lead to risks in some situations. She became more selective about her respondents as she had obtained a desirable number of participants, and some of the young people who wanted to be included were not suitable for the study. Jamieson (2000: 67) also points out that

> The apparent threat in this situation arose from the fact that these people had volunteered on the understanding they would be interviewed and that they would be paid for this. The potential participants were understandably disappointed when told they were unsuitable for interview; being turned down meant they were not getting money which many were relying on to help buy them their drugs for that day.

As Lee (1995: 41) also points out, payment for participating in research, particularly in disadvantaged locations, often catches the attention of 'ineligible' participants. These people may become angry and react in a threatening way when they are not included in the research project.

Sensitivity to the Needs and Lives of the Participants

Being sensitive to the needs of the participants is an essential aspect in conducting research with the 'vulnerable' groups (Moore and Miller 1999; Moore 2002; Meadows et al. 2003; Jewkes et al. 2005). Women, for example, have traditionally been made silent and powerless. In many societies, women are still treated as objects to be seen but not to be heard. Shulamit Reinharz and Susan Chase (2002: 225) suggest that in some societies, 'women's voices must not be heard in public as they are defined as erotic and dangerous'. This historical context may help to explain why in the interviews, many women may become silent or reluctant to speak even though they are willing to participate in the study. Reinharz and Chase (2002: 225) comment that we, as researchers who interview women, need to understand the impact of being involved in the research on the woman herself. 'She may discover her thoughts, learn who she is, and find her voice'. We 'need to be aware that women who have never had an opportunity to express themselves may not know what to do when given that opportunity'. Belenky and colleagues (1997) discovered this in their study with women who grew up in violent families and had no external support.

It is a common practice in qualitative research that data collection takes place at the site where the participant feels most comfortable, which usually is the home of the participant (see Moore 2002; Herzog 2005). In her study with visually impaired older women, Linda Moore (2002: 563) conducted all interviews at the women's homes. She offered to meet the women in local libraries or quiet restaurants, but this was dismissed by the women. Only after the women started to talk about their visual loss did Moore realise the importance of a familiar setting for people with visual impairment. Moore (2002: 563) tells us, 'some women explained how each item of furniture in their homes was carefully placed. Several described having visual images of room layouts in their minds. Clearly, everyday surroundings were important to the comfort and functioning of these women'.

However, in some sensitive research when privacy and high confidentiality are involved, this may prove otherwise. In their study on violence, drugs and street-level prostitution among impoverished Hispanic women in the inner city of Hartford, Connecticut, Nancy Romero-Daza and colleagues (2003: 240) pointed out that the majority of the participants wanted to be interviewed at the Hispanic Health Council – a community-based agency that they could access easily. They were also more familiar with the agency and hence felt more comfortable being there. This setting also provided confidentiality for the participants. Very often, their family members did not know about the sex work in which the participants were involved.

Where sensitive issues exist, the research processes may be traumatic for the participants. In research relating to women's experiences of violence, for example, the women may experience distress, anxiety and flashbacks. The researchers need to be prepared for this possibility. In case the women find the interviews to be overwhelming, the researchers need to be able to offer referrals for support such as counselling services, information, contacts and local support groups (Cutcliffe and Ramcharan 2002; see also Chapter 4 in this volume). Otherwise, the interview may be harmful to the participants (Brzuzy et al. 1997). In a particular study that one of my honours students and I carried out with women who have experienced a miscarriage (Abboud and Liamputtong 2003), we compiled a list of loss and grief counsellors to whom the women could be referred if necessary. Fortunately, none of the women in this study required a referral. Had it been needed, we would have been able to provide prompt assistance to a distressed woman.

Rosanna Hess (2006) undertook her research on post-abortion experience in Ohio. As the research topic is extremely sensitive, the women were clearly informed that they could stop anytime and request further help if the interviews were too distressful. In a consent form, Hess (2006: 582) included the following information:

> The decision of the abortion experience is distressful for some women. You may find that reliving that time of your life may cause emotional stress for you. If this is the case for you, and the stress is too great, you may ask to stop and resume at a later time. You are free to withdraw from this study at any time, without any penalty. Should you experience a level of distress that requires professional help, referral services can be recommended.

In their study on child rape, Rachel Jewkes and colleagues (2005: 1811) point out that interviews with children who have been abused must be 'approached with great sensitivity to avoid re-traumatising the children'. It was essential to give the children a chance to speak about their experiences through the research, but we must be cautious about the needs of these children too. All interviews were undertaken by trained social workers, who were very familiar with the field. They also knew what was appropriate, or was not, when they approached and had discussions with abused children and their families.

When conducting research with the chronically ill and handicapped people, Jan Morse (2002: 321) points out that 'the process of interviewing itself triggers memories' of their illnesses or injuries. The participants may cry, and the researchers should be prepared to offer comfort and tissues to wipe the tears. Morse also warns us that novice researchers conducting sensitive research may be reluctant to console the distressed participants as they fear this action may 'contaminate the data' or 'lead the participant'. Morse argues that this is unlikely. Rather, Morse contends, as researchers, we 'should respond humanly and kindly when the participant becomes emotional' (Morse, 2002: 321).

Researchers may ask the participant if she or he wishes to rest and then continue when the participant is ready to do so.

Priscilla Pyett (2001: 114–15) points out that in her study with female sex workers she and a co-researcher were extremely cautious and sensitive about asking certain questions. The study aimed to investigate the health of women in sex work, but it would be insensitive to ask the women about their health as 'health was too private. The women would be very sensitive about their nutrition, dental hygiene, and reproductive health, all of which were likely to be very poor'. However, the researchers could ask them about any sexual or drug-using practices. Through consultation and negotiation, the solution was to ask a simple question 'How are you?' The women would be more likely to raise health issues, which will allow the researchers to follow up. In the same study, Warr and Pyett (1999: 293) point out that all interviews were undertaken in a familiar site chosen by the participants, which was usually in a café of a welfare agency. During the interview, the women were told that they could stop the tape recorder or 'stop the interview at any time if they became anxious, distressed or required reassurance on any matter'. Additionally, the interviews were done as 'conversations' (Kvale 1996; Hirst 2004) to allow the participants to talk about their intimate matters. And each interview lasted only 20 minutes to one hour in order not to interrupt their working time too much.

There are other practical sensitivities that I wish to point out here. Researchers should be aware of the time that is required for vulnerable people to participate in the study (Booth 1999). Moore and Miller (1999: 1039) warn us that, as researchers, we must consider the time of day when we attempt to recruit our potential participants and when we wish to obtain our data as these events may influence the decisions of some participants – whether they wish to participate or not. It is more likely that older persons and those with disabilities may refuse to be involved in research if it is seen as interfering with their routines or treatments. Logistical factors including inaccessible research sites, cost of public transport, parking distances, and weather conditions might also influence people's decisions (Meadows et al. 2003). These issues are more problematic for many 'doubly vulnerable individuals'. Therefore, researchers should be particularly cautious when planning recruitment and data collection. Having said this, I must give an interesting example from Jamieson's study (2000: 68) with young men in crime. Previous experience indicated that late morning would be a suitable time to interview young people as they are more likely to be up, but still at home. Jamieson followed this experience and she would usually turn up at the home of these young men and find that they were out of bed but 'were in various states of undress'. This could be embarrassing for her as a young female researcher, but it could also be a threatening experience as well, particularly if there were a few of them in the same house.

In research involved with older people, Clare Wenger (2002) cautions us that when approaching older people at home, we should remember that older people may have mobility and hearing difficulties. It may take them a long time to answer a knock on the door. It is recommended that researchers should show the older people their identification cards to verify their profession. Particularly if their children are cautious about the presence of a stranger at home, older people may wish to see some forms of identification and this may facilitate future research projects at home (Moore 2002; Wenger 2002).

Linda Moore (2002) provides valuable insights and strategies for researchers who wish to conduct research with older people with visual impairments. Moore (2002: 562), in her study with visually impaired older women, suggests that there were some strategies adopted on the days of planned interviews to address the vulnerability of the participants and these strategies were to enhance the safety and security of these people. Immediately before the interview, the respondents were telephoned and told that the researcher would soon be knocking at their doors. At the participant's door, it was important for the researcher to identify herself. Most women wanted to see a proper identification before opening their doors. All interviews were carried out during the daylight hours so that the women could see better when they opened their doors.

Moore (2002: 561) was particularly cautious about the vulnerability of women with visual impairments. She carefully drafted a consent form to reflect the special needs of the visually impaired research participants. For instance, even though she planned to read the consent form to the participants, 'the form was constructed to maximise participants' visual capabilities should they choose to follow along during the reading of the consent'. The consent form 'was printed on plain white paper using black bold-faced print, size 18 font, Times New Roman type'. She also 'avoided script typeface because they are difficult to decipher for individuals with visual impairments. A large "X" was placed next to the signature space to assist the participants in affixing their signatures'. Moore (2002: 562) contends that:

> Careful attention to the issue of participant vulnerability and to safety and security issues was crucial to the success of the study. Attention to such details can foster participant access and enhance the bond of trust that is imperative between the qualitative researcher and participant.

Conclusion

There are many challenges for sensitive researchers to consider when research-ing vulnerable and difficult-to-access people. Sensitive researchers need to forge a new way to enhance their success in gaining access and for building trust and rapport with these people. Respect for the research participants is essentially important. They need to carefully consider particular needs of research participants and give something back for their part in helping to make their research possible. Yet, these issues are not simple and straightforward. Although at times these may be difficult, I would argue that they are challeng-ing and they will enable researchers to carry out their research sensitively and successfully.

TUTORIAL EXERCISES

1. If you are a researcher or postgraduate student who is asked to undertake a research project on the lived experience of living with HIV/AIDS among young men and women or with women who have experienced rape, how would you go about planning and conducting this sensitive research with the groups in ways that will also address their vulnerability?
2. When researching these vulnerable groups, what salient issues might be considered in order to ensure that your research project will be carried out ethically, sensitively and successfully?

SUGGESTED READINGS

Campbell, R., 2002, *Emotionally Involved: The Impact of Researching Rape*, Routledge, New York.

Douglas, J.D. (ed.), 1972, *Research on Deviance*, Random House, New York.

King, R.D. and E. Wincup (eds), 2000, *Doing Research on Crime and Justice*, Oxford University Press, New York.

Lambert, E.Y. (ed.), 1990, *The Collection and Interpretation of Data from Hidden Populations*, National Institute on Drug Abuse, Rockville.

Lee, R.M., 1995, *Dangerous Fieldwork*, Sage, Thousand Oaks, CA.

Miller, J.M. and R. Tewksbury (eds), 2001, *Extreme Methods: Innovative Approaches to Social Science Research*, Allyn and Bacon, Boston.

Renzetti, C.M. and R.M. Lee (eds), 1993, *Researching Sensitive Topics*, Sage, Newbury Park.

Schwartz, M.D. (ed.), 1997, *Researching Sexual Violence against Women: Methodological and Personal Perspectives*, Sage, Thousand Oaks.

Wolf, D.R., 1991, 'High-Risk Methodology: Reflections on Leaving an Outlaw Society', in W.B. Shaffir and R.A. Stebbins (eds), Experiencing Fieldwork, Sage, Newbury Park, pp. 211–23.

4

The Sensitive and Vulnerable Researcher

Chapter Objectives   71
Introduction   72
The Sensitive Researcher and Self-disclosure   72
The Researcher as a Person: Social Locations and Gendered
    Experiences   74
Safety Issues – Risk and Harm of the Researcher   76
'Labour Pains' – Emotional Experiences: The Impact of
    Conducting Research with Vulnerable People   82
The Other Vulnerable Researcher – A Transcriber   88
The Vulnerable Researcher: The Need for Support   90
Safeguard the Vulnerable Researcher   91
Conclusion   93

Data collection can be an intense experience, especially if the topic that one has chosen has to do with the illness experience or other stressful human experiences. The stories that the qualitative researcher obtains in interviews will be stories of intense suffering, social injustices, or other things that will shock the researcher.

(Morse and Field 1995: 78)

Each field situation is unique and presents a multitude of problems for the researcher... The [researcher] deals with people, and because of this, fieldwork is subject to all of the complexities, ambiguities, and unpredictability inherent in any form of social interaction.

(Mann 1976: 95–109)

Chapter Objectives

This chapter aims to

- Discuss important issues pertaining to the researcher who may also be as vulnerable as the research participants.
- Provide a discussion on the issue of self-disclosure of the researcher.
- Point to danger and harm and emotional experiences in carrying out sensitive research.
- Provide a discussion on the impact of sensitive research on the other researcher – transcribers.
- Discuss some strategies to protect the vulnerable researchers.

Introduction

Researching vulnerable and difficult-to-access groups requires extraordinary special considerations and substantial demands on the researchers. Most often, the researchers are confronted with what Alty and Rodham (1998: 275) call 'the Ouch! Factor'. Accordingly, the 'Ouch! Factor' refers to 'certain experiences encountered in the process of conducting qualitative research' which may include 'a short sharp shock to the researcher to those situations and experiences that can develop into a chronic ache if not addressed early'. Essentially, an 'Ouch! Factor is an obstacle to research, which requires the researcher to step back and reconsider the options'. While this can seem like a daunting enterprise, it is also a challenging one (Lee 1993; Warr 2004). In this chapter, I will discuss some important issues which may have an impact on the ways the sensitive researchers undertake their sensitive research and some which may impact on their physical and emotional well-being.

The Sensitive Researcher and Self-disclosure

In conducting sensitive research with vulnerable and hard-to-access groups, self-disclosure is essentially important (Letherby 2000; Tewksbury and Gagné 2001; Johnson 2002; Kong et al. 2002; Wenger 2002; Perry et al. 2004; Weston 2004; Dickson-Swift 2005; Galvin 2005; Hesse-Biber and Leavy 2005). Although it is seen as 'contamination' in conventional research (Dunbar et al. 2002: 286), it encourages the participants to elaborate on their subjective experiences. Researchers need to be more open to their participants, that is, they need to be willing to share their experiences with the participants (Vance 1995; Letherby 2000; Perry et al. 2004; Weston 2004). This will facilitate rapport and trust among the participants. As Virginia Dickson-Swift (2005: 101) remarks in her research on doing sensitive research, her participants believed that there was 'a need to create some sort of "level playing field," acknowledging that self-disclosure could enhance rapport, show respect for the participants and validate the participants' stories'. Shulamit Reinharz and Susan Chase (2002: 227) suggest that researchers' self-disclosure occurs when the researcher 'shares ideas, attitudes, and/or experiences concerning matters that might relate to the interview topic in order to encourage respondents to be more forthcoming'. Christopher Dunbar and colleagues (2002: 286) contend that to employ an approach which Jack Douglas (1985) refers to as 'creative interviewing', the researcher 'forges common ground to share with the respondent, so that the subjects behind both interviewee and interviewer share a familiar, if sometimes uncomfortable, narrative space'. In order to encourage self-disclosure, as Jack Douglas (1985: 51) puts it, is to get 'deep-deep probes into the human soul' and the researchers need to 'know thyself' (see also Holstein and Gubrium 2004). Douglas (1985: 25, original emphasis) says,

> Creative interviewing...involves the use of many strategies and tactics of interaction, largely based on an understanding of friendly feelings and intimacy, to optimize *cooperative, mutual disclosure and a creative search for mutual understanding.*

In undertaking a study on sexual abuse or domestic violence, for example, the researchers might disclose their own experiences of having been sexually or physically abused. This self-disclosure may put the participants at ease, and hence help them to tell their stories (Reinharz 1992; Letherby 2000). In her recent study on disability and identity, Rose Galvin (2005: 395–96) tells us that 'because I am disabled myself I looked upon the dialogues as a space in which to share our stories and to reflect on the various ways in which disability had affected our identities'. Clare Wenger (2002) found in her studies with older people that when she revealed to them that she was divorced, the participants tended to bring out their lived experiences of family life more and admitted that they too were divorced when at the beginning this disclosure was not forthcoming. Wenger (2002: 272) contends that the researcher's self-disclosure encourages the exchange from the participants as 'resistance to self-disclosure by the interviewee . . . can create a feeling of imbalance and increase the distance between interlocutors'. Wenger (2002: 272) also suggests that 'there needs to be giving as well as receiving in these exchanges. Reciprocity is needed to maintain the relationship'.

According to Dunbar and others (2002), the researcher's self-disclosure is particularly essential when he or she is undertaking research with minority groups. Similar to other marginalised individuals, people of ethnic minorities tend to perceive outsiders with suspicion: 'years of misrepresentation and misinterpretation have legitimated scepticism and distrust' (Dunbar et al. 2002: 291). Dunbar and colleagues (2002: 291) believe strongly that 'it is important to the success of the interview for the researcher to disclose something about him- or herself to the interviewees. This is foundation work: that is, it tells the interviewees where the researcher is coming from'.

In conducting sensitive research with gay men and lesbians, the need for self-disclosure is of particular importance (Kong et al. 2002; Perry et al. 2004; Weston 2004). Prior to being involved in the research, gay men and lesbians wish to know 'where both the researcher and the teller of that life are coming from, what kind of relationship they are having together, and how intimate details will be used and represented?' As Dan Mahoney (in Kong et al. 2002: 249–50) has found, his self-disclosure was an effective approach when he was trying to persuade a gay couple to participate in his study. He writes,

> Adam [a participant] went about asking for clarification about the nature of the research and what I meant by storytelling. I took the opportunity to speak about the book I was writing on gay men and their families, and my interest in writing about experiences of gay men we haven't heard about before. James [Adam's partner'] sat and took it all in. He wanted to know about my personal background, why I was studying in England, and why on earth I was living in Colchester. I gave him a short biography of my life. More disclosure about my life precipitated more answers and questions about me and my research interests. I was getting the impression that they were warming up to the idea of being interviewed.

Travis Kong and colleagues (2002: 252) also suggest that researchers should construct 'an empathic, emotional orientation' while undertaking sensitive research with queer participants. When researchers invite gay people to disclose themselves, the gay people need to know if the researcher 'will be open to their lived experiences and is prepared to cofacilitate the interpretations of those events... Deep levels of disclosure will come about only if the subject senses shared understanding from the interviewer' (see also Perry et al. 2004). Kate Weston (2004: 202) too contends that her lesbian identity essentially assisted in recruiting and building up trust and rapport with gay men and lesbians in her study in San Francisco. She points out that 'many participants mentioned that they would not have talked to me had I been straight and one or two cited "bad experiences" of having had their words misinterpreted by heterosexual researchers'.

In their research on sexuality with gay men, lesbians and bisexual young people, Catherine Perry and colleagues (2004) write that when the young people learned that Perry was a lesbian, they became more open with their views. Perry et al. (2004: 141) state that 'it appeared that the researcher was able to establish a degree of trust and rapport, and in so doing elicited depth and detail from the interviewees; it appeared that participants felt encouraged to share more of their experiences because they believed that she would "understand" what they were trying to convey'.

Some writers may argue that such self-disclosure has ethical implications as it might be perceived as the exploitation of participants (Hart and Crawford-Wright 1999). However, Wenger (2002) suggests that it is up to the researchers to consider this themselves. It can be difficult in practice in certain situations for researchers to know how much to disclose and what kind of disclosure is appropriate. In some situations, it is appropriate to adopt a 'tight-lipped approach' (Blum 1999: 214). For Donna Eder and Laura Fingerson (2002: 228), researchers must 'think carefully about whether, when, and how much disclosure makes sense in the context of particular research projects and with specific participants' (see also Tewksbury and Gagné 2001). I too believe that this strategy should be adopted so that neither party will feel constrained or embarrassed.

The Researcher as a Person: Social Locations and Gendered Experiences

In doing sensitive research, Reinharz and Chase (2002: 233) suggest that it is essential for the researchers to consider the social locations of themselves and of the research participants, as this may influence their research relationship. This is applicable when women study men and men study women (see Willot 1998; Anderson and Umberson 2004), and in cross-cultural research where ethnicities and social class of the researcher and the researched can be of marked difference.

Shulamit Reinharz and Susan Chase (2002: 231) contend that if social locations of the researchers and the researched differ extremely, 'uncertainty and discomfort are likely to arise'. But others suggest otherwise. Linda Blum (1999: 213) admits that in the course of interviews of African-American women regarding their breastfeeding experiences, she 'learned most from those facets of African-American women's stories which [she] had the most trouble hearing'. Anne Phoenix (1994) also told us that in much of her research with women, some white respondents were surprised to learn that she, the researcher, was black. Phoenix contends that racial difference can be either inhibiting or liberating for researchers who come from non-white backgrounds.

Kimberly Huisman (1997) carried out research on wife battering in Asian communities on the East Coast of the United States. To gain access to potential research participants who work with battered Asian women, Huisman volunteered to assist at domestic violence shelters where the women sought help. She was the only white academic woman who was working at the shelter. Huisman felt that her race and position was perceived with 'extreme caution and distance'. People often questioned her for her reason to work at the shelters. It took a considerable amount of time and effort for her to build up trust and rapport with workers at the shelter.

In her study with Latino women in New York, Esther Madriz (1998: 5) was extremely cautious about the class differences between herself as a researcher and the women of low status. Due to her middle-class background and her position as a professor in a university, she stood in stark contrast to the women who mainly worked as cleaners, street vendors and nannies. Most of the women were just staying-home mothers. However, Madriz (1998: 5) tried to reduce this difference by carefully dressing in the manner of most Latino women who are cautious about the way they dress. She also referred to the women and herself by first names and used informal Spanish pronouns. And by sharing the language with the women, the gap between herself and the women was markedly minimised.

Gender differences between the researcher and the researched play an important role in conducting sensitive research with vulnerable groups or where research revolves around sensitive gendered experiences (see Anderson and Umberson 2004). At a very basic level, the gender of the researchers may influence their own perceptions of the worldview, experience and performance of their research participants. As Kerry Daly (1992: 10) asks, 'How is the interview discourse different when it is man to man versus woman to woman or woman to man?' Maureen Padfield and Ian Procter (1996) conducted a joint study of young women's work and family lives. Both researchers are experienced field workers who adopt a feminist standpoint in their research approach and hence encourage women to talk freely in the interview process. An issue regarding an abortion was not asked directly in the interview, but when comparing their interviews, they found that women who had had abortions tended to reveal this to Maureen Padfield rather than to Ian Procter. This suggests that the gender of the researcher affected the voluntary sharing of such sensitive and personal experiences as abortion.

In researching older people, and particularly older women living alone, Clare Wenger (2002: 264) argues that older people tend to accept women better than men into their homes, but they may also mistrust young women. In one of Wenger's studies, she used two male colleagues as interviewers where the research involved a brief encounter which did not require the researcher to enter the home of the older participants. She was later told by one participant that she made a mistake by sending two men to ask questions, as the men frightened a number of older people in her area. Even though the two men were established academics with gentle personalities, to older women who lived alone in their homes, 'men clearly could not be trusted' (Wenger 2002: 264). Wenger's (2002: 264) own experience suggests that the interviewers who gain the highest success in acceptance by older people are 'middle-aged or older women with outgoing personalities'. Prager (1995) too argues that older researchers are 'qualitatively and empirically more complete and useful' when it comes to researching vulnerable older participants.

A similar issue emerges when doing research with the difficult-to-access group of gay men and lesbians (Perry et al. 2004). The rise of a lesbian and gay movement from the 1960s onwards has led to a new research direction and strategy. More self-identified gay researchers employed qualitative research methodology and the implication was that only gay and lesbian researchers could undertake qualitative research because they have an in-depth and genuine understanding of issues regarding gay men and lesbians. To put it simply, only those who 'have been there' would understand what it is like to be gay and lesbian.

Safety Issues – Risk and Harm of the Researcher

> Risk and danger to the personal security of the researcher is an issue gaining greater recognition within the social sciences ... Research can be threatening to the researcher as well as the participants and that researchers may be placed in situations in which their personal safety is jeopardised.
>
> (Jamieson 2000: 61)

Researching some vulnerable and hard-to-reach populations may present a danger to the personal safety of the researcher (Adler 1990; Sluka 1990, 1995; Renzetti and Lee 1993; Lawrinson and Harris 1994; Lee 1995; O'Neill 1996; Craig et al. 2000; Jamieson 2000; Kenyn and Hawker 2000; Lee–Treweek 2000; Lee–Treweek and Linkogle 2000a; Seal et al. 2000; Dickson-Swift 2005). Researchers who carry out research into sexual behaviour, for example, as David Seal and colleagues (2000: 11) point out, 'may be particularly vulnerable to the potentially volatile nature of fieldwork. In addition to the normal difficulties of fieldwork, they must study a behaviour that is deeply private, secretive, and taboo'. Margaret Melrose (2002: 337) also argues that research in the areas of hard drugs, criminal activities and the world of prostitution may 'lead researchers into dubious moral territory' and hence 'may present the researcher with "anonymous" dangers because the researcher is present in an otherwise avoidable, potentially dangerous, situation'.

There are numerous dangers involved in researching vulnerable and difficult-to-reach populations. Danger, according to Lee-Treweek and Linkogle (2000a: 1) relates to 'the experience of threat or risk with serious negative consequences' which may affect the researchers. They may have to deal with difficulties and dangers in the field during their data collection process (Adler 1990; Dunlap et al. 1990; Sluka 1990, 1995; Lee 1995; O'Neill 1996; Calvey 2000; Jamieson 2000; Hopper and Moore 2001; Warr 2004; Dickson-Swift 2005). Maggie O'Neill (1996: 132), in her research with street prostitutes in Nottingham, tells us that

> The issue of personal safety of the researcher is illustrated by my own experience whilst accompanying a health outreach worker in the spring months of 1992. We witnessed at very close range a violent assault on a woman prostitute and attended court four times until the case was finally dealt with. This was the last occasion I visited the street as part of my research.

O'Neill lives in a Victorian terrace house and has to park her car on the street. Some nights before the first three court cases, the car was smashed. This frightening incident prompted her to think about the nature of her research and its danger. O'Neill has two small children. She is not only worried about her own safety, but also that of her children and partner. A similar issue is raised by Boynton (2002) in her research in the red-light area in a West Midlands town in England.

Deborah Warr (2004) refers to some of the danger that she had encountered in her work with street sex workers in Australia. She went with an outreach worker to observe the lives of the street workers. The nature of her research necessitated observations very late at night. This led her to experience 'occupational irritations common to street work', even though it was not at the same level as that those women have to deal with. Warr (2004: 580) tells us that

> For one thing, there was the gathering cold as the night closed in, despite my being dressed far more warmly than most of the women we encountered. I also experienced the thick darkness of streets specially chosen for the privacy they afforded, and I feared being mistaken for a sex worker by 'hoons', troublemakers whose sport is to drive by and throw eggs or buckets of water at waiting workers. On one occasion, we also endured the ignominy of being stopped and questioned by the police.

Sometimes, the processes involved in collecting data lead to dangers in fieldwork. For example, researchers may have to manage relationships with individuals or groups who act in a threatening way (see Calvey 2000; Jamieson 2000; Hopper and Moore 2001). At other times, however, the difficulties and dangers may come merely from when researchers are trying to get to their fieldwork or research sites. Sam Punch (personal communication in Lee-Treweek and Linkogle 2000a: 2) was physically attacked by dogs as she walked to remote households in villages when researching childhood in rural Bolivia. I too was attacked by a dog when I went to interview a Thai mother in a suburban area in Bangkok. This incident left me with open wounds on one of my legs which took a few months to heal. Richard Wright and colleagues (2001: 99) had to deal with many potentially dangerous accounts during their fieldwork including an instance where the participants turned up for their interviews with firearms and on another occasion when they were caught in the middle of a fight between their participants and others. Janet Jamieson (2000: 68), in her research with young men in crime, had to travel to crime-prone/disadvantaged areas in Scotland to interview the young men. She elaborates on this:

> Whilst visiting participants' homes the threat of attack or theft on the street was also of great concern... The study necessitated my carrying valuable equipment in the form of tape recorder and laptop computer and I received numerous warnings from the participants about the threat of theft... There was also the general threat of carrying money and equipment about the research sites. Luckily for me I did not experience theft whilst in the field. Given that neither the money nor the equipment was my property, and the equipment was insured, I would have simply handed it over and extricated myself from the situation as quickly as possible.

Those who conduct research in other cultural and social settings, apart from having to deal with the feelings of dislocation and isolation, may also experience some physical dangers due to political and physical environments. Stephanie Linkogle (2000), while carrying out her fieldwork in Nicaragua, had to deal with not only dangers due to political violence within the country, but also due to some day-to-day hazards. In their research with AIDS victims in rural China, Yun Lu and colleagues (2005) had to travel by foot, bicycle or by a *beng-beng che* (a riding cart pulled by a motorcycle-bike). However, very often they had to walk to the village as no *beng-beng che* drivers wanted to get into what they called the 'village of plague'. There was one occasion that they managed to rent a *beng-beng che*, but the driver stopped five miles away from the village and told them that he would not go any farther. Hence, once again they all had to walk to their research site.

The intimate and personal nature of the questions that the researchers are asking as well as the physical environment in which the research occurs may lead to physical danger of researchers undertaking projects with some hard-to-reach groups (Parker and Ulrich 1990; Lee 1995; Calvey 2000; Jamieson 2000; Langford 2000). Very often, the researchers travel to talk to their participants at their homes, and this can be dangerous. Terry Arendell (1997) went to interview a man about living with a chronic illness in his apartment in a middle class neighbourhood in the United States only to find that he was not interested in being interviewed. He had agreed to take part in her research project because he wanted sex with her. Arendell escaped unharmed but very emotionally disturbed by the incident. Janet Jamieson (2000: 66), in her study on young men and crime in Scotland, elaborates on her experience in one of the interviews: a male resister in his twenties who lived alone.

> On arrival at the address there was a delay in his opening the door of the flat and when I finally entered his home he insisted on locking the door from the inside... During the

course of the interview the young man acknowledged that he had mental health problems which, I felt, explained his edginess on initial contact and his obvious discomfort and agitation prior to, and to a lesser extent, during the interview. Furthermore, his locking of the door and his palpable discomfort when he could not see the external door were explained by the fact that he felt victimised by local residents in the area in which he lived. Despite knowing this information I was concerned and felt threatened and the interview was undertaken with as much brevity as possible. Thus, I balanced my own misgivings and anxiety with the need to complete the interview process and fulfil the demands of the research.

There were also unfortunate incidents where the researchers could not escape harm in their fieldwork. Mary Ellen Conaway (1986) and Jennifer Huff (1997) were physically molested and sexually harassed, and Eva Moreno (1995) was raped. These incidents may be rare, but it clearly points to some dangers that researchers working on sensitive areas may have to confront.

There are also times when researchers are threatened by partners of women who participate in domestic violence research (Parker and Ulrich 1990; Bergen 1993). Raquel Bergen (1993: 199) points out that researching marital rape with women who have been sexually assaulted also poses a potential threat to her as a researcher. She remarks that the threat occurred because most interviews were undertaken in the homes of the participants; a place where their (ex)husbands could arrive anytime. Although Bergen felt safe carrying out the interviews, she says 'the possible threat of angry men finding me interviewing their (ex)wives about their experiences was something daunting'.

Researchers may be confronted with legal issues. It is possible that during the research process, the participants may reveal some contentious issues, such as child abuse, which the researchers are required to report to the police under mandatory reporting rules (Morse and Field 1995; Socolar et al. 1995; Steinberg et al. 1999). In Australia, the National Health and Medical Research Council (NHMRC) has warned researchers who undertake research with the vulnerable that 'mandatory reporting of information that has been revealed by a participant may be required' by the court (NHMRC 2002: 132). Because of this legal requirement and also our responsibility as sensitive researchers, we need to inform the participants. This may mean that we will lose our participants, but this is not as detrimental as if our research participants were harmed by the research process.

Information gathered in some sensitive research such as drug use or illegal activities may be subpoenaed for testimony in court cases (Brajuha and Hallowell 1986; Shaffir and Stebbins 1991; Ferrell and Hamm 1998; Marquart 2001; Scarce 2001; Wright et al. 2001; Volker 2004). Researchers have been imprisoned because they refused to provide information to the court of their researched participants. The cases of Mario Brajuha (Hallowell 1985; Brajuha and Hallowell 1986) and Rik Scarce (2001) are two good examples to cite here. Brajuha was a postgraduate student researching a restaurant that was burnt down. It was suspected by the police that it was mob arson and the police took the matter to the court in order to obtain Brajuha's research data. Brajuha, however, refused to surrender his data because he had to protect his participants and as a result, he was jailed. Similarly, Rik Scarce (2001) carried out his research with environmental activists, a controversial movement at the time. He is the first sociologist who was imprisoned for 159 days because he refused to provide his confidential research data to law enforcement authorities. The activists he interviewed collectively practised radical tactics; they made use of 'direct action' such as speech making to street theatre, property destruction, civil disobedience and letter writing. The University campus where Scarce was studying was raided by and Animal Liberation Front (ALF). One evening, he was summoned to the University police station because he knew one of the suspected cases and his research involved radical groups. He was questioned and later on was ordered to appear before a federal grand jury meeting. Scarce (2001: 262) bitterly laments:

> The subpoena frightened me terribly. Though I knew little about grand juries, it was clear to me that they had extraordinary powers and that in a clash with one I would likely have to go to jail rather than discuss aspects of my research that were confidential. It took me nearly two weeks to find an attorney experienced with grand jury procedures, and by then I had lost ten pounds and was getting almost no sleep.... I constantly felt sick to my stomach. In short, I was falling apart.

It was clear at the beginning of his ordeal that he would, and could, not cooperate if the law enforcement authorities wanted to access his data which was collected with his promises of confidentiality. Later on, Scarce had to appear before the grand jury and this meeting lasted for nearly 8 hours (Scarce 2001: 265).

> The government was treating my testimony seriously. I answered all of the prosecutor's questions regarding nonconfidential matters, but I refused to answer thirty-two questions that probed confidential communications... It was my refusal to answer these questions that led to my jailing.

James Marquart (2001: 44), however, was fortunate enough not to be caught in a legal matter as Scarce was. During his fieldwork in a Texas prison, he saw many illegalities but he acted like he 'did not see them'. He said in order to 'block or neutralize the moral predicament of seeing "too much," I kept quiet and simply observed'. During his fieldwork, an attorney in the Special Master's Office, asked him to testify against the Texas Department of Corrections, but he told the attorney that he 'had nothing to say'. He believed what he had collected in the prison was confidential but anticipated that he might be jailed for refusal to testify in court, but fortunately this did not happen. Richard Wright and others (2001) also warn researchers about the possibility of being coerced by legal enforcement in their inquiries with domestic burglars. They were aware of the intrusions from criminal justice officials which could jeopardise their research. As part of their fieldwork was to visit with their participants the sites of recent burglaries, the threat of being confronted with the police was great. Thus, they had made some negotiations with police authorities not to interfere with the research fieldwork prior to commencing their research. They were then not subjected to police coercion.

It is possible too that the research participants may disclose some illegal activities to the researchers during the data collection period (Adler 1990; Lee 1993; Ferrell and Hamm 1998; Melrose 2002; Volker 2004). This may pose danger to the researchers. As Terry Williams and others (1992), in their research involving the drug culture on crack houses in New York City found, secret police tapped their phones and followed them around while they were conducting their research. Patricia Adler (1990: 105) points out that researchers are likely to confront dangerous situations when researching deviant and illegal activities. Members of these groups may harm a researcher if they believe the researcher has done something to cause harm and this can be just a simple misunderstanding. Alder and her co-researchers were forced to escape their home on a number of occasions when fierce arguments occurred among group members due to misunderstandings. Adler (1990: 106) also points to danger from the police. They were concerned that the local police would discover the nature of their study and confiscate their data.

Being vulnerable to social stigma may also occur with researchers who undertake sensitive research. This has been referred to as 'stigma contagion' (Kirby and Corzine 1981: 3); that is, researchers become stigmatised like those whom they carry out their research with (see Reavey 1997; Boynton 2002; Melrose 2002; Fisher and Ragsdale 2005). Erving Goffman (1963) refers to this as 'a courtesy stigma' (see also Mattley 1997). As Mitchell Miller and Richard Tewksbury (2001: 206) suggest, 'this is the idea of "guilt by association": it is assumed that the only people who would want to study and hang around with "those types of peoples" are others who are also "those types" '. Researchers who examine issues confronting female sex workers may be assumed to be prostitutes. In the same manner, researchers doing their research on homosexuality may be seen by others as homosexual. And if you are a woman researching abortion, it might be assumed that you have had an abortion too. The stigmatised lists can go on. Tewksbury and Gagné (2001: 84) contend that 'when a researcher seeks and gains entrée to stigmatised populations, members often assume or believe that the researcher is actually or potentially a member of the community . . . This assumption may well be because of the strength of the stigma felt by community members. Because they themselves are discredited in society, it is not surprising that such individuals may believe that only similarly stigmatised persons would be interested in them and their experiences'. Therefore, it is not surprising to see that in their study of the transgender community, Richard Tewksbury and Patricia Gagné (2001) were both seen as transgendered individuals and in Tewksbury's study with persons with HIV disease (1994), he was believed to be HIV-positive. This matter is really clear in Gagné's experience, as indicated in her study with battered women who had received clemency. She was introduced to a support group for women who had killed or attempted to kill their abusers as 'This is Dr. Gagné. She's one of us' (Tewksbury and Gagné 2001: 85). In Kathleen Ragsdale's study with sex workers in Belize (cited in Fisher and Ragsdale 2005: 11), she and her co-researcher unexpectedly came across this social stigma. It was perceived by most key informants in Belize City that researching sex work by female researchers was 'unusual', and in some cases it was 'deemed risqué or aberrant' when they compared the researchers' attempts with 'traditional gender norms for Belizean women'.

Researchers working with vulnerable people may be exposed to what Morse and Mitcham (1997: 650) refer to as the 'compathy' phenomenon. Accordingly, compathy is 'the acquisition of the distress and/or physiological symptoms (including pain) of others by an apparently healthy individual following contact with the physical distress of another'. When we see others experience pain or distress, we may ourselves have the 'compathetic response'; that is, we may feel the pain or distress too. The compathetic response may arise from our direct observation, listening to or hearing the stories, reading stories about distressing experiences, and remembering or thinking about the distressing stories (Morse and Mitcham 1997; Morse et al. 1998; Morse 2000; Melrose 2002). This compathy phenomenon is clearly one of the effects of working with the vulnerable on sensitive researchers, as they often work with distressing and traumatic situations like pain, abuse, loss, grief and death. Through our in-depth discussions, observations and stories being told by our research participants, we too become vulnerable to this compathetic response. As Jan Morse (2000: 540) points out, 'if the researcher is working with his or her emotional pain, for example, the pain caused by listening to descriptions of the dying of the participant's child, then the researcher may also become engulfed with shared suffering. This has a profound effect on the researcher'. Morse (2000: 540) tells us precisely that 'sharing the world of the ill has its own risks for the researcher. I know from personal experience that when working with transcripts or videos of patients in distress, researchers must actively steel themselves and block the compathetic response so that the pain experience is not shared'. The compathy phenomenon has also been referred to as 'emotional contagion' (Miller et al. 1988), 'vicarious traumatization' (McCann and Pearlman 1994; Dane 2000), 'pain by proxy' (Moran-Ellis 1996) and 'labour pains' (Melrose 2002, see later section).

'Labour Pains' – Emotional Experiences: The Impact of Conducting Research with Vulnerable People

> The emotions of researching emotionally difficult topics are often over-looked in academic discourse. Yet, the emotionally engaged researcher bears witness to the pain, suffering, humiliation, and indignity of others over and over again.
>
> (Campbell 2002: 150)

All too often, sensitive researchers neglect to discuss their emotional experiences of doing research (Dunbar et al. 2002). This is mainly due to their fears about being accused of having 'bias' (Campbell 2002). But this has begun to change as more qualitative researchers have started to write about their subjective experiences and how they are affected by the field relationships in their field-work (see Kleinman and Copp 1993; Moran-Ellis 1996; Mattley 1997; Stanko 1997; Letherby 2000; Lather 2001; Campbell 2002; Melrose 2002; Grinyer 2005; Hallowell et al. 2005). Margaret Melrose (2002) names this emotional distress as 'labour pains' or 'emotional labour'. Melrose (2002: 345) contends that emotional labour involved in interviewing sensitive issues is indeed 'hard work' and it can be 'sorrowful and difficult', as it involves 'dealing with the participants' feelings about "telling" and with the feelings involved in the researcher by "hearing" such accounts of appalling abuse'. The researchers may experience 'subjective distress' because they have to 'endure and share the pain' of their research participants. Thus, these labour pains are real for many sensi-tive researchers who carry out their research with extremely vulnerable people. Researching child prostitution, Melrose (2002: 337) points out, 'is an emotionally sensitive area to investigate. When conducting research of this kind, researchers may be entering an emotionally charged experience where anxiety levels are unpredictable and this level of sensitivity makes it a potentially threatening excursion for both researchers and researched'. See also a chapter on 'Emotions' in Nina Hallowell and colleagues (2005: 11–41), where several sensitive researchers tell their emotional stories in conducting their research with vulnerable people.

Researchers have discussed how the process of conducting research in sensitive issues has affected them personally (Riessman 1990; Moran-Ellis 1996; Rowling 1999; Calvey 2000; Lankshear 2000; Letherby 2000; Gilbert 2001a; Lather 2001; Campbell 2002; Melrose 2002; Dickson-Swift 2005; Hallowell et al. 2005). And for some researchers, this may also have an impact on other parts of their lives (Moran-Ellis 1996; Jamieson 2000; Lankshear 2000; Letherby 2000). Katherine Riessman (1990: 225) say, in her writing about the experiences of divorce of women, that the interviewing process had an effect on her as an interviewer. She says 'listening to people's painful accounts of their marriage and trying to probe sensitively for their understanding of what had happened was sometimes difficult'. Lather (2001) tells us that listening to the stories of women living with HIV/AIDS brought many tears to her eyes. Not only that, she realised that in working with these women, she had to manage her own relationship to loss. Due to this, she began to think whether and how she could even continue to work on the project.

In doing sensitive research with vulnerable people, researchers may be involved in a number of emotional experiences. Some researchers have talked about their emotional distress when their participants die (Dunn 1991; Cannon 1992; De Reave 1994; Beaver et al. 1999; Rowling 1999; Campbell 2002; Gair 2002; Warr 2004). Others point to their emotional exhaustion (Parker and Ulrich 1990; Cannon 1992; Gregory et al. 1997; Letherby 2000; McCosker et al. 2001; Melrose 2002; Johnson and Clarke 2003; Dickson-Swift 2005) and guilt (Rubin and Rubin 1995; Melrose 2002; Warr 2004). In Rubin and Rubin's study (1995), one participant committed suicide not long after revealing some secret stories in the interview. The timing of this participant's death made Rubin and Rubin wonder if the death was linked with the interview. And this does not leave them with a good feeling at all.

Some researchers cry with their participants in the interview (Matocha 1992; Burr 1995; Stanko 1997; Lather 2001). They have feelings of helplessness (Cannon 1992; Melrose 2002), pain and anger (Rothman 1986; Kitson et al. 1996; Stanko 1997; Haris and Huntington 2001; Hubbard et al. 2001; Rosenblatt 2001; Campbell 2002; Melrose 2002). Dunn (1991: 390), for example, was 'choked with emotion', and Rowling (1999: 172) had tears in her eyes, while collecting data in their research.

The emotionally draining experience during the course of doing sensitive research of some researchers deserves greater detail here. In her work with women who have experienced infertility, miscarriage and child death, Gayle Letherby (2000: 103) laments, 'half way through the fieldwork I felt very low ... The emotional involvement and emotional work involved in the fieldwork also led to emotional exhaustion'. And when May, one of the participants, talked about the feelings when she failed to conceive a child as 'her time in the wilderness', Letherby felt that that was her own story. For Kathleen Gilbert (2001a), the emotional distress has resulted in many disturbing dreams during her fieldwork on the study of loss, grief and coping of parents who lost a child in pregnancy. Julia Brannen (1988: 562) tells us that the emotional drain from listening to research participants' stories and distress for a long period was so great that she believed that 'no psychiatrist or psychotherapist would work (or be allowed to work) under these conditions'.

In Linda Matocha's study (1992) on the effects of AIDS on family members responsible for care of PWAs, the PWAs were often very ill, and within the two-year fieldwork, they all had died. In carrying out this study, Matocha (1992: 72) tells us,

> I experienced strong emotions while conducting this research. I cried, laughed, and exhibited anger and confusion along with each participant. I did not remain untouched or removed from the participants. The sessions were full of sharing ... Family secrets were shared. This was important information, but frequently there was an accompanying burden of knowledge placed on me.

In her research with women working on the streets, Deborah Warr (2004: 583) contends that because researchers are immersed in the data and the research participants in their research, the stories they are given or hear and see often stay with them, and this can be emotionally heavy. Warr interviewed one sex worker who was only 14 years old. The girl told Warr that she had a regular customer who would pick her up very early on Saturdays. Each time, the man gave her a wrist bracelet as a gift. The girl then rolled up her sleeve on the left arm to show Warr the gifts she had received from this man. Warr (2004: 583) remarks: 'I was shocked to see that they reached almost to her elbow! For me, the benign bracelets became symbols of her stolen youth as well as of the man's selfish and exploitative desires'. After this incident, she would see a lot of girls and young women wearing similar bracelets. This may make the girl similar to other women but her situation was dramatically different from those girls. Warr (2004: 583) says:

> I felt angry with the unknown man when I imagined him procuring more bracelets in preparation for his weekend trysts. Most of all, I was overwhelmed by the futility of research and its inability to change anything in the lives of the women we were interviewing.

One important study on the emotional impacts of carrying out sensitive research with vulnerable people is that of Rebecca Campbell (2002). Campbell (2002) individually interviewed 12 researchers in her study about their experiences of doing research with rape survivors at the end of her project. This was to give her research team a chance to 'talk, reflect, vent' their personal experiences in doing this kind of research. Many of the researchers in Campbell's project remarked that they were personally impacted by their involvement in the research, including by feelings of numbness and not wanting to react. Some talked about physical and emotional safety. Some had to hold their thoughts in abeyance while other had outbursts like anger and crying. Campbell alerts us that although not all researchers may experience emotional distress in doing research with vulnerable people, we must appreciate that it can potentially have an impact on the researchers. Campbell suggests that researchers working with vulnerable people and 'emotionally difficult topics,' (like being a rape victim in her study) need to develop some strategies to make the impact minimal for them before embarking on this type of research. This may prevent some emotional distress and hence harm on the part of the researchers.

A similar but more recent study on the impact of researching vulnerable people on the researchers is that of Barbara Johnson and Jill Clarke (2003). Johnson and Clarke interviewed researchers whose research was on sensitive areas including HIV/AIDS, cancer, death and dying. Johnson and Clarke (2003: 423) argue that these types of research topics potentially have an 'emotional and moral unease' impact on the researchers. The research participants in this study made remarks on this impact such as being unprepared to carry out the research and worried about being in 'uncharted territory' (Johnson and Clarke 2003: 425). Many had problems with the conflict of their roles as a researcher and as a friend in their attempts to build up rapport. Feelings of isolation and lack of emotional and practical supervision were raised by the participants. Clearly, this study points to the many emotional burdens of researchers who work in this vulnerable area of research.

Often, these researchers have to 'pent up' their emotions and find ways to release them when they return home (Campbell 2002; Gair 2002; Melrose 2002). Some researchers argue that very often, researchers have to 'hide' the truth, pretend not to know or suppress their feelings in order to protect their research participants. This can leave researchers with emotional problems and physical danger too. And when it comes to the time of analysing the data and writing, Adler (1990: 107) laments, 'we were torn by conflicts between utilizing details to enrich the data and glossing over descriptions to guard confidences'. This problem has been the experience of many researchers dealing with hard-to-reach people or very sensitive research topics (see Humphreys 1970, 1975; Scarce 2001; Melrose 2002).

When the research is completed, researchers may experience some difficulties with leaving the field (Stebbins 1991; Cannon 1992; Booth 1998; Russell 1999; Robertson 2000; Baca Zinn 2001; Hubbard et al. 2001; Kondo 2001; Boynton 2002; Cutcliffe and Ramcharan 2002; Dickson-Swift 2005). Through the process of extensive involvement with the researched participants in qualitative research in general and through established rapport developed with vulnerable people in particular, the participants may not wish to end their involvement (Hesse-Biber and Leavy 2005). Very often, researchers working with vulnerable people develop friendships with their research participants (Acker et al. 1991; Stebbins 1991; Watson et al. 1991; Cannon 1992; Boynton 2002; Gair, 2002). And this may make leaving the field difficult for some researchers. But as Carol Warren (2002: 96) suggests, 'like most things, qualitative interviews come to an end ... but sometimes ... interviewers do not necessarily end their relationship with respondents at the conclusion of their interview'. This is referred to as the 'unfinished business' (Burr 1995: 174). Researchers may have 'on-going feelings of concern for the fate of each person' (Burr 1995: 177). Wendy Booth's research with people with learning difficulties (1998) did not end when the study was completed. Booth suggests that when researchers take on research with some vulnerable people, sometimes relationships may need to be maintained, and this is both necessary and ethically responsible. In her case, the relationships with some research participants continued for more than 10 years. At the time she published her work in 1998, she stated, 'the reality is that 11 years on from the first project, I am still contacted by, and in contact with, five women who chose to attach their own "terms and conditions" to their participation in my research' (Booth 1998: 134; see also Stalker 1998).

Emotional feelings such as depression and guilt amongst the researchers when leaving the fieldwork have also been reported in some studies (Cannon 1989, 1992; Glesne and Peshkin 1992; Burr 1995; Miller 1997; Letherby 2000; Sque 2000; Boynton 2002; Melrose 2002; Dickson-Swift 2005; Sin 2005). Gayle Letherby (2000: 101), in her study with women who cannot have children or have lost children through miscarriages and child death, laments that 'I did wonder sometimes if I had encouraged respondents to re-live difficulty experiences and then abandoned them to come to terms with their distress alone. I still feel uncomfortable about this aspect of the research'. In her study of breast cancer, Sue Cannon (1989: 74) admits that it was extremely difficult for her to leave the field. During the course of her study, 21 women died. This has greatly affected Cannon's emotions. She tells us that she felt sad, depressed, shocked, angry and at a great loss. This research had greatly impacted her life and, because of this, it was difficult for her to finish her research with the women. In Petra Boynton's research with sex workers (2002: 10), she contends, 'we felt depressed, deflated and lethargic following the end of the data collection phase. We were concerned about the safety of the women we had interviewed and wanted to know they were "okay" '. Magi Sque (2000: 32), in her research with bereaved relatives of organ donors, talks about her guilt feeling – 'at times I felt guilty about my comparative riches. For instance, I was deeply touched by a young mother whose baby son died as a result of an unusual accident. She told me how resentful and angry she felt when she saw other people, including her own sister, with their children; somehow, I felt almost guilty that, as far as I knew, my sons were at home and well'. And Margaret Melrose (2002: 347) admits that 'to walk away from some of the young people after an interview was, to say the least, difficult, when one knew that they would be going out afterwards to suffer the same kinds of abuse they had just been describing. My feelings often seemed to parallel those expressed by my participants, that is, anger, guilt, powerlessness and frustration'. Whenever she saw men in 'grey suits' in the street, they reminded her of the abuse that young girls received from these men, and she had to 'suppress the desire to scream' at them. The kind of emotional distress (labour pains) that sensitive researchers experience in researching vulnerable people, Melrose argues, can seriously damage the health of researchers.

The impacts of sensitive research on the researchers extend beyond researchers who use reactive research methods to those who adopt an unobtrusive method in their research with vulnerable people (Alexander et al. 1989; McCarroll et al. 1995; Milling-Kinard 1996; Driscoll et al. 1997). These unobtrusive researchers experience similar physical and emotional impacts to those who use in-depth interviews and other qualitative methods in their studies. In their research on researchers who reviewed case records of sexual assault and rape victims, Alexander and colleagues (1989) assert that these researchers experienced emotional distress and had sleeping problems like the experiences of those researchers who had a direct contact with the vulnerable research participants. Similarly, Milling-Kinard (1996) reports feelings of sadness, anger, frustration and helplessness among the researchers who reviewed the records of children experiencing abuse.

Many researchers undertaking research with vulnerable people are not well prepared to deal with sensitive and often delicate situations in their research (Rowling 1999). Very often too, researchers underestimate their emotional well-being in undertaking research with vulnerable people. Janet Robertson's study with mature women with bulimia (2000) is a good example of my point here. Robertson was an ex-bulimic person, but she considered herself as recovered from the illness. Due to her personal experience, Robertson decided to undertake research on this issue hoping that her research will help other women to be free from their silent voices. However, this was not so. This is what Robertson (2000: 533) says:

> I felt secure in the knowledge that I considered myself 'recovered'. Consequently, I was rather shocked when I realized during a period of my intense interviewing and

transcribing that I was experiencing a return of the feelings that I remembered from when I was 'bulimic' ... The dominant image of the researcher as 'in control and successful' meant that it was not easy to admit to feelings of vulnerability, even to myself.

This is also the experience of others such as Burr (1995), Kiesinger (1998) and Hubbard et al. (2001). In her work with critically ill patients, Burr (1995: 174) tells us that her level of preparedness, training and skills is inadequate for the extensive disclosure that her participants bring out. Kiesinger (1998: 73) was not prepared for the intensive emotionality of her researched participants. Hubbard and colleagues (2001: 128) felt unprepared for dealing with participants who cried when talking about the deaths of their fathers. This level of emotional unpreparedness has great impact on the researchers. One of the research teams reveals her feelings that after the interview she would be 'crying in private confines of her car'.

I must also point out that there are times when the researchers may feel that doing research with the vulnerable is rewarding too (see Kondora 1993; Hutchinson et al. 1994; Cook and Bosley 1995). According to Hutchinson and colleagues (1994), there are some positive aspects including the sense of purpose, being able to help people who are more marginalised than the researches, catharsis, empowerment, healing, and having a voice heard (see also Brannen 1988, 1993; Cowles 1988; Lee and Renzetti 1993; Owens 1996; James and Platzer 1999; Sque 2000; Dickson-Swift 2005). Feelings of being privileged are also mentioned by some (Cannon 1992; Rosenblatt and Fischer 1993; Sullivan 1998). Sullivan (1998: 74) tells us that 'at the forefront of my mind was always the thought that to be permitted a private view of another person's past, their pain, and their sorrow, was a privilege'. Sometimes the researchers may be a concern of the research participants. The participants in Letherby's study (2000) were worried about her emotional well-being when they were discussing their distressing experiences of miscarriage, chid death or infertility treatment. They were concerned that what they were telling Letherby would upset her because she had lost a child through a miscarriage and thereafter been unable to have children.

These kinds of privileged feelings have also been my own experiences in working with vulnerable women from ethnic communities (see Liamputtong Rice et al. 1994; Liamputtong Rice 1996, 2000). Very often, I would leave the participants with feelings of gratitude and debt to these individuals who gave me the opportunity to share many intimate details of their lives.

The Other Vulnerable Researcher – A Transcriber

In doing qualitative research, often there are others who also play an important role during the life of the research and this includes transcribers and research assistants (Burr 1995; Kitson et al. 1996; Gregory et al. 1997; McCosker et al. 2001; Gilbert 2001b; Darlington and Scott 2002; Warr 2004; Benoit et al. 2005;

Dickson-Swift 2005). Issues confronting research assistants are largely similar to those confronted by researchers that I have discussed (see also Benoit et al. 2005). Here, I wish to examine the issues facing transcribers who transcribe our tape-recorded interviews.

Data gathered in qualitative research requires a transcription for in-depth analysis. It is likely that some transcribers will become emotionally distressed if they have to listen to and type powerful and often distressing stories of the researched participants (Matocha 1992; Cameron 1993; Gregory et al. 1997; McCosker et al. 2001; Darlington and Scott 2002; Gair 2002; Warr 2004; Benoit et al. 2005; Dickson-Swift 2005). As Deborah Warr (2004: 586) asserts, transcribers are 'absorbing the voices and stories of research', just as are the researchers who are eliciting the stories in their data collection processes. For example, the transcribers who are involved in sensitive research like domestic violence and murder, experience emotional and physical symptoms such as headaches, gastrointestinal upsets, exhaustion and depression, and sleep problems and nightmares (Cowles 1988; Burr 1995; Gregory et al. 1997; Ridge et al. 1999; McCosker et al. 2001). Miriam Cameron (1993: 224) talked with the transcriber who transcribed interview tapes on living with AIDS and this is what she said:

> When you are plunged into the dictation equipment, you are living somebody else's experience. You hear if they hurt or don't hurt and they're happy or sad. I wanted to tell somebody, but I couldn't because of confidentiality ... I felt that I got to know them as persons because they really opened up.

In researching the effects of AIDS on family members responsible for care of PWAs, Linda Matocha (1992: 72) employed two people to transcribe the data for her. She instructed both transcribers to maintain confidentiality of the researched and the content of the data. She tells us that 'the transcriptionists experienced powerful emotions and high stress. They grieved and became angry as the lives of the participants unfolded, and I spent hours listening to them and assisting them to resolve feelings'. Similarly, in Cecilia Benoit and others' research (2005) with sex workers, as a number of transcribers were ex-sex workers, what they heard from the tape brought them back to their own stressful experiences while working in the trade. Deborah Warr (2004: 585–86) asked one of the transcribers in her research about how she felt listening to the stories of disadvantaged young people. The transcriber responded with a story that she could not forget and she called it the 'chin-ups story'. It was a story of a young homeless man who would hang off the side of a bridge by his fingertips; he was practicing chin-ups. He would do the chin-ups until his arms ached and he felt as if he was almost falling from the bridge as a way for him to tempt his fate. Warr (2004: 586) tells us that: 'the woman who had done the transcribing described to me the tremendous edge in the young man's voice, which made his story ring true for her, and the despairing image she had of him hanging from the bridge, inviting his hands to slip but still not wanting to choose death'. Warr (2004: 586) puts it succinctly that 'clearly, transcribers who work with sensitive data are also absorbing the voices and stories of research'. They are indeed affected by emotional problems as researchers are.

The Vulnerable Researcher: The Need for Support

What I have discussed thus far clearly points to the need for support for researchers who are doing their research with vulnerable people and on sensitive issues (see also Renzetti and Lee 1993; Payne 1994; Rubin and Rubin 1995; Moran-Ellis 1996; Schwartz 1997; Lee-Treweek 2000; Letherby 2000; Sque 2000; Gilbert 2001a,b; Meadows et al. 2003; Perry et al. 2004; Warr 2004; Dickson-Swift 2005). Very few research projects provide mentors who can talk with researchers about how to deal with the emotional burden generated from their interviews with vulnerable research participants (Schwatz 1997). There appear to be very few support programmes for researchers who work with the vulnerable and this also includes research students. Jan Morse (2000: 540) firmly asserts that

> Most of you, I know, will be able to recall large blocks of quotations and hear the participant's voice in your head many years after conducting a heart-wrenching interview. Yet, oddly, how advisors should be monitoring and debriefing their student researchers is not discussed in the literature.

Some suggestions have been made to assist and support researchers working with the vulnerable and these include access to a professional confidant (Brannen 1988; Kitson et al. 1996; Robertson 2000), formal supervision (both academic and therapeutic supervision) (Etherington 1996; James and Platzer 1999; Meadows et al. 2003; Warr 2004; Dickson-Swift 2005), regular meetings (Meadows et al. 2003; Jewkes et al. 2005) and emotional support (Moran-Ellis 1996; Sque 2000; Ellsberg et al. 2001; Gilbert 2001b). With a few exceptions, most of the support currently available for researchers who work with the vulnerable is from friends, family members and some colleagues (Lee-Treweek 2000; Letherby 2000; Ellsberg et al. 2001; Melrose 2002). It is essential that a formal support guideline should be developed to assist the vulnerable researchers to be less vulnerable in their research enterprise and this may include some of the points I have mentioned above. Catherine Perry and colleagues (2004: 146) suggest forming a small team of researchers to support those who carry out 'sensitive and emotionally laden' tasks. Perry and others, in their research on sexuality with gay, lesbian and bisexual young people (2004: 146) tell us

> We have found that supportive and constructive teamwork, which actively brings researchers and their emotions center stage, can be beneficial in enhancing the integrity of the research as well as in sustaining researchers through difficult periods.

In the study on child rape undertaken by Rachel Jewkes and colleagues (2005: 1811), meetings of research teams were done on a regular basis. In each meeting, all the researchers reported on each interview they had carried out and any support that they needed was discussed. The research team made sure that no one on the team would be unduly distressed by the interviews and support was provided to all members. Cowles (1988), Stoler (2002) and Warr (2004) suggest that there should be a debriefing session with a therapist and colleagues after a stressful data collection period.

Jo Moran-Ellis (1996) recommends that researchers who carry out sensitive research need emotional support, and this support should form part of the context within which the research is undertaken. In her research on violence against women and children, she strongly argues that:

> I propose that all research that is concerned with violence against women or children should have, as part of the method and as part of the process of conducting research, a clear mechanism for giving support to all staff engaged on the project, including support/administrative staff as well a researcher. I would go so far as to say that no research proposal should be approved by a funding body unless it has this support clearly built into the structure, and that in referring such research proposals this is a point that should be made.

Others suggest that it is imperative that researchers working with vulnerable people need good training in carrying out this type of research (Anderson and Hatton 2000; Sque 2000; McCosker et al. 2001; Meadows et al. 2003; Dickson-Swift 2005). Extensive training for the researchers is needed. But this training needs to go beyond the methodological issues and include things like how to manage distress and end difficult interactions (Lee-Treweek and Linkogle 2000b). Not only good training on how to handle the research processes, but also training on how to deal with delicate and distress situations is advocated. Some suggest that researchers working with the vulnerable need good counselling skills as well (Lee 1993; Coyle and Wright 1996; Sque 2000; McCosker et al. 2001).

Safeguard the Vulnerable Researcher

The discussions in this chapter point to the need for some strategies to safeguard researchers. In particular, when planning research involving dangerous fieldwork, safeguard strategies are essentially important (Kenyan and Hawker 2000; Craig et al. 2001). David Calvey (2000: 57) suggests that the use of practical equipment such as mobile phones, the selection of setting, and letting someone know your whereabouts are necessary (see also Jamieson 2000). He also suggests that researchers may need to be 'artful and skilled in impression management in the field' such as planning about cover stories and leaving the field when necessary.

It was recognised in Jamieson's (2000: 63) study of young men's resistance to, desistance from and persistence in offending in Scotland that there were risks to the researchers during the fieldwork because the interviews were carried out in unfamiliar locations and often after working hours. The young people in their research involved in some 'risky' behaviour. Hence, she and her co-researchers planned several safety procedures in order to reduce the threat to themselves as researchers. They tried to conduct their interviews within office hours as much as possible. They carried mobile phones while they were out in the field. They made sure they had access to a car. They informed office staff at the university about their whereabouts. And if they were very concerned about a particular interview, the office staff would be alerted. The use of 'partnered interviews' was also adopted. Jamieson and another researcher made special attempts to be in the same area in order to minimise the likelihood of physical threat and their fears of actual risks. However, in reality, adherence to all these precautions may not be too practical and researchers may have to find other ways to reduce potential risks. In her work, Jamieson (2000: 69) suggests the following to safeguard researchers' safety:

* Have a thorough and careful research plan.
* Be always conscious about safety in the field.
* Keep alert to some likely risks.
* Be prepared to respond to threat, even if one has to leave the research field.

Petra Boynton (2002: 8) suggests several strategies for researchers working in the red-light area who, like their research participants, often work on streets late into the night. These include the following:

* Do not work alone. This can be done by informing others of the location that the researcher will be working on that particular day or night, or working in pairs with another researcher.
* Always carry a mobile phone while in the field.
* Discuss any problems emerging in the field with the research team members.
* Use comfortable clothes that provide confidence while in the field.
* Try to be 'visible' in the field and at work.
* If the interview is done inside the home setting or office, try to stay near the door.
* If essential, seek advice and use support from security services such as the police.

Terry Williams and colleagues (2001: 219) provide simple styles of safety in doing research with crack dealers in New York City and other difficult-to-access groups such as burglars, robbers and drug sellers. Amongst these, style and demeanor are essential. 'First impressions are very important', they recommend. Researchers should feel that they belong to the research setting by wearing clothes that are appropriate to the environment. What the researchers wear and their behaviour will be seen as their 'willingness to fit into the social setting'. This may also prevent drawing unnecessary attention from the local people. Williams and colleagues (2001: 219) point out that 'failure to establish this presence, and especially being perceived as a victim, by those in the drug business for instance, may greatly increase personal dangers of theft/robbery and difficulty in establishing rapport with potential subjects'. They also provide other recommendations which are similar to what Jamieson has given. (See also Craig et al. 2000; Kenyon and Hawker 2000).

For transcribers, David Gregory and colleagues (1997) suggest several strategies to reduce any harm and these include the following:

* Before taking up a job, transcribers need to be fully informed about the nature of research and the data they will be working with.
* The researcher needs to organise regular debriefing sessions with the transcribers.
* They should be alerted about difficult interviews they will be transcribing.
* They should be prepared for the termination of the research they are working on.

In order to help their RAs with emotional distress, Cecilia Benoit and colleagues (2005: 274) assign two transcribers to work together to ensure that they have each other for companionship when dealing with difficult material. One of the transcribers remarked on this that, 'I think that working in a team is very effective if something's upsetting to you or it triggers up a memory because you have someone to bounce [it] off [and] you can talk about it'.

Conclusion

> Sensitive research often also has potential effects on the personal life, and sometimes on the personal security, of the researcher.
>
> (Lee 1993: 1)

As I have discussed throughout this chapter, undertaking sensitive research with vulnerable people places a great many demands, physically and emotionally, on the researcher. Conducting sensitive research has a great impact on the researcher's personal lives (Lee 1993). In his well-known book, Raymond Lee (1993: 16) warns us that, as researchers, we 'need to find ways of dealing with the problems and issue raised by research on sensitive topics. The threats which the research poses to research participants, to the researcher and to others need to be minimized, managed or mitigated'. Virginia Dickson-Swift (2005) alerts us that as researchers, we must prepare ourselves for physical and emotional danger in our fieldwork and find ways to disengage ourselves when our research ends. One way to do this is to tell the stories of the vulnerable researchers to others – to let our stories and our voices be heard in a similar manner to the way we make the voices of our research participants heard in our research endeavours. Amanda Coffey (1999: 1) convincingly suggests that

> It has become increasingly fashionable for individual researchers to 'personalise' their accounts of fieldwork. But there has been little systematic attempt to reflect upon their experiences and emotions that are reported in any overarching collective or epistemological sense. All too often, research methods texts remain relatively silent on the ways in which fieldwork affects us, and we affect the field.

TUTORIAL EXERCISES

1. You are assigned to conduct a project with women who have experienced domestic violence, drug users and dealers and street sex workers. How do you plan to do this in a way to minimise danger and harm that may occur to you in the fieldwork?
2. You are about to embark on a research project with homeless young people who have been sexually abused. What issues are you likely to encounter and how will you deal with these?

SUGGESTED READINGS

Arendell, T., 1997, 'Reflections on the Researcher-Researched Relationship: A Woman Interviewing Men', *Qualitative Sociology*, 20(3): 341–68.

Campbell, R., 2002, *Emotionally Involved: The Impact of Researching Rape*, New York: Routledge.

Hallowell, N., J. Lawton and S. Gregory, 2005, Reflections on Research: The Realities of Doing Research in the Social Sciences, Berkshire: Open University Press.

Kleinman, S. and M.A. Copp., 1993, *Emotions and Fieldwork*. Newbury Park, CA: Sage Publications.

Lee, R.M., 1995, *Dangerous Fieldwork*, Thousand Oaks, CA: Sage Publications.

Paterson, B., D. Gregory and S. Thorne, 1999, 'A Protocol for Researcher Safety', *Qualitative Health Research* 9(2): 259–69.

Pyett, P., 2001, 'Innovation and Compromise: Responsibility and Reflexivity in Research with Vulnerable Groups', pp. 105–19, In *Technologies and Health: Critical Compromises*, edited by J. Daly, M. Guillemin and S. Hill, Melbourne: Oxford University Press.

Warr, D.J., 2004, 'Stories in the Flesh and Voices in the Head: Reflections on the Context and Impact of Research with Disadvantaged Populations', *Qualitative Health Research*, 14(4): 578–87.

Williams, T., E. Dunlop, B. Johnson and A. Hamid, 1992, 'Personal Safety in Dangerous Places', *Journal of Contemporary Ethnography*, 21(3): 343–74.

5

Traditional Interviewing Research Methods Appropriate for Researching Vulnerable People

Chapter Objectives   95
Introduction   96
In-depth Interview   96
What does an In-depth Interviewing Method Offer?   96
Case Examples of Sensitive Research Using In-depth Interviews   97
A More Innovative Interviewing Method   100
Telephone Interviewing   100
Interview Proxies   101
Conjoint In-depth Interviews   102
Flexibilities in Doing Sensitive Research: Something to Think About?   104
Focus Group Interviews   105
The Nature of a Focus Group Method   105
Case Examples of Sensitive Research Using Focus Groups   108
Oral and Life History   111
What is Oral and Life History Research?   111
Case Examples of Sensitive Research Using Oral History   114
Conclusion   116

Research designs that move beyond the more traditional methods of epidemiological studies to include qualitative designs...that involves the subject as participants in the research design and implementation...present possibilities for understanding the experiences of vulnerable populations.

(Flaskerud and Winslow 1998: 9)

Chapter Objectives

In this chapter, readers will learn about traditional interviewing methods in the social sciences and these include the following:

- An in-depth interviewing method.
- Innovative interviewing methods.
- Focus group interviews.
- Oral and life history.

Introduction

As I have pointed out in Chapter 1, qualitative inquiry is appropriate for researching vulnerable people. The most commonly used qualitative approach is that of orthodox interviewing methods in social science and these include an in-depth interviewing method, a focus group and oral or life history. In this chapter, I will focus on the use of these traditional interviewing methods in researching vulnerable and hard-to-reach research participants. In the sections that follow, I will detail these methods and provide some empirical examples.

In-depth Interview

> The doing of interviews is personal, interactional, and emotional. It is embodied work that can have implications for the researcher as well as the researched. How does the researcher present him- or herself? How is the interaction embodied? How are feelings presented and managed?
>
> (Kong et al. 2002: 250)

What does an In-depth Interviewing Method Offer?

An in-depth interviewing method is most commonly utilised by qualitative researchers. It is sometimes referred to as an intensive interview (Hesse-Biber and Leavy 2005: 119). Within this method, it is assumed that people have particular and essential knowledge about the social world that is obtainable through verbal messages. It necessitates 'active asking and listening'. The process involves a meaning-making effort which is started out as a partnership between the researchers and their participants. In-depth interviews aim to elicit rich information from the perspective of a particular person and on a selected topic under investigation. Similarly, Nancy Schoenberg and colleagues (2005: 92) contend that in-depth interviews allow researchers to access complex knowledge from an insider 'without the preconceived biases inherent in using existing structured instruments that may contain items irrelevant to local populations'. In-depth interviews, they maintain (2005: 93), permit the participants to freely articulate their worldviews while allowing researchers to remain focused on the research topic.

In-depth interviews, according to John Johnson (2002: 103), usually connote a face-to-face and one-on-one interaction between a researcher and a respondent. In-depth interviews 'seek to build the kind of intimacy that is common for mutual self-disclosure'. They require a grander expression of the self of the participant than other interviewing methods do. According to Sharlene Hesse-Biber and Patricia Leavy (2005: 123), in-depth interviews are particularly valuable for 'accessing subjugated voices and getting at subjugated knowledge'. Therefore, they are suitable for collecting stories from vulnerable and marginalised people. Indeed, the method is more preferable amongst sensitive researchers who wish to be close to their participants in order to allow them to speak about their lived world in greater depth (Birch and Miller 2000; Nicholson and Burr 2003; Hesse-Biber and Leavy 2005; Liamputtong and Ezzy 2005). This is echoed by Johnson (2002: 104) who suggests that researchers who use in-depth interviewing techniques are searching for great depth of information and knowledge from the participants. This information often concerns 'personal matters, such as an individual's self, lived experience, values and decisions, occupational ideology, cultural knowledge, or perspective'. As the method 'seeks "deep" information and understanding' (Johnson 2002: 106; Hesse-Biber and Leavy 2005), it permits researchers to make sense of the multiple meanings and interpretations of a specific action, occasion, location or cultural practice. Additionally, in-depth interviews are closely related to feminist research (Oakley 1981, 1988; Reinharz 1992; Edwards 1993; Renzetti 1997; Weston 2004; Hesse-Biber and Leavy 2005; Liamputtong and Ezzy 2005). The method represents what Graham (1983: 136) refers to as 'a female style of knowing' and Smith (1987: 105) calls 'the standpoint of women'.

Often, an in-depth interview method is adopted in sensitive research with vulnerable participants (see for example, Bergen 1993, 1996; Booth and Booth 1994a,b; Hutchinson et al. 2002; Nicholson and Burr 2003; Cooper et al. 2005; Mosack et al. 2005; Schoenberg et al. 2005; Sharpe et al. 2005; van Kesteren et al. 2005; Varas-Diaz et al. 2005; Ware et al. 2005; Potts et al. 2006). In-depth interviewing methods require sensitive researchers to 'hear' the data. And this means we need to attend to what the participants tell us. But at the same time, our own lived experiences may assist us to 'hear' the data better. For example, when Jack Douglas (1985) carried out in-depth research on the nature of love and intimacy, he tells us that his own deeply hidden and conflicted feelings about his mother's occupation as a prostitute permitted him to 'hear' crucial issues in the in-depth interviews.

Researchers have successfully use in-depth interviews to elicit sensitive information from men on issues including sexuality, perceptions of contraception, abortion and fatherhood (see Allen and Doherty 1996; Marsiglio et al. 2000, 2001; Körner et al. 2005). Other researchers have used in-depth interviews to explore sensitive issues including sexual assault (Esposito 2005), domestic violence (Taylor et al. 2001; Davis 2002; Wuest et al. 2003), sexuality (Lowe 2005), living with cancer (Manderson et al. 2005), living with Hepatitis C (Crockett and Gifford 2004; Treloar and Fraser 2004; Waldby et al. 2004), harm reduction and women in prison (Rehman et al. 2004), experiences with abortion (Aléx and Hammarström 2004) and coping with Anorexia Nervosa (Honey and Halse 2006). However, in the next section, I shall provide more details of some empirical research projects using in-depth interviewing methods.

Case Examples of Sensitive Research Using In-depth Interviews

Tim and Wendy Booth (1994b) provide an excellent review of their research procedure, utilising in-depth interviews with people with learning difficulties. Booth and Booth's study of 33 parents with learning difficulties involved between 1 and 20 interviews with each of their subjects, as well as numerous phone calls and short visits. Booth and Booth (1994b: 416) explored the experience of childrearing and parenthood among parents with learning difficulties in order to develop 'a set of "good practice principles," grounded on parents' perceptions of their own needs, for the guidance of service providers and practitioners'. Typically, they used multiple interviews about sensitive and personal topics, and established trust and rapport and obtained consent, which was seen as an integral process by Booth and Booth (1994b). Access was granted through an introduction by a professional worker who was known to the family being studied. This worker asked if the families were willing to meet the researchers, and if they agreed, the researcher was then given their name and contact numbers. This approach provided excellent solutions to some of the problems associated with confidentiality as participants' names were only released with their consent. It also provided a personal introduction, which improved levels of trust in the interview and facilitated an easier first interview.

Many qualitative projects involve one-off interviews that could be described as 'hit and run' approaches (Booth and Booth 1994b: 417). However, Booth and Booth wanted to establish a greater level of intimacy to gain a more sympathetic understanding of the meaning and significance of events for the people themselves. They, therefore, spent considerable time developing this trust, often devoting the entire first interview to establishing rapport. This paid significant dividends, as details of some participants' experiences began to emerge only in later interviews when greater trust had been gained. Another result was the higher level of personal involvement with their research participants. For example, they sometimes assisted participants with current demands, such as responding to a drug overdose in the family or helping to fill out official forms. Booth and Booth (1994b: 418) stated that 'to maintain a detached stance at these times was not possible in human terms nor desirable on research grounds'. The more personal nature of the relationships that were established also meant that the researchers had to take more time and care in withdrawing from the relationship.

While many interviewers emphasise the value of using tape recorders, Booth and Booth note that they deliberately chose not to record in some situations. Not recording allowed greater freedom to move around the respondent's house and to continue discussions in noisy environments (for example, while children were playing), as well as providing more scope in the type of discussion. They point out that interviewers should be skilled at taking notes after an interview, so that these interviews would still yield valuable data.

In their study of sexual scripting of gay men, David Whittier and Rita Melendez (2004) conducted unstructured, longitudinal interviews concerning men's sexual lives, behaviour, desires and fantasies, which were carried out over a period of time with 23 gay men in Houston, Texas. In particular, sexual history and multiple follow-up diary interviews were undertaken. The men were recruited face-to-face in gay locales including bars and gyms as well as by a snowball technique. The men were informed that they would meet with the researcher on a weekly basis to discuss their thoughts and feelings about masturbation and interpersonal sexual encounters as well as their fantasies, wishes and desires. In the study, two men identified themselves as Latino and the rest were White. Three men were in their twenties, five in their thirties, and eleven in the forty-plus age group. An unstructured, flexible interview schedule was employed to elicit information. In the first interview, the men were asked to tell the story of their sexual lives. All men went through an average of 6.5 follow-up interviews when they were asked to capture any sexual experience since the last interview, including masturbation and sexual encounters with others, in as much detail as possible. Whittier and Melendez (2004: 131) found that 'intersubjectivity, or what individuals thought others thought of them was a common process in the men's intrapsychic sexual scripting'. The men made sense of their sexual lives and the other men they were attracted to by referring to social structures, such as gender, ethnicity, class and age. In their conclusion, Whittier and Melendez (2004: 141) asserted that sexual desires did not simply emerge from these gay men's lives, but appeared as part of their lives.

In their study exploring how women in geographically isolated settings in Northern Canada maintain their health, Beverly Leipert and Linda Reutter (2005) adopted a feminist grounded theory method using in-depth interviews to elicit information from the women. Twenty-five women who came from diverse backgrounds living in northern British Columbia took part over a 2-year period. Leipert and Linda Reutter interviewed each woman three times. The first interview was carried out in the community of each participant, often her home or the hotel room where Beverly Leipert stayed during the fieldwork. Because of distance and weather problems, part of the second interview and all of the third set of interviews were conducted by telephone. Interviews were directed by open-ended questions which asked for their definitions of health, effects of context on health and their decisions and measures to maintain and enhance their health. After each interview, a summary of the analysis of the interview was given to each woman. In subsequent interviews, each participant was asked to comment on the completeness and accuracy of the analysis.

The findings of Leipert and Reutter (2005: 51) showed that the central problem for these women was vulnerability to health risks, particularly 'physical health and safety risks, psychosocial health risks and risks of inadequate health care'. Vulnerability to health risks was the consequence of their marginalisation within the northern context. This was featured as physical and social isolation; restricted options of education, services and consumption goods; limited power and their own silences. The marginalisation was also the result of the northern context, particularly the physical, socio-cultural, political and historical circumstances. The women adopted the central process of developing 'resilience' to deal with their vulnerabilities, using strategies of 'resilience', which involved 'becoming hardy, making the best of the north, and supplementing the north'. The degree of vulnerability experienced by the women and their opportunities to develop 'resilience' were influenced by their degree of marginalisation and their personal resources, including financial situation, social support, the level of education and their own health.

Leipert and Reutter (2005: 63) contended that in–depth interviews assisted them to illuminate understanding of the vulnerability of these women and observe the ways the women established 'resilience' in order to maintain their health. Their findings would help the northern women, their partners, friends, and families, health care practitioners, and policy makers to have bet-ter understanding about the women's lived experiences, to prevent their health vulnerabilities, and to strengthen their strategies of 'resilience'. They con-cluded that 'the use of a feminist qualitative research method was very useful in this study, as it provided clear access to women's voices and perspectives and was an important vehicle for women's empowerment'.

A More Innovative Interviewing Method

Here, I wish to point to some innovative approaches, structured loosely within the interviewing methods. Some of these methods may have been used in positivist science but are often neglected in the interpretative tradition.

Telephone Interviewing

Although telephone interviewing has been utilised in quantitative research, it has also been used as a way to obtain sensitive information from hard-to-reach participants (see Tourangeau and Smith 1996; Greenfield et al. 2000; Rhode et al. 2002; Perlis et al. 2004; Pridemore et al. 2005). Telephone interviewing has also becoming increasingly popular as a qualitative research method for relatively well-defined research topics and when interviews are likely to be of short duration. Telephone interviewing is considered an appropriate and practi-cal method for conducting research with older people about function and affect (Shuy 2002; Wenger 2002). It is argued that people tend not to reject a friendly voice on the telephone. Loneliness in some people, including older people, will encourage them to enter into conversation with other people. For this reason, Clare Wenger (2002) suggests the use of telephone interviews. Wenger (2002: 263) contends that older people are more likely to answer questions asked over the telephone if the questions are not too intrusive or personal or to do with finances and properties. However, it is imperative that researchers skilfully estab-lish rapport prior to asking specific questions. In addition, researchers must be aware that not all older people have access to telephones, particularly those who come from low socio-economic and ethnic backgrounds. Additionally, some older people may have a hearing problem, and so they may have difficulties in conversing on the telephone, misunderstand the questions and hence give misleading responses, or not hear incoming calls (Wenger 2002).

In Langford's study (2000) with women who have experienced domestic violence, some women were interviewed via telephone despite his original

plan for in-depth face-to-face interviews at the place organised for the participants. Langford (2000) points out that the need for telephone interviewing
became obvious when some women who were interested in participating
expressed their fear of leaving their homes to attend an interview. They felt that
they could be safely interviewed over the telephone within their own home.
These women were then interviewed via telephone. However, in this unusual
circumstance, it was decided that for safety reasons, no follow up calls would
be conducted if the telephone conversation was unexpectedly terminated.
Fortunately, the telephone interviews (only two cases) proceeded without
interruptions.

In a recent study on disability and identity, Rose Galvin (2005) used
telephone interviews as one of the research methods to access the narratives of
disabled people. Due to her own disability, travelling around to gather in-depth
information from research participants would become problematic for Galvin.
Hence, in this study, Galvin conducted 52 lengthy telephone interviews with
24 participants and invited 12 people to respond to the question. 'How has [the
illness or disabling condition] affected the ways in which you see yourself and
how others treat you?' Galvin (2005: 393) found that identity relevant to
independence, work and appearance/sexuality were the major areas that were
affected by people's disabilities. These areas were greatly impacted by the
negative attitudes of others in society, 'each of which were related to qualities
which could be argued to represent the pivotal characteristics separating the
"afflicted and the marginalised" in contemporary Western society'.

Interview Proxies

Innovative researchers have adopted proxy interviews as a way to elicit
information from some vulnerable participants. Wenger (2002: 268) suggests
an innovative method of 'using interview proxies' with older participants who
are also experiencing speech impairments such as those who suffer a stroke or
are in the advanced stages of Parkinson's disease. Attempts to speak will make
these people tired easily. Hence, interview by proxy may be appropriate for this
group of vulnerable people. Usually, spouses or close relatives are their proxies.
If this is not possible, the proxy can be the person who is closest to the
participant. It is essential to note that questions asked in proxy interviews
should be 'questions of fact' (e.g. Can the person handle eating by him or
herself?), rather than 'questions requiring subjective answers involving feelings
or attitudes' (e.g. Is the person feeling depressed or sad?). If this type of question
is necessary, the researcher must acknowledge this in his or her interpretation
of the interview data.

Clare Wenger (2002) suggests that a proxy interview should only be
conducted when it becomes obvious that the speech impaired persons will
have difficulty responding to the researcher's questions. It is also important that
after the interview has been conducted, the speech impaired people should be
given opportunities to review the responses made by their proxies. This can be

done by the researcher audibly reading the responses and the participant may nod or shake his or her head to indicate agreement or disagreement. Wenger (2002: 268) contends that this will provide better data and at the same time the older people have good opportunities to be involved in the interview: 'something many speech impaired people enjoy'.

Jan Morse (2002) also advocates proxy interviews when conducting research with chronically ill and dying people. Morse (2002) argues that we may have no option but to elicit information from significant others who have a close contact with the ill individuals who are unable to express themselves. Under such circumstances, the narratives and feelings of the others surrounding the seriously ill and dying are important.

Rosaline Dworkin (1992) suggests using proxy interviews in research with people with mental illnesses. Dworkin (1992: 72) contends that some individuals living with mental illnesses may not be able to respond intelligibly because of the magnitude of symptoms they are experiencing or the side effects of the medication they are taking. Under these circumstances, sensitive researchers may think about interviewing a 'significant other', usually a member of the immediate family, about the sick individual. The use of proxies is very similar to the way anthropologists collect data in their fieldwork when they interview 'key informants', who often provide information about other people within the group to which they belong.

When choosing proxies, Dworkin (1992: 73) contends, sensitive researchers need to consider the relationship of the proxy to the participant. More accurate information may be gained from spouses and offspring than from parents and siblings. Also, 'any proxy will have access to only certain kinds of information. Easily hidden behaviour may not be within the proxy's ability to disclose'. Similar to Wenger (2002), Dworkin (1992) asserts that proxies cannot provide accurate data regarding the attitudes, beliefs and perceptions of research participants. Hence, sensitive researchers may consider working with proxies for data on 'social functioning' in preference to the 'subjective states' of the respondents.

Conjoint In-depth Interviews

Some sensitive researchers have adopted conjoint in-depth interviews in their research with vulnerable people (see Sandelowski et al. 1992; Booth and Booth 1994a; Seymour et al. 1995; Dunne 2000; Morris 2001). Sara Morris (2001: 565) contends that joint interviews generate data that not only provide rich information but also offer 'additional avenues of relevant enquiry'. Morris (2001: 565) points out that the joint interviewing method is generally more accepted by the participants as it provides a more comfortable situation for them, for example, when one of the participants is in poor health or when space is limited. It is suitable for cross-cultural research, where people will not talk alone with the researcher. And it is cost effective in terms of time and travel (see also Seymour et al. 1995 and Song 1998 for more details of this method).

From her research with cancer patients and their carers, Morris (2001: 565) suggests that 'having two people present offered the chance to observe some of the ways in which people confront the cancer experience as a shared one and where there may be differences'. Among the participants in her study, the existence of another person in the interview did not prohibit discussion about sensitive topics, such as death and difficult emotions. It was apparent that, at times, it encouraged more disclosure. Morris (2001: 565) concludes that joint interviews are 'particularly appropriate to research questions where a socially defined relationship or situation is to be explored – in our case, the patient and carer roles arising from the cancer diagnosis'.

In Margaret Sandelowski and colleagues' study (1992) on transition to parenthood of infertile couples, conjoint interviews were adopted. Sandelowski and others (1992: 305) contend that 'the interviews were conjoint, intensive, and intended to create an atmosphere conducive to free expression'. Two of the researchers carried out the interviews and they interviewed the same couples throughout the research fieldwork. The couples were encouraged to 'reach a natural end in their talk', and then prompted with some clarification or elaboration of the issues they had brought up.

Sandelowski and colleagues (1992: 305–06) assert that conjoint interviews were adopted rather than individual in–depth interviews due to several practical and ethical reasons. First, infertility tends to be seen as the problem of a couple. This makes it appropriate to 'treat the couple as a unit of study during the interviews'. Second, they realised that men are underrepresented in studies concerning infertility, partly because of the men's reluctance to take part in such research projects. Sandelowski and colleagues assumed that through the men's wives, they would be able to access men who were not willing to participate in the study by conducting conjoint interviews. Third, they realised that infertility may disrupt a partnership between husbands and wives, and hence, they did not wish to further disrupt the partnership by interviewing men separately from their partners. Conjoint interviews may cherish openness and trust critical to a family study (1992: 306) (see LaRossa and LaRossa 1981; Morris 2001). Fourth, conjoint interviews provide researchers with a better presentation of data. When individuals talk about their experiences, this often invokes responses from their partners and both can elucidate, endorse, correct or challenge each other's stories. During the conjoint interviews, couples frequently reminded each other about the correct events. They also talked about many things that they had not previously talked about. Last, the interchange between a couple during a conjoint interview provides additional data. As couples tell their stories, they also reveal conduct that would normally be hidden from a stranger in the private worlds of marriage and family. Sandelowski and colleagues (1992: 306) concluded that, 'conjoint interviewing permitted us to witness how partners acted together, how they sought to help or influence each other, and how they handled disagreements arising in the interview situation'.

Tim and Wendy Booth (1994a: 39) use joint interviews with parents with learning difficulties as well as individual interviews. They argue that joint interviews provided some benefits in this study.

> People with a common background and shared experience sparked off each other; mutual prompting encouraged the disclosure of things that might otherwise have been overlooked; often there was a degree of cross-questioning and challenging that an interviewer would not have entertained. Joint interviews involving relatives provided a fuller picture of the family as a unit. Also informants who lacked confidence or were a little reticent were put at their ease by having a familiar face present.

Booth and Booth (1994a: 39) maintain that joint interviews are valuable for disclosing new paths of enquiry. They include this method as part of their interviewing approach. Sara Morris (2001), in her research on the needs of cancer patients and their caregivers, used a joint interview method as well as individual interviewing.

Flexiblities in Doing Sensitive Research: Something to Think About?

In conducting qualitative research, as Morse (2000) comments, those who are able to articulate their experiences and elaborate their everyday worlds are good participants. However, this assumption may become problematic when the participants are seriously injured or ill and are undergoing physical changes caused by illness or injury. These physical changes inhibit their ability to speak, and as a result, the ill and the seriously injured are often unable to be interviewed. But, as Morse (2002) suggests, with effort these barriers to communication can be overcome. The participants may communicate using pencil and paper, or by signalling with nods or winks. Although it can be difficult and tedious, the acutely ill or seriously injured may have a chance for self-expression and their (silent) voices can be heard. Interestingly, being able to move only one eyelid, the biography of illness of Jean-Dominique Bauby (1997) has been written by applying this innovative technique.

When conducting an in-depth interview with vulnerable people, if the participant becomes too emotionally involved to the extent that he or she cannot be interviewed in-depth, the researchers should consider alternative means of obtaining their information. Jan Morse (2002: 321) provides an example from her student's work, who attempted to interview a farmer who lost his son and became too overwhelmed with sadness each time he attempted to articulate his loss. The student gave the farmer a tape-recorder and asked him to bring it with him when he walked on the farm and when he felt he could tell his story.

In their study with AIDS victims in rural China, Yun Lu and colleagues (2005: 1154) employed several qualitative methods for their data collection including individual interviews, focus groups, field notes and letters. They also used a 'speak-alone monologue' with one participant, who over the course of several days, used an audiotape to record his lived experience of living with AIDS. The man was given a tape recorder with 90 minute tapes and some instructions about the interview questions. This allowed him to be able to tell his stories whenever he was able to without interrupting his daily life.

In Melissa Buujtjens and Pranee Liamputtong's study (2005) of women who experienced postnatal depression, all the women were interviewed in-depth about their experiences of living with the illness. In the process of talking about these debilitating experiences, many women became distressed. The interview had to be stopped immediately and time was taken to wait for the women to be ready to talk. But very often, the women themselves would suggest that they go for a walk during the interview. The walk permitted the women to feel more relaxed and, hence, they were able to articulate many detailed stories of their suffering after giving birth.

Focus Group Interviews

> Focus groups are a profound experience for both the researcher and the research participants that generate a unique form of data. They tell the qualitative researcher things about social life that would otherwise remain unknown.
>
> (Hesse-Biber and Leavy 2005: 197)

The Nature of a Focus Group Method

Some sensitive researchers argue for the need to use focus group interviews when researching sensitive issues and working with vulnerable people (Zeller 1993; Kitzinger 1994a,b, 1995; Wellings et al. 2000; Owen 2001; Seymour et al. 2002, 2004; Warr 2005). These researchers suggest that focus group interviews allow group dynamic and shared lived experiences (Kitzinger 1994a,b, 1995; Lichtenstein and Nansel 2000; Wellings et al. 2000; Seymour et al. 2002, 2004; Hirst 2004; Stephens et al. 2004; Wilkinson 2004; Hesse-Biber and Leavy 2005; Hyde et al. 2005; Warr 2005). Jenny Kitzinger (1994a: 108, original emphasis) contends that 'group work ensures that priority is given to the respondents' hierarchy of importance, *their* language and concepts, *their* frameworks for understanding the world'. As such, focus groups access the element that other methods may not be able to reach. It permits researchers to disclose aspects of understanding that often remain hidden in the more conventional in-depth interviewing method. Sharlene Hesse-Biber and Patricia Leavy (2005: 199) argue that group work is inviting to sensitive researchers 'working from "power-sensitive" theoretical perspectives' including feminism and postmodernism. Group work may reduce the imbalance in power relationships between the researcher and participants that gives the researcher an 'authoritative voice' – an issue that most feminist and postmodern researchers are concerned about. Focus groups, on the other hand, 'create data from multiple voices'.

Focus groups, according to Sue Wilkinson (2004: 279), inexorably decrease the power and control of the researchers. Due to the number of participants instantaneously involved in the group interaction, the balance of power transposes from the researcher. The researcher's authority is 'diffused' when the research commences in a group, rather than in a one-to-one setting (Frey and Fontana 1993: 26). Because the goal of a focus group is to give opportunities for an interactive exchange of opinions, it is less influenced by the researcher, particularly when compared with an in-depth interview. Focus group positions 'control over [the] interaction in the hands of the participants rather than the researcher' (Morgan 1988: 18, 2002; Warr 2005; Hesse-Biber and Leavy 2005). Sue Wilkinson (2004: 282–83) succinctly concludes that:

> In sum, feminist focus group researchers recognize that focus groups shift the balance of power and control toward the research participants, enabling them to assert their own interpretations and agendas. . . . This reduction in the relative power of the researcher also allows the researcher to access better, understand, and take account of the opinion and conceptual worlds of research participants, in line with the suggested principles of feminist research.

The interaction between participants themselves substitutes their exchange with the researchers, and this leads to more focus on the points of view of the respondents (Hesse-Biber and Leavy 2005; Warr 2005). Focus groups provide an opportunity for researchers to listen to local voices (Murray et al. 1994). Jeanette Norris and others (1996: 129) too maintain that a focus group method is a research tool that gives 'a "voice" to the research participant by giving her an opportunity to define what is relevant and important to understand her experience'. The focus group method allows researchers to pay attention to the needs of 'those who have little or no societal voice' (Rubin and Rubin 1995: 36; Madriz 1998, 2000; Shalhoub-Kevorkian 2003; Kossak 2005).

Focus groups are a crucial research method for eliciting information from members of groups who are normally hard to reach, including the 'disadvantaged or disfranchised' (Winslow et al. 2002: 566; see Kitzinger 1995; Smithson 2000; Wellings et al. 2000; Wilkinson 2004; Lu et al. 2005; Warr 2005). Focus groups, Wendy Winslow and colleagues (2002: 566) contend, 'can evoke a level of candor (truthfulness) and spontaneity from members that provide data not accessed by more conventional interview technique. With a supportive group, people might be encouraged to discuss sensitive issues'.

Bronwen Lichtenstein and Tonia Nansel (2000: 120) suggest that focus groups allow 'peer group support and reassurance'. As such, its structure empowers group members to share their views and experiences. This is especially crucial when the area of examination may be perceived as sensitive or uncomfortable for the respondents. In their study on end of life care, Jane Seymour and others (2004: 60) also contend that focus groups are seen as potentially effective tools for researching sensitive topics because the group process prompts participants to examine the issues in their own terms. Focus groups help them to generate questions and priorities which are relevant to the areas under exploration and which could be further investigated during the research process. They also suggest that when carefully undertaken, focus groups allow crucial ways of gaining access in research to individuals who are relatively marginalised. Focus groups provide opportunities to 'open up' discussions on sensitive issues which are rarely referred to and not well understood.

Kaye Wellings and others (2000: 255) conducted three different studies on sensitive issues using focus groups. Their analyses of these studies attest that not only this method can draw out responses and views about sensitive topics, but also that the 'dynamics' of the focus group can yield information which is not attainable by other research methods. Wellings and others (2000: 256) maintain that 'the use of focus groups, by revealing conflicts and contradictions between what is personal and private and what is public and open, may provide insights which may not be obtainable through the use of other methods'.

In their study on subjective experiences of stigma amongst schizophrenia patients, Beate Schulze and Matthias Angermeyer (2003: 301) contend that focus groups permit entrance to research participants who may find face-to-face interaction of in-depth interviews to be intimidating. This is particularly so for people with schizophrenia. Focus groups create layers of communications and, therefore, provide respondents with a safe environment where they can articulate their experiences, opinions and beliefs in the company of people who share similar experiences and hold similar beliefs. This results in a familiar atmosphere and it is helpful in encouraging people to discuss any difficult and unpleasant topics such as the stigma of living with mental illnesses and HIV/AIDS, or being street sex workers or having the experience of domestic violence.

Jeffrey Borkan and others (2000: 209) suggest that focus groups offer 'an enjoyable forum for interaction' among respondents and permit some data quality control because 'extreme views are often muted or marginalized by the majority'. They also offer the respondents with the possibility for connecting with others and the continuous establishment of opinions during the group sessions – something not permissible in an in-depth interview method. In their research on sexuality among school children in Ireland, Abbey Hyde and colleagues (2005: 2593) use focus groups to elicit information from these young people. Hyde and others (2005: 2588) argue that interactions in focus groups allow the young people to challenge each other 'on how aspects of their sub-culture are represented within the focus group, in a way that is normally beyond reach within individual interviews'. Interactions can also reveal vulnerabilities of some participants, and when this happens, the others will share their vulnera-bilities. The following is an example from Hyde and others' work (2005: 2593). When the young people in one focus group were asked about what would be the biggest fears of having sex, the group responded this way:

P: That you have a small willie;
P: Yeah like fellas think more about that than getting the girl pregnant, . . .
     when you're actually doing it than getting a disease.
P6: Yeah, you do think more of, 'Oh crap what if I have a small willie?'
P4: But you can't help it can you, not saying I have or anything!

Hyde and colleagues (2005: 2593) argue that focus groups potentially permit participants to bring their fears, vulnerabilities and uncertainties out to the surface. It is extremely unlikely that in everyday conversations among young men themselves, their fears and vulnerabilities about the size of their penises will be shared. They may also be unaware that performance anxiety is a typical source of anxiety among young boys of their age.

In sum, the focus group method has its suitability for examining 'sensitive' issues or its use in research involving 'sensitive' populations, because people may feel more relaxed about talking when they see that others have similar experiences or views (Zeller 1993; Wellings et al. 2000).

The focus group method has been used in research concerning vulnerable people or sensitive topics. Examples are domestic violence (Petersen et al. 2004), incest survivors (Barringer 1992), rape and sexual abuse (Lira et al. 1999), safe sex practices among lesbians (Lampon 1995), immigrant and refugee women perceptions of sexuality and gender-related issues (Espin 1995), men and unemployment (Willott and Griffin 1997), men talking about sex (Crawford et al. 1994), men and postnatal depression (Davey et al. 2006), sexual decision making (Zeller 1993; Robinson 1999), gay identity (Mao et al. 2002), young people and menstruation (Lovering 1995), reasoning about abortion (Press 1991), living with mental illnesses (Koppelman and Bourjolly 2001; Schulze and Angermeyer 2003; Lester and Tritter 2005), living with HIV/AIDS (Lather and Smithies 1997; Lichtenstein 2000), death and dying (Steinhauser et al. 2000) and end of life decision-making (Morrow 1997).

Focus groups have also been used in research with difficult-to-reach and high risk families in an inner city (Lengua et al. 1992), ethnic gay men (Mays et al. 1992, Lichtenstein 2000; Mao et al. 2002), the elderly (Chapman and Johnson 1995, Quine and Cameron 1995), low-income minority groups (Jarrett 1993, 1994), women in rural countries and communities (Wong et al. 1995, Pini 2002), and dying patients (Raynes et al. 2000). Focus groups have been employed in research concerning children and adolescents (see Wight 1994; Charlesworth and Rodwell 1997; Mauthner 1997; Costley 2000; Banister et al. 2002; Eder and Fingerson 2002; Heary and Hennessy 2002; Hennessy and Heary 2005; Hyde et al. 2005). In the following section, I shall outline some empirical research in more detail.

Case Examples of Sensitive Research Using Focus Groups

A recent interesting focus group research is that of Jane Seymour and colleagues (2002, 2004) on end of life care with older people in Sheffield, England. They conducted 8 focus groups with 32 older persons recruited from 6 community associations in Sheffield. Instead of just having questions posed and getting the participants to discuss, they also used a computer-based Power Point (© Microsoft) 'slide show' in their group discussions. Due to their interest in new health technology, Seymour and colleagues (2002: 522) realised that visual presentations are an effective and interesting means of exchange with their participants. They wished to make sure that their respondents had sufficient knowledge and information to talk about the issue. They also wanted to ensure that they had a way of 'bringing back' the discussion if it went out of their control. Hence, their Power Point 'slide show' offered 'a simple pictorial aide-mémoire' that comprised the following themes (Seymour 2002: 522):

- The best place to be cared for (e.g. home, hospital, nursing home or hospice).
- The use of technology to extend life (e.g. resuscitation and artificial feeding).
- The use of technology to provide comfort (e.g. terminal sedation and morphine).
- Who makes the decision? (e.g. clinical staff, patient or relative, with material on communications and advanced care planning).

One slide that Seymour and colleagues used to help the participants to talk about advance care statements contained a photograph of a man with early Alzheimer's disease and a portrayal of his plan to end his life (Lesley Dennis, a person with dementia):

> I have decided that life will end for me when they try to use life support systems. You should think about this and act to define how things will work for you. Then you need to talk to others about your concerns while you are still able. Complete an advance directive and enduring power of attorney.

Although Seymour and colleagues acknowledged that their approach was rather structured and might not allow the participants to discuss other issues of concerns, it was beneficial in many ways. For example, presenting potentially risky material using television-like technology created a more comfortable situation and offered a 'frame' for subsequent discussions. They found that both the computer and protection equipment attracted curiosity and discussion and were valuable as an 'ice-breaker' (2002: 522). The material provided useful flexibility and, thus, the pace of the discussion could be varied. Particular images or words could be revisited or skipped over. If the discussion became too personal, it was sometimes necessary to interrupt or stop. The slides permitted this possibility. Seymour and others (2002: 522–23) remarked as follows:

> Unexpectedly but importantly, we realised that the participants viewed the slide show as similar to watching television. Most people are comfortable and familiar with television, and many of us sometimes watch programmes that include taboo or 'risky' material. By showing such material in this way, it may be de-personalised, and it clearly generates a lot of interest. They were most revealing, and gave us insight into the types of needs that people have for information about end of life care.

At the end of the session, the participants were debriefed over lunch. They were offered opportunities to follow up some discussions that had been raised in the group shortly after the focus group discussion. They were also provided with the names and contacts of bereavement care organisations. Seymour and colleagues (2002: 524) concluded that most participants enjoyed the group sessions and found the discussions interesting and extremely informative. See also their recent writing (2004) on the results of this study.

Focus group interviews have been used widely in social science research in Western societies, and recently they have been increasingly adopted in cross-cultural research. Jeffrey Borkan and colleagues (2000: 209) used the focus group method in their study on perceptions of health services amongst the Negev Bedouin Arabs in Israel. They conducted 12 focus groups (158 participants) with the assistance of specially trained local moderators and observers. Each group met for three to seven sessions. The focus groups method was chosen in this study because the nature of interaction in the focus group resembles the pattern of socialisation within the Bedouin. Tribal members of the same gender often meet for leisure and discussions in their tents, home or *shieg* (desinated structure). The Bedouin would then be more comfortable to discuss in groups than in an individual interview situation. Borkan and colleagues, however, suggested that orthodox focus groups needed to be modified to suit the local setting. They (2000: 209) strongly contended that a direct application of Western research methods of data collection to tra-ditional societies was 'fraught with difficulties'. For example, drawing group members from total strangers, as suggested in orthodox focus group methods, would be problematic. They asserted that 'in tightly knit traditional tribal soci-eties in which social interaction and settlement patterns are strictly regulated, disclosure to strangers, and in some cases even interaction, is unacceptable, even forbidden'. Borkan and colleagues modified several aspects in their focus group research with the Bedouin in order to make it more culturally appropriate. However, in their conclusion, Borkan and colleagues (2000: 207) contended that their study, the first of its kind with the Negev Bedouin, suggested that the 'focus group method, if properly modified to cultural norms, can be a valuable research tool in traditional communities and in health service research'.

Gisele Maynard-Tucker (2000) conducted focus groups regarding the knowledge of AIDS among high risk groups, sex workers and STD patients in Antananarivo, Madagascar for the World Bank/Futures Group International in 1996. Focus group discussions with sex workers and their clients were planned to be carried out in a private room in a restaurant in the red–light district. For 6 days, focus groups were organised from noon to 2 pm. Sex workers were informed about the research in the streets and bars the night before by a health promoter who was known to the women. Many promised to attend, but few actually turned up. Later, it became clear that these women spent all night working and they would sleep in the morning. In the end, women were recruited from the streets and bars closer to the research venue. The choice of restaurant where focus groups were held with the women assisted recruitment as it was convenient for them to attend. Lunch was served after the session and it was during this lunch time that the women talked freely about their lives, expectations, difficulties and sexual behaviours. The women felt more at ease during a social gathering than in a formal focus group discussion.

Oral and Life History

> Narrative is present in every age, in every place, in every society.
>
> (Barthes 1977: 79)

> Storytelling is in our blood. We are the storytelling species... We are recognising more readily now that there is something of the gods and goddesses inside us, in the stories we tell of our own lives. Life storytelling gives us direction, validates our own experience, restores value to living, and strengthens community bounds.
>
> (Atkinson 2002: 122)

What is Oral and Life History Research?

Oral and life history research is an inquiry involving collecting personal stories from an individual over his or her life course. Oral and life history is a specific method of interviewing which requires the researcher and respondents to invest lengthy periods together in a process of telling and listening of life stories. It is 'a collaborative process of narrative building' (Hesse-Biber and Leavy 2005: 152). Storytelling, Hesse-Biber and Leavy (2005: 149) suggest, is a fundamental aspect of the human experience. People convey meaning through storytelling. This means of transmitting knowledge has allowed researchers to develop research techniques that provide an opportunity for people to express their voices. Oral and life history, Andrea Fontana and James Frey (2005: 709) point out, is popular amongst feminist scholars. It is perceived as 'a way of understanding and bringing forth the history of women in a culture that has traditionally relied on masculine interpretation'. Gluck (1984: 222) says this succinctly: 'refusing to be rendered historically voiceless any longer, women are creating a new history – using our own voices and experiences' (see also Gluck and Patai 1991).

The difference between a life story and an oral history, as Robert Atkinson (2002: 125) suggests, is on its emphasis and scope. An oral history often emphasises a particular part of an individual's life, for example, work life or a specific function in some aspect of a community life. The main focus of an oral history is on the community or about a particular historical event, juncture, period or location memorised by individuals (see Candida Smith 2002). However, when an individual's entire life is a focus, it is essentially marked as a life story or life history.

Oral and life history, Sharlene Hesse-Biber and Patricia Leavy (2005: 156) maintain, affords researchers a means to invite their participants to tell their story of their past. But the individual story is often tied to historical existences and, therefore, goes beyond his or her experience. Oral and life history, as such, 'allows for the merging of individual biography and historical processes. An individual's story is narrated through memory'. Oral and life history is especially crucial for studying how individuals experience social changes as well as social and personal problems emerging from these changes (see Slater's work 2000, later on). As Robert Atkinson (2002: 126) contends, oral and life history interviews allow the participants to speak about their stories on their own terms, so they are able to recount their stories in the way that they choose to tell them. Life stories, hence, function as ideal vehicles for understanding how people perceive their lived experiences, and how they connect with others in society. Life stories, Atkinson (2002: 137) claims, 'make connections, shed light on the possible paths through life, and, maybe most important, lead us to the human spirit, to our deeper feelings, the values we live by, and the eternal meaning of life'.

Oral and life story, according to Hesse-Biber and Leavy (2005: 151), is a particular type of 'intensive biography interview'. During an oral and life history project, researchers invest a lot of time with research participants in order to gain comprehensive knowledge about their lived experiences or specific aspects of their lives. Oral and life history permits researchers to obtain in-depth information about the lives of the participants from their own perspectives. Through this method, the participants convey 'their perspective and their voice on their own life experiences' to the researchers. Researchers learn how the participants feel about things, what they consider important in their lives, how they see the relationship between different life experiences, their difficult times and the meanings they have constructed as a member of society. Ingrid Botting (2000), for example, was interested in domestic servants who relocated themselves from coastal communities to a mill town in Newfoundland in order to seek employment in the 1920s and 1930s. Oral history was used by Botting (2000) in her attempt to make sense of the experiences of migration and domestic work among these female workers, who represented a large number of women workers during that period. Botting's work is valuable in helping us to understand the meaning of being a woman from a given social class in a particular time, place, and work, from the woman's own perspective. Susan Chase (2005) includes life and oral history in her 'narrative inquiry'. Narrative inquiry, according to Chase (2005: 651), is embodied as 'an amalgam of interdisciplinary analytic lenses, diverse disciplinary approaches, and both traditional and innovative methods—all revolving around an interest in biographical particulars as narrated by the one who lives them'.

Daniel Detzner (1992: 88) contends that oral history research is grounded in symbolic interactionist framework. This theoretical perspective suggests that people act according to the meanings they attribute to expressions, phenomena, other persons and things. Meanings are constructed from the language and behavioural interplays between individuals and the groups to which each individual belongs. Meanings are constructed and re-constructed over time through the cultural and personal experiences of each individual. In research with older people, for example, researchers can perceive the narration of life histories in old age as in the present and collect interpretations of reality that these people have constructed over their life courses.

Based on feminist framework and being predominantly a feminist method, as Hesse-Biber and Leavy (2005: 151) suggest, oral history permits researchers to access the invaluable knowledge and rich life experiences of marginalised individuals and groups which would otherwise remain hidden. Particularly, the method affords a means of reaching unprivileged voices. Oral histories offer 'the collaborative generation of knowledge' between the participant and the researcher, and this can be an empowering experience for the researched as they are able to gain insight into their own 'pivotal moments' in their lives (Hesse–Biber and Leavy 2005: 151).

Oral history has the potentiality to decentre the researcher's 'authority' (Hesse–Biber and Leavy 2005: 172). Oral history argues that the participants have personal accounts, ideas and emotional lives that can assist researchers to have a better understanding about the social reality of the participants. Researchers argue that the participants have unique and invaluable knowledge in oral history. Only the narrator has access to his or her own story, and each person takes the role of narrator. The method, therefore, permits the participants to uphold authority over their knowledge during the research process. This is in line with the feminist and multicultural framework. Hesse–Biber and Leavy (2005: 173) claim that 'by changing the locus of knowledge and constructing engaged researchers and narrators, oral history lends itself to collaboration and the oppositional possibilities inherent in a collaborative knowledge-building process'. The oral history approach has been particularly embraced by social movement scholars (Hesse–Biber and Leavy 2005). It is, therefore, essentially invaluable for researching vulnerable people.

Life history, Prue Chamberlayne and Annette King (1996: 96) contend, enables researchers to discover both collective and individual untold stories. As such, it offers great value 'for purposes of empowerment and identity'. Life history 'gives voice to the dispossessed', and hence, it is valuable for research involving vulnerable people (see Sparkes 1994; Beverley 2000; Frank 2000; Tierney 2000; Langellier 2001; Loseke 2001; Auerbach 2002; Banks-Wallace 2002; Gamson 2002; Behar 2003; Crawley and Broad 2004; Haglund 2004; Marston 2005). According to Roxanne Struthers and Cynthia Peden-McAlpine (2005: 1265), indigenous culture has embraced oral tradition as a means to convey and transmit information since 'time immemorial'. Oral history is essentially a way for indigenous people to tell their stories and has long been utilised in research with indigenous populations (see Einhorn 2000; Struthers 2000; Struthers and Eschiti 2005). Indeed, as Susan Chase (2005: 669) puts it, ' "giving voice" to marginalized people and "naming silenced lives" ' have been the main aim of life history research for many decades.

Oral history, Hesse–Biber and Leavy (2005: 156–57) suggest, is very useful for studying social, political and economic changes. They assert that 'in this time of world change, oral history helps us understand both the shared and the personal impact of social upheaval on the individual living within it'. For example, oral history would be a great method for discovering the experiences of the US occupation, the shift of political regime and the rebuilding of their country among Iraqi people. How do these people adjust to these great social changes? How do they cope with it? How do different people respond to these changes? And to what extent are their personal relationships such as courtship, marriage and family relationships influenced by these changes? And we may extend these questions to vulnerable individuals living in many other societies where major political changes are occurring, like Afganistan, East Timor and some war-torn countries in Africa.

Case Examples of Sensitive Research Using Oral History

Kristin Haglund (2004) conducted life history research on the experiences of sexual abstinence among young people in the United States. Life history, Kristin Haglund (2004: 1309) pointed out, is a suitable method for examination of an extensive range of psychosocial events. Many psychosocial incidents do not occur suddenly. Often over time, they happen gradually in response to a number of influences. The life history method permits examination of such events, as the researchers gain lifelong information which allows them to examine diverse experiences and relationships, and to explore changes occurring over time. Haglund (2004: 1309) also suggested that life history gives information that assists researchers to obtain deep knowledge into how past phenomena occur and their influence on the lives of research participants. Knowledge of the experiences of other individuals allows researchers to gain more understanding about a wide range of human conditions (see also Sandelowski 1991; Cole and Knowles 2001; Haglund 2003). In adopting life history as her method, Haglund (2004: 1310) contended,

> I assumed sexual abstinence to be a developmental phenomenon, a state of being that had progressed over time in accordance with the biological processes of growth and maturity and that a variety of contexts had influenced. To discover how abstinence developed over time, I determined that lifelong data were required. Asking young women about their current states of being without exploring their pasts and their futures would have been inadequate. Therefore, the life history approach appeared to be the ideal means to collect a broad, comprehensive data field from which I might eventually glean understanding about the lives of sexually abstinent youth.

Using oral history as a method, Rachel Slater (2000) undertook a project to examine the experiences of urbanisation under apartheid among four black South African women. The four women had their own individual experiences, but also shared many experiences, and these were disclosed during the life history interview. Slater found that structural constraints shaped the economic realities of these women in extreme ways. The women also disclosed that their lives were ultimately influenced by not only the shared social reality, but also their own agency. Slater (2000: 38) elaborated, 'life histories enable development researchers to understand how the impact of social or economic change differs according to the unique qualities of individual men and women. This is because they allow researchers to explore the relationship between individual people's ability to take action (their agency), and the economic, social, and political structures that surround them'.

Daniel Kerr (2003) undertook an oral history research project adopting collaborative analysis in his work with homeless people in Cleveland. Kerr spent many years working with homeless people in the Cleveland Homeless Oral History Project. Kerr wished to carry out research which allowed meaningful exchange among homeless individuals in Cleveland which would lead to the development and implementation of policy changes which would reduce homelessness in urban areas in the United States. Kerr contended that traditional homeless research has failed to construct dialogues on a street level. Therefore, without extensive input from the homeless themselves, the results have not led to appropriate social policy to improve the life of these marginalised people.

Kerr had to relinquish the traditional authoritative position of the 'researcher as knower' and work closely with the homeless so that trends could be revealed, theories generated and appropriate policy changes advocated and effectively implemented. Kerr (2003) remarked that through their participation, the respondents were empowered. The research process permitted the homeless to be their own agents for social change within the area which was directly relevant to their daily lives and helped them escape being the victims of an oppressive system in the society.

Another interesting research using life history approach is the study by Debra Gimlin (2000) on plastic surgery in Long Island, New York. Gimlin (2000: 77) contended that plastic surgery is seen as 'the ultimate symbol of invasion of the human body for the sake of physical beauty'. This interpretation is often seen from the physiological and cultural discourse point of view. Women's subjective experiences of having undergone plastic surgeries are largely ignored in the literature. Gimlin conducted biographical narratives with 20 women who were clients of a plastic surgeon in Long Island. The women were of Asian or European-American backgrounds. The surgeries these women had included breast augmentations, face-lifts, eye reshaping, tummy tucks, nose jobs and liposuctions.

The women's narratives suggested that plastic surgery allowed them 'to successfully reposition their bodies as "normal" bodies' (p. 77). The women did not just embark on plastic surgery, but did so only after serious thinking and extensive researching. Gimlin (2000: 96) argued that 'the women's decisions to undergo surgery were shaped by broader cultural considerations – by notions of what constitutes beauty, by distinctively ethnic notions of beauty, and, most importantly, by the assumption that a woman's worth is measured by her appearance'. The women were 'savvy cultural negotiators' who attempted to do as well as they were able to within a cultural boundary that restricted their choices. Although these women knew that the surgery might turn out to be wrong, it was a realistic goal to achieve, at least for the time being.

Gimlin (2000: 97) also contended that the women had to work hard to 'reattach the self to the body'. They had to convince themselves that the new given bodies are connected to the self – that 'they are innocent of the charges of inauthenticity' (p. 97). To do this, Gimlin (2000: 97) argued, the women 'invoke essentialist notion of the self and corresponding notions of the body as accidental, somehow inessential, or a degeneration from a younger body that better represented who they truly are'.

Conclusion

> When a researcher is willing to get his/her hands dirty by becoming involved in the worlds they are studying, they are much better able to understand what they are studying. And sometimes being involved in 'different' world allows researchers to both gain information they would not otherwise be able to get, as well as to be better able to understand what they are seeing, hearing, feeling, and experiencing.
>
> (Miller and Tewksbury 2001: 118)

In this chapter, I have outlined and provided empirical researches concerning traditional interviewing methods in the social sciences. I have also incorporated what I call a more innovative interviewing method in the chapter. The three methods have been extensively adopted in qualitative research and many sensitive researchers have also used them to collect sensitive information from vulnerable people. I hope that in this chapter, I have provided readers with some basic ideas of each methodology. Selecting which method is best-suited for your research project, is a matter of thinking carefully about what each one may offer you. Then design the research accordingly.

TUTORIAL EXERCISES

1. You are asked to undertake a research project on the lived experience of being homeless among young people from diverse cultural and linguistic backgrounds and you have only one year to complete your project. How will you design this research project? What method(s) will you use? What are the rationales of using such method(s)?

2. As a sensitive researcher, you know that each research method offers particular strengths and weaknesses. If you plan to conduct a research project on sexuality, domestic violence or gay identity, how would you go about this?

SUGGESTED READINGS

Booth, T. and W. Booth., 1994b, Use of Depth Interviewing with Vulnerable Subjects', *Social Science and Medicine*, 39(2): 415–24.

Gubrium, J. and J. Holstein. (eds), 2002, *Handbook of Interview Research: Context & Method*, Thousand Oaks, CA: Sage Publications.

Hesse-Biber, S.N. and P. Leavy, 2005, *The Practice of Qualitative Research*, Thousand Oaks, CA: Sage Publications.

Kerr, D., 2003, 'We Know What the Problem Is: Using Oral History to Develop a Collaborative Analysis of Homelessness from the Bottom Up', *The Oral History Review*, 30(1): 27–45.

Kitzinger, J., 1994a, 'The Methodology of Focus Groups: The Importance of Interaction Between Research Participants', *Sociology of Health and Illness*, 16(1): 103–21.

Liamputtong, P. and D. Ezzy., 2005, *Qualitative Research Methods*, 2nd edition. Melbourne: Oxford University Press.

Montell, F., 1999, 'Focus Group Interviews: A New Feminist Method', *NWSA Journal*, 11(1): 44–70.

Potts, A., V.M. Grace, T. Vares and N. Gavey, 2006, "Sex for Life"? Men's Counter-Stories on "Erectile Dysfunction," Male Sexuality and Ageing', *Sociology of Health and Illness*, 28(3): 306–29.

Rickard, W., 2003, 'Collaborative With Sex Workers in Oral History'. *The Oral History Review*, 30(1): 47–59.

Shalhoub-Kevorkian, N., 2003, 'Liberating Voices: The Political Implications of Palestinian Mothers Narrating their Loss', *Women's Studies International Forum*, 26(5): 391–407.

Wilkinson, S., 2004, 'Focus Groups: A Feminist Method', pp. 271–95, In *Feminist Perspectives on Social Research*, edited by S.N. Hesse-Biber and M.L. Yaiser, New York: Oxford University Press.

6

Flexible and Collaborative Investigative Methods

Chapter Objectives   118
Flexible Investigative Methods   118
Ethnography   119
Case Examples of Sensitive Research Using Ethnography   122
Ethnomethodological Standpoint – Covert Participant Observation   127
Case Example of Sensitive Research using
    Covert Participation Observation   128
Participary Action Research (PAR)   129
Case Examples of Sensitive Research Using PAR   133
Conclusion   137

A philosophical system claims uniformity of method, but a truly philosophical spirit will rather aim at flexibility. This flexibility is not a random flexibility, but a uniform or 'methodical flexibility' in which the method changes from one topic to another because form and context are changing.

(Collingwood 1950: 192)

We both know some things, neither of us know everything. Working together we will both know more, and we will both learn more about how to know.

(Maguire 1987: 40)

Chapter Objectives

In this chapter, readers will learn about more flexible and collaborative research methods in researching vulnerable people. The focus of this chapter is on the following methods:

- Ethnography.
- Covert participation observation.
- Participatory action research.

Flexible Investigative Methods

Most researchers who undertake sensitive research with vulnerable people call for flexible and collaborative investigative methods. There may be times when a single interviewing method may not work well but require more flexible and collaborative efforts. It is argued that any one method cannot fully 'capture the richness of human experience' (Eder and Fingerson 2002: 188; see also Silverman 1993; Hammersley and Atkinson 1995). Researching young children, for instance, using only the in-depth interviewing method may not elicit a full and accurate lived story of the children. Sensitive researchers may need to use a method that includes participant observation commonly used in ethnography, as 'children's experiences are grounded in their own peer cultures and life experiences' (Eder and Fingseron 2002: 188). A short period of participant observation, Eder and Fingerson (2002: 182) suggest, may set 'the ground' for the in-depth interview (a primary data collection method). But in some cases, the researchers may wish to use participant observation as the main methodology and additional data may be obtained through in-depth interviews. In research that involves certain groups of vulnerable people who are marginalised, such as aboriginals and poor people living in slums, not only a more flexible, but also a more collaborative research method is crucial if the research process is to provide benefit to the participants. In this chapter, I shall point to two qualitative research methods which provide more flexibility and that require more collaboration in researching vulnerable people. These are ethnography and participatory action research.

Ethnography

> The ethnographic method provides the researcher with an important window into understanding the social world from the vantage point of those residing in it. Ethnographies provide the reader with an in-depth understanding of the goings on of those who inhabit a range of naturally occurring settings.
>
> (Hesse-Biber and Leavy 2005: 269–70)

Ethnography, according to Paul Atkinson and Martyn Hammersley (1994: 248), is a social research genre that has several main components:

- An attempt to uncover the nature of particular social phenomena is a strong focus of the method.
- There is a tendency to work with a small number of people, perhaps just one, in great detail.
- Explicit interpretation of the meanings and functions of human actions is at the core of analysis.
- Descriptions and explanations of the events take priority.

However, ethnography is often adopted in the field of anthropology. Researchers carry out their research 'on foreign cultures in order to capture understanding of the "native" population – the customs, values, artefacts associated with a given group and its wider culture' (Hesse-Biber and Leavy 2005: 230). Ethnography, as Hesse-Biber and Leavy (2005: 230, original emphasis) put it, 'aims to get an in-depth understanding of how individuals in *different cultures* and *subcultures* make sense of their lived reality'. The method is, therefore, well-suited to carry out research with vulnerable people in cross-cultural arenas.

James Spradley (1979) contends that ethnography is not only for understanding the human being, but also for serving the needs of humankind. He precisely emphasises the synchronisation of these two uses of ethnographic research. According to Spradley (1979: 10–16), ethnography is particularly invaluable in many ways:

- It helps to understand human behaviours. Therefore, it helps to understand complex societies where cultural diversity is great.
- It helps to discover human needs. And therefore, it helps to find ways for meeting these needs.

Spradley's argument for ethnography is particularly applicable to multicultural societies of the United Kingdom, Canada, the United States and Australia, where there are large numbers of immigrants who have come from diverse social and cultural backgrounds. Ethnography permits researchers to understand the needs and behaviours of the immigrants and this, in turn, helps to fulfil their needs. This can be seen clearly in the case of a woman from my ethnographic study among the Hmong community in Melbourne, Australia. Through my immersion in the community, I discovered a Hmong woman who had suffered badly from soul loss as a result of having a caesarean operation with her last birth in a maternity hospital. As a consequence of my ethnographic approach, I realised that the solution for the woman was to take her back to the hospital in order to perform a soul calling ceremony for her. Through negotiation with health care providers and the permission of the hospital, this ceremony was eventually performed. Because she was able to observe her cultural practices, the woman has been well since then (see Liamputtong Rice et al. 1994 for further details).

The essence of ethnography is 'the emphasis on interpretation' – obtaining interpretations and meaning from the perspective of those from whom researchers wish to learn (Hesse-Biber and Leavy 2005: 270). Within the tradition of the ethnographic methodology, participant observation is an essential component in ethnography. It is a means for the researcher to fully comprehend the standpoint of the participants and hence assist accurate interpretations of their data (Hesse-Biber and Leavy 2005; Liamputtong and Ezzy 2005). Erving Goffman (1961) studied the social world of inmates at a mental institution. He wished to understand the social lives of these inmates and hence immersed himself in their world. This is what Goffman said (1961: ix–x):

> My immediate object in doing fieldwork at ... was to try to learn about the social world of the hospital inmate, as this world is subjectively experienced by him ... It was then and still is my belief that any group of persons – prisoners, primitives, pilots, or patients – develop a life of their own that becomes meaningful, reasonable, and normal once you get close to it, and that is a good way to learn about any of these worlds is to submit in the company of the members to the daily round of petty contingencies to which they are subject.

A researcher, who uses ethnography as a method in his/her research, is referred to as an ethnographer. Literally, the word 'ethnography', according to Amir Marvasti (2004: 36), means 'to write about people or cultures, from the Greek words *ethnos* (people) and *graphei* (to write)'. At the heart of this ethnographic method, Marvasti (2004: 36) contends, are two activities: participating and observing. Ethnographers, Hesse-Biber and Leavy (2005: 230) suggest, ' "go inside" the social worlds of the inhabitants of their research setting, "hanging out" and observing and recording the ongoing social life of its members by providing "thick descriptions" of the social context and the everyday lives of the people who inhabit these worlds'. The ethnographer writes the ethnography from all the data collected: from people's daily lives to their specific rituals. In order to write up this data correctly and clearly, they have to first make sense of it all. The ethnographers, Marvasti (2004: 48) points out, 'examine how people make sense of their world in their native circumstances'.

In researching drug users, for example, Adler (1990: 99) points out that 'the highly illegal nature of the occupation makes drug dealers and smugglers secretive, deceitful, mistrustful and paranoid. To insulate themselves from the straight world, they construct multiple false fronts, offer lies and misinformation, and withdraw into their group'. Adler attempts to enter this hidden world by taking 'a membership role' in the research setting. And this is done through participant observation by submerging in the research setting. Although Adler did not get involved in any deal, she participated in numerous activities of the drug dealers. She attended their social gatherings, travelled with the groups and watched them as they planned and carried out their business.

Often the ethnographic method is employed in research involving vulnerable or hard-to-reach people. This can be traced back to the work of Charles Booth, in his study of underclass people in London in 1902. Booth, as Emerson (2001: 9) tells us, utilised interviewing methods and direct observation to document in-depth accounts of the lives of the London poor. Employing direct observation, Booth and his colleagues 'entered directly into the world of the poor'. In their ethnographic research with women living with HIV/AIDS, Patti Lather and Chris Smithies (1997) interviewed and participated in the daily lives of these vulnerable women who had been rendered silent by their marginalisation. The women provided in-depth details of their lived experiences of living with HIV/AIDS. Ethnography has been and is still a popular method in researching the so-called 'deviant' groups such as gangs, drug dealers, commercial sex workers and so on. See Dick Hobbs (2001) in his detailed review on ethnography and the study of deviance.

Most often, ethnographers tend to work in the field alone. But Adler (1990) suggests that a team field research approach may be crucial in some research projects. If researchers wish to have a deep understanding about the complex but hidden realities of some hard-to-reach groups, a research team comprising different genders, ages and backgrounds may be beneficial as the team can provide multiple perspectives into the complexity of their world. This is particularly crucial in research involving deviant groups. As a female researcher doing research with difficult-to-reach populations like drug dealers, Adler (1990: 108) tells us about the benefit of having a team on the research:

> I profited from having my husband serve as partner in this project. It would have been impossible to examine this world as an unattached female without failing prey to sex role stereotyping, which excluded women from business dealings. Acting as a couple allowed us to relate in different ways to both men and women. We protected each other when we entered the homes of dangerous characters, buoyed each other's courage, and helped each other keep the conversation going.

Case Examples of Sensitive Research Using Ethnography

James Marquart (2001: 36) undertook research to explore the methods of prisoner control and discipline, official and unofficial, in a large maximum security prison in Texas. He tells us, 'I worked as a researcher-guard for nineteen months... and collected ethnographic materials while working, participating, and observing in a variety of location and activities (e.g. cell blocks, dormitories, visitation areas, recreation periods, dining halls, shower rooms, solitary confinement, disciplinary hearings and hospital). I eventually obtained unlimited access to the unwritten and more sensitive aspects of guard work, prisoner control, and the guard culture'. With this type of research, Marquart argues, complete participation by immersion in the prison scene was essential, hence the choice of ethnography with extensive participant observation was adopted. He also suggests that often ethnographic reports failed to discuss important issues in research in prison such as 'the activities of entering the prison, negotiating a research role, establishing field relationships, studying social control and order, and exiting the field'. Immersion in the prison scene placed some unusual demands on him as a researcher and as a person, not often encountered by other qualitative researchers (cf. Van Maanen 1982). Marquart (2001: 36) terms his method as 'a prison methodology'.

Over the course of 17 years, Columbus Hopper and Johnny Moore (2001) conducted an ethnographic study of women in outlaw motorcycle gangs in Mississippi, Tennessee, Louisiana and Arkansas, using a participant observation method and in-depth interviews with outlaw bikers and their female associates. Hopper and Moore (2001: 141) tell us that 'during the course of our research, we have attended biker parties, weddings, funerals, and other functions in which outlaw clubs were involved. In addition, we have visited gang clubhouses, gone on "runs", and enjoyed cookouts with several outlaw organizations'.

As I have discussed in Chapter 3, accessing some hard-to-reach groups like the outlaw motorcycle gangs can be extremely difficult. But Hopper and Moore were able to make contacts with bikers through the assistance of Johnny Moore, an ex-biker and a former club president. Moore was also able to obtain permission for the research team to enter biker clubhouses, which to an outsider was 'a rare privilege'. Because of the nature of the gang life (the gangs were more active at this time), most of the fieldwork was carried out on weekends. The bikers normally held a big party one weekend of each month, but more often when the weather was good. Hopper and Moore were invited to join them in many of their parties. This comprised their crucial participant observation. They tell us that 'at some parties, such as the "Big Blowout" each spring in Gulfport, there were a variety of nonmembers present to observe the motorcycle shows and "old lady" contests and to enjoy the party atmosphere. These occasions were especially helpful in our study because bikers were "loose" and easier to approach while partying' (p. 141). Hopper and Moore also contend that their research necessitated informal research procedures like participant observation in ethnography because most bikers would not permit tape recording or note taking in the field.

Maggie O'Neill (1996: 134) undertook an ethnographic approach to document the voices of women working as prostitutes. O'Neill (1996) conducted 'lifespan narratives' with street prostitutes in Nottingham. In this study, O'Neill (1996: 131) tells us that the lifespan narratives were, however, undertaken only as guided conversations. She remained silent as much as possible and would only gently say a few words in order to encourage the participants when they paused or stopped talking. The women's own stories, their narratives, feelings and interpretations were the focus. She contends that 'documenting women's experiences through lifespan narratives, biographies becomes political when contextualized within feminist theory/methodology. Feminist research methodologies are ways of envisioning and grounding knowledge and providing ways of locating and contextualizing women's experiences'.

O'Neill (1996) adopted a very flexible approach with this study. She told us that employing an ethnographic method to the recording of the voices of women working as sex workers had led to different types of data. She remarked that the information she collected was governed by many factors. First the location, which was determined by whether the information was collected on or off-street. Second was the time factor – whether the interview was carried out in the early or latter stage of her research. Early data came from her notes which were taken on-street, but the latter data was recorded on tape in the form of lifespan narratives. Third, her relationship with the women as well as the women's perceptions of trust and risk inherent in the relationship with her as a researcher dictated the type of data she elicited from the women. At the beginning of her research, longer off-street interviews were recorded by taking notes as the women did not wish to have their stories recorded on tapes. She also recorded her encounters with the women on streets in the form of short notes which were written in the car, between locations, or from memory upon returning home. Longer lifespan narratives were taped, lasting between 1.5 and 3.5 hours. The lifespan interviews were conducted almost 2 years after she had commenced the initial work. This was the evidence of trust that she had developed with the women in the local area.

Because ethnography is a traditional method in anthropology, it is not surprising that cross-cultural sensitive research relies heavily on the ethnographic method (see Glantz et al. 1998; D'Cruz 2004; Hoeyer et al. 2005; Martinez 2005;

Stevens and Capitman 2005). Namino Glantz and colleagues (1998), in their research on reproductive health in Chiapas, Mexico, tell us that because there was a limited understanding of the local cultural interpretations of reproductive health issues and, more importantly, because the topic of reproductive health was particularly sensitive to women in Chiapas, they chose to use ethnographic methods in their research. They adopted ethnography to examine a range of reproductive and sexual health issues including domestic violence.

Ethnography was particularly selected for their study due to its immense suitability for exploring an intimate and sensitive issue like domestic violence. This issue is often hidden and people would not talk about it easily, or if they wanted to, they would only do so in private. In their research, Glantz and others (1998) used focus groups and in-depth interviews as their main data collection method. They found that the women discussed openly about pregnancy, birth and childrearing in a group setting, but were reluctant to talk about their bodies, sexuality and marital relationships. Hence, individual focused ethnographic interviews were carried out to allow the women to tell their personal stories in a more private setting. Additionally, they found that the women tended to express themselves better when they commented on the experiences of other people. Glantz and colleagues (1998) developed a number of innovative techniques to allow the women to express their views. They developed questions that initiated discussions on sensitive issues by first framing them in general or abstract terms or by using hypothetical characters in tangible situations. For example, the participants were invited to comment on various phases of their lives and were then asked to evaluate each situation. One question, for example, was 'could you tell me what your family was like before you got married?' This was followed by 'when you lived with them, what were your relationships like?' Glantz and others (1998: 380) contended that in responding to these questions, the women often talked about sensitive issues such as domestic violence, abandonment and alcoholism – issues which might not have come out if they were asked with a more direct questioning technique.

Premilla D'Cruz (2004) carried out an ethnographic research project in India on the family experience of caregiving for those with HIV/AIDS. D'Cruz (2004) undertook multiple session in-depth interviews and participant observations with 19 family members who were giving or receiving care. Due to the stigma attached to AIDS, recruiting family members was a challenging task for D'Cruz, but through trust building and rapport, she managed to secure the consent of these 19 families. Within this study, D'Cruz (2004) adopted phenomenology as her theoretical standpoint due to her interest in understanding the experience and subjective meanings and interpretations of caring for people infected with stigmatised illness. Interviewing the participants at home allowed D'Cruz to record 'ethnographic observations' which assisted her to have a full understanding of the 'situational context' of the care. D'Cruz suggested that her study permitted in-depth knowledge about the ways of people taking care of those living with HIV/AIDS and the diverse ways in which carers experienced their roles as caregiver within a particular social context of the disease.

Joyce Stevens and John Capitman (2005) conducted an interesting study relating to drug use in minority communities in the United States. They argued that drug use and drug trafficking is prevalent in many African–American communities, particularly those in urban settings. Hastings neighbourhood, an anonymous name for an African–American community in a large northeaster metropolitan area in the United States, is a good case example. Stevens and Capitman (2005) pointed out that there have been numerous ethnographic studies examining the everyday lives of African–American individuals and the world in which they lived – a world where they bought, used, and sold drugs. But most of these studies have not explored the impacts of the activities on 'the social and moral fabric' of these people or their community as a whole. In this study, Stevens and Capitman (2005) used ethnographic methods to elicit individuals' stories of the consequences of drug use in the neighbourhood and drug trafficking within the locations where they resided and operated.

In this study, Stevens and Capitman (2005) employed participant observations, field trips, individual interviews and a focus group. They used the term 'ethnographic geographical community mapping' for their data collection procedure. This is what they did:

> To gain greater access to a study sample, neighbourhoods were selected for geographical density and concentrated drug trafficking and drug use occurrences. We reasoned that public housing sites met these criteria because of the density of dwelling units and shared neighbourhood characteristics. Moreover, observational field trips and participant observation rendered the identification of specific neighbourhood community resources, including churches and neighbourhood social, recreational, and health resources.

All research members, the researcher, project coordinator and four community researchers (all were African–American), collected neighbourhood mapping data. All community researchers were experienced women who had extensive knowledge of the Hastings community. They were living and working within the research community. Their residency within the Hastings community permitted them to produce 'a multivocal text'. In-depth interviews were conducted with 25 key informants, and 1 focus group interview was carried out.

Their study showed 'loss trauma within familial and communal contexts' (p. 280). The participants 'expressed losses of physical space, social networks, and familial attachments' (p. 282). Their narratives, Steven and Capitman (2005: 280) say, 'exemplify a discourse from which to view the psychosocial impact of inner-city drug activities as a man-made social disaster, characterized by the trauma of personal, familial, physical, and spatial loss. This view of social disasters also reveals victim vulnerability and the consequential communal and individual responses of recovery'. Stevens and Capitman (2005) argued strongly that their findings have great ramifications for social work professionals who work with communities that are affected by drug use and profiteering and wish to 'reconstruct' these communities.

Rebecca Martinez (2005) utilised ethnography in her research on how women in Venezuela perceived their cervical cancer. In its early stage, cervical cancer is symptomless and hence it can occur without the victim feeling ill. However, nowadays it can be detected through medical technology. The women in her study were confronted with 'disparate and contradictory physical and psychological states of well-being, sickness, and disease'. In this study, Martinez (2005: 797) inquired how women attempted to make sense of and deal with cervical cancer in the context of their daily lives. Martinez (2005) referred to this as 'living on the borderlands of health, disease, and illness, where all these states are experienced concurrently and boundaries between them blur'. Martinez (2005) carried out ethnographic interviews with the women who sought treatment for cervical cancer and pre-cancerous abnormalities. She participated in hospital activities and observed interactions between the patients and their doctors during their appointments, examinations and treatments. She also carried out her research in more informal situations such as in waiting rooms and hallways. She interviewed both the women with suspicious lesions on their cervixes and the doctors who treated these women.

Martinez (2005: 797) found that the women tried to understand their medical experiences, but they did so with little information from their treating doctors. Each consultation occurred within a short period and the women felt they could not ask questions. They said their doctors seemed very busy and hence they felt they could not impose on their busy schedules. Due to their social class, they were seen as low and uneducated, and they were not provided with information about their cancer. A general idea from the doctors who treated these women was that they would not be able to fully understand and absorb information told about their conditions and they might become irrational and depressed, and could defy medical knowledge by not seeking treatment. The women were generally silent in their interactions with doctors; they asked their doctors very few questions, but this did not mean that they were not interested in their health. Rather, they developed their own strategies for obtaining clinical information about their medical conditions and actively sought to make sense of their experiences. For example, they tried to read the body language of their doctors or they overheard conversations among their doctors during medical consultations, and then made their own assumptions about their conditions. In fact, through ethnographic interviews, Martinez found that the women wished to have more basic information about their diagnoses and treatments. In her conclusion, Martinez (2005: 807) strongly argued that

> Without an ethnographic account of the subtle ways in which women actively seek out information, one might conclude that they are disinterested in their health due to their silence in the medical encounter. However, in critically observing their actions and asking them about their experiences, we gain a more complex understanding of how it is that these women try to make sense of their situations as they confront complex interrelations between the ostensibly contradictory states of well-being, illness, and disease.

Ethnomethodological Standpoint – Covert Participant Observation

> The goal of any science is not wilful harm to subjects, but the advancement of knowledge and explanation. Any method that moves us toward that goal is justifiable.
>
> (Denzin 1968: 504)

It has been debated in literature that research with some hard-to-reach groups requires a covert participant observation. Many social researchers argue that covert participant observation is 'ethically indefensible' (Calvey 2000: 46), and hence should not be permitted. But the nature of the group that researchers wish to examine would render difficulty in gaining access and securing informed consent in overt participant observation. As Mitchell Miller (2001: 13) succinctly puts it, 'it is unfortunate that covert research is so rarely conducted because a veiled identity can enable the examination of certain remote and closed spheres of social life, particularly criminal and deviant ones, that simply cannot be inspected in an overt fashion. Consequently, covert research is well-suited for much subject material of concern to criminology and the criminal justice sciences'.

According to Miller (2001), covert participant observation may take the form of disguise, but the researcher is always immersed in the field location. Essentially, it is 'opportunistic research' (Ronai and Ellis 2001) conducted by 'complete-member researchers' (Adler and Adler 1987) who explore their research study while participating as full members in the research setting. Miller (2001: 14) contends that 'admission to otherwise inaccessible settings is gained by undertaking a natural position and then secretly conducting observational research'. The aims of covert participant observation do not differ from those of overt participant observation: that is to explore, describe and occasionally evaluate the situation. In a way, Miller (2001) argues, covert participant observation equates to participant observation employed in ethnography, except that the research participants lack knowledge of the real role of the researchers.

A major controversial issue about covert participant observation is the ethical concern of 'deception'. Deception is seen as being equal to immorality and this is the reason why many researchers reject covert observation as a legitimate form of research in the social sciences. Miller (2001: 17) contends that 'the major objection is that deceptive techniques often violate basic ethical principles including informed consent, invasion of privacy, and the obligation to avoid bringing harm to subjects'. This method will certainly be sanctioned by most ethics committees in the current climate of researching vulnerable people. But Miller (2001: 17) argues that covert participant observation should not be dismissed totally. There are times when covert participation can be valuable. This is mainly because individuals or groups engaged in illegal or unconventional activities, such as drug dealers and users, or inmates and undercover police, will not agree to participate in a study by more overt methods. See also Erving Goffman (1961), Laud Humphreys (1970, 1975), Terry Williams (1996) and Carol Ronai and Carolyn Ellis (2001).

Covert participation observation places more demands on the researchers and can be difficult. A full participation in research settings may contain many risks (Miller and Selva 1994; Calvey 2000; Miller 2001). For example, researchers undertaking their covert participation in the area of criminal activities, may place themselves in real or perceived wrong-doings. Before embarking on any research using covert participation, researchers need to carefully consider the possibility of being arrested or legally sanctioned as well as their moral decision. Miller (2001: 19) points out that the most problematic aspect of using covert participation remains its ethical issues. He suggests that this could be dealt with by being more cautious about the research process and consequences and adhering to scientific guidelines for qualitative research. He contends that 'the spirit of selecting methods on technical merit and relevance to research objectives rather than ethical pretense is an outlook consistent with the goals of social science'.

Case Example of Sensitive Research using Covert Participation Observation

David Calvey (2000) carried out a covert participant observation in his study of 'bouncers' (door supervisors) in the entertainment and leisure industries in Manchester, England. Bouncers, according to Calvey (2000: 440), tend to be seen as having an association with criminality in the form of organised criminal gang activities. Particularly in the entertainment context, bouncers are perceived to have their link with the sale of popular 'dance drugs'. To research this area, as Calvey (2000: 46) puts it, is 'to step into a dangerous world where attempts at regulation have not been as successful as was hoped'.

In his study, Calvey (2000: 46) adopted an ethnomethodological standpoint theorised by Garfinkel (1996). This standpoint requires the researchers to take the issue of description seriously. The description is grounded in the 'lived experiences' of the research participants. The researchers begin and remain with the participants' perspectives throughout their research processes. Following this standpoint, Calvey (2000: 46) contended, his moral objective was to 'describe as faithfully as possible the natural setting of door work in a manner which does not trivialise, diminish or caricature the observed phenomena'. Hence, this was his defence for using a covert participant observation. He worked as a bouncer and carried a tape recorder in his jacket. As he worked alongside other bouncers, he took extensive notes of incidents that happened without the knowledge of other bouncers, club and pub owners and customers.

Calvey (2000: 46–47) defended his covert methodology of this study by arguing that although some researchers may see covert research as unethical, his concern was about the authentic lived experience within a dangerous field research, and it would have been impossible to obtain access to his research site by other means. Calvey (2000: 47) convincingly argued that

> An overt role would have been inappropriate for this topic as the participants are reluctant to give any information about their work activities to external agencies. Even if they did

it would be highly selective and artificial. Covert participant observation was the richest way to engage with the participants in any meaningful sense. To get closer to and understand the experience of being a bouncer, one needed to do minimum damage to the natural settings of bouncing. The practical concerns, and the aim to understand the setting without disturbing it, problematised the issue of informed consent.

Participatory Action Research (PAR)

In doing research, I am educating and being educated with the people.

(Paulo Freire 1982: 30)

Those promoting participatory action research believe that people have a universal right to participate in the production of knowledge which is a disciplined process of personal and social transformation.

(Paulo Freire 1997: xi)

Participatory action research (PAR), according to Nazilla Khanlou and Elizabeth Peter (2005: 2334), is perceived as 'a more inclusive form of inquiry' (see Stringer and Genat 2004). PAR can be seen as a means of 'bringing participation into action research'. As such, PAR is not a method of undertaking research, but more like 'an orientation to research' (see Minkler and Wallerstein 2003).

Mary Brydon-Miller (2001: 77) suggests that PAR is a research methodology in which the differentiation between the researcher and the participants is questioned due to the fact that the participants are permitted the opportunity to take more active roles in pinpointing issues impacting on their lives, their families and their communities. Researchers adopting this methodological approach clearly aim to work collaboratively with people who have traditionally been oppressed and exploited. Collectively, fundamental social change can be achieved through PAR. And this is what sensitive researchers aim for in their research endeavours.

PAR arises from two research approaches, namely, action research (AR) and participatory research (PR) (Khanlou and Peter 2005: 2334). PR's philosophy is grounded in the power of emancipation derived from the 'Southern tradition' of research (Wallerstein and Duran 2003). The term PR originates from the work of Marja Lissa Swantz in Tanzania in the early 1970s (Brydon-Miller 2001; Park et al. 2003). Orlando Fals-Borda and Rajesh Tandon have adopted a similar approach in their work in Colombia and India (Hall 1997; Lykes 2001). The original work was associated with oppressed peoples in less developed societies. The aim of PR is 'structural transformation' (Khanlou and Peter 2005: 2334), and its target groups are 'exploited or oppressed groups' including immigrants, labourers, indigenous peoples and women (Hall 1981: 7).

Generally, PAR involves individuals, groups and communities who are vulnerable and oppressed. Therefore, it is essential that great care is taken to ensure that these vulnerable participants will benefit from the research and not be further exploited or marginalised. The ideals of PAR are that the participants who are directly involved in the research should be benefited (Hall 1981; Renzetti 1997; Pyett 2002; Wahab 2003; Schneider et al. 2004; Beardwood et al. 2005; Kemmis and McTaggart 2005; Khanlou and Peter 2005).

Although PAR primarily aims for 'improving people's well-being', it also has 'political overtones' (Khanlou and Peter 2005: 2335). PAR, Kemmis and McTaggart (2000: 597) suggest, is 'emancipatory'. PAR 'aims to help people recover, and release themselves, from the constraints of irrational, unproductive, unjust, and unsatisfying social structures that limit their self-development and self-determination'. Knowledge obtained through and from PAR 'is focused upon action, not understanding alone' (Khanlou and Peter 2005: 2335). This is particularly conducive to researching with vulnerable groups who may benefit from participating in PAR projects. For example, Barbara Schneider and co-researchers (2004: 564) suggest that PAR has become a crucial method of undertaking research with people with disabilities. PAR is valuable for sensitive researchers as it can contribute to a better understanding of the issues confronted by people with disabilities and their lived experiences (see Campbell et al. 1998; Balcazar et al. 1999; Stewart and Bhangwanjee 1999; M. Richardson 2000; Krogh 2001; Minkler and Wallestein 2003).

PAR has also been employed in research concerning people living with schizophrenia (see Davidson et al. 2001; Schneider et al. 2004). In their research with people with schizophrenia, Larry Davidson and co-researchers (2001: 164) contend that 'conventional approaches to research on mental illness provide yet one more source of the loss of self, unwittingly undermining rather than promoting recovery by treating the person with the disorder as a passive object to be investigated and acted upon by others'. They propose a research method which will enhance recovery by exploring and safeguarding a functional sense of self. They adopted PAR as their methodology because the approach has its focus on the agency of an individual living with the illness. It also engages the person as 'an active collaborator' in the research process. They insist that adopting PAR as a method for people with mental illnesses adds crucial knowledge to our understanding of the health issue of these vulnerable people. It also contributes greatly to the recovery of the person living with such illness.

Recently, we have also seen more of the adoption of PAR in research with children. The central argument for this is that it facilitates children's capacity to participate in research, rather than being a subject of investigation as in the past (Hill 1997; Johnson et al. 1998; O'Kane 2000; Punch 2002). PAR, Punch (2002: 325) argues, 'not only provide[s] opportunities for children to express themselves, but [is] also a potential source for empowering them for a fuller participation in society and for decision-making in matters which affect them'.

PAR commits to producing 'the political nature of knowledge' and empha-sises 'a premium on self-emancipation' (Esposito and Murphy 2000: 180). Therefore, PAR is ideally a sensitive method used with and for vulnerable people and particularly those vulnerable groups in cross-cultural settings (see also Khanlou and Peter 2005). In their work regarding non-Western participants, Esposito and Murphy (2000: 181) suggest that researchers using PAR are typically

> Comprised of both professionals and ordinary people, all of whom are regarded as authoritative sources of knowledge. By making minorities the authorized representatives of the knowledge produced, their experiences and concerns are brought to the forefront of the research. The resulting information is applied to resolving the problems they define collectively as significant. As a result, the integrity of distinct racial group is not annihilated or subsumed within dominant narratives that portray them as peripheral members of society.

Esposito and Murphy (2000: 182) suggest that PAR offers opportunities for discussion. Information is not just simply transmitted between researchers and participants. Rather, 'information is cocreated,...data are coproduced intersubjectively in a manner that preserves the existential nature of the information'. Sensitive researchers employing PAR, Bishop (2005: 120) points out, are not simply knowledge gatherers and data processors; they are also required 'to be able to communicate with individuals and groups, to participate in appropriate cultural processes and practices, and to interact in a dialogue manner with the research participants'.

PAR is more meaningfully harmonised with the expectations and concerns of local people (Lomawaima 2000). Researchers actively involve themselves in the local situations and attempt to find solutions to enhance the well-being of local communities, rather than simply treating the local communities as sites for data collection (Bishop 2005). Researchers, Lomawaima (2000: 15) contends, bring out the 'possibilities for directly meaningful research – research that is as informative and useful to tribes as it is to academic professionals and disciplinary theories'.

PAR, according to Zohl dé Ishtar (2005a: 364), is 'unique to every moment, every circumstances. It is flexible, adaptive and sensitive to its hosts'. PAR involves local hosts in all aspects of research development from the beginning to the end. It depends heavily on the people's 'common sense' (Fals-borda 1991: 149), and their 'critical consciousness' (Gianotten and de Wit 1991: 65). PAR methodology allows the local people to 'discover and apply their half-hidden science – their own "people's knowledge" – for their own benefit' (Fals-borda 1991: 149).

PAR allows the local people (the researched) and the researcher to have their 'freedom to explore and to recreate' (Fals-borda 1991: 149). It requires that the researched and the researcher work collaboratively to find new knowledge and practical solutions to end their problems (Fals-borda 1991; Pyett 2002; Schneider et al. 2004; Beardwood et al. 2005; dé Ishtar 2005b: 364; Khanlou and Peter 2005). It commits to 'the principle of autonomy and ownership in collective research' (dé Ishtar 2005a: 364). The Indigenous Self-determination (PAR) carried out by Zohl dé Ishtar (2005a,b,c), for example, has resulted in the establishment of the Kapululangu Women's Law and Culture Centre in the Great Sandy Desert in Western Australia.

PAR, Kemmis and McTaggart (2000: 572) contend, emerges deliberately as a means for resisting traditional research practices which are seen by some vulnerable participants as 'acts of colonization' when research aims and policy agendas are imposed on a local community and far removed from local concerns or needs (Tsey et al. 2004). In PAR, local people are the experts in their own lives. They, hence, should be actively involved in making decisions, planning the research, implementing and reviewing change. As such, research is not isolated from their everyday experience, as is often the case with conventional research carried out solely by external researchers. PAR is essentially an appropriate research methodology for working with indigenous people and in cross-cultural research where the researched participants are extremely oppressed by social structures and other political and economic forces.

Basing on the same epistemological perspective of PAR, Kaupapa Māori research methodology has emerged (Bishop 2005; Denzin 2005; Smith 2005). Kaupapa Māori research, according to Russell Bishop (2005: 114), 'is oriented toward benefiting all the research participants and their collectively determined agendas, defining and acknowledging Maori aspirations for research, while developing and implementing Māori theoretical and methodological preferences and practices for research'. Linda Tuhiwai Smith (1999: 183) asserts that Kaupapa Māori research allows the researched and the researchers to be able to work together in order to set strategies for 'the priorities, policies, and practices of research for, by, and with Māori'. Graham Smith (1992: 1) refers to Kaupapa Māori research as 'the philosophy and practice of being and acting Māori', where 'Māori language, culture, knowledge and values are accepted in their own right' (p. 13). Through emancipation, Kaupapa Māori research permits oppressed, silenced and marginalised groups such as the Māori to have more control of their own lives and their community (Smith 2000).

Ultimately, PAR as Cornwall and Jewkes (1995: 1674) contend, is about

> Respecting and understanding the people with and for whom researchers work. It is about developing a realization that local people are knowledgeable and that they, together with researchers, can work toward analyses and solutions. It involves recognizing the rights of those whom research concerns, enabling people to set their own agenda for research and development and so giving them ownership over the process.

Following Budd Hall's writing (1981), Mary Brydon-Miller (2001: 80) suggests that PAR has the following three basic tenets:

- It emphasises individuals, groups, and communities who have traditionally been oppressed or exploited.
- It attempts to pinpoint both the particular concerns of the local people and the pivotal origins of their oppression and aims to achieve positive social change.
- It is a form of research, education, and action which requires that all participants contribute their special knowledge and skills and through this contribution, all participants gain valuable knowledge and are reformed.

I wish to point out here that sensitive researchers have started to use more innovative methods in PAR (see Chapter 7 in this volume). Within the participatory rural appraisal approach, some innovative methods have been increasingly employed in PAR. These include seasonal calendars (Welbourn 1992), body mapping (Cornwall 1996), modelling (Marindo-Ranganai 1996), the use of Internet (Ferri 2000) and photovoice method (Wang 1999, 2003; Wang et al. 2004). Marindo-Ranganai provides an account of an interesting PAR project in Zimbabwe, which attempted to obtain demographic data on fertility, population size and mortality in order to create a community-based information system. Through participatory modelling, area maps were drawn and quantitative data on birth and deaths among children within the communities were collected, despite the fact that most participants, particularly women, were illiterate.

PAR researchers also use community meetings and different types of community events, such as theatre, storytelling, puppet shows, songs, drawing and painting and educational camps, as means of gathering data among illiterate people (Brydon-Miller 2001). The use of drama as a method in a PAR project concerning AIDS education programmes in black secondary schools in KwaZulu, South Africa was adopted by Preston-Whyte and Dalrymple (1996) and Dalrymple and Preston-Whyte (1992). Ethnodrama was used by Mienczakowski and Morgan (2001) in their PAR project in Australia.

Many of these so-called 'unconventional' methods employed in PAR are essential if sensitive researchers want to offer local people the chance to fully participate. Salazar (1991) argues that it is crucial for 'oppressed' people to be able to find a way to tell their stories and this may help them to break 'a culture of silence' resulting from centuries of oppression. See also, the recent works of Dickson (2000), Lykes (2001), Swantz et al. (2001) and Tsey et al. (2002, 2004).

Case Examples of Sensitive Research Using PAR

Barbara Beardwood and colleagues (2005) conducted a PAR project with injured workers who encountered numerous problems including difficulties in returning to work, and with compensation, medical and rehabilitation systems in Toronto, Canada between 1999 and 2001. These injured workers are double marginalised in the health and social care system. Beardwood and others (2005: 31) elaborate as follows:

> Some injured workers are viewed as the underserving injured. They are treated with suspicion, because their injuries from the late modern workplace have no specific etiology, might be multicausal, are frequently invisible, and do not fit any template of recovery. Furthermore, they never completely reassimilate into the workplace and are accommodated either with difficulty or not at all … They find it difficult to regain some semblance of their former lives. They become powerless and dependent. They lose control over their bodies and become dependent on health professionals and bureaucrats, and sometimes their employers, to be able to function physically and financially.

Following PAR methodology, the injured workers were actively involved in all the research processes: setting up the research agenda, designing the research questions and methodology, collecting the data, analysing, interpreting and reporting the research findings. At the beginning of the research, they attempted to engage injured workers in identifying the research agenda. Due to this, a conference for injured workers who had experienced difficulties with either compensation or returning to work was organised by the main research team comprising an academic researcher and representatives of the injured worker organisation. Beardwood and co-researchers recruited potential participants by several means: using contacts in the injured worker community, mailing out flyers to key locations, contacting key newsletters, conducting direct and targeted telephone calls, and placing advertisements in a local news-paper. At the conference, the participants were separated into small groups. They were invited to identify their main concerns, develop the main themes of their concerns, set up questions from the themes, and discuss the way they could obtain answers to these questions. In their study, the injured workers were asked to suggest the way they wanted to be involved in the project. Those injured workers who agreed to take part in the research were given a status as 'peer researchers'. The group had 12 members including 7 peer researchers, 4 academic researchers and 1 community legal worker. All peer researchers were given training in qualitative research methodology and conducting in-depth interviews.

Beardwood and colleagues (2005: 33–34) tell us that despite some complications and difficulties in the undertaking of the research project, the process of PAR assisted all those involved in the project (the researchers and the injured workers) to have a deeper knowledge about the complex reality of being an injured worker within the existing system of work and societal expectations. The research findings were not only disseminated amongst the academic community, but also the compensation system and the injured worker communities and the report was released at a public meeting. The main finding of this study, as Beardwood and colleagues (2005: 31) point out, was that the injured workers see themselves as 'victims twice over': victims of the workplace and 'victims of a system that implies they are fraudulent and that, in their eyes, refuses them support and impedes their rehabilitation'.

Using PAR methodology, Barbara Schneider and colleagues (2004) conducted research on the ways schizophrenia patients communicate with their health professionals. The research was conducted by members of the Unsung Heroes Peer Support Group for people with schizophrenia in Calgary, Canada. All members were schizophrenic. PAR in this research context, required that members of the research group meaningfully engage in all stages of the research process. Group members selected the issue of concern, in this case their experiences with medical professionals. They also chose their preferred method of data collection; and they selected an in-depth interviewing technique. They carried out in-depth interviews with each other. They also wrote and performed a readers' theatre presentation of their results and recommendations about the way they would like to be treated by medical professionals. Schneider and colleagues (2004: 563) tell us that

> The participatory approach taken in this project not only had the potential to contribute to an understanding of the experiences of people with schizophrenia but also offered the people involved an opportunity to overcome the isolation so characteristic of schizophrenia by connecting with others in the same situation to research a topic of importance to them.

The research points to the essence of good communication that people with schizophrenia receive from medical professionals. Good communication with medical professionals is crucial for people living with schizophrenia. Obtaining information about diagnosis, medication, and available support, and being treated with dignity and respect allowed people with schizophrenia to accept their illness, learn to live with it and come to terms with having schizophrenia. The research offers a 'transformative experience to group members and its contributing to change in the practice of health care for people with severe mental illnesses' (Schneider et al. 2004: 562).

Participatory Action Research has been hailed as appropriate for research involving vulnerable people in cross-cultural research including research with indigenous people (Dickson 2000; Tsey and Every 2000; Lykes 2001; Tandon et al. 2001; Tsey et al. 2002, 2004; Minkler and Wallerstein 2003; Holkup et al. 2004; Marshall and Batten 2004; dé Ishtar 2005a,b,c; Hewitt and Stevens 2005; Khanlou and Peter 2005; Mosavel et al. 2005). It is suggested by Marshall and Batten (2004: 3) that sensitive researchers need to adopt a participatory methodology, which will ensure 'a more equitable relationship among parties through its partnership constructs'. This is precisely what Komla Tsey and co-researchers (2002: 283) contend in their PAR project with indigenous men in Australia:

> PAR seeks explicitly to address and transform social inequalities. The approach, which integrates scientific investigation with skill development and political action, is widely acknowledged as an appropriate methodology in the context of indigenous research, not least because of its potential to empower those participating in the research.

One indigenous participant in their study, who is an educator, said it clearly:

> We (indigenous people) can use research ourselves to gain accurate knowledge of our own realities, so that we are empowered to find our own solutions . . . Participatory action research creates opportunities for these aspirations to be met.

One man from the Yarrahah Men's Group, who took part in Tsey's project (2002: 283) talked about the empowerment of the group because of their participation in this PAR project:

> This process has empowered participants to really develop the future of Yarrabah Men's Group, never before have they had such opportunity to have input into the program and

I find the process to be excellent, because what we discuss are about ourselves and the first step in man finding his rightful role we need to face our problems honestly and admit them and move forward to find solutions and these steps reveal leadership that lies in each of the men.

The study carried out by Zohl dé Ishtar with indigenous Australians (2005a,b) is an excellent example of PAR in cross-cultural research. She names the methodology adopted in this study as 'Living On the Ground' method. It is essentially based on the philosophy of PAR, but contains an element of participant observation of ethnography as well. dé Ishtar (2005a,b) worked with the women elders of Wirrinamu in Western Australia's Great Sandy Desert, one of the most remote Aboriginal settlements. The research was carried out as her doctoral thesis and it was a result of her involvement, as a co-ordinator, in the Kapululangu Women's Law and Culture Centre which was created by the women elders as a way to preserve their cultural heritage for their younger generations. A *Tjilimi* (women's camp) was established as a site where women's religious and cultural rites could thrive as the women elders observed, performed and relished their customs. It was a place where the women elders passed on their cultural knowledge and skills to their middle-generation daughters. dé Ishtar resided in this *Tjilimi* with 13 women for 2 years, participating in their daily living, gathering bush food, taking part in secret ceremonies, as well as managing the finances and administration of the Centre.

As the Kapululangu was initiated by the women elders, Zohl dé Ishtar (2005a: 358) had to plan a research design that would directly engage the elders but would not be too intrusive into their lives, and which mirrored their cultural practices. She tells us, 'my project needed to be flexible, responsive and responsible to the elders' needs, both immediate and longer term, and to resonate with their lives and include their realities – their concepts of the meaningful'. The outcome was, therefore, 'a methodology which responded to the depth of indigenous women's knowledge and the passion of feminist commitment'. Hence, indigenous self-determination or PAR was chosen as a way for her to gather data in this research. Her choice of research methodology resonated with the philosophy and principles of researching Maori, posited by Linda Tuhiwai Smith (1999, 2005) and Russell Bishop (2005).

In this research, strategies which depended on the elder's capabilities to identify their needs and to directly participate in practical activities which would lead to desirable output were developed. The women elders called this strategy 'kapululangu'. It was 'based on the notion of self-determination: the inalienable right of a people to define their own needs and to determine what actions they are going to take to fulfil those needs' (dé Ishtar 2005a: 364). Through a series of gatherings, the women talked about the problems faced by them and their families, named what they believed to be the origins of those problems, and made decisions on some solutions that they believed might reduce and eradicate their problems. From these attempts, Kapululangu was born. In these gatherings, the women pinpointed several concerns about their younger generations and these included petrol sniffing, alcoholism, teen pregnancy and domestic/family violence. Their immediate concerns were about the well-being of the children and youth. The women elders believed strongly that the trauma experienced in their community was due to the fact that people in their locality began to 'lose' their cultural life. And this was mainly because people's connection with their land declined, and they had few chances to acquire and observe their cultural rites. The women elders, therefore, wished to pass on their cultural knowledge to their grandchildren in order to 'bring them up properly'. To accomplish this, the children needed to be taken out camping to learn about the country, to hear the women's stories and to learn about hunting and dancing. The children must be taught how to help their men in carrying out similar work with the boys and young men. The women elders decided that the Kapululangu Women's Law and Culture Centre needed to be established and with this, they decided that a *Tjilimi* must also be set up so that they and their young women could reside together, and this would enable their grandchildren to have opportunities to practise and enjoy their culture and women's Yawulyu (law, ritual practice).

In arguing for the essence of 'Living On the Ground' methodology, Zohl dé Ishtar (2005a: 359) maintained, 'I sought to develop a research methodology which drew upon the women elders' knowledge and way of knowing and, fitting with indigenous process, incorporated the women elders' world-view, their cultural base and their ways of being'. However, it was also crucial that she must base her methodology on her own perspectives and the processes of knowledge which derived from her experience as a 'feminist *Kartiya* (White)'. The methodology must incorporate her ways of thinking and acting and her obligations and accountabilities to the women elders and her own cultural influences. 'Living On the Ground', dé Ishtar (2005a: 359) suggested, was 'grounded in relationship, bridged indegenous and feminist knowledge, required the researcher to be passionately involved, and produced tangible outcomes which immediately benefited the project's host'. Moreover, 'Living On the Ground' located the researcher 'within the terrain of indigenous people'. dé Ishtar (2005b: 360) contended, the process of this methodology could 'contribute towards culturally unburdened communications, for it is not only enlightening but it also challenges culturally-held perceptions, beliefs, and misunderstandings'.

Conclusion

Like theoretical perspectives, specific methodological approaches are various ways of viewing and interpreting the world. They are not necessarily correct or incorrect, but rather they often grasp at different aspects of reality.

(Rank 1992: 296)

In this chapter, I have referred to the use of multiple methods in conducting research with vulnerable people and these include the traditional anthropological method of ethnography and a more collaborative methodology of participatory action research (PAR). I argue that there may be times when a single interviewing method like an in-depth interview, focus groups and life history may not work well with some vulnerable people. This would necessitate a research method which is more flexible and collaborative like those in ethnography and PAR.

I have also pointed to the possibility of covert participation observation methods in researching some difficult-to-access groups. Although this method is seen to be somewhat unethical by researchers, those who advocate the method argue that it may offer some means for sensitive researchers to access hard-to-reach groups. Sensitive researchers need to think carefully about which method will be best for them to use to work with vulnerable individuals and groups and the moral and ethical issues that go with the method.

TUTORIAL EXERCISES

1. You have recently obtained a job as a researcher in order to under-take a project with homeless young people in an inner city of your country. Which research method will best provide you with in-depth and accurate information about their lived experiences, needs and so that the lives of these marginalised people can be improved?
2. Supposing that you have to engage in an attempt to empower women living in extreme poverty in Honduras in order to help these women to be able to take a more active role in improving their health and well-being. How will you plan your project? What method will you adopt in order to answer your questions and give you the outcome you wish to obtain?

SUGGESTED READINGS

Atkinson, P., A. Coffey, S. Delamont, J. Lofland and L. Lofland (eds), 2001, *Handbook of Ethnography*, London: Sage Publications.

Booth, C., 1902, *Life and Labour of the People of London*, London: Macmillan.

Bryman, A. (ed.), 2001, *Ethnography Volume I*, London: Sage Publications.

Coffey, A., 1999, *The Ethnographic Self: Fieldwork and the Representation of Identity*, London: Sage Publications.

dé Ishtar, Z., 2005a, 'Living On the Ground: The "Culture Woman" and the "Missus"', *Women's Studies International Forum*, 28: 369–80.

dé Ishtar, Z., 2005c, *Holding Yawulyu: White Culture and Black Women's Law*, North Melbourne: Spinifex Press.

Emerson, R.M. (ed.), 2001, *Contemporary Field Research: Perspectives and Formulations*, 2nd edition, Prospect Heights, IL: Waveland Press.

Ferrell, J. and M.S. Hamm (eds), 1998, *Ethnography at the Edge: Crime, Deviance, and Field Research*, Boston: Northeastern University Press.

Fife, W., 2005, Doing Fieldwork: Ethnographic Methods for Research in Developing Countries and Beyond, New York: Palgrave Macmillan.

Hammersley, M. and P. Atkinson, 1995, *Ethnography: Principles in Practice*, 2nd edition, Routledge, London.

Lather, P. and C. Smithies, 1997, *Troubling the Angels: Women Living with HIV/AIDS*, Boulder, CO: Westview.

Laureau, A. and F. Schultz (eds), 1996, *Journey Through Ethnography: Realistic Accounts of Fieldwork*, Boulder, CO: Westview Press.

Minkler, M., and N. Wallestein, 2003, *Community-Based Participatory Research for Health*, San Francisco: Jossey-Bass.

Smith, S.E., D.G. Willms and N.A. Johnson (eds), 1997, *Nurtured by Knowledge: Learning to Do Participatory Action-Research*, New York: Apex Press.

7

Innovative and Alternative Research Methods in Consideration

Chapter Objectives   140
Introduction   141
Photographic Method   141
Photoethnography   141
Photo Elicitation   143
Reflexive Photography   144
Video Diaries   147
Drawing Method   148
Diaries as a Research Method   151
Arts-based Method   154
Online Research   156
Conclusion   161

My 'method' is not fixed . . . It is based on what I read and how it affects me, that is, on the surprise that comes from reading something that compels you to read differently . . . I therefore have no method, since every work suggests a new approach.

(Barbara Christian, in Sandoval 2000: 68)

Artistically crafted novels, poems, films and paintings, and photography have the capacity to awaken us from our stock responses . . .

(Eisner 1995: 2)

Chapter Objectives

In this chapter, readers will be introduced to innovative research methods in researching vulnerable people including the following:

- The use of photographic method.
- Drawing method as a research tool.
- Diaries as research method.
- Arts–based research method.
- Online method.

Introduction

There are some situations where no conventional qualitative method will work and can be alienating for some vulnerable people. It is essential that researchers adopt unconventional alternative approaches. Travis Kong and colleagues (2002) suggest that in conducting research with gay and lesbian people, researchers may need to explore other innovative methods such as drama, poetry, diary, documentaries and the Internet. Claire Renzetti and Raymond Lee (1993) comment that numerous innovative methodologies, such as the use of visual imagery, group diaries, drama, conversation and textual analysis, and associative writing which have been utilised in feminist methods (Cook and Fonow 1984; Reinharz 1992; Olesen 2000), are particularly appropriate for researching sensitive topics with vulnerable people. This is what Norman Denzin (1999c) has advocated. Susan Finley (2005: 689) asserts that Denzin (1999c: 568, 572) encourages a new movement in qualitative research and asks sensitive researchers to 'take up their pens (and their cameras, paintbrushes, bodies, and voices) so that we may undertake "our own ground level guerrilla warfare against the oppressive structures of our everyday lives" '. In this chapter, I shall point to a number of innovative ways that sensitive researchers can utilise in research with vulnerable and marginalised people.

Photographic Method

In this section, following Barbara Harrison's (2002: 858) suggestion, I discuss the use of visual images and techniques as 'a resource': that is the use of the visual imagery as a tool to access information about topics of examination. These visual records may be carried out by either the researcher or the research participants (Banks 2001).

Photoethnography

An early example of this method was of Douglas Harper (2001, 2002, 2005), who took photographs of the 'subjects world' and then used the photographs to talk with his participants to make sense of the visualised world. In a sense, the photographs were field notes which necessitated the translation of their meaning from the research participants. Lopez and colleagues (2005) suggest that photographs which capture events and symbols of individuals have been used to inspire these people to talk about the meanings of their lived experiences. This tool makes it possible for vulnerable research participants to tell their own stories (see also Hagedorn 1994).

In her study of gendered notions of pain, Gillian Bendelow (1993) argues that visual imagery methods provided her participants with an appropriate means to talk about their sensitive and private issues in public. Bendelow (1993) contends that often for people, perceiving pain involves their emotions and feelings, and therefore, to elicit and to measure pain can be problematic. There is a need to find a means through which pain sufferers will be able to express their own definition of their pain. Visual imagery was, therefore, chosen as a way to allow the participants to talk about their pain. The participants (11 women and 11 men) were given a series of pictures illustrating different types of pain, and were asked to articulate their views on the pictures. With each set of pictures, the participants were asked the following questions (Bendelow 1993: 219):

- What is happening to the people in the picture?
- Is anyone in the pictures in pain?
- Is there more pain in one picture than the other?

All the pictures were then shown to the participants and they were asked to articulate on the following two questions:

- Who is in the most pain out of all the images?
- With whom do you identify most?

The visual images acted as 'equalisers' in this research process. Almost all participants were able to express their opinions about the pictures which they viewed; their opinions were 'very rich and philosophically profound' (Bendelow 1993: 227). Additionally, it was therapeutic both for the participants and for herself as a researcher. The participants remarked that the speculation of the misery of the people in the photographs assisted them to put their own problems into perspective. It also provided them with an opportunity to deal with the feelings of the personal events that had bothered them.

In her research on sexual violence and abuse with women with learning disabilities, Michelle McCarthy (1996) points out that it is common for people with learning disabilities to have difficulty thinking in abstract terms and understanding abstract subjects. It does not mean, however, that people with learning disabilities have different feelings from other people. Rather, they may have more problems with their understanding and expression of feelings. Because of this, McCarthy (1996: 120) contends, 'I have found it invaluable to work with visual aids such as pictures showing different sexual acts, images of sexual abuse, aspects of relationships . . . The advantage of visual materials like these is that they can help facilitate communication for people who find it difficult to express themselves verbally and/or who lack a good vocabulary on sexual matters'. As these visual images are difficult to find, particularly images which are not racist, sexist or homophobic, she and her colleague had to develop their own photographs. McCarthy's work (1996) was based on her fieldwork conducted with 60 women with learning disabilities and it was carried out over a 4-year period. Most participants had mild or moderate learning disabilities and nearly half also had mental health problems. From this research, McCarthy (1996: 124) reveals that sexual violence committed against women with learning disabilities abounded and frequently was of a most serious nature such as vaginal or anal rape. This often started when the women were at a very young age, and occurred over long periods of time. People with learning disabilities, McCarthy concludes, are especially vulnerable to abuse. Her study is confirmed by earlier studies including that of Crossmaker (1991).

Photo Elicitation

Another way of using photographs as a research tool is by asking the participants what they see in the photographs – a method which has been referred to as 'photo elicitation' (Weiniger 1998; Smith and Woodward 1999; Harper and Faccioli 2000; Sustik 1999; Bender et al. 2001; Harper 2001, 2002, 2005; Salmon 2001; Harrison 2002). Photo elicitation, according to Douglas Harper (2002: 13), 'is based on the simple idea of inserting a photograph into a research interview'. He suggests that the difference between interviews using words alone and interviews also using images is the ways individuals react to these two 'symbolic representation' formats. To Harper, images speak louder than words. He says this clearly,

> Images evoke deeper element of human consciousness than do words; exchanges based on words alone utilize less of the brain's capacity than do exchanges in which the brain is processing images as well as words.

Photo elicitation, Barbara Harrison (2002: 864) suggests, is the 'reflexivity between image and verbalisation which produces the data for the investigator'. Harrison (2002: 864) contends that personal orientations can be examined by inviting people to tell researchers what they see in the photographs. The photographic images can be used as an 'eliciting technique' in in-depth interviews or ethnographic field work. In photo elicitation, Harper (2002: 13) suggests that a particular form of representation of the photograph used 'evokes information, feelings, and memories' of individuals. As such, photo elicitation broadens the scope of conventional research methods. Photo elicitation, Harper (2002: 15) contends, is based on a postmodern ground, where the research participants have more authority than the researcher. In using photo elicitation as a method, the authority of the researcher is decentred, and this helps to empower the research participants, particularly those who have been silenced in society. This makes the method essentially suitable to vulnerable people.

This method is employed as researchers have a desire to understand the world as seen by their research participants (Harper 2005). In his study of the meaning of change in dairy farming in northern New York (2001), Harper used photo elicitation as a means to collect stories from elderly farmers. His aim was to examine changes which occurred in agriculture, how these happened, and what these changes meant for people who lived through them (Harper 2005). Older farmers were shown photographs of the 1940s, (a period when they had been young adult farmers) and were invited to talk about stories, events or usual activities, and the photos prompted their memories. The farmers provided explanations about the secular aspects of farming, including the social side of shared agricultural work. More importantly, however, the farmers elaborated on 'what it meant to have participated in agriculture that had been neighbour based, environmentally friendly, and oriented toward animals more as partners than as exploitable resources' (Harper 2005: 757). Here, Harper (2005: 757) argues for the necessity of the photo elicitation method in his study since 'photographs proved to be able to stimulate memories that word-based interviewing did not. The result was discussions that went beyond "what happened when and how" to themes such as "this was what this had meant to us as farmers" '.

In what he refers to as 'auto-photography', Ernst Thoutenhoofd (1998) used photographs to explore the worlds of deaf people in his study. For deaf people, Thoutenhoofd (1998: paragraph 1.3) contends, 'photograph (like all visual representation) offers a mode of expression with characteristics present in visual/gestural language itself. This is so by reference to iconic and symbolic form, but also by reference to placement, spatial arrangement, viewpoint shifts and temporal sequencing'. Three photographic projects were carried out in this research: those taken by himself as a documentary, those taken by a group of hearing and non-hearing A level students as an autophotography and images used in magazines targeting deaf audiences.

Here, I will focus my discussion on the autophotography project. Two groups of 10 A-level students, one group of deaf students and another one of healing students, at local schools were invited to take photographs of their social events in a 1-month period. The students were given cameras and films. They were then asked to choose what they believed to be the four best photographs and their reasons for selecting them. In this study, Thoutenhoofd (1998: paragraph 1.9) attempted to obtain an understanding of what deaf people themselves decided on about which visual documents would be relevant to their lives as deaf people as well as to examine the possible rationale of the results pattern. Autophotography, as Thoutenhoofd (1998: paragraph 3.5) claims, provides the opportunity to address issues which have been neglected in studies concerning deafness:

> If we look sympathetically at the idea that the 'Deaf way' hinges on an ability to literally see its phenomena, we should be willing to bracket (or abandon altogether) verbally-based, or rather, literally dependent research methods in favour of other forms of inquiry.

See also the interesting work by Anne Sustik (1999) in her autophotographic research of the adjustment of life in the United States among refugees from the former Soviet Union.

Reflexive Photography

Another way of using photographs as a resource is to ask the research participants to take their own photographs instead of the researcher. As Sol Worth and John Adair (1972) refer to these research participants as 'native filmmakers' in their research with Navaho people, we may refer to them as 'native photographers' in this book. The idea is, as Barbara Harrison (2002: 861) suggests, that the produced image may tell us more about what cultural groups perceive as most important for themselves and their cultures. And this, I would argue, gives voices to the researched.

Barbara Harrison (2002: 865) contends that photographic projects, like those of painting and drawing explicitly aim to 'use self-generated imagery to symbolise and make visible aspects of the self in social and physical environments'. Ziller (1990) refers this as 'photobiography', and Douglas (1998) calls it 'reflexive photography'. The camera allows the research participants to be able to address their identities. In his work, Robert Ziller (1990) invited students from four ethnicities to take photographs depicting what the United States meant to them and then reflected on their photos. Their photographs remarkably differed from those taken by white American students. Katie Douglas (1998) too invited black students to take photographs of a predominantly white university and to reflex on them in the subsequent interviews, hence the term reflexive photos. Douglas argues that this method allows a deeper level of reflective thinking than a lone interview can offer (Hurworth 2003: 2). Hagedorn (1994: 44) argues that photography reveals 'unfamiliar and unknown aspects of human health experience'. In what she called 'a hermeneutic photography study', Hagedorn (1994) invited eight families to take photo-graphs of their experiences of caring for a child with a chronic illness. This elicited 'spontaneous story telling' (Hagedorn 1994: 48) from the families, as the photos 'provide symbols of experience which represented the meaning of that experience' (Harrison 2002: 865). Hagedorn then used these photographs for the families to further reflect on and provide their interpretation. In Hedy Bachk's (1998) work regarding the creation and interpretation of schoolgirl culture in Canada, four girls were given disposable cameras and asked to take pictures which depicted their lives inside and outside the classrooms. Each girl took about 80–120 photographs. These photographs, in combination with interview transcripts, were used to produce visual narratives of these girls. Helene Berman and colleagues (2001) used photo elicitation with recently arrived refugee children, aged 11–14, from Bosnia who are living in Canada. The children were given disposable cameras and told to take pictures of places, events and people. These photos were then used for discussions in later interviews.

Virginia Morrow (in Hallowell et al. 2005: 131–32) similarly used photo elicitation in research with children (12–13 years old) and young people (14–15 years old) in two schools in a town in the southeast of England. As part of a larger study on the relationship between health and social capital, the children were asked to provide their narratives about neighbourhoods. The study employed several methods to examine the views of children about places that were important to them, but included visual methods comprising of map-drawing and photo elicitation. Morrow wanted to examine how young people perceive their local environments in a way that allowed them to have direct control of what they wanted to represent. Morrow states that drawing is less suitable to older children and she wanted the children to have fun as well. The children were, therefore, given disposable cameras and asked to take photos of their localities. They were asked to take about six photos for the research but allowed to use the rest of the film to take photographs of anything and keep them for their own use. The children were told not to take photos of people for ethical reasons. Once the films were processed, they were returned to the children to take out the non-research photos. The children sorted the research photos and wrote captions on the back of each photo using self-adhesive notes to describe what the photo represented and why they were taken, and then returned them to Morrow (about 100 in all).

Alan Radley and Diane Taylor (2003a,b) conducted their study about how people remember their time as hospital in-patients and to what extent this memory assisted them with recovery. The photographic method was selected for this study as the researchers attempted to learn about the experiences derived by the patients in the physical setting of the hospital ward. Radley and Taylor (2003a: 131) contend that 'the ward situation, with its particular architecture and array of medical technology, provides the setting in which initial recovery takes place. We wanted to know about this, and to know how individuals make sense of this experience in the days and weeks after discharge'. Nine patients who were in hospital for at least 1 week were invited to take part in this study. Once they agreed to participate, they were told that the research was about their experiences in the ward and they were asked to take up to 12 pictures that they believed were important about their hospital stay. These pictures could be spaces or objects which were parts of the hospital, but they must also take pictures of the objects that they had brought in with them. No photographs of people were taken due to the hospital's restriction. The researcher stayed with the patients when they took the pictures. An interview was conducted shortly after the photographs were developed with each patient while they were still in the hospital. The interview was open-ended but limited to the description of the photographs they had taken. They were asked what each photograph showed, what was being captured in particular, and to provide their explanations of the places or objects pictured. All photographs were then spread out and the patients were asked to select the one which was most important in illustrating their experience of being in hospital and their reasons for this. Four weeks after returning home, each patient was interviewed about his or her recovery and memories of being in hospital. All the photographs were laid out and the patients were asked to pick the picture that best depicted their experience of being in hospital. The patients were asked to reflect on the picture: what was the picture about, why was it taken, what memories did it bring back and how they felt about it. The photographs, Radley and Taylor (2003a) contend, made legible the images of the patients' hospital experience and the part these images played in their accounts of their recovery. Radley and Taylor (2003a: 129) conclude, 'the use of photographs is particularly useful in showing how remembering involves an ongoing transfer between different kinds of representation, including the narrative exploration of the movement of objects between hospital and home'.

In their most recent paper, Alan Radley and colleagues (2005) used a similar photo-production technique to show how homeless people visualise their lives on the streets and in hostels in London. Photo production provided the participants an opportunity to reveal their every day situations and to tell their stories as seen through their own eyes. Asking the participants to capture their world, Radley and others (2005: 277) suggest, provided homeless people 'the opportunity to "turn upon" their environment and to provide an account of how and why they did so'. Radley and others (2005) further argue that the use of cameras allowed them to capture spaces and places of homeless people and there were two important reasons for this. For one, it represents locations which are indistinguishable from homelessness. It also reveals other settings that homeless people hold in common with non-homeless individuals. Twelve home-less people were given cameras and asked to take pictures which would represent a typical day as homeless people. The photos were developed and then used to discuss their lived experiences in a subsequent in-depth interview 1 or 2 days later. At this interview, each homeless person was asked about the photographs which were set out in front of him or her. He or she was asked to tell what the photograph showed, what it focused on and to respond to the person, place or object of the photograph. All the photographs were spread out and the participants were then asked to select the photographs that would best depict their experience of homelessness. Radley and others argue that this methodology provided them with both visual and textual data so that researchers would have a better understanding of the ways that homeless people engaged with the city and domiciled people. Radley and colleagues (2005) conclude that this research revealed different ways that homeless people attempt to make their home in the city and to survive amongst domiciled people in this suburban area.

Video Diaries

Another aspect of the photographic method is provided by video diaries. An interesting study using 'video diaries' is that of Michael Rich and Richard Chalfen (1998) who carried out research with children suffering from asthma. In this study, Rich and Chalfen (1998: 54) asked children and adolescents who were experiencing asthma to record their own lives and their worlds; the children were asked to create their visual narratives via video cameras to create 'video diaries' of their everyday lives with asthma. This method draws on the tradition of personal narratives and the telling of a story. But a story is recorded in words and pictures. The children were given some directions about the pictures to be taken, including the tours of their homes. Rich and Chalfen (1998: 51) conclude in their study that the video diary method not only produces important and useful research findings, it also generates 'visual docu-ments of the child's illness experience that can serve as tools for influencing policy, advocating for patients, and educating health care providers, patients, and their families'. Video diary reveals some never before captured situations of these young people: their social isolation, irresponsibility of parents and others. These emerging issues help adults to have a full understanding of the ways the children manage their debilitating illness. The video diaries provided the children who participated in this study with the sense of being more active and having some control over the research process. This in turn helped them to have greater control over their ill health. See also a recent study of Barbara Gibson (2005) in Toronto, who examined the identities of young men with Duchenne muscular dystrophy (DMD) who rely on mechanical ventilation.

Drawing Method

Although the drawing method is still largely marginalised in social science research, innovative researchers have adopted drawings as a means to elicit information from some vulnerable groups. More often, however, they combine drawings and writing together or drawings are used in conjunction with in-depth interviews (Guillemin 2004a,b; Prendergast, in Hallowell et al. 2005: 134–37). Marilys Guillemin (2004a: 273), for example, suggests in her methodology on researching illness experience that the use of drawings as a research method 'is best suited as an adjunct to other social science methods. The use of an integrated approach that involves the use of both visual and word-based research methods offers a way of exploring both the multiplicity and complexity that is the base of much social research interested in human experience'.

Primarily, the use of drawings as a research method has concentrated on research with children (see Swart 1990; Oakley et al. 1995; Herth 1998; Punch 2002; Prendergast, cited in Hallowell et al. 2005: 134–37). This is perhaps due to a belief that drawings are most suitable for individuals who are unable to easily express their emotions and beliefs using written or spoken words, and these include young children and perhaps some vulnerable groups such as those with language problems (immigrants and people with disabilities). In Kaye Herth's study on homeless children (1998), she used drawings and semi-structured interviews to learn about their meanings of hope, and strategies that these children adopted to maintain their hope, from 60 homeless children aged 6–16 years currently living in homeless shelters in one Midwestern state in the Unite States. Herth invited the children to describe their hopes through drawings. The children were given art materials for their drawings and at the end of the session they all were given a copy of their drawings to keep. Herth (1998: 1053) contends that 'an understanding of hope from the perspective of homeless children could provide a basis upon which to develop intervention that engenders hope and to develop programmes that build on the hopes that children had already developed'.

The draw and write method has been widely used with children in studies concerning health, illness, death, drug use and cancer (see Williams et al. 1989; Wetton 1992; Oakley et al. 1995; Pridmore and Bendelow 1995; Bendelow et al. 1996; Bendelow and Pridmore 1998; Wetton and McWhirter 1998; Backett-Millburn and McKie 1999; France et al. 2000). It is argued that the drawing and writing method will give a voice to children and reveal the wealth of knowledge held by the children. In their study, Wetton and McWhirter (1998) asked the children to draw and write something next to the drawing. One child drew a person who has dropped a bag of drugs and another one drew a picture of him/herself doing something that makes him/her healthy. This 'draw and write' method is seen as a good starting point for in-depth interviews with the children. It is a quick and cheap method to do with children. The authors argue that their research is an attempt to examine children's ideas and knowledge of health from their everyday world. However, there is a warning about this method too. Wakefield and Underwager (1998) contend that draw-ing/visual image has been used with children who have been abused and it yields comprehensive results. But it should not be seen as a means for children to tell their stories because images may also elicit fears, anxieties and fantasy.

Shirley Prendergast (in Hallowell et al. 2005: 134–37) developed what she refers to as a 'visual life-line' in her research with young homeless people who were also lesbian, gay and bi-sexual (LGB). This visual life-line is adopted from the life history method, which allows participants to tell their story in their own way. The visual life-line allows young people to be able to 'reflect upon experiences as dynamic processes unfolding over time' (p. 136). This is how she did it.

She organised key interview questions along stage or age-related groups, including, the primary school years, life at home as a child, the transition to secondary school, experiences as a teenager in and out of school and leaving home. Common themes were used across these sessions and included peer and parental expectations, fitting in, gender constraints, labelling of difference, coping strategies and support. A large sheet of flip-chart paper and several coloured felt pens were used at the commencement of each session. First, she drew a line right across the middle of the sheet. Then a smiling baby was drawn on the left-hand side, a mark in the middle, and a smiling person on the right-hand side. She pointed out to the young people: 'This was you as a baby, this is you at about the end of primary school, and this is you now'. She then invited the young people to tell her about important moments and events in their life and they could begin wherever they wanted along the line. Prendergast (in Hallowell et al. 2005: 136) elaborates:

> Using different-coloured pens, we each added words, places, names and dates, funny or sometimes sad faces to the line. We made no prior assumptions about what was important or significant: narratives were respondents-led and we (carefully) followed. With both heads bent over the paper, constant eye contact was obviated and silent reflection was possible, crucial factors for people who are shy, or thinking about difficult things. Looking together, patterns might become visible, for example: 'There seems to be a big gap here between the ages of 11 and 16...'; 'Yes, so much happened to me that year'; 'I had forgotten, s/he was a very important person'; 'It looks as though things are a bit better now'.

Often, as she and the young people became more confident with each other, they would be sitting on the floor and working on a coffee table rather than a desk. When the young people were asked to choose to work with a female or male researcher, most often they wanted to work with both. Additionally, the friendly 'group' feeling sessions gave the young people space to reflect on their thoughts and feelings. Paradoxically, these sessions were effective ways for people who wanted to participate in the study, and at the same time were very anxious and found it difficult to articulate their thoughts and feelings.

At the end of the session, the paper was turned over and the life-line was continued. She then said: 'Now here is your life going on. Where do you want to be in five years, what are your hopes and dreams?' The participants would, without hesitance, go on to reflect on 'a time of greater agency and positive aims and achievements' (p. 137). Prendergast contends that these sessions were extremely valuable for young people who had experienced countless distressing and painful events in their lives with social workers, agency workers for the homeless and the police. But they had never had opportunities to talk about their happier times, achievements and future hopes. Prendergast (in Hallowell et al. 2005: 137) concludes that

> We cannot underestimate the significance of our more inclusive methodology for enabling the positive insights young people gave us as they told us their stories. As the interviews unfolded and respondents began to draw on a wider context and range of experience in the construction of their life-narratives, we believe that many were empowered as they began to reflect differently upon their lives. Overall, we found the shared task of filling in and reflecting on these emerging stories to be a liberating, absorbing and inspiring way of working, for us and we believe for our respondents too.

The use of drawings as a research method has also been used with some vulnerable adults (see Guillemin 1999, 2004a; Victoria and Knauth 2001). Marilys Guillemin (2004a) used drawings as her research method in her studies on menopause and heart disease with Australian women (see also Guillemin 1999, 2004b). In both researches, Guillemin was interested in exploring how women understood and experienced their illness conditions. In the menopause study, 53 women were individually interviewed and asked to draw their understanding of their menopause. In the heart disease study, 32 women completed a questionnaire, and were individually interviewed and requested to draw how they visualised their heart disease. The women in both studies were given a blank, unlined A5 card and a packet of 12 coloured felt pens. Most often, the women would laugh nervously and say 'I can't draw', but most drew some types of images as they saw it. Their drawings produced 'powerful and vivid embodiments' of illness among the women (p. 276). After the drawing was done, each woman was asked to describe her image. All women were asked about the content of their drawings, the choice of colour, and the composition of the drawings. This discussion was taped for data analysis.

Guillemin (2004a: 272) concludes that drawing methodology provides 'a rich and insightful research method to explore how people make sense of their world' and hence, it is suitable for conducting research with vulnerable people. It is interesting to see that in the menopause study, the drawings revealed many layers of women's understanding and experiences of menopause. The most common and notable perception of menopause was framed within a context of hormone deficiency. It was also important to note that the women made no drawings of hormones, hormone replacement therapy or doctors at all. Guillemin finally makes a case for drawings methodology stating that it provides valuable resource for sensitive researchers. However, in her study, Guillemin suggests that the use of drawings method was most effective when combined with in-depth interviews; the participants' drawings continue smoothly from their narratives.

In their study on images of the body, sexuality and reproduction amongst low-income people in Brazil, Ceres Victoria and Daniela Knauth (2001) used drawings and interviews as their methods to collect information on the female reproductive system from their research participants. Ninety-nine women and 103 men living in four shantytowns in Brazil were asked to draw women's reproductive systems. They were asked to make a graphic representation of the reproductive system in an empty silhouette. From their participations, 55 drawings were produced. The drawings were then used in the interviews to examine their perceptions of the female reproductive system. The researchers aim to encourage the participants to discuss the reproductive system. They also wanted to find out the extent to which biomedical perspectives of anatomy and physiology had been accepted, rejected or re-interpreted by these vulnerable people. Victoria and Knauth recorded the comments elicited from the drawings. The interpretation of the drawings and of the comments was done both together and separately. This provided important understanding of the various ways in which people perceive the functions of their bodies and reproductive systems.

They found that the drawings of women's reproductive system by most men tended to represent 'external' body parts. But the women tended to draw the 'hidden' nature of the internal body parts. The women tended to have more contact with the health system, and most women drew basic biomedical body parts. However, their verbal expressions revealed other notions and values as well as the physical experience of their bodies. Even when the women discussed their reproductive organs or represented them in drawings using the biomedical model, often they included their own meanings 'based on physical sensations they had experienced or emotional and social experiences' to them (p. 30). Also, the pictures of the female reproductive body drawn by men revealed the primacy of sexuality of the women's bodies, and that these men lacked biomedical knowledge of a woman's body. Victoria and Knauth conclude that health professionals need to pay more attention to the way in which people perceive the reproductive body if they wish to improve health care for poor people.

Diaries as a Research Method

The diary has been adopted as a research method in researching sensitive topics and with vulnerable people (Verbrugge 1980; Corti 1993; Marino et al. 1999;

Clayton and Thorne 2000; Jones 2000; Backman and Walther 2001; Punch 2002; Keleher and Verrinder 2003; Jokinen 2004; Miller and Timson 2004; Galvin 2005; Jacelon and Imperio 2005; Milligan et al. 2005; Alaszewski 2006; Hyers et al. 2006). Diaries, Jacelon and Imperio (2005: 992) contend, give researchers hints about the events which are important for the participants as well as their attitudes toward those events. Hesse–Biber and Leavy (2005: 383) point out that people may record their feelings, experiences, observations and thoughts about a particular aspect of their lives in a diary. The method can provide researchers with in-depth understandings of, for example, the experience of living with an HIV-positive person, dealing with daily discrimination and caring for a child or parent dying of AIDS and so on. Hence, the diary method can be an invaluable vehicle to gather information on some sensitive issues and from hidden and hard-to-reach populations. There are two types of diary methods: solicited and unsolicited (personal diaries). In this book, I refer to the solicited diary method, as it is written with the purpose of research in mind (Elliott 1997; Jacelon and Imperio 2005). The participants explicitly write their diaries as data for the researcher with full knowledge that their writing will be used in research and will be read and interpreted by another person (Jacelon and Imperio 2005).

Helen Keleher and Glenda Verrinder (2003) conducted their research on health needs among families in rural Victoria, Australia, using the diary method. One hundred and eighteen families living in rural and remote areas kept records of the families' health needs, perceptions of health and health behaviours of members, and the ways they dealt with their health needs. Families with preschool and school-age children were contacted for this study. They invited these families to continuously write in their diaries everyday for 16 weeks. The families were asked to record any illnesses in the family, the attempts adopted to keep the family healthy, the use of health services, and their own reflections on other services which could have been helpful to the family for some health or illness conditions. The diaries had both open and closed-ended questions. Keleher and Verrinder provided the diaries to the family in booklet form. Information regarding the study and guidelines for the participants to complete the diary each week was also prepared for the participants. The diary was separated into weekly sections and it was made up of two facing pages. There were 16 questions in each weekly section. Nine of the questions required a simple mark only. The other six questions needed the participants to write a one-word or short answer. The rest of the questions were open-ended, and the participants were encouraged to write as much (or little) as they wanted.

Kelehear and Verrinder discovered many surprising findings from diaries that the families kept over the 16 weeks. Somehow, these unanticipated outcomes may not be too surprising as their participants were rural dwellers who are marginalised in Australian society. They have little access to health, education, and other support services and experience isolation due to distance and financial difficulty. Kelehear and Verrinder (2003: 440) contend that, 'the diary was more than just a data collection tool, because it became the intermediary for a supportive relationship between the participants and the researchers. Furthermore, participants were enabled through their diary keeping to reflect on their own health and that of their family members, which seemed to enhance their capacity for observation about the issue they were experiencing'. They admit that in their study it was both challenging and rewarding with the writing of diaries as a method for data collection. But they believe that the method offers a wide application ability and is a very useful research tool. As long as the process is carried out sensitively, this will result in qualitatively rich data.

Similar to the drawing method, the diary method tends to be used in conjunction with other orthodox and alternative methods, such as an in-depth interview, life history, ethnography and PAR, in social science research. Through diaries, Jacelon and Imperio (2005: 991) contend, the researcher can collect data about the day-to-day events of participants, and then further investigate those events in subsequent interviews (see also Elliott 1997). In their study with women who sell sex in Uganda, Gysels and others (2002: 181) utilised a combination of life histories, participant observation and sexual diaries for the collection of information on the survival strategies and risk. In this study, the life history interview method was used so that a participant was able to 'articulate her daily activities and past experiences, explain choices and reflect on consequences'. The life history interviews were conducted over 2 years and on average, each woman was interviewed five times. The researchers also travelled with the women when they visited home villages and met their family members and they also provided medical assistance for the women and their family when needed. Gysels and colleagues also used diaries as a method of data collection. Women kept detailed records of income and expenditure in one diary and sexual activities in the other. The diaries were kept for 3 months and the diary entries were checked every day during this period. The diary method proved to be a fruitful method of indirectly obtaining additional information on numbers of casual sexual partners and the income that these generated.

In their recent study on strategies adopted by older adults to manage their chronic health problems, Cynthia Jacelon and Kristal Imperio (2005) used solicited diaries as part of their data collection. They claimed that using solicited diaries in conjunction with interviews (initial and follow-up) provided a rich source of information regarding day-to-day activities of older adults. The solicited diaries were guided by open-ended questions in order to encourage the participants to concentrate on their daily activities and reflect on their values. Ten participants, who were 75 years or older with at least one self-identified chronic health problem, were interviewed and asked to keep solicited diaries for two weeks. The participants were given three options for their diary maintenance: written, audio-taped or telephone conversation. This was done to overcome some difficulties with writing a diary for some participants. The second interview was undertaken in order to follow-up and clarify information gathered in the first interview and to get the participants to elaborate on what they have written in their diaries. The researchers telephoned to remind the participants who selected written or taped diaries about four times during the two weeks to maintain their diary writing. For those who chose the telephone interview diary, the researchers telephoned every second day. All participants were provided with essential equipment to maintain their diaries. A notebook and pen were given to those who keep writing diaries and a tape recorder and two 60 minutes cassette tapes to those who wished to keep recorded diaries.

Sensitive researchers have adopted the diary as a trustworthy means of data collection with a low level of recall error (Keleher and Verrinder 2003), particularly if the diary is entered on the day that the event takes place and if the participants receive regular support and encouragement from the researcher throughout the diary-keeping time. However, the diary method may not be suitable for people who cannot write or have difficulty in articulating their feelings in writing (Meth 2003). But this can be overcome by using audio-diary; that is, the participants may record their inputs with a tape-recorder rather than by writing in a diary. This is what Jacelon and Imperio (2005) have done in their research with older adults suffering chronic illness, as mentioned above. See also Christine Milligan and colleagues (2005) for their study using diary techniques with older people and Rose Galvin (2005) on people with disability.

Arts-based Method

Arts-based research methods, Susan Finley (2005: 681) contends, are becoming 'socially responsible, politically activist, and locally useful research methodologies'. Norman Denzin (2000: 261) argues that arts-based research is essentially 'a radical ethical aesthetic'. The representations of the world in arts-based method is grounded in 'a set of interpretive practices that implement critical race, queer, and Third World postcolonial theory'. Tom Barone (2001: 26) suggests that arts-based research methods are valuable for 'recasting the contents of experience into a form with the potential for challenging (sometimes deeply held) beliefs and values'.

Arts-based inquiry, according to Finley (2005: 682), is one of many new forms of qualitative methodology. Yvonna Lincoln (1995) suggests that this method is situated within a tradition of participatory action research in social science. Researchers adopting this line of inquiry call for a 'reinterpretation of the methods' as well as its ethics concerning human social research. They attempt to develop inquiry involving action–oriented processes which provide benefits to the local community where the research is undertaken. Historically, arts-based inquiry, as it is adopted by social science researchers situates neatly within a postmodern framework which shapes 'a developing activist dynamic among both artists and social researchers'. Arts-based research,

Finley (2005: 686) maintains, is 'not exactly art and certainly not science', but it is carried out to 'advance human understanding'. Primarily, arts-based researchers attempt to 'make the best use of their hybrid, boundary-crossing approaches to inquiry to bring about culturally situated, political aesthetics that are responsive to social dilemmas'.

Susan Finley (2005: 689) provides an extremely interesting arts-based research project; the project that she claims as 'an example of radical, ethical, and revolutionary arts-based inquiry'. The project has been ongoing within different communities of low-income children and their families (both sheltered and unsheltered), street youths including 'unaccompanied minors, run-away and throwaway children, travellers, and other people between 17 and 24 years of age who live on the streets' and people living in tents. The At Home At School (AHAS) programme was set up as a means to empower children who live in shelters and transitional housing to become active learners in school. This field-based community project brings together children from preschool through to eighth grade, their families, as well as preservice and inservice teachers.

Due to their homelessness, the children in her research have been criminalised in American society, marginalised in schools, and have experienced disrupted lives in moving between homes and schools as they and their families tried to find affordable homes. Some are also stigmatised by their addictions, incarcerations of parents and siblings, and other social identifications of their poverty. Through the year, the children participated in an arts-based research during after-school educational programmes. Additionally, they took part in a 6-week intensive summer school programme. The programme included visual arts, drama, literature, gardening and computer technology.

Apart from her attempt to strengthen academic achievement as a way to create self-esteem in the young people who attended AHAS, Finlay aims to help them to pay attention to the relationship between themselves and society. This is in order to assist them to redirect the anger that they have about themselves and their parents towards the persistent poverty that demolishes them. It is the way for the children to see themselves and society in terms of political struggle. Doing so may help them to think about what they can do and will be in their lives as well as to question their lifelong poverty destiny. Finlay's task is to give the children some mechanisms for creating 'new autobiographical images', and then to promote ongoing preparations that these children and their families might use to improve their lives.

Art is an intimate and personal experience which allows individuals to be able to express ways of being and knowing effectively. Hence, the arts-based method was introduced in the curriculum as a means for the children and their teachers to construct their own 'mystories'. Mystory performances, Finlay (2005: 690) suggests, are

> Personal cultural texts (e.g. narratives, paintings, poetry, music) that contexualize important personal experiences and problems within the institutional settings and historical moments where their authors (e.g. painters, collagists, dramatists) find themselves. They

attempt to make sense of seemingly senseless moments in life, to capture frustrations, and turmoil and open them for critical critique. They open a liminal space, and create an open and dialogic text, where a diverse group of people can be brought to collective understanding of the sites of power, of conflicts between the empowered and the powerless, and from this point of understanding can begin to address the need for social change.

During weekly sessions for the whole year, children painted self-portraits, pictures of objects and so on to tell their life stories. The project was completed by a day of communal painting. Five mural panels (4 × 4 feet) with the theme of 'the story of us' were constructed. The session was followed up with narratives from the children describing what they intended to convey when they began painting and the meanings they constructed during the process of painting. Through painting, one young person was able to express his anger and frustration with his physically small body. It was his personal story, but it tied him with the community as his teachers were able to understand his seemingly unfounded anger. Being able to tell his life story, the child discovered compassion and understanding among his teachers and peers. He had fewer outbursts of his anger and his school performance gradually improved. Painting portraits, Finley (2005: 691) contends, is just one of the means for the children to tell 'the story of us'. Movie making, writing and rap and blues were also occasionally performed. Through these innovative ways, a community in which personal storytelling is rewarded is constructed.

In this project, Finley (2005: 692) aims to prepare the children to 'become lifelong activists who are equipped for guerrilla warfare against oppression'. This is achievable because of the fact that the children are able to 'name their oppressors, dispute oppressive practices that are stereotyped or systematized into seeming normality, imagine a life lived otherwise, and then construct and enact a script that shifts them into an alternative space'. Art, in whatever forms, is a means for the children to reflect on their lives, to express their feelings and communicate with others. Finlay (2005: 692) asserts that social change can be performed by starting with 'artful ways of seeing and knowing ourselves and the world in which we live'. See also the recent work of Ephrat Huss and Julie Cwikel (2005) on the application of arts-based research to Bedouin women's drawings in Israel.

Online Research

> Internet technologies have the potential to shift the ways in which qualitative researchers collect, make sense of, and represent data.
>
> (Markham 2005: 794)

Innovative research methods have also embraced the use of computers and the Internet as a means to collect information from vulnerable people and difficult-to-reach groups (Oringderff 2004; Liamputtong and Ezzy 2005; Turney and Pocknee 2005; Liamputtong 2006). We now are not only able to make contact with other human beings but also to obtain knowledge swiftly (Plant 2004). I contend that, as sensitive researchers, we need to engage in what Murray (1995: 11) refers to as 'the fourth revolution' in 'the production of knowledge', which is 'vital to our understanding of how language, society and technology intersect'. Researchers cannot ignore considering the electronic communication as a research resource and tool (Strickland et al. 2003; Turney and Pocknee 2005). This is particularly so for sensitive researchers who, as O'Dochartaigh (2002: 7) suggests, are 'concerned with understanding different aspects of collective human behaviours', such as those of vulnerable and marginalised groups.

Conducting research online has many advantages over more conventional research methods (Liamputtong and Ezzy 2005; Liamputtong 2006). Online communication can reach a large number of people across different geographical and socio-cultural boundaries (Punathambekar and Fraley 2000; Thomas et al. 2002; Hessler et al. 2003; Moloney et al. 2003; Oringderff 2004). The most powerful advantage of online research is its lower cost (Mann and Stewart 2000). Richard Hessler and colleagues (2003) used email as a research tool for their online research on risky behaviours with young people precisely due to their limited research budget. Mann and Stewart (2000: 80) also argue that 'the global range of the Internet opens up the possibilities of studying projects which might have seemed impracticable before'. Caroline Bennett (1998), for instance, managed to talk online with men from the United States, the United Kingdom, and Australia. Fiona Stewart and colleagues (1998) too undertook their virtual focus group with young women from Fiji, China, Malaysia and Australia. And Gillian Dunne (1999) was able to conduct in-depth interviews with gay fathers from different international locations including the United Kingdom, New Zealand, Canada and the United States.

Online research offers a 'democratisation of exchange' more than traditional research methodologies (Selwyn and Robson 1998: 2; Ferri 2000). Roger Boshier (1990: 51), for example, asserts that online communication such as email 'provide[s] a context for the kind of non-coercive and anti-hierarchical dialogue that ... constitutes an "ideal speech situation," free of internal or external coercion, and characterised by equality of opportunity and reciprocity in roles assumed by participants'. More importantly, when communicating electronically, race, gender, age, sexuality and disability can be muted (Spender 1995; Seymour and Lupton 2004). Online communication has advantages for individuals with disabilities in the sense that other users will not know that the person they are communicating with has a disability (Grimaldi and Goette 1999). Hence, the marginalities of people with disabilities are eliminated in their interaction with others. This is particularly useful when researching vulnerable groups like people with stigmatised illness and disabilities. The characteristic nature of online communication technologies indeed eliminates the traditional biases that occur with face-to-face research methods. Participants can reply when they feel comfortable or decide how they will respond. As such, the main advantage of online communication, particularly email, is its 'friendliness' to the participants (Selwyn and Robson 1998; Liamputtong 2006).

More importantly, online research provides possibilities to reach a terrain of vulnerable participants, such as mothers at home with small children, people with disabilities, older people, and people from socially marginalised groups such as gays and lesbians, who may not be easily accessed in face-to-face research methods (Mann and Stewart 2000; see also Grimaldi and Goette 1999; Ferri 2000; Davis et al. 2004; Elford et al. 2004; Seymour and Lupton 2004; Liamputtong 2006). These vulnerable individuals can make contact with others from their familiar and physically safe locations (see Correll 1995; Spender 1995; Hoffman and Novak 1998; Adler and Zarchin 2002; Thomas et al. 2002; Im and Chee 2006; Merkes 2006). Online communication offers a possibility to participate in research for those who are unable to leave their homes due to their health reasons (Finn 1999). People with disabilities can have access to email and necessary online information and respond without having to leave home or be mobile (Grimaldi and Goette 1999; Seymour and Lupton 2004). Online research also permits researchers a possible vehicle for connecting with people situated within areas with restricted access such as hospitals, schools, cult and religious groups, bikers, surfers, punks and so on. This issue can be seen clearly in Sweet's personal experience in moderating an online focus group. Sweet (cited in Mann and Stewart 2000: 18) tells us that in one of her online focus groups, 'one participant excused himself to take a shot of his insulin and returned promptly. He, in fact, would have been unable to attend a two hour group an hour away with his unpredictable diabetes condition. He was a great participant online'.

Online research, Chris Mann and Fiona Stewart (2000) assert, provides the possibilities of carrying out research within politically sensitive or dangerous areas. Due to the anonymity and physical distance, both the researchers and the research participants are protected (see Coomber 1997, for example). Some highly sensitive and vulnerable participants, such as political and religious dissidents or human rights activists, will be more likely to participate in online research without excessive risk. Researchers can access censored and politically sensitive information without being physically in the field. People living or working in war zones, or sites of criminal activity or places where diseases abound can be accessed without needing to combat the danger involved in actually visiting the area. Online communication also permits researchers to distance themselves physically from research sites. This helps to eliminate the likelihood of suspicion that might alienate some participants. Additionally, communication with both police and criminals can be undertaken without being sighted or without leaving themselves open to charges of spying.

Online research preserves the anonymity of the research participants (Illingworth 2001; Liamputtong 2006). The anonymity of the technology has permitted some researchers to reach members of socially marginalised communities including mothers (O'Connor and Madge 2001; Madge and

O'Connor 2002), lesbians (Bromseth 2006), gay men (Campbell 2004; Elfords et al. 2004), gay fathers (Dunne 1999), men who avoided discussing emotions if interviewed face-to-face (Bennett 1998), young people engaging in risky behaviours such as sex, drinking, drugs and fast driving (Hessler et al. 2003; Hessler 2006), older people (Merkes 2006) and people with disabilities (Ferri 2000; Seymour and Lupton 2004; Holge-Hazelton 2006). The Internet has been used as a means to access and interview vulnerable people with specific health problems such as panic attacks (Stones and Perry 1998), infertility (Epstein et al. 2002), chronic illness (Holge-Hazelton 2006), HIV (Lombardo and Gillett 2006), stigmatised illness (Berger et al. 2005) and multiple sclerosis (Solomon 2006). The e-mail journal approach which was adopted in the work of Richard Hessler and colleagues with young people (2003) was anonymous enough to permit these young people to share sensitive views and activities with adult researchers. Hessler et al. (2003) contend that this situation would have been difficult to achieve with conventional face-to-face research methods (see also Hessler 2006). In an online synchronous focus group undertaken by Punathambekar and Frawley (2000), it was found that the participants openly articulated their view much more than in a face-to-face situation. In particular, opinions considered politically incorrect which would not be easily said in a face-to-face method were in fact expressed. The anonymous nature of online interaction permits the elicitation of viewpoints on sensitive topics and issues that traditional focus groups may have difficulty in accessing (Punathambekar and Frawley 2000; Turney and Pocknee 2005).

In their research, Barbara Thomas and colleagues (2002) employed the Internet to examine women's knowledge and perceptions about breast health education and screening and the support that influences their participation in these practices. Thomas et al. (2002) suggest that women across North America participated in this sensitive research precisely due to the anonymity of their participation. Similarly, as Nicola Illingworth (2001: paragraph 7.1) points out in her research on women's perceptions of assisted reproductive technologies, 'because of the sensitive nature of this research, a number of respondents emphasized their reluctance to participate had this research been conducted in a more conventional, face-to-face setting'. In fact, Illingworth asserts, 'online participation offered personal anonymity in a very emotive field'.

Here, I wish to discuss a few case examples of sensitive research using online methodology. An innovative example can be drawn from Richard Hessler and colleagues' work (2003). They undertook research on the Internet with young people about their risky behaviours. In their earlier work Hessler and colleagues (1998) experienced difficulty in trying to carry out face-to-face interviews between adult researchers and children. The presence of an adult researcher and the way questions were asked were intimidating experiences for many children. Hessler and colleagues discovered that they could collect better data if there were fewer adult researchers. This experience led Hessler and colleagues to use e-mail and daily diaries as their tools for data collection in their study about the risky behaviours of young people (Hesslear et al. 2003). Hessler et al. (2003: 113) write, 'this approach removed the adult researchers physically, it was familiar to adolescents – more so, say, than a formal interview – it was an immediate motivator to write and file the daily diary, and it had a comforting air of informality'. For 10 weeks, and through e-mail, Hessler and others were able to collect diary documents from 31 young people. Hessler and colleagues contend that some of the stories they collected would not have been identified had they conducted personal face-to-face interviews.

Beth Ferri (2000) carried out a participatory action research via an e-mail discussion group with women who were recruited from existing email discussion groups targeting women or individuals with disabilities. Prior to online discussion, all the women were interviewed by phone to document their biographical data and to explain about the study, their involvement in the study, and the logistic processes in accessing electronic mail. Ferri collected information from each woman in her 'closed' discussion list four days a week for eight weeks. After all identifying material had been removed, Ferri sent everyone's responses in 'a digest format' (p. 132). Ferri (2000: 132) contended that 'this method allowed responses to be collected and sent out to participants in one group message per day. My comments and questions followed the flow of the discussion, as I attempted to draw connections among their different voices, and facilitate a dialogue'. Having based her research on participatory action research methodology, one of Ferri's aims was to 'explore the potential of electronic mail to transgress boundaries between the researcher and the researched', and 'the product and the process of constructing knowledge' (p. 130). As the women in the study could access the daily flow of conversation, this allowed them to respond to, comment on and challenge the responses of others in the group. As such, the online discussion yielded an interactive and rich data. Ferri (2000: 131) found that 'electronic communication afforded greater flexibility than arranging face-to-face or phone contacts, especially for a group discussion'. In the middle of the data collection period, a summary of themes emerging from the group discussion was sent to all women and they were asked to respond to Ferri's analysis. The same process was repeated at the end of the project. The women had opportunities to reflect on any of the themes and elaborate on their experiences in participating in this online research. Ferri (2000: 131) also asserted that the use of online research 'facilitated collaboration, as all participants are able to communicate with one another and assist in the analysis as it unfolded'.

Recently, Wendy Seymour and Deborah Lupton (2004) examined disability, risk and technology in Adelaide, South Australia. In stage 1 of the research, 15 in-depth offline interviews were conducted with people with a range of disabilities. A further 20 participants were recruited from a disability list server – an Internet site concerning people with disabilities. Eight men and 12 women took part in their online research. Seymour and Lupton (2004) used a threaded discussion online site which allowed participants to carry out their asynchronous online discussions. Seymour and Lupton (2004: 293) contended that 'participants could enter the site as often as they wished, enabling both researcher and researched to extend on a particular topic, to delete or qualify a point, or to clarify their responses over time'. Although they had prepared a question to ask in each interview, 'the openness of the medium encouraged discursive, rather than didactic communication. The ongoing exchange offered the participants a significant opportunity to influence the research outcomes'. Because the participants were able to respond at the time that suited them, the researchers obtained a large amount of data. The shortest interview was done over 22 days and the longest one extended over 75 days. On average, the duration of the interviews was 42.6 days. This might also indicate that people with disabilities benefited from communication online. In their conclusion, Seymour and Lupton (2004: 303) contended that cyberspace 'can be re-positioned to work in the interests of people with disabilities... Text-based, interactive, virtual performance provides the means for people with disabilities to actively engage in the task of breaching the divide' of 'the able-bodied-disabled distinction'. As such, 'techno-sociality and virtual participation promise new avenues for personal fulfilment and political action, and point to new ways of being and having a body' among people with disabilities.

Conclusion

> 'A method is an interpretation'. The choice of one method over another is not simply a technical decision, but an epistemological and theoretical one. This means that, as feminists considering the use of innovative or unusual methods, we need (as much as with conventional methods) to be aware of the epistemological commitments and value assumptions they make.
>
> (Wilkinson 2004: 271–72)

As with any research method, I am in no way suggesting that all of these innovative methods will suit all vulnerable people. What I can say, however, is that researching vulnerable people may require different approaches from those used in normal circumstances and that often, sensitive researchers have to be innovative, as I have outlined in this chapter.

And of course, there are other creative and innovative methods that sensitive researchers may wish to experiment with that I have not been able to include in this chapter (as you know, there is always a space limit), like López and colleagues (2005), Kralik and colleagues (2000), Harris (2000, 2002) and Warkentin (2002), who propose to use photovoice, pen pals, letter writing and writing competitions and as many more data collection strategies. I would suggest that we do our own experiment with our creative methods and then document it so that other researchers may be able to see and follow our steps. This is the only way we can make our research sensitive to our vulnerable research participants.

As a sensitive researcher, as Samantha Punch (2002: 338) suggests, our choice of innovative methods primarily depends on the age, experience, preference and social status of the research participants. The cultural environment and the physical setting of the research, the questions we pose, and our competence as researchers, also determine the methods we select. However, regardless of the innovative methods we may choose, showing respect to individuals and taking into account the group differences such as class, age, gender, disability, ethnicity and culture are important fundamental aspects of research involving vulnerable people.

TUTORIAL EXERCISES

1. You are assigned to conduct research with children living with autism. It may be problematic to carry out in-depth interviews or focus groups with these vulnerable children. What other innovative methods might be more sensitive and appropriate to researching these groups? Design a project on innovative methods as outlined in this chapter.
2. At a certain point, you may need to reach some marginalised groups such as men living with disabilities, people with drug addictions and old person living in rural areas. How will you go about collecting data with these people? Discuss.

SUGGESTED READINGS

Bendelow, G., 1993, 'Using Visual Imagery to Explore Gendered Notions of Pain', pp. 212–28, In *Researching Sensitive Topics*, edited by C.M. Renzetti and R.M. Lee, Newbury Park: Sage Publications.

Campbell, J.E., 2004, *Getting It On Online: Cyberspace, Gay Male Sexuality, and Embodied Identity*, New York: Harrington Park Press.

Guillemin, M., 2004a, 'Understanding Illness: Using Drawings as a Research Method', *Qualitative Health Research*, 14(2): 272–89.

Harrison, B., 2002, 'Seeing Health and Illness Worlds – Using Visual Methodologies in a Sociology of Health and Illness: A Methodological Review', *Sociology of Health and Illness*, 24(6): 856–72.

Jacelon, C.S. and K. Imperio, 2005, 'Participant Diaries as a Source of Data in Research with Older Adults', *Qualitative Health Research*, 15(7): 991–97.

Keleher, H.M. and G.K. Verrinder, 2003, 'Health Diaries in a Rural Australian Study', *Qualitative Health Research*, 13(3): 435–43.

Liamputtong, P., 2006, *Health Research in Cyberspace: Methodological, Practical and Personal Issues*, New York: Nova Science Publishers.

López, E.D.S., E. Eng and N. Robinson, 2005, 'Quality of Life Concerns of African American Breast Cancer Survivors Within Rurual North Carolina: Blending the Techniques of Photovoice and Grounded Theory', *Qualitative Health Research*, 15(1): 99–115.

Mann, C. and F. Stewart, 2000, *Internet Communication and Qualitative Research: A Handbook for Researching Online*, London: Sage Publications.

Radley, A. and D. Taylor, 2003a, 'Remembering One's Stay in Hospital: A Study in Photography, Recovery and Forgetting', *health: An Interdisciplinary Journal for the Social Study of Health, Illness and Medicine*, 7(2): 129–59.

Seymour, W. and D. Lupton, 2004, 'Holding the Line Online: Exploring Wired Relationships for People with Disabilities' *Disability & Society*, 19(4): 291–305.

Victoria, G.C. and D. Knauth. 2001. 'Images of the Body and the Reproductive System among Men and Women Living in Shantytown in Porto Alegre, Brazil', *Reproductive Health Matters*, 9: 22–33.

8

(Re)Presentation of Vulnerable Voices – Writing Research Findings

Chapter Objectives   164
Introduction   165
Autoethnography   166
Short Story and Fiction   170
Performances and Staged Plays   172
Story-Telling and Public Performance   173
Performance Ethnography   174
Ethnodrama   176
Poetic Representation   178
(Re)Presentation of Voices: The Researcher's Perspective   182

We imagine a form of qualitative inquiry in the 21st century that is simultaneously minimal, existential, autoethnographic, vulnerable, performative and critical...It seeks to ground the self in a sense of the sacred, to connect the ethical, respectful self dialogically to nature and the worldly environment...

(Lincoln and Denzin 2000: 1052)

What we are presenting is not a distorted view of reality but the reality which engages the people we have studied, the reality they create by their interpretation of their experience in terms of which they act. If we fail to present this reality, we will not have achieved full sociological understanding of the phenomenon we seek to explain.

(Becker 1963: 174)

Chapter Objectives

In this chapter, readers will learn about innovative and different ways of representing the voices of research participants. These include the following:

- Autoethnography.
- Short story and fiction.
- Performance and staged plays.
- Poetic representation.
- Discussions on representation of voices from the researcher's perspective.

Introduction

One of the most disputatious issues of postmodern-informed research centralises on how research data should be represented (Fontana 2002). Adopting a postmodern perspective, I argue that there are so many ways to do our research, many new ways to learn and many ways to represent what we learn from our research participants. I believe it is appropriate to 'open' up discussions on an old issue but a new direction in qualitative research: How do we (re)present the voices of our research participants – the 'Other's voice' in Lincoln and Denzin's terms (2000: 1050)?

In the current 'crisis of representation' (Lincoln and Denzin 2000: 1050), the use of alternative forms of data collection clearly influences the ways we present our findings. As Susan Finley (2005: 682) questions, 'how should research be reported?' She asks: Do the traditional methods of dissemination suffice enough for broader readers which includes vulnerable people themselves? How do researchers write their interpretations 'without "othering" their research participants, exploiting them, or leaving them voiceless in the telling of their own stories?' How do researchers make their work accessible and of use to their respondents rather than generate writing in the tradition of academic writing in order to advance their career? In other words, how do we write up and disseminate our findings in a way that we can give voice to our research participants who are vulnerable and marginalised?

We are, Andrea Fontana (2002: 170) suggests, 'moving toward the literary'. Based on the postmodern framework, writing becomes more engaging with 'new, experimental, and highly controversial forms of representation'. Laurel Richardson (2002) adopts a postmodern approach as her framework in her alternative representations of research findings. This is echoed in her recent publication (2002: 878):

> The core of that position is the doubt that any discourse has a privileged place, any method or theory a universal and general claim to authoritative knowledge. Truth claims are suspected of masking and serving particular interests in local, cultural, and political struggles…Once the veil of privileged truth is lifted, the opportunities for addressing how we think, who can legitimately think, and what we can think are legion; with this comes the possibility of alternative representations of research material.

Sensitive qualitative researchers, hence, have come up with experimental forms of representing research data (Ellis and Bochner 1992, 1996, 2000; Ellis 1993, 1995a,b, 2004; Richardson 1994a,b, 1997, 2002; Van Maanen 1995; Ely et al. 1997; Lincoln and Denzin 2000; Ellis and Berger 2002; Richardson and St. Pierre 2005). After being rejected by several local journals a few years ago, I submitted a piece of work based on my personal experiences and the findings of my research with Thai immigrant women to a prestigious journal in social work in the United States (see Liamputtong 2000). Inspired by C. Write Mills's words (1959: 216, 2000) 'you must learn to use your life experience in your intellectual work: continually to examine and interpret it', I wrote subjectively, beginning each section with poems, or some beautiful writings of some well-known and not so well-known writers. I followed with the usual academic writing woven with my personal experiences. The editor wrote to me to say that he had always been looking for an alternative form of presenting research findings. My piece fitted well with his philosophy. The way I constructed this piece of work is the way Cotterill and Letherby (1993: 67) suggest in their writing, that 'feminist research involves weaving the stories of both the researcher and her respondents'. I wove my personal trouble with those of my participants in my attempt to shed light on the lives and voices of migrant mothers who are marginalised in so many ways. I incorporated many details of my personal story in the original piece, but to get it published, I had to omit many things (too personal and too long, as I was told). At the time, it was painful for me to write it but in the end the paper speaks for me and my lived experience. Like Laurel Richardson (in Richardson and St. Pierre 2005: 965) who tells us about her negative experience with her department chair and dean: 'writing the story was not emotionally easy, in the writing, I was reliving horrific experiences, but writing the story released the anger and pain'. This was how I felt when I wrote that piece. And this is precisely what Richardson (2000: 930) has articulated in her alternative form of writing: 'writing is always . . . situational, and that our Self is always present, no matter now much we try to suppress it . . . Writing from that premise frees us to write material in a variety of ways: to tell and retell'.

This new trend in representing the voices of our participants is what Laurel Richardson (1994b) refers to as 'experimental writing' (see also Van Maanen 1995; Glesne 1997; Lincoln and Denzin 2000; Fontana 2002; Olesen 2005; Richardson and St. Pierre 2005), and recently, she (2000) has renamed it CAP ethnography (see also Richardson and St. Pierre 2005). These new forms of writing, Douglas Ezzy (2002: 151) asserts, 'are deliberate attempts to reposition the author and the reader'. They blur the boundaries between science and art (Glesne 1997), and as Paul Stoller (1989: 9) contends, combine 'the strengths of science with the rewards of the humanities'. Elliot Eisner (1998: 235) advocates the use of the arts to address the representational crisis: 'art, music, dance, prose, and poetry are some of the forms that have been invented to perform this function'. This is what Zali Gurevitch (2000: 3) refers to as 'the serious play of writing'. Writing in this way, as Ivan Brady (2000: 957) asserts, 'invites us to live through other experiences vicariously and to come away with a deeper understanding of . . . the human condition'. Susan Finley (2005: 683) suggests that the move towards ethics of care among sensitive researchers in social science posits 'narrative discourse (storytelling) to the forefront of social science research'. In what follows, I shall discuss some of these approaches in more detail.

Autoethnography

Within the postmodern approach, autoethnography has become a popular writing form among sensitive social scientists, but more so among ethnographers (see Ellis 1993, 1995a,b, 1997, 1998, 2001, 2002, 2004; Ronai 1995, 1996, 1998; Sparkes 1996; Ellis and Bochner 1996, 2000; Spry 1997, 2001; McGinnis 1999; Richardson 1999; Ronai and Ellis 2001; Holman Jones 2005; Muncey 2005; Ellingson 2006). Autoethnography is more about the researcher's own self while in fieldwork, but it also incorporates his or her life as the researched within wider social and cultural contexts. As Caro Grbich (2004: 64) suggests, autoethnography often 'involves personal narratives of the author's life experiences within a particular cultural setting'. According to Carolyn Ellis and Art Bochner (2000: 739), autoethnography is an

> Autobiographical genre of writing and research that displays multiple layers of consciousness, connecting the personal to the cultural. Back and forth, autoethnographer gaze, first through an ethnographic wide-angle lens, focusing outward on social and cultural aspects of their personal experience; then, they look inward exposing a vulnerable self.

In recent writing, Stacey Holman Jones (2005: 764) contends that autoethnography is

> A balancing act. Autoethnography and writing about autoethnography, that is. Autoethnography works to hold self and culture together, albeit not in equilibrium or stasis. Autoethnography writes a world in a state of flux and movement – between story and context, writer and reader, crisis and denouement. It creates charged moments of clarity, connection, and change.

With this form of writing, researchers write about themselves while they participate and observe the social world in which they themselves are situated. Researchers who write in this form, Marvasti (2004: 58) points out, are doing a 'moral project'. Researchers are not just telling readers about the world, 'but they want to change it. They use personal experiences, be it pleasant or painful, to both inform their readers about sociological topics and to emotionally stimulate them. They want their readers to learn through feeling'. The focus of autoethnographic texts, Stacey Holman Jones (2005: 767) contends, is on 'how subordinated people use deliberately subtle and opaque forms of communication – forms that are not textual or visual – to express their thoughts, feelings, and desires by performing these practices on the page and on stage'. Autoethnographic texts, Holman Jones (2005: 776) maintains, 'are personal stories that are both constitutive and performative. They are charged exchanges of presence or "mutual presentness." They are love letters – processes and productions of desire – for recognition, for engagement, and for change... Written and experienced in this way, autoethnography becomes an intimate provocation, a critical ekpharasis, a story of and with movement'.

Carolyn Ellis is a pioneer on autoethnography and has written extensively on this. In her earlier work, she writes about her pain of dealing with the death of her brother in an airplane crash (1993), the gradual death of her beloved husband who was affected by a terminal illness (1995a) and her difficult incident with a friend who was dying of AIDS (1995b). Laurel Richardson (1999) writes a personal story of her ill fortunes with colleagues at her faculty after a car accident. In his presentation of 'The Art of Leaving', Troy McGinnis (1999) writes about his encounter with an intimate situation between his wife and his best friend. Norman Denzin (1999a,b) writes about his hideout in Montana. Lisa Tilman-Healy (1996) emotionally constructs her autoethnography of living with an eating disorder and Aliza Kolker (1996) writes about coming to terms with cancer.

An emotional but provocative personal narrative of Carol Ronai (1996) is a clear reflection of utilising personal lived experiences as a rich source of data. In this writing, Ronai tells us about her intimate relationship with her mentally retarded mother — the relationship that allowed her to be sexually abused by her own father. In this work, Ronai brings us through a 'layered account' of her personal life: as a victim, a detached researcher and a sociologist. Ronai (1996: 121) moves fluidly between these roles while taking us through her emotional journey. She uses her personal life as both the location and the source of her data. In one section, she talks about her violent father Frank Gross Rambo, who 'had a police record as a child molester, a rapist, and an exhibitionist'. This is what Ronai writes:

> Even though we were on public assistance, our lives were much calmer during the time he was in prison. Her [mother] beating me was an enormous betrayal. Yes, I needed to be disciplined, but this was not a spanking. This was the kind of beating Frank dished out . . .

Carolyn Ellis (1995a: 121–22) provides an autoethography — her emotionally distressed account of the experience of caring for a dying person (her late husband Gene):

> She's in the lobby of the theatre with her partner, who is critically ill with emphysema. He has refused to let her retrieve his battery-powered wheelchair from the car, though he is having trouble breathing and his oxygen canister, which he needs to walk, is low on oxygen. On the way out of the theatre, he carries the oxygen tank on his shoulder and insists that she carry his cane, which opens up into a chair. Enter the scene briefly as she — struggling for some measure of independence from the weight of her caretaking role as well a distance from the oddity of how they appear to others — walks away from her partner momentarily to greet some friends she sees across the lobby.

> Their conversation is interrupted by a loud voice yelling, 'Help! Help!' Embarrassed and angry, she rushes to him. 'The chair. I need the chair', he gasps, point to the cane. She unfolds it and he sits down quickly in the middle of the lobby. She narrows her shoulders and looks to the floor, trying to make herself invisible to the people staring at her.

> Between gasps, he says in a loud voice filled with hatred, 'You castrating bitch'. With that, she storms out of the theatre, not waiting to see if he is okay. At that moment, she hates him.

Autoethnography, to my understanding is similar to the term 'autobiography' used by some social scientists (see Mykhalovskiy 1996; Letherby 2000; Miller et al. 2003). Gayle Letherby (2000) refers autobiography to both the way researchers collect data and represent the voices of the research participants. Increasingly, Letherby (2000: 109) contends, researchers embody parts of their own 'self' in their research and writing. However, researchers still tend to keep this outside the main writing of their studies (see also Ellingson 2006). Many researchers still feel uneasy with this new way of writing. This may have something to do with their personal reasons (in terms of privacy). But it is more about academic reasons. Researchers who adopt this type of writing may be criticised for their 'self-indulgence and intellectually sloppy work' (see also Ellis and Ellingson 2000). And this may create 'professional dangers' to many of us, as I will point out in the latter section.

Here, I wish to extend Letherby's suggestion with another aspect of autoethnographic writing. In her recent writing, Laura Ellingson (2006: 303) suggests that researchers may 'write autoethnographically about the research process' (see also Ellis 1997). She points out that short descriptions about the experiences in the researchers' fields and their reflections should be included in writing up qualitative data using 'a layered organization' (see also Ellis and Bochner 2000: 739). Ellingson (2006: 303) asserts,

> Autoethnographic methods acknowledge the dialogic construction of patients' construc- tions of meaning of their illness with researchers' embodied experiences. Rather than simply the narrator or reporter of findings, the researcher is the main character of a story that parallels the academic narrative contained in the research report. In layered accounts, researchers alternate sections of an article that is written using social science conventions (i.e. citation of relevant research and theory, presentation of a research question, explanation of methods) with brief narratives that show rather than tell about aspects of the research; alternatively, such narratives can be placed at the beginning or end of the conventional analysis.

In her writing on a geriatric oncology programme, Ellingson (2005) does so. For example, when she walked into the examination room of one patient, she was 'hit' by a strong smell and she felt imposed to cover her nose. She writes about this experience in her book (2005: 86). She suggests that this experience made her understand the situations that both the patients and health care providers have to deal with in their daily lives and this has guided her on the way she writes her research findings. Ellingson (2006: 304) tells us, 'the odor affected my body, and I garnered insights about the patient and health care team members as we all coped with the unpleasant problem. Tales of my embodied experience in the clinic demystify the process of my research and writing because they make it clear that my body could not be separated from and dominated by my mind's more logical perspective'. See a similar reflection from Emily Martin's work (1995) in her study of the cultural construction of the immune system in America.

Ellingson (2006: 304) contends that autoethnographic writing should also be adopted with the subjective experiences of writing research findings:

> Writing is done with fingers and arms and eyes: It is an embodied act, not mental conjuring, and we should reflect on the experience of writing our research just as we reflect on our experience of being at a research site.

Short Story and Fiction

> [S]tories are an attempt to tell a truth by creating material in which that truth can be enacted...the lines are so fine between my creative nonfiction and my fiction that the only way I can explain it is by intent.
>
> (Ortiz Cofer 1997: 58)

Social scientists have used a short story and fiction to represent the voices of vulnerable people (see Banks and Banks 1998; Diversi 1998; Goldstein 2003). Marcelo Diversi (1998) adopts short stories to describe the lives of children who live on the streets of Campinas, Brazil. In this piece of writing, Diversi presents four short stories in order to reveal the cultural narratives shaping the everyday lives of street children and hence allow people to have better understanding about the lived experiences of these children. Diversi (1998: 132) wants to 'give voice' to the street children and to provide readers with accurate representations of the lived experiences of these children, representations which reveal 'the depth of their humanness and that transcend the limited, stereotypical image of "little criminals" prevalent in the national and local dominant narratives'. Diversi tells us that he does not wish to represent the voice of these children from a theoretical perspective as this will 'bury their voices beneath layers of analysis'. In order to represent the children without losing their voices, he transgresses the boundaries of conventional forms of writing in the social sciences. For this purpose, the short stories form is chosen. Diversi (1998: 132) tells us, 'I employed short story techniques such as alternative points of view, dialogue, unfolding action, and flashback to attempt to create the tension, suspense, delay, and voice that compose a good short story and that are inseparable from lived experience'. In arguing for using a short story to represent the voice of these street children, Diversi (1998: 132) says this clearly:

> The short story genre has the potential to render lived experience with more verisimilitude than does the traditional realist text, for it enables the reader to feel that interpretation is never finished or complete. Short stories that show, instead of tell, are less author centered, which, in turn, invites interpretation and meaning making...This invitation is crucial to avoid authorial omnipotence...and to avoid 'closing off or nailing down an interpretation without allowing alternative views to creep into view'.

In Donna Goldstein's work (2003), women living in urban shantytowns of Brazil amidst poverty, trauma and tragedy used black humour and laughter as a means of telling their stories. The black humour and laughter used by these women, Goldstein (2003: 12–13) contends, are 'windows into the sense of injustice oppressed peoples feel about their conditions...Their laughter contains a sense of the absurdity of the world they inhibit'. The black humour and laughter emotionally unchain their frustration and marginalisation as a result of severe poverty and social despair. In this work, Goldstein (2003) writes up the women's stories, black humour and laughter as a series of humourous short stories. Presenting the women's stories this way can be dangerous as it may create uneasy feelings among readers. However, Goldstein suggests that in order to prevent our wrong assumptions about these poor women, readers must posit the women's stories within the context of their severe poverty. Goldstein (2003: 45) remarks,

> The women I knew often joked and laughed about child death, rape, and murder in a way that made me feel and may make the reader feel ill at ease. These jokes and accompanying laughter create a seemingly paradoxical emotional aesthetic that calls for contexualization of Brazil's urban poor and feeling the sense of frustration and anomie that accompanies their often desperate political and economic situation.

Fiction has also been adopted by sensitive researchers to represent the voices of their research participants (see Banks and Banks 1998; Linstead 1998; Banks 2000). The fiction written by Steven Banks (2000) is interesting as he constructs what he refers to as 'accidental fiction'; a fiction that is based on the annual summer holiday and written from letters sent to a number of family members. In this fiction, Banks creates and shows five letters which were written over 6 years. The centralised identity of the letters was Ginny Balfour who was a mother. Her annual experiences, as perceived by herself, represented many other families who wrote the letters. Banks (2000: 392) tells us that Ginny's letters speak about 'an interpersonal drama that instantiates in specifically intimate and public expressions the pathos, courage, disillusionment, concepts, optimum, and faith – that is, the quotidian struggles – of a particular life'. Banks' research reveals moral quality and family virtue. He contends that the letters were written with purpose; they revealed sad stories, commanded the interpretation of readers, and yet sustain fictional ecstasy.

Paul Rosenblatt (2002: 903) uses the term 'fictional researcher' to represent sensitive researchers who re-present their work through fiction. In his study with farm workers who have lost a family member in a fatal farm accident, Rosenblatt writes the incident up as a detective novel. Writing the novel, Rosenblatt (2002: 901) remarks, prompted him to provide more context for the circumstances of the people he had interviewed. This enables him to portray characters with greater texture than he could have done in traditional research writing. He tells us,

> I talk about how people sit as they talk, what they ask me, how they smell, how their language changes as who is present changes, how their dogs are players in family experience, their use of facial tissues when they cry, how they slide by family disagreements during a family interview, the ways they can blithely and aunapologetically be inconsistent, and how much they seem trapped by culture, neighbours, property ownership, and much else into thinking along certain lines and not others.

Rosenblatt (2002: 902) admits that by representing his research findings as fiction, he can also write about 'the starts, stops, blind alleys, mistakes, and evolution of an investigative journey' in a way that he cannot do so in writing research reports within the conventional style.

Performances and Staged Plays

> I think theatre is primarily a site for liberation stories and a sweaty laboratory to model possible strategies for empowerment.
>
> (Tim Miller 2002, in Holman Jones 2005: 763)

Performance, as Holman Jones (2005: 777) points out, 'has long been a site and means for negotiating social, cultural, and political dialogue'. In the United States in particular, activist theatre has been identified with social movements including 'the labor movement of the 1930s, the civil rights and feminist movements of the 1960s and 1970s, and the AIDS activism of the 1980s' (Cohen-Cruz 2001: 95). Activist theatre was at its peak during the late 1960s and early 1970s. The aims of these 'actor-based, movement-linked companies' were clear – to 'get the United States out of Vietnam, enforce equal rights for all people regardless of race or ethnicity' (Cohen-Cruz 2001: 98). Augusto Boal (1979) established the 'theatre of the oppressed', which is grounded in the liberation impulses of Paulo Freire. The theatre was used by Boal to 'blur the line' between the off-stage audience and the on-stage actors. The theatre of the oppressed, Kamberelis and Dimitriadis (2005: 891) contend, is 'a public, improvisational, and highly interactive form of theatre with strong transformative and pedagogical impulses and potential'.

Theatrical performance is often used as a form of 'political analysis, catharsis, and group healing by indigenous peoples who have experienced ethnic, cultural, and social displacement; poverty; and horrendous acts of violence' (Tedlock 2005: 470). Norman Denzin (2005: 999), in his recent writing on performance ethnography, suggests that performance ethnography can be conceived as 'a pedagogy of freedom'. As he puts it, 'performance texts provide the grounds for liberation practice by opening up concrete situations that are being transformed through acts of resistance'. As such, performance ethnography 'advances the causes of liberation'.

Performance shuns written words but shows research findings as stage performances (Saldaña 2005). In Marianne Paget's work (1990: 142), she contends that through a performance, 'an audience could react to complexity textured characters. The layers, the dimensions of live actors performing, would signal so much more than I could communicate in writing. There is something odd about privileging an analysis of discourse in its least robust form, a written text, exploring it in great detail while ignoring the speakers' miens and intentions'. This is because, as Michal McCall and Howard Becker (1990: 118) point out, performance science is seen as a means of 'presenting the "multivocality" of texts, as opposed to the privileged monotone of "scientific representations"'.

Norman Denzin (2003a,b) suggests that sensitive researchers should write about their research findings using performances as vehicles to reach wider audiences and provide opportunities for those who have been oppressed and not had their voices heard. Andrea Fontana and James Frey (2005: 714) echo this: 'in performance, we infuse in our relationship to them, that is, not merely to create new sociological knowledge but also to use that hand to grasp and pull the downtrodden out of the mire in which they are suffocating'. They express this beautifully:

> Performance does not become fixed in a written text to be read later; rather, performance is doing, is not, and has feelings, passions, joy, tears, despair, and hope. Performance can reach to people's hearts and not only their minds. Performance can be a powerful instrument for social reform, for righting some wrongs, and for helping those in need.

In the following sub-sections, I will discuss different, but sometimes overlapping types of performances which have been adopted to represent the voices of vulnerable research participants.

Story-Telling and Public Performance

Writing a story-telling method and performing the story has been adopted by sensitive researchers. With this writing, researchers describe the actors' characters (research participants), the scenes in which they collect their data and their own roles in the enactment of the story. Very often, the researchers' selves are at the centre of the stories. The following example presented by Amir Marvasti (2004: 129) is adopted from the personal experience with abortion of Carolyn Ellis and Art Bochner (1992).

Telling and Performing Personal Stories: The Constraints of Choice in Abortion

The Story
Scene 1: The Pregnancy Test and the Test of Pregnancy
Scene 2: Making the Decision
Scene 3: Dealing with the Decision
Scene 4: The Pre-abortion Procedure
Scene 5: The Abortion
Epilogue

In this performance, Ellis and Bochner tell the story of a decision that they had to make when they discovered that Ellis was pregnant after their 10-week relationship. This experience had a great impact on Ellis's relationship with Bochner and their personal lives and led them to write a story.

> With a self-consciously therapeutic motive, we decided to try to understand about our experience to try to understand what had happened at a deep emotional level. We wanted to reveal ourselves to ourselves as we revealed ourselves to others. Hoping to provide companionship to others who may have been similarly bruised by the ambivalence and contradictions associated with the constraint of making such a choice, we attempted to share the complex emotions that were part of this experience so that readers might experience our experience – actually feel it – and consider how they might feel or have felt

in similar situations. We tried to write in an open, revealing way that would connect us to readers, especially those who had themselves suffered the complexities of abortion. We hope to tell enough in our story so that readers might . . . connect our emotions to the cultures in which they arise.

(as told in Ellis and Berger 2002: 863)

Ellis and Bochner wrote their story as a script which had critical scenes as given above, and then performed at a social science conference. The performance of their story was an essential part of their 'attempt to cope with and bring closure' to their experience (Ellis and Berger 2002: 864).

In their participatory action research with people with schizophrenia, Schneider and co-researchers (people who suffer schizophrenia) (2004) performed in public as a way to disseminate their findings. The research team constructed a script for a reader's theatre presentation for the group members to perform. Although the script was written by Schneider, who is a university researcher, the group suggested the contents of the script which incorporated many direct quotations from interview transcripts. The performance was moving and powerful. They have performed seven times and the play has been seen by many hundreds of health professionals. Schneider and co-researchers (2004: 576) contend,

> Our research is contributing to change in the practice of health care for people with severe mental illnesses through our influence on the psychiatrists and other professionals who see our performances . . . Our presentation offers them an understanding of the other side of the doctor-patient relationship and of the importance of communication in developing the therapeutic relationship.

After one performance, a psychiatrist told the group that because of the performance he has changed the way he interacts with his patients. Schneider and co-researchers (2004: 576) suggest that there was no other stronger evidence to show that their participatory research had accomplished their aims to empower people and improve their lives. Their research project has helped to empower a small group of extremely marginalised people who live with schizophrenia. It assisted them to speak about their treatment experiences to psychiatrists and other mental health professionals. Through this, the treatment of people with mental illnesses by their health care professionals has changed.

Performance Ethnography

Performance ethnography, Bryant Alexander (2005: 411) suggests, 'is literally the staged re-enactment of ethnographically derived notes. This approach to studying and staging culture works toward lessening the gap between a perceived and actualized sense of self and the other'. Ethnographers write up in-depth information they have gathered from carrying out interviews and participant observations with the group of people they learn from. Arguably, culture 'travels in the stories, practices, and desires of those who engage it', and by using performance ethnography, audiences who wish to have better understanding of the lived experiences in other cultures are given 'a body-centered method of knowing' (Alexander 2005: 411). The aim of performance ethnography is to 'capture the multivoices of complex social situations' (Coffey 1999: 150).

Joni Jones (2002) contends that performance ethnography is 'a form of cultural exchange', and to Jim Mienczakowsi (1995, 1996, 1997, 2001, 2003), Linda Park-Fuller (2003), Barbara Tedlock (2005) and Johnny Saldaña (2005), it is a theatre form which promotes emancipation. In performance ethnography, Bryant Alexander (2005: 412) suggests, theatre is used to 'illuminate cultural politics and to instill understanding with the potential to invoke change and have a positive effect on the lived conditions of self and others' (see also Boal 1985, 1995, 1998; Dolan 2001a,b; Spry 2001; Park-Fuller 2003; Schneider et al. 2004; Tedlock 2005). Alexander (2005: 413, original emphasis) maintains that 'in a literal sense of the aphorism "walking a mile in someone else's shoes," performance ethnography most often entails an embodied experience of the cultural practices of the other. This practice has the intent to allowing the participants in and audience of the performance the opportunity to *come to know culture differently*'. The following example provides a remarkable example of performance ethnography taken from Alexander (2005: 413–14) – an example that I deeply believe vividly shows audiences the many difficulties faced by migrant street vendors who are extremely marginalised in the US society.

Performing Street Vendors

A group of students (three men and two women) perform an ethnography focusing on the lived experiences of migrant streetside vendors. In the Los Angeles area, there are many immigrant Mexican street vendors, both women and men, who hang around the entrances and exits of major interstates and highways, trying to sell anything they can, such as bagged oranges, cherries, peanuts, flowers, handmade cultural artefacts and clothing. This reminds me of many streets in Thailand as well where I grew up. The students have undertaken ethnographic interviews and immersed themselves in the areas as part of their participant observation in order to learn about the real lived experience of these street vendors. Alexander (2005: 413) writes,

> The narratives are delivered through impassioned voices, in Spanish and with Spanish accents, then translated by another vendor (student performer). The narratives reveal the multiple reasons for which the vendors come to this circumstance: Some work to send money back to their families in Mexico or to support their families here in the United States. Some are trapped in a type of slave labor with the coyotes (smugglers of human chattel from Mexico) who helped them cross the border. Others labor because they have no other marketable skills. Through the performance and written reflective essays, the students articulate and claim a new understanding of the lives of particular others. The efforts of street vendors are not seen as what is casually assumed or asserted to be their culture, but acts of survival and sustenance grounded in their current predicament and their relation to space, place, and time.

The performance of these students brings the voices of these marginalised street vendors into a public place – the classroom. Alexander (2005: 414) contends that the student performance 'serves as product and process, a performative representation of their knowing, a starting point of their understanding, and a method of engaging others in the issues that undergird cultural experience'. This piece of performance ethnography assists in developing 'a critical site, an instance in which embodied experience meets social and theoretical knowing to establish a critical dialogue between researcher-performers and observers'.

In sum, performance ethnography as Bryant Alexander (2005: 428, 419) writes, is 'a moral discourse', as it attempts to reduce gaps between what we know and what we do not know. It explores and interprets the lived experiences of research participants, and connects social and geographical distance through 'vivid description, narration, and embodiment'. This helps readers/audiences to see possible realities through the 'visualization of experience'. Alexander's final conclusion (2005: 434) speaks clearly for the suitability of performance ethnography in the representation of the voices of the marginalised and vulnerable people:

> Performance ethnography can help us to understand the lived cultural experiences of others, but it also can help us to claim the joint culpability of history's legacy. It can then help us to strategize possibility, ways in which collective social action might lead to a more compatible human condition.

Sometimes, performance ethnography is referred to as ethnodrama, ethnotheatre, epic, playback, applied and confrontational theatres, theatre of the oppressed and theatre for social change (see Mienczakowsi 1997, 2001, 2003; Mienczakowsi et al. 1996; Saldaña 1999, 2005; Tedlock 2005; Stuttaford et al. 2006).

Ethnodrama

Ethnodrama is another staged performance form of representation of research findings. Ethnodramas, as Jim Mienczakowsi (2001: 468, original emphasis) puts it, 'are about the *present moment* and seek to give the text back to the readers and informants in the recognition that we are all co-performers in each other's lives'. Explicitly, ethnodrama is about decoding and translating the experiences of research participants through theatrical practices. It attempts to present research findings in a language and manner which is more accessible to diverse audiences (see also Mienczakowsi 1998). Mienczakowsi (2001: 469), however, argues that ethnodrama is different from other forms of ethnographic performance due to its 'overt intention', which is 'not just transgressively to blur boundaries but to be a form of public voice ethnography that has emancipatory and educational potential'. In ethnodrama, the audiences engage with research material. This leads to a greater possibility for changing social understanding than using a traditional form of written text (Stuttaford et al. 2006). Ethnodrama, Mienczakowsi (1997) contends, is a way to provide in-depth understanding into the lives of those who are marginalised and disempowered. And for Norman Denzin (2005: x), ethnodrama, 'can help enact a politics of resistance and possibility by giving a voice to the previously silenced, by creating a space for audiences and performers to actually engage in meaningful dialogue and discourse' (see also Madison 2005; Saldaña 2005). In their work relating to health issues, Mienczakowsi and others (2002: 34) write,

> Performed data has an empathetic power and dimension often lacking in standard qualitative research narratives. Data as performance has a demonstrable potential to construct explanations from within for particular health consumption groups. It also possesses the potential to destablize sensitivities. To remain true to the informants who contribute data to our research we require a new aesthetic through which we may interpret and consume these research explanations: the ethnodrama.

Ethnodrama has been adopted by sensitive researchers as a way to create constructed catharsis, a form of 'emotional unravelling', among the audience (Mienczakowsi et al. 2002: 42). Catharsis, according to Mienczakowski and others (1996: 443), is 'a staged (semiotically presented) revelation that intentionally confronts the emotional construction of self for audience members and actors and may...present a prerequisite of epiphany'. Responses to emotional stimuli are collectively shared by the audiences (Mienczakowsi et al. 2002). Indeed, they argue, 'catharsis as emotional unravelling' can be a desirable and deliberate aim if researchers attempt to empathetically and effectively show to audiences the lived realities of specific health issues for health care professionals and consumers (Mienczakowsi et al. 2002). In their earlier study, Mienczakowski et al. (1996) adopted this technique in the health area to illuminate the emotions and powerlessness experienced by people with traumatic brain injury. In his other studies, Mienczakowski portrayed the experiences of people undergoing detoxification (1996), schizophrenic illness (1992) and suicide attempts (Morgan et al. 1999). The actors in his studies may or may not have had the health conditions they are acting out. When the focus is community education, the audiences of these performances are usually health practitioners, students, carers and other interested public. This is what Jim Mienczakowsi and others (2002: 37) refer to as the 'seeing words – hearing feelings approach'. They contend that their ways of representation are to ensure 'the veracity and integrity of our scripts and performances through the inclusion of informants' explanations of their health experiences, be they suicide attempts, cosmetic surgery, rape, or drug and alcohol detoxification processes, and the translation of informants' experiences into the public performance of the resulting ethnodrama texts'.

The project on experiences of schizophrenia, *Syncing Out Loud* (Mienczakowski 1992) was performed for a season within a university and also at Wolston Park Hospital, a large psychiatric hospital in Queensland. Viewed from within 'an emancipatory critical social framework', it was intended to be a valuable occasion for the consumers of the hospital (Mienczakowski 2001).

And in their ethnodrama on the experiences of people undergoing detoxification, *Busting*, Jim Mienczakowski and Steve Morgan (1993) commence with a scene developed from a description given at a night beach party by one informant about herself. In this scene, a teenage girl drinks Bourbon alone. The images of this girl and other women drinking alone in different drinking contexts are illuminated by an adjacent slide show. The girl dances to music and she is then approached by a drunken man who offers her a bottle and attempts to have sexual intercourse with her. But his drunken state and her vomiting stop his attempt…

There are many other performing texts and I suggest that readers seek more information. Due to space constraints, I am unable to include them in greater detail. See, for example, Ross Gray and Christina Sinding (2002) who performed their research with and about women diagnosed with metastatic breast cancer. Gray and Sinding also video-taped the performance, and showed it in many venues. In reporting on a study of transsexuals, Andrea Fontana, in her work with Robert Schmidt (1998, 1999), wore a white mask and black clothing to represent Farinelli the castrato. An interesting and recent performance by Maria Stuttaford and colleagues (2006) in South Africa is another great example of ethnodrama. They call it 'applied theatre'. Under a tree without any technology, the field researchers and audiences performed 'Xiseveseve' (Coming Together to Share) in six local communities as a means for dissemination of their research findings and validation of their data.

The book edited by Johnny Saldaña (2005) is a good collection of different ethnodramas which represent the voices of many vulnerable and marginalised people including the homeless, prison inmates, illegal immigrants and others.

Poetic Representation

For quite some time, poetry as an innovative representation of the voices of research participants has been used by some sensitive researchers (Richardson 1994a; Glesne 1997; Poindexter 1998). Poetry, according to Laurel Richardson (2002: 879) 'belongs to both written and oral traditions. It can be read silently, read aloud, or performed'. Poetry, unlike traditional social science writing, is acceptable in many different settings. It can provide 'theoretic understandings to life' for readers/audiences in settings such as in poetry bars, theatres, stylistic conventions, street scenes, policy-making scenes, and the media. Poetics, to Andrea Fontana and James Frey (2005: 720), 'encapsulate in a welter of feelings and emotions a life story, an epiphanic moment in the life, a tragedy, a moment of sorrow, or a moment of utter joy'. Ethnopoetry, in Amanda Coffey's term (1999: 151), permits 'a mechanism to capture the pauses, rhyme and rhythm of everyday life and conversation'. Poetic writing is often 'striking and emotive', and hence it offers a better means to evocatively represent qualitative data. Laurel Richardson's poetry of Louisa May's life (see later) is a good example of what Coffey suggests.

Poetic expressions have recently become popularised as an effective way to represent the voices of marginalised people. For people who 'speak in "nonscience" voices' like the poor, the sick, the working-class, the minorities and the less educated, their voices are marginalised (Richardson 2002: 880; see also Danforth 1997; P. Smith 1999). Poetic representation makes a way for sensitive researchers 'to write about, or with, people in ways that honor their speech styles, words, rhythms, and syntax' (Richardson 2002: 880). According to Carol Grbich (2004: 104), 'the poetic text sits in a changing network of texts, interrelating and blurring traditional boundaries and allowing multiple selves and voices to emerge'. Richardson (2002: 879) too suggests that 'poetic representation also may be used as one of the discursive practices within outer oppositional paradigms whose goals are to challenge the power relationships inscribed through traditional writing practices'.

Laurel Richardson has been a leading sensitive writer using poetry as a representational form (see Richardson 1992, 1994a,b, 1996a,b, 1997, 1999, 2000, 2002; Richardson and St. Pierre 2005). In the past 15 years, Richardson has been exploring alternative forms of presenting research findings. Her work has inspired many followers who believe in different and better ways of representing the voices of their research participants (see Glesne 1997; Poindexter 1998; P. Smith 1999; Dickson 2000). Her 36 hours of interviews with an unwed mother, named Louisa May, was turned into a five-page poem 'Louisa May's Story of Her Life' (Richardson 1992; see also 1997, 2002). In this poem, Richardson (1992: 126) used only Louise May's words, voice and necessitation. However, she relied on poetic tools like 'repetition, off rhyme, meter, and pauses' to turn into Louise May's narrative. This process, according to Richardson, (1992: 136), reduces the centring of self: 'in writing the Other, we can (re)write the Self'. From her interview with Louisa May, Laurel Richardson (2002: 888) converts the sad and powerful tale of Louise May into a poem.

So, the Doctor said, 'You're pregnant.'
I was 41, John and I
had had a happy kind of relationship,
not a serious one.
But beside himself with fear and anger,
awful, rageful, vengeful, horrid.
Jody May's father said,
'Get an Abortion.'

I told him,
'I would never marry you.
I would never marry you.
I would never.

'I am going to have this child.
I am going to.
I am. I am.

'Just Go Away'.

The poem captures the 'soul' of Louisa May. Through this poem, readers/audiences get to know Louisa May and her feelings. And this brings about deep empathy for Louisa May among readers/audiences; as Fontana and Frey (2005: 720) write, 'our heart goes out to her'.

Richardson (2002: 880) contends that introducing research findings as sociology poems changes people's ways of hearing because boundaries are broken. Representing Louisa May's story as a poem helps social workers and policy makers to change their stereotypical perception about single mothers. For feminist researchers, this representation is 'a method for "demasculinizing" the production of social research'.

Phil Smith's writing on the story of Food Truck (1999), a 65-year-old man with developmental disability who has been residing in Landon (a home for the mentally retarded people) for 40 years, offers some provocative thoughts about the way sensitive researchers write to represent the world of their research participants. This is what Smith writes before he begins the poem:

> So here's a story that I got from Food Truck. I couldn't help writing it; it wouldn't let me go. It's his story, his words. It's my story, my words. None of it is fiction. It's all fiction.

In Food Truck's Party Hat, Smith (1999: 248–59) opens the writing with

> He looks me square in the face, square as a man can whose head doesn't ever stop bobbing and weaving, swooping and diving.
> His head is a butterfly looking for nectar in a field of flowers,
> a swallow in the darkening sky searching out mosquitoes,
> a surfer climbing up and down green waves under a setting sun,
> Food Truck's blue eyes look for mine
> while his smile and almost-white hair slide and weave and float in the air in front of me.

And he ends the story with:

> Food Truck looks up
> he says quietly
> in a voice falling apart
> tumbling in on itself
> Grandma's not feeling good
> huge old man tears
> flow out from his eyes
> drip down his cheek
> to make a small wet mark on his shirt.
> All I can ever think to do
> all I can ever do
> is
> rub
> the back
> of his
> neck.

Phil Smith (1999) tells us that his experiences with traditional scientific writing persuade him to find a different means of representation for Food Truck's world as he does not wish Food Truck to be harmed by his research. He wants to take a '*nam shub*' form of representation – a Sumerian term meaning 'speech with magical force' (Stephenson 1992: 211). Smith wants to write a *nam shub* which will transform the way people think about and behave toward people with developmental disabilities. In reading Smith's poem about Food Truck, Richardson (2002: 886) admits that 'we are changed by the writing; we feel differently about the developmental disabled', and because of this 'the cultural narratives' about the disabled 'have been resisted'. She strongly argues that this would not have occurred if Smith had written Food Truck's world in traditional social science writing.

In her participatory action research with Aboriginal Grandmothers, Geraldine Dickson (2000: 194) not only analyses and writes up her research findings in a conventional way (presenting with themes emerging from the data), but also uses poetry to represent the voices of these marginalised grandmothers. Dickson (2000: 194–95) says, 'the poetry is mine, reflecting my musings on what I heard in the grandmothers' words and actions and what I imagined might be in their minds and thoughts but may have been left unsaid'. The following example is from Dickson's finding. When the grandmothers spoke of their well-being, self-esteem and self-respect, one woman told Dickson (p. 198),

> I feel good now. It seems like my health . . . .[has] improved because that helps you when you go out and you're among . . . older women. You forget about . . . yourself. It's just like it's a new me, a new person. That's the way I feel. It's just helped me a lot, you know.

In her writing, Dickson represents this narrative with the following poem:

I Feel Good Now

It doesn't take much–
a little attention and caring.
kind words, warm clasp.
That was enough for
reserve to drop
a face to open.
a smile to break.
A glow spreads on one to all.

As in Richardson's verse, Dickson's poem succinctly reflects the troubled feeling of this grandmother and at the same time it is more interesting and fascinating. Dickson (2000: 212) strongly believes that when working with people who have been oppressed and silenced for too long, attention to that which is not said is essential. Therefore, other means need to be developed which will give voice to the one that is not easily expressed. Brady (2000: 956) too suggests that by representing people's expression through poetry, researchers 'attempt to say things that might not be said as effectively or at all any other way'. And this is consistent with qualitative researchers' attempts to 'discover and examine critically all of the ways a subject (including social and cultural relationships) can be represented'. In Dickson's work, poetry representation is strongly advocated.

Poetic representation, according to Richardson (2002: 881), provides opportunities for sensitive researchers to develop alternative ways to reveal the lived experiences of vulnerable people.

> Poetry's task is to re-present actual experiences – episodes, epiphanies, misfortunes, pleasures; to retell those experiences in such a way that others can experience and feel them. Poems, therefore, have the possibility of doing for social research what conventional social research representation cannot.

But Richardson (2002: 877) does not claim that poetic representation is the only, or the best, means to represent social research knowledge. However, she maintains that poetic representation is a feasible method for understanding the realities of research participants beyond the discursive practices of social scientific traditions. It, therefore, should be of value to sensitive researchers who are concerned with the challenges of the development of knowledge.

(Re)Presentation of Voices: The Researcher's Perspective

> Qualitative writing may be seen as an active struggle for understanding and recognition of the lived meanings of the lifeworld, and this writing also possesses passive and receptive rhetoric dimensions. It requires that we be attentive to other voices, to subtle significations in the way that things and others speak to us. In part, this is achieved through contact with the words of others. These words need to touch us, guide us, stir us.
>
> (van Manen 2006: 713)

Laurel Richardson (1996b), Norman Denzin (1996) and Corrine Glesne (1997) explicitly argue that qualitative researchers should be encouraged to experiment with these new forms of writing in their work, like Richardson (1994b) who raises essential questions like how should researchers create texts which are essential and make a difference. I also encourage sensitive researchers to reflect on these questions in their writing. Richardson (1994b) suggests that we need to break free from traditional forms of writing and re-create texts which are not only intellectually produced, but also emotionally engaging. This is the point Rebecca Campbell (2002: 121) also advocates in her work on rape research.

Here, I wish to tell a tale of Christopher Dunbar (in Dunbar et al. 2002: 294), who uses the story to capture the lived experiences of young black Americans. Dunbar initially aims to collect data and write up a traditional ethnography as most ethnographers would do. However, Dunbar (in Dunbar et al. 2002: 294) contends, when the stories started to emerge, they revealed new aspects of the lives of these young people. Therefore, stories are chosen as a way to represent the voices of these young vulnerable people. He tells us,

> Stories and performance texts helped me to represent these experiences in an evocative way. This approach allowed me to rework the data so that they highlighted the triumphs and tragedies that constituted the lives of these children. My intent was to bring their experiences to life for the reader rather than simply attempt to explain them. Turning simple tales of suffering, loss, pain, and victory into evocative performances sometimes moves audiences beyond just emotional catharsis, to reflective critical action. I wrote collective stories from the data in an effort 'to give voice to silenced people to represent them as historical actors'.

Dunbar (in Dunbar et al. 2002: 295) contends that with performance texts, he was able to challenge the traditional form of representation which is heavily influenced by rules of 'realistic interpretation and meaning'. Performance texts offer him with a means to transform 'the chaotic, unstructured, spontaneous moments of students into evocative performances'.

But as Douglas Ezzy (2002: 152) suggests, I do not mean that all qualitative researchers need to turn into 'poets, novelists or dramatists'. This is precisely what Richardson (2002: 877) recently suggests in her attempt to promote the use of poetry to present research findings: that poetry is the only means researchers adopt to represent their research findings. But she does claim that poetic representation is a 'viable method for seeing beyond social scientific conventions and discursive practices, and therefore should be of interest to those concerned with epistemological issues and challenges'. Ezzy cautions us that experimental writing is not easy. Although the rewards it brings are rich, it can be problematic in many ways and its risks are significant. Creating a performance text, Virginia Olesen (2005: 245) contends, is not easy. It requires great stylistic skills. Sensitivities are also crucial if the writing is not to be out of its depth or be seen as 'sophomoric' by readers/audiences who are more familiar with the traditional form of research writing. In advocating autobiography, Letherby (2000: 109–110) warns us that the method is fascinating, but researchers need to carefully and seriously consider the professional and emotional risks in using 'the self' in research. Some argue that this form of writing 'passes the litmus of scientific writing' and it should not be considered as sociological writing (Marvasti 2004: 129). This new form of re-presentation, particularly autoethnography, has also been accused of being 'self-indulgent writing of the self' (see Coffey 1999: 155–56; Letherby 2000; Saldaña 2005).

There is another thorny issue that I wish to discuss here. Research findings tend to be written up and published in academic refereed journals with prestigious status. This is recognised as the best way to go about for academic researchers. But as Sommer (1999) argues, this typical academic 'dissemination' model of research is deficient. General public and health and service providers may not have access to research findings which are published as papers in academic journals. Additionally, the implications for practice or change may not be clear to non-academics in journal articles (Marshall and Batten 2004).

All too often, researchers write theoretically and/or use academic jargon in their articles to satisfy the academic life, but this makes it difficult to follow. This has deterred many service providers from reading them. Marshall and Batten (2004) propose that a 'translation' from research context to the society should be done in the form that the general public and non-academics find more accessible, like community newsletters or displays. Emily Paradis (2000: 842–43) too contends that instead of publishing our findings in academic journals, we may return it to the community in the forms of reports, articles in local newspapers, public forums and action adapted to the needs of community. This will reach those who may be able to make some changes for the vulnerable groups with whom the researchers have worked.

Here, I want to give you one excellent argument about this issue. In his recent piece, Johnny Saldaña (2005: 82) re-presents the work of Elissa Foster from *Qualitative Inquiry* (see Foster 2002), but he stripped all references from the piece in order to make the performance flow as in drama. He points out that some social science researchers may argue that art-based work is not 'academic' or 'rigorous' enough when the presenter does not cite references or discuss its theoretical framework. But Saldaña (2005: 82) argues:

> I say that without these references, ethnodrama breaks free from the shackles of traditional, hegemonic academia and transcend into a more aesthetic and evocative form, one that is no less credible or trustworthy than the juried journal article.

So, how we, as sensitive researchers, write and represent our findings depends on our political agenda, what we intend to do for people who kindly offer knowledge and time to us, and our own research aims (Glesne 1997; Ellis and Berger 2002; Ezzy 2002; Richardson 2002; Chase 2005). The decision to represent our findings is 'an ethics decision' (Markham (2005: 811). Researchers should not underestimate the consequences of our research on the participant and the society. The choices we make about how to write about the participants, about ourselves and about the cultural context of their studies will lead to how these are perceived and reacted to by readers, policy makers and the service providers. Susan Chase (2005: 671) too puts it this way:

> I am not suggesting that we should all aspire to off-Broadway performance or to best-sellerdom for our work; rather, I am suggesting that we need to think more concertedly and broadly about whom we write for and speak to – and how we do so. For many of us, this may mean thinking about how to create public spaces in our local communities where the personal narratives and collective stories of marginalised people can be heard by those who occupy more powerful subject positions and social locations.

Corrine Glesne (1997: 11) tells us that when people ask her about the way to write, she would say 'it depends on the inclination of the presenter, the nature of the data, the intended purpose for writing up one's research, and the intended audience'. These alternative forms of representation may not suit every one (Glesne 1997; Brady 2000). As Laurel Richardson (1990: 16) tells us, 'how we are expected to write affects what we can write about'. Many may argue that it is easy to write whatever and however we want to write, but we may have to perhaps consider our own future career path (see Letherby 2000; Paradis 2000; Foley and Velenzuela 2005). 'Real' academic publications, however dry they are, are still essential for many who attempt to secure their tenure or to find the next employment or to obtain research funding. That means we may need to write in such a way that it will be published in so-called 'scientific journals' or as dictated by the editors of publishers. The experiences of Letherby (2000) speak for this. In her work, Letherby (2000: 106) warns us that 'writing auto/biographically brings the danger that you will be accused of being non-academic and producing what Katz Rothman (1986: 53) calls "sensational journalism" in order to deal with your own personal problems'. One piece of her work that she wrote with Cotterill (Cotterill and Letherby 1993) on the links between feminist research and auto/biography, was strongly criticised by a non-sociologist, who said that their 'approach was "grossly self indulgent" and "sickly self-advertisement" ' (Letherby 2000: 107). Letherby (2000: 107) laments, 'once the research becomes a product, the writer is vulnerable. When doing research on an issue with which one has a personal involvement and when writing in part about "oneself," it is easy to feel that criticism is directed not only at your academic work but at you personally'.

In representing the voices of the vulnerable people, sensitive researchers also make themselves vulnerable (Behar 1996; Paradis 2000). Sensitive researchers often write extensively about their emotions, beliefs, thoughts, relationships in research and their changeable (often unstable) interpretive decisions. Embarrassing and shameful incidents are often included. Writing this way, these researchers are vulnerable to the criticism of self-indulgence, and to charges that they disclose aspects of their lives that are too personal and hence not of interest to other so-called 'scientific readers'. But these researchers will argue that if readers are to truly understand the participants' stories, the readers need to know about the stories and positions of the researchers. They attempt to demolish 'the myth of the invisible omniscient author' (see also Tierney and Lincoln 1997; Frank 2000; Shostak 2000; Tierney 2002).

Laurel Richardson (1997) has echoed this all along, and in my career path, I have had to deal with what I call 'academic arrogance'. I often write in a way that is accessible to research communities and health and welfare professionals who provide care for vulnerable people. This means that I write simply, with minimal jargon and more practical applications than theory. The accusation that I often hear is that I am not theoretical enough and what is the use of research findings when they do not provide new theories. I argue that as long as my writing is used to improve the health and well-being of vulnerable people, it is more moral than striving to discover new theories. And is not this the aim of a feminist standpoint? And is not this what we call postmodern research when our findings will be used by and for different people in the society?

Then, how can we experiment with our writing? There is no need to feel despair. At least we can use this form of writing in our theses (as long as our supervisors support this trend – see Emily Paradis 2000 for example), reports and books (if we can find commissioning editors who have the same visions as us). I have been doing this in my own writings. My first book, which was targeted to help health professionals in birthing services, begins with the Women's Stories, followed with themes emerging from the stories and some practical suggestions and resources (see Liamputtong Rice 1993). Comments that I received from readers about this book were that it was like reading a novel. The book was entertaining, and yet the stories were serious enough to make the readers think about caring for women from non-English speaking backgrounds. Carolyn Ellis and Art Bochner and Laurel Richardson have shown us that personal lives can be woven into our writing. Their works clearly illustrate my argument. Sharlene Hesse-Biber and Patricia Leavy (2005) suggest that we may be able to move between traditional and experimental forms of writing at different points during the research process. And I add that we may do so at different points in our working lives. For those who need to have publications to secure tenure, they may wish to start with the traditional form, and as they move into a more secure position, they may like to experiment with their writing. This opportunity will never be lost if we are committed to it.

However, Gayle Letherby (2000: 107) had the opposite experience. She was told by some academic counterparts that an auto/biography is 'sloppy sociology', and when she attempted to get her thesis published, she was told by the commissioning editor that she must not include the autobiography if she wanted her work to be accepted. Well, this is precisely the reaction I received when I first submitted my paper on motherhood (Liamputtong 2000) to a local Australian journal. I was told bluntly that it contained too many of my personal details and that readers would not want to hear my private story. I then had to omit many of my details in an attempt to get the paper published. In the end, the paper was published in an international journal, but I wished that my 'Story' would be echoed more in the way that I had wanted, as it would be a better reflection of a life of an immigrant minority woman in Australia.

Nevertheless, it is encouraging to see that there are many prestigious qualitative journals, which are more open-minded, and accept academic papers written in these alternative forms. Glesne (1997: 11) tells us that she sent her paper on poetic representation to *Qualitative Inquiry* – 'a journal – and presumably a readership – open to experimental forms of representing research'. There are many prestigious journals where we may submit our new forms of writing and these include: *Qualitative Inquiry, Symbolic Interaction, Sociological Quarterly, Qualitative Sociology, Text and Performance Quarterly, Journal of Contemporary Ethnography, American Anthropologist, Journal of Ageing Studies*, and *Family & Society* (which has accepted my alternative writing work). These journals regularly publish alternative forms of representation 'not because it is trendy to do so' but because 'social scientists have far too long ignored these important forms of [research] representation and interpretation' (Norman Denzin, personal communication, cited in Brady 2000: 962). Like Laurel

Richardson (2000: 931), I would suggest that we may write our work in a conventional academic form for the sake of our future. But if circumstances permit, we should try out different ways of writing because it is a powerful means to expand our interpretive skills, raise our consciousness and bring a fresh and more interesting perspective to our research. This way, we may bring to the fore the many silent voices of our research participants, the Others, for whom we attempt to provide a better world in our research agenda.

> Writing is never innocent. Writing always inscribes. One can write in ways that reinscribe the discourses of academia and social sciences as the only legitimate form of knowledge, or one can write in ways that empower those whose 'ideas and beliefs are not cast in the rhetoric of science'.
>
> (Richardson 2002: 879)

The struggle and crisis of representation will continue into the next moment, the Eighth and Ninth moments – 'a fractured future', in social science (Lincoln and Denzin 2005: 1123). I wish to finish off this chapter with a nice suggestion from Lincoln and Denzin (2005: 1124):

> Attention to the representations we make, to the possibility that messages may further disenfranchise or oppress when they begin circulating in the wider world, and respect for wisdom of people who are not like us, who know all too well the unfortunate images that surround their lives, may be the starting of our performance of justice. It is a place to begin.

TUTORIAL EXERCISES

1. Consider that you have done a piece of research on mental health with indigenous people. How would you write up your findings in a way that will better re-present their lived experiences?
2. Assume that you have obtained good data on living with chronic illnesses among older gay men. Using your own imagination, construct a poem or a stage performance that will really tell the stories of these vulnerable people.

SUGGESTED READINGS

Banks, A. and S.P. Banks, 1998, *Fiction and Social Research: By Ice or Fire*, Walnut Creek: AltaMira Press.

Denzin, N.K., 2003, *Performance Ethnography: Critical Pegagogy and the Politics of Culture*, Thousand Oaks, CA: Sage Publications.

Diversi, M., 1998, 'Glimpses of Street Life: Representing Lived Experience Through Short Stories', *Qualitative Inquiry*, 4(2): 131–47.

Ellis, C., 2004, *The Ethnographic I: A Methodological Novel About Teaching and Doing Autoethnography*, Walnut Creek, CA: AltaMira Press.

Ellis, C. and A.P. Bochner (eds), 1996, *Composing Ethnography: Alternative Forms of Qualitative Writing*, Walnut Creek, CA: AltaMira Press.

Glesne, C.E., 1997, 'That Rare Feeling: Re-Presenting Research Through Poetic Transcription', *Qualitative Inquiry*, 3(2): 202–21.

Lather, P. and C. Smithies, 1997, *Troubling the Angels: Women Living with HIV/AIDS*, Boulder, CO: Westview.

Mienczakowski, J., 1995. 'The Theatre of Ethnography: The Reconstruction of Ethnography into Theatre with Emancipatory Potential', *Qualitative Inquiry*, 1(3): 360–75.

Miller, L.C., J. Taylor and M.H. Carver, 2003, *Voices Made Flesh: Performing Women's Autobiography*, Madison, Wisconsin: The University of Wisconsin Press.

Richardson, L., 1997, *Fields of Play: Constructing an Academic Life*, New Brunswick: Rutgers, University Press.

Richardson, L., 2002, 'Poetic Representation of Interviews', pp. 877–91, In *Handbook of Interview Research: context & Method*, edited by J.F. Gubrium and J.A. Holstein, Thousand Oaks, CA: Sage Publications.

Ronai, C.R., 1996, 'My Mother is Mentally Retarded', pp. 109–31, In *Composing Ethnography: Alternative Forms of Qualitative Writing*, edited by C. Ellis and A.P. Bochner, Walnut Creek, CA: AltaMira Press.

Saldaña, J. (ed.), 2005, *Ethnodrama: An Anthology of Reality Theatre*, Walnut Creek, CA: AltaMira Press.

Smith, B., 1999, 'Food Truck's Party Hat', *Qualitative Inquiry*, 5(2): 244–61.

A Closing Word.... For Now

Qualitative researchers' concerns for social justice, moral purpose, and 'liberation methodology' will mark [the] next moment with passion, urgency, purpose, and verve.

(Lincoln and Denzin 2005: 1123)

As an artist, one needs to have a good knowledge about colour and skills in the methods of painting. As sensitive researchers, we need to have extensive knowledge and well-developed skills in the principles of sensitive research methodology. As artists mix and blend paints and apply their skills to create good and interesting art, sensitive researchers also need to be creative and artistic in their approach to all aspects of the research endeavours (Dunlap et al. 1990: 122). The artistic researchers need to be creative and innovative in their research process. And this is what I have done in this book, pointing to many 'artistic blends' in being a sensitive researcher and in carrying out research with vulnerable people.

As I have stated at the beginning of this book, I have argued that it will become difficult, or even impossible, for sensitive researchers to avoid carrying out research regarding vulnerable populations in the present climate of the 'moral discourse' moment of the postmodern world (Lincoln and Denzin 2000: 1048). There are more marginalised people as the gaps between the rich and the poor, the haves and have nots, women and men, the old and the young and so on are widening, yet their voices are still largely muted. The lists can go on. In previous chapters, I have discussed salient issues in doing research with these groups. In particular, as we have seen, sensitive researchers have invented alternative forms of data collection methods to suit the needs of these people. These non-traditional means of data collection are what Glesne (1997: 2) refers to as 'experimental forms'. We have recognised the use of photographs, drawings, dramas, story-telling and so on as research methods in order to be more sensitive to the needs of research participants. We have also seen that sensitive researchers make use of technology in their attempt to access some marginalised people via online research. I have also suggested different ways to represent the voices of research participants within the crisis of representation. For their own reason, qualitative researchers are motivated to experiment with form, whatever forms they may be (Lincoln and Denzin 2000). Clearly then, future sensitive qualitative research may involve more of this kind of research agenda and methodology.

Chih Hoong Sin (2004: 272) warns us that we, as sensitive researchers, need to be 'more reflective and reflexive' in the way we undertake our research. Pierre Bourdieu (1977) says clearly that we need to stand back and look closely at the relationships of our methodology and the data we collect because this will permit us to carry out good research that will be beneficial to those we work with in our research projects. The challenge for us, as Fiona Devine and Sue Heath (1999: 3) contend, is to deal with 'the mundane messiness' of our sensitive research by speaking loudly about the ethical, practical and theoretical concerns that emerge in the research process. I believe I have done just that in this book.

Researching the vulnerable populations requires careful consideration and planning. The complex issues and dilemmas that the researcher has to deal with may make the enterprise too daunting for the researcher (Alty and Rodham 1998). But I contend that well-planned research is possible. However, it needs extra thought and preparation, an artistic blending process and perhaps a great deal of sense of good humour (Frijda 1986; Dunlap et al. 1990; Alty and Rodham 1998). But researching vulnerable people can be both a fascinating and a rewarding enterprise. We are privileged to have an opportunity to work with people who are normally made silent by oppressive social structures. This is a highly rewarding goal that we can obtain. It is promising to see that there has been a tendency, and acceptance, of how personal feelings direct our research, particularly in research relating to the 'vulnerable' (Ellis 1991; Ellis and Bochner 1992, 2000; Melrose 2002). Carolyn Ellis (1991: 125) says it all:

> We can view our own emotional experience as a legitimate sociological object of study and focus on how we feel as researchers as a way of understanding and coping with what is going on emotionally in our research.

Through the experiences of our former sensitive researchers we, as new researchers, may learn about the essence of our 'experience'. As C. Wright Mills (1959: 197) teaches us, we need to trust our experience, but we also must be sceptical of our own experience, as 'experience is so important as a source of original intellectual work'. I hope that my discussions in this book will be a learning experience for all novices and even the experienced researchers who wish to work in sensitive research and with vulnerable people.

On conducting research among vulnerable individuals and groups, this book has raised many salient issues. Lessons can be learnt from previous works and the experiences of others and, therefore, pitfalls can be avoided. I hope that when you embark on research with any vulnerable group, this book will provide some insights for the success of your sensitive work. It is our task, as sensitive researchers, and our moral obligations, that we carry out our research in a manner that creates opportunities for vulnerable people to be heard.

Glossary

Arts-Based Inquiry   It is one of many new forms of qualitative methodology. The method is situated within a tradition of participatory action research in social science. Researchers adopting this line of inquiry call for a 'reinterpretation of the methods' as well as its ethics concerning human social research. They attempt to develop inquiry involving action-oriented processes which provide benefits to the local community where the research is undertaken.

Autoethnography   Within the postmodern approach, autoethnography has become a popular writing form among sensitive social scientists, but more so among ethnographers. With this form of writing, researchers write about themselves while they participate and observe in the social world in which they themselves are situated.

Confidentiality   Confidentiality aims to conceal the true identity of people who partici- pate in the research. Revealing true identities of the research participants may lead to danger and other negative consequences for these people. Confidentiality is extremely important with some vulnerable groups, particularly those who are marginalised and stigmatised in the society.

Decentring   This is the process of taking the researcher from a position of central authority and this in turn permits the voices of the research participants to be heard more in representation of research findings.

Ethical Issues   In carrying out research with vulnerable people, researchers need to be more ethically responsible for their lives and well-being so that they do not make them more vulnerable. Although ethical issues are important for all research, sensitive researchers must be more cautious about the confidentiality, privacy, anonymity and safety of their participants.

Ethnodrama   Ethnodrama is about decoding and translating the experiences of research participants through theatrical practices. It attempts to present research findings in a language and manner which is more accessible to diverse audiences. In ethnodrama, the audiences engage with research material. This, therefore, leads to greater possibility for changing social understanding than in a traditional form of written text.

Ethnography   The method used to discover and describe individual social and cultural groups. Crucial features include the use of participant observation with other qualitative methods in the fieldwork including in-depth interviewing, focus groups and unobtrusive methods.

Feminist Methodology   Within feminist methodology, women and their concerns are the focus of investigation. A clear intention of feminist research is to undertake research which is beneficial for women, not just one about women. Feminist methodology argues that the process of research is as important as its outcome. Feminist research opposes research methods which are the products of standard research like those of positivist science. Feminist research calls for qualitative inquiry which is less structured and more flexible than that of the positivist science. Primarily, but not exclusively, feminist methods are qualitative. Feminist research aims to give voice to the marginalised. A feminist methodology aims to construct knowledge which may benefit women and other minority groups.

Focus Group Interviews   A particular method requiring group discussion. Typically, there is a moderator who acts as the leader of the group. The participants (usually between 8 and 10 in number) express their views via interaction in the discussion of the issues in a group.

Grand Narratives   The large frames of authoritative understanding/knowledge that dominate belief systems in societies.

In-depth Interviewing Method   Within this method, it is assumed that people have particular and essential knowledge about the social world that is obtainable through verbal messages. It necessitates 'active asking and listening'. The process involves a meaning-making effort which is started out as a partnership between the researchers and their participants. In-depth interviews aim to elicit rich information from the perspective of a particular person and on a selected topic under investigation.

Informed Consent   A process that precedes the data collection. The people to be involved in the research process are informed of the aims and methods of the research and then asked for their consent to participation in the research project.

Innovative Research Methods   There are some situations where no conventional qualitative method will work and can be alienating for some vulnerable people. It is essential that researchers adopt unconventional alternative approaches. Innovative research methods proposed in this book include the following: the use of photographs, drawings, diaries, arts-based research and the online method.

Mini-Narratives   Belief systems constructed by particular groups. These narratives stand in contrast with meta-narratives – the term used by Jean Francois Lyotard (1979) which refers to 'the grand unifying theories and universal claims to truth', which is seen as a feature of modern thought (Grbich 2004: 131).

Moral Issues   These are debates regarding research with vulnerable people. Should researchers carry out investigative work with some extremely vulnerable populations such as frail elderly people, people suffering from mental illness or those who experience extreme loss or grief, or those who are homeless or terminally ill? These people are already vulnerable in many ways. Sensitive researchers believe that the benefits of undertaking the research need to be measured against the risks to the participants who are involved in the research.

Online Research   Online research embraces the use of the computer and the Internet as a means to collect information from vulnerable people and difficult-to-reach groups. Online communication has emanated as an important tool because it permits the researcher and the research participants to exchange information directly using text via keyboards. The most commonly adopted text-based modalities are email and online or real-time chat.

Oral and life history   It is an inquiry that involves collecting personal stories from individuals over their life course. Oral and life history is a specific method of interviewing which requires the researcher and respondents to invest lengthy periods together in a process of telling of and listening to life stories.

Participatory Action Research   A method in which research and action are joined in order to plan, implement and monitor change. The informants become co-researchers and hence have their voices heard in all aspects of the research. The researcher becomes a participant in the initiatives and uses his or her research knowledge and expertise to assist the informants in self-research.

Photovoice Method   Photovoice method, which has been known as autodriving and photo novella, rejects traditional paradigms of power and the production of knowledge within the research relationship. Photovoice methodology allows people to record and reflect the concerns and needs of their community by taking photographs. It also promotes critical discussion about important issues through the dialogue about photographs they have taken. Their concerns may reach policy makers through public forums and the display of their photographs. Using a camera to record their concerns and needs permits individuals who rarely have contact with those who make decisions over their lives to make their voices heard.

Poetic Representation   The new way of presenting research findings using poetry. Poetic writing is often 'striking and emotive', and hence it offers a better way to evocatively represent qualitative data. Poetic expressions have recently become popularised as an effective way to represent the voices of marginalised people.

Positivism   An approach to research that believes social science research methods should be scientific in the same way as the physical sciences such as physics or chemistry. This approach largely dominates quantitative researches. However, qualitative researchers reject the arguments of positivism, pointing out that meanings and interpretations cannot be measured like physical objects.

Postmodernism   Postmodernism rejects the idea that there is a single reality or truth, but states rather that there are many realities and many truths. People have different stories, and hence different ways of saying, expressing and telling their stories. All stories and ways of doing are legitimate. Researchers adopting the postmodern theoretical paradigm reject the grand narratives of positivist science which ignore the differences between individuals and the social contexts of these individuals. Instead, they attempt to deconstruct the grand narratives in order to remove the established power of objectivist science.

Reflexivity   An acknowledgment of the role and influence of the researcher on the research project. The researcher is involved in a constant process of reflectivity and self-criticism. The place and power relations in the research process are continuously questioned throughout the research process. The role of the researcher is subject to the same critical analysis and scrutiny as the research itself.

Self-Disclosure   The sharing of personal details with others. Researchers need to be willing to share their experiences with the participants. Self-disclosure of the researcher encourages the participants to elaborate on their subjective experiences. Being more open to the participants will also facilitate rapport and trust among the participants.

Sensitive Research   Research is deemed sensitive 'if it requires disclosure of behaviours or attitudes which would normally be kept private and personal, which might result in offence or lead to social censure or disapproval, and/or which might cause the respondent discomfort to express' (Wellings et al. 2000: 256). Sensitive research may include research which involves the private sphere of an individual. Sensitive research includes studies which are 'intimate, discreditable or incriminating' (Renzetti and Lee 1993: ix). Sensitive research is 'research which potentially poses a substantial threat to those who are or have been involved in it' Lee (1993: 4). And this includes not only the research participants but also the researchers.

Subjectivity   It is an awareness of oneself as a subject and as a self-conscious person. In research, subjectivity is always situated within a particular context of the phenomena under examination. Different individuals will have different subjectivities.

Vulnerable People   Individuals who are marginalised and discriminised in society due to their social positions based on class, ethnicity, gender, age, illness, disability and sexual preferences. Often, they are difficult to reach and require special considerations when they are involved in research. The term is also used to refer to people who are difficult to access in societies.

References

Abboud, L.N. and P. Liamputtong. 2003. 'Pregnancy Loss: What it Means to Women who Miscarry and Their Partners'. *Social Work in Health Care* 36(3): 37–62.

Acker, J., K. Barry and J. Essevald. 1991. 'Objectivity and Truth: Problems in Doing Feminist Research'. Pp. 133–53. In *Beyond Methodology: Feminist Scholarship as Lived Research*, edited by M.M. Fonow and J.A. Cook. Bloomington: Indianna University Press.

Adler, C.L. and Y.R. Zarchin. 2002. 'The "Virtual Focus Groups": Using the Internet to Reach Pregnant Women on Home Bed Rest'. *Journal of Obstetrics, Gynaecologist and Neonatal Nursing* 31: 418–27.

Adler, P.A. 1990. 'Ethnographic Research on Hidden Populations: Penetrating the Drug World'. Pp. 96–111. In *The Collection and Interpretation of Data from Hidden Populations*, edited by E.Y. Lambert, Rockville, MD: National Institute on Drug Abuse.

Adler, P.A. and P. Adler. 1987. 'The Past and Future of Ethnography'. *Journal of Contemporary Ethnography* 16: 4–24.

Alaszewski, A. 2006. *Using Diaries for Social Research*. London: Sage Publications.

Alderson, P. 2000. 'Children as Researchers: The Effects of Participation Rights on Research Methodology'. Pp. 241–75. In *Research With Children*, edited by P. Christensen and A. James. London: Farmer Press.

Aléx. L. and A. Hammarström. 2004. 'Women's Experiences in Connection With Induced Abortion – A Feminist Perspective'. *Scandinavian Journal of Caring Science* 18: 160–68.

Alexander, B.K. 2005. 'Performance Ethnography: The Reenacting and Inciting of Culture'. Pp. 411–41. In *The Sage Handbook of Qualitative Research,* 3rd edition, edited by N.K. Denzin and Y.S. Lincoln. Thousand Oaks, CA: Sage Publications.

Alexander, J.G., M. de Chesnay, E. Marshall, A.R. Campbell, S. Johnson and R. Wright. 1989. 'Parallel Reactions in Rape Victims and Rape Researchers'. *Violence and Victims* 4(1): 57–62.

Allen, D.A. and W.J. Doherty. 1996. 'The Responsibilities of Fatherhood as Perceived by African American Teenage Fathers'. *Families in Society* March: 142–55.

Allen, K.R. and A.J. Walker. 1992. 'A Feminist Analysis of Interviews with Elderly Mothers and their Daughters'. Pp. 198–214. In *Qualitative Methods in Family Research*, edited by J.F. Gilgun, K. Daly and G. Handel. Newbury Park, CA: Sage Publications.

Allen, K.R. and K.M. Baber. 1992. 'Ethical and Epistemological Tensions in Applying a Postmodern Perspective to Feminist Research'. *Psychology of Women Quarterly* 16: 1–15.

Alty, A. and K. Rodham. 1998. 'The Ouch! Factor: Problems in Conducting Sensitive Research'. *Qualitative Health Research* 8(2): 275–82.

Anderson, D.G. and D.C. Hatton. 2000. 'Accessing Vulnerable Populations for Research'. *Western Journal of Nursing Research* 22(2): 244–51.

Anderson, K.L. and D. Umberson. 2004. 'Gendering Violence: Masculinity and Power in Men's Accounts of Domestic Violence'. Pp. 251–70. In *Feminist Perspectives on Social Research*, edited by S.N. Hesse-Biber and M.L. Yaiser. New York: Oxford University Press.

Arendell, T. 1997. 'Reflections on the Researcher-Researched Relationship: A Woman Interviewing Men'. *Qualitative Sociology* 20(3): 341–68.

Atkinson, P. and M. Hammersley. 1994. 'Ethnography and Participant Observation'. Pp. 248–61. In *Handbook of Qualitative Research*, edited by N.K. Denzion and Y.S. Lincoln. Thousand Oakes, CA: Sage Publications.

Atkinson, P., A. Coffey, S. Delamont, J. Lofland and L. Lofland. (eds). 2001. *Handbook of Ethnography*. London: Sage Publications.

Atkinson, R. 2002. 'The Life Story Interview'. Pp. 121–40. In *Handbook of Interview Research: Context & Method*, edited by J.F. Gubrium and J.A. Holstein. Thousand Oaks, CA: Sage Publications.

Atkinson, R. and J. Flint. 2001. 'Accessing Hidden and Hard-to-Reach Populations: Snowball Research Strategies'. *Social Research Update* 33: 1–4. Available at: http://www.soc.surrey.ac.uk/sru/SRU33.html (Accessed 29/11/2005).

Atlas, B. and R. Molloy. 2005. *Photo Voice*. Paper presented at the Melbourne Interest Group in International Health, the University of Melbourne, Melbourne, 9 August.

Auerbach, S. 2002. ' "Why Do They Give the Good Classes to Some and Not to Others": Latino Parent Narratives of Struggles in a College Access Program'. *Teaches College Record* 104: 1369–92.

Baca Zinn, M. 2001. 'Insider Field Research in Minority Communities'. Pp. 159–66. In *Contemporary Field Research: Perspectives and Formulations*, 2nd edition, edited by R.M. Emerson. Prospect Heights, IL: Waveland Press.

Bach, H. 1998. *A Visual Narrative Concerning Curriculum, Girls, Photography etc.* Alberta: Canada International Institute for Qualitative Methodology/Qualitative Institute Press.

Backett-Millburn, K. and L. McKie. 1999. 'A Critical Appraisal of the Draw and Write Technique'. *Health Education Research* 14: 387–98.

Backman, C.G. and S.M. Walther. 2001. 'Use of a Personal Diary Written on the ICU During Critical Illness'. *Intensive Care Medicine* 27: 426–29.

Baez, B. 2002. 'Confidentiality in Qualitative Research: Reflections on Secrets, Power and Agency'. *Qualitative Research* 2(1): 35–58.

Bagley, A. 2000. 'The Educational Self-Perceptions of Children With Down Syndrome'. Pp. 98–111. In *Researching Children's Perspectives*, edited by A. Lewis and G. Lindsay. Buckingham: Open University Press.

Baker, L., T. Lavende and D. Tincello. 2005. 'Factors that Influence Women's Decisions About Whether to Participate in Research: An Exploratory Study'. *Birth* 32(1): 60–66.

Balcazar, F., C.B. Keys, D.L. Kaplan and Y. Suarez-Balcazar. 1999. 'Participatory Research and People with Disabilities: Principles and Challenges'. *Canadian Journal of Rehabilitation* 12: 105–12.

Banister, E., B. Tate, N. Wright, S. Rinzema and L. Flato. 2002. 'Data Collection Strategies for Accessing Adolescent Women's World'. *Health Care for Women International* 23: 267–80.

Banks, A. and S.P. Banks. 1998. *Fiction and Social Research: By Ice or Fire*. Walnut Creek: AltaMira Press.

Banks, M. 2001. *Visual Methods in Social Research*. London: Sage Publications.

Banks, S. 2000. 'Five Holiday Letters: A Fiction'. *Qualitative Inquiry* 6(6): 392–405.

Banks-Wallace, J. 2002. 'Talk that Talk: Storytelling and Analysis Rooted in African American Oral Tradition'. *Qualitative Health Research* 12: 410–26.

Barnard, M. 2005. 'Discomforting Research: Colliding Moralities and Looking for "Truth" in a Study of Parental Drug Problems'. *Sociology of Health & Illness* 27(1): 1–19.

Barone, T. 2001. 'Science, Art, and the Pre-Disposition of Educational Researchers'. *Educational Researcher* 30(7): 24–29.

Barringer, C.E. 1992. 'Speaking of Incest: It's Not Enough to Say the Word'. *Feminism and Psychology* 2: 183–88.

Barthes, R. 1977. *Image, Music, Text* (Translated by S. Heath). New York: Hill & Wang.

Bauby, J-D. 1997. *The Diving Bell and the Butterfly: A Memoir of Life in Death*. (Translated by J. Leggatt). New York: Random House.

Baylis, F., J. Downie and S. Sherwin. 1998. 'Reframing Research Involving Humans. Pp. 234–59. In *The Politics of Women's Health*, edited by S. Sherwin. Philadelphia: Temple University Press.

Beardwood, B.A., B. Kirsh and N.J. Clark. 2005. 'Victims Twice Over: Perceptions and Experiences of Injured Workers'. *Qualitative Health Research* 15(1): 30–48.

Beauchamp, T.L., B. Jennings, E.D. Kinney and R.J. Levine. 2002. 'Pharmaceutical Research Involving the Homeless'. *Journal of Medicine and Philosophy* 27(5): 547–64.

Beaver, K., K. Luker and S. Woods. 1999. 'Conducting Research with the Terminally Ill: Challenges and Considerations'. *International Journal of Palliative Nursing* 5(1): 13–17.

Becker, H.S. 1963. *Outsiders: Studies in the Sociology of Deviance*. New York: Free Press.

Behar, R. 1996. *The Vulnerable Observer: Anthropology that Breaks Your Heart*. Boston, MA: Beacon.

Behar, R. 2003. *Translated Woman: Crossing the Border with Esperanza's Story*. Boston, MA: Beacon.

Belenky, M.F.B., B.M. Clinchy, N.R. Goldberger and J.M. Tarule. 1997. *Women's Ways of Knowing: The Development of Self, Voice, and Mind*, 10th Anniversary Edition, Basic Books, New York.

Bell, S. 2002. 'Sexualizing Research: Response to Erich Goode'. *Qualitative Sociology* 25: 535–39.

Bendelow, G. 1993, 'Using Visual Imagery to Explore Gendered Notions of Pain'. Pp. 212–28. In *Researching Sensitive Topics*, edited by C.M. Renzetti and R.M. Lee. Newbury Park: Sage Publications.

Bendelow, G. and P. Pridmore. 1998. 'Children's Images of Health'. Pp. 128–40. In *Health Matters: A Sociology of Illness, Prevention and Care*, edited by A. Petersen and C. Waddell. Sydney: Allen & Unwin.

Bendelow, G., A. Oakley and S. Williams. 1996. 'It Makes you Bald: Children's Beliefs about Health and Cancer Prevention'. *Health Education* 96(3): 8–15.

Bender, D.E., C. Harbour, J.M. Thorp Jr and P.D. Morris. 2001. 'Tell Me What You Mean by "Si": Perceptions of Quality of Prenatal Care among Immigrant Latina Women'. *Qualitative Health Research* 11(16): 780–94.

Bennett, C. 1998. *Men Online: Discussing Lived Experiences on the Internet*. Unpublished honours dissertation, James Cook University, Townsville, Queensland, Australia.

Benoit, C., M. Jansson, A. Millar and R. Phillips. 2005. 'Community-Academic Research on Hard-to-Reach Populations: Benefits and Challenges'. *Qualitative Health Research* 15(2): 263–82.

Bergen, R.K. 1993. 'Interviewing Survivors of Marital Rape: Doing Feminist Research on Sensitive Topics'. Pp. 197–211. In *Researching Sensitive Topics*, edited by C.M. Renzetti and R.M. Lee. Newbury Park: Sage Publications.

Bergen, R.K. 1996. *Wife Rape: Understanding the Responses of Survivors and Service Providers*. Thousand Oaks, CA: Sage Publications.

Berk, R.A. and J.M. Adams. 2001. 'Establishing Rapport with Deviant Groups'. Pp. 58–71. In *Extreme Methods: Innovative Approaches to Social Science Research*, edited by J.M. Miller and R. Tewksbury. Boston: Allyn and Bacon.

Berman, H., M. Ford-Gilboe, B. Moutrey and S. Cekic. 2001. 'Portraits of Pain and Promise: A Photographic Study of Bosnian Youth'. *Canadian Journal of Nursing Research* 32(4): 21–41. (Online)

Beverley, J. 2000. 'Testimonio, Subalternity and Narrative Authority'. Pp. 555–65. In *Handbook of Qualitative Research*, 2nd edition, edited by N.K. Denzin and Y.S. Lincoln. Thousand Oaks, CA: Sage Publications.

Beyrer, C. and N.E. Kass. 2002. 'Human Rights, Politics and Reviews of Research Ethics'. *Lancet* 359(9328): 246–51.

Biernacki, P. and D. Waldorf. 1981. 'Snowball Sampling: Problems and Techniques of Chain Referral Sampling'. *Sociological Methods and Research* 10: 141–63.

Birch, M. and T. Miller. 2000. 'Inviting Intimacy: The Interview as Therapeutic Opportunity'. *International Journal of Social Research Methodology* 3(3): 189–202.

Birman, D. 2005. 'Ethical Issues in Research with Immigrants and Refugees'. Pp. 155–77. In *Handbook of Ethical Research with Ethnocultural Populations and Communities*, edited by J.E. Trimble and C.B. Fisher. Thousand Oaks, CA: Sage Publications.

Bishop, R. 2005. 'Freeing Ourselves from Neocolonial Domination in Research: A Kaupapa Māori Approach to Creating Knowledge'. Pp. 109–38. In *The Sage Handbook of Qualitative Research,* 3rd edition, edited by N.K. Denzin and Y.S. Lincoln. Thousand Oaks, CA: Sage Publications.

Blum, L.M. 1999. *At the Breast: Ideologies of Breastfeeding and Motherhood in the Contemporary United States*. Boston, MA: Beacon.

Boal, A. 1979. *Theatre of the Oppressed*. London: Pluto Press.

Boal, A. 1985. *Theatre of the Oppressed* (Translated by C.A. McBride and M-O. Leal McBride). New York: Theatre Communication Group.

Boal, A. 1995. *The Rainbow of Desire: The Boal Method Theatre and Therapy.* (Translated by A. Jackson). New York: Routledge.

Boal, A. 1998. *Legislative Theatre: Using Performance to Make Politics.* (Translated by A. Jackson). New York: Routledge.

Bolton, R. 1995. 'Tricks, Friends, and Lovers: Erotic Encounters in the Field'. Pp. 140–67. In *Taboo: Sex, Identity and Erotic Subjectivity*, edited by M. Wilson and D. Kulick. Boston: Routledge.

Bond, J. and L. Corner. 2001. 'Researching Dementia: Are There Unique Methodological Challenges for Health Services Research? *Aging and Society* 21: 95–116.

Booth, C. 1902. *Life and Labour of the People of London*. London: Macmillan.

Booth, S. 1999. 'Researching Health and Homelessness: Methodological Challenges for Researchers Working with a Vulnerable, Hard-to-reach, Transient Population'. *Australian Journal of Primary Health* 5(3): 76–81.

Booth, T. and W. Booth. 1994a. *Parenting Under Pressure: Mothers and Fathers With Learning Difficulties*. Buckingham: Open University Press.

Booth, T. and W. Booth. 1994b. 'Use of Depth Interviewing with Vulnerable Subjects'. *Social Science and Medicine* 39(2): 415–24.

Booth, W. 1998. 'Doing Research with Lonely People'. *British Journal of Learning Disabilities* 26: 132–34.

Borkan, J.M., M. Morad and S. Shvarts. 2000. 'Universal Health Care? The Views of Negev Bedouin Arabs on Health Services'. *Health Policy and Planning* 15(2): 207–16.

Borrayo, E.A., L.P. Buki and B.M. Feigal. 2005. 'Breast Cancer Detection Among Older Latinas: Is It Worth the Risk?'. *Qualitative Health Research* 15(9): 1244–63.

Boshier, R. 1990. 'Socio-Psychological Factors in Electronic Networking'. *International Journal of Lifelong Education* 9(1): 49–64.

Bosk, C.L. 2002. 'Obtaining Voluntary Consent for Research in Desperately Ill Patients'. *Medical Care* 40(9) Supplement: V-64-V-68.

Bostock, L. 2002. '"God, She's Gonna Report Me": The Ethics of Child Protection in Poverty Research'. *Children & Society* 16(4): 273–83.

Botting, I. 2000. 'Understanding Domestic Service Through Oral History and the Census: The Case of Grand Falls, Newfoundland'. *Feminist Qualitative Research* 28(1,2): 99–120.

Bourdieu, P. 1977. *Outline of a Theory of Practice*. Cambridge: Cambridge University Press.

Bowser, B.P. and J.E. Sieber. 1993. 'AIDS Prevention Research: Old Problems and New Solutions'. Pp. 160–76. In *Researching Sensitive Topics*, edited by C.M. Renzetti and R.M. Lee. Newbury Park, MA: Sage Publications.

Boynton, P.M. 2002. 'Life on the Streets: The Experiences of Community Researchers in a Study of Prostitution'. *Journal of Community and Applied Social Psychology* 12(1): 1–12.

Brady, I. 2000. 'Anthropological Poetics'. Pp. 949–79. In *Handbook of Qualitative Research*, 2nd edition, edited by N.K. Denzin and Y.S. Lincoln. Thousand Oaks, CA: Sage Publications.

Braidotti, R. 2000. 'Once Upon a Time in Europe'. *Signs* 25: 1061–64.

Brajuha, M. and L. Hollowell. 1986. 'Legal Intrusion and the Politics of Fieldwork: The Impact of the Brajuha Case'. *Urban Life* 14: 454–78.

Brannen, J. 1988. 'The Study of Sensitive Subjects'. *The Sociological Review* 36: 552–63.

Brannen, J. 1993. 'The Effects of Research on Participants: The Findings from a Study of Mothers and Employment'. *The Sociological Review* 41(2): 328–46.

Brigham, L. 1998. 'Representing the Lives of Women with Learning Difficulties: Ethical Dilemmas in the Research Process'. *British Journal of Learning Disabilities* 26: 146–50.

Brody, B. 1998. *Ethics of Research: An International Perspective*. New York: Oxford University Press.

Bromseth, J. 2006. 'Researcher/Woman/Lesbian? Finding a Voice in Creating a Researcher Position, Trust and Credibility as a Participant Researcher in a Mediated Mailing-List Environment for Lesbian and Bisexual Women in a Time of Conflict'. Pp. 85–104. In Health Research in Cyber Space: Methodological, Practical, and Personal Issues, edited by P. Liamputtong. New York: Nova Science Publishers.

Brown, H. and D. Thompson. 1997. 'The Ethics of Research with Men Who Have Learning Disabilities and Abusive Sexual Behaviour: A Minefield in a Vacuum'. *Disability and Society* 12(5): 695–707.

Brydon-Miller, M. 2001. 'Education, Research, and Action: Theory and Methods of Participatory Action Research'. Pp. 76–89. In *From Subjects to Subjectivities: A Handbook of Interpretive and Participatory Methods*, edited by D.L. Tolman and M. Brydon-Miller. New York: New York University Press.

Bryman, A. (ed.). 2001. *Ethnography Volume I*. London: Sage Publications.

Brzuzy, S., A. Ault and E.A. Segal. 1997. 'Conducting Qualitative Interviews with Women Survivors of Trauma'. *Affilia* 12(1): 76–83.

Burr, G. 1995. 'Unfinished Business: Interviewing Family Members of Critically Ill Patients'. *Nursing Inquiry* 3: 172–77.

Buujtjens, M. and P. Liamputtong. In press. 'When giving life starts to take the life out of you: Women's experiences with postnatal depression following childbirth'. *Midwifery*.

Byrne, A. and R. Lentin. (eds). 2000. *(Re)searching Women: Feminist Research Methodologies in the Social Sciences in Ireland*. Dublin: IPA.

Calhoun, T.C. 1992. 'Male Street Hustling: Introduction Processes and Stigma Containment'. *Sociological Spectrum* 12: 35–52.

Calvey, D. 2000. 'Getting on the Door and Staying there: A Covert Participant Observational Study of Bouncers'. Pp. 43–60. In *Danger in the Field: Risk and Ethics in Social Research*, edited by G. Lee-Treweek and S. Linkogle, Routledge: London.

Cameron, M. 1993. *Living with AIDS: Experiencing Ethical Problems*. Newbury Park, CA: Sage Publications.

Campbell, J.E. 2004. *Getting It On Online: Cyberspace, Gay Male Sexuality, and Embodied Identity*. New York: Harrington Park Press.

Campbell, M., K. Copeland and B. Tate. 1998. 'Taking the Standpoint of People with Disabilities in Research: Experiences with Participation'. *Canadian Journal of Rehabilitation* 12: 95–104.

Campbell, R. 2002. *Emotionally Involved: The Impact of Researching Rape*. New York: Routledge.

Campbell, R. and D.A. Salem. 1999. 'Concept Mapping as a Feminist Research Method: Examining the Community Response to Rape'. *Psychology of Women Quarterly* 23: 67–91.

Campbell, R. and S.M. Wasco. 2000. 'Feminist Approaches to Social Sciences: Epistemological and Methodological Tenets'. *American Journal of Community Psychology* 28(6): 773–91.

Cancian, F.M. 1992. 'Feminist Science: Methodologies that Challenge Inequality'. *Gender & Society* 6: 623–42.

Candida Smith, R. 2002. 'Analytic Strategies for Oral History Interviews'. Pp. 711–33. In *Handbook of Interviews Research: Context & Method*, edited by J. Gubrium and J. Holstein. Thousand Oaks, CA: Sage Publications.

Cannon, L.W., E. Higginbotham and M.L.A. Leung. 1988. 'Race and Class Bias in Qualitative Research on Women'. *Gender & Society* 2: 449–62.

Cannon, S. 1989. 'Social Research in stressful Settings: Difficulties for the Sociologist Studying the Treatment of Breast Cancer'. *Sociology of Health and Illness* 11(1): 62–77.

Cannon, S. 1992. 'Reflections on Fieldwork in Stressful Settings'. Pp. 147–82. In *Studies in Qualitative Methodology: Volume 3: Learning About Fieldwork*, edited by R.G. Burgess. Greenwich: JAI Press.

Carrier, J. 1999. 'Reflections on Ethical Problems Encountered in Field Research on Mexican Male Homosexuality: 1968 to present'. *Culture, Health & Sexuality* 1(3): 207–21.

Cassell, J. and A. Young. 2002. 'Why We Should Not Seek Individual Informed Consent for Participation in Health Services Research'. *Journal of Medical Ethics* 28: 313–17.

Chamberlayne, P. and A. King. 1996. 'Biographical Approaches in Comparative Work: The "Culture of Care" Project'. Pp. 95–104. In *Cross-National Research Methods in the Social Sciences*, edited by L. Hantrais and S. Mangen. London: Pinter.

Chapman, T. and A. Johnson. 1995. *Growing Old and Needing Care: A Health and Social Care Needs Audit*. London: Avebury.

Charlesworth, L.W. and M.K. Rodwell. 1997. 'Focus Groups With Children: A Resource for Sexual Abuse Prevention Program Evaluation'. *Child Abuse and Neglect* 21: 1205–26.

Chase, S.E. 2005. 'Narrative Inquiry: Multiple Lenses, Approaches, Voices'. Pp. 651–79. In *The Sage Handbook of Qualitative Research,* 3rd edition, edited by N.K. Denzin and Y.S. Lincoln. Thousand Oaks, CA: Sage Publications.

Christian, C.G. 2005. 'Ethics and Politics in Qualitative Research'. Pp. 109–64. In *The Sage Handbook of Qualitative Research,* 3rd edition, edited by N.K. Denzin and Y.S. Lincoln. Thousand Oaks, CA: Sage Publications.

Clayton, A. and T. Thorne. 2000. 'Diary Data Enhancing Rigour: Analysis Framework and Verification Tool'. *Journal of Advanced Nursing* 32(6): 1514–21.

Coffey, A. 1999. *The Ethnographic Self: Fieldwork and the Representation of Identity*. London: Sage Publications.

Cohen-Cruz, J. 2001. 'Motion of the Ocean: The Shifting Face of U.S. Theater for Social Change since the 1960s'. *Theater* 31(3): 95–107.

Coles, A. and J. Knowles. (eds). 2001. *Lives in Context: The Art of Life History Research*. Walnut Creek, CA: AltaMira.

Collingwood, R.G. 1950. *An Essay on Philosophical Method*. Oxford: The Clarendon Press.

Conaway, M.E. 1986. 'The Pretense of the Neutral Researcher'. Pp. 52–63. In *Self, Sex and Gender in Cross-Cultural Fieldwork*, edited by T.L. Whitehead and M.E. Conaway. Urbana: University of Illinois Press.

Coney, S. 1988. *The Unfortunate Experiment*. Auckland, Penguin Books.

Cook, A.S. and G. Bosley. 1995. 'The Experience of Participating in Bereavement Research: Stressful or Therapeutic?'. *Death Studies* 19: 157–70.

Cook, J. and M. Fonow. 1984. 'Knowledge and Women's Interests: Issues of Epistemology and Methodology in Feminist Sociological Research'. *Sociological Inquiry* 56: 2–29.

Coomber, R. 1997. 'Using the Internet for Survey Research'. *Sociological Research Online* 2(2). Available at: http://www.socresonline.org.uk/socresonline/2/2/2.html (Accessed 12/6/2004).

Cooper, H., L. Moore, S. Gruskin and N. Krieger. 2005. 'The Impact of a Police Drug Crackdown on Drug Injectors' Ability to Practice Harm Reduction: A Qualitative Study'. *Social Science and Medicine* 61: 673–84.

Corbin, J. and J. Morse. 2003. 'The Unstructured Interactive Interview: Issues of Reciprocity and Risks When Dealing with Sensitive Topics'. *Qualitative Inquiry* 9: 335–54.

Cornwall, A. 1996. 'Towards Participatory Practice: Participatory Rural Appraisal (PRA) and the Participatory Process'. Pp. 94–107. In *Participatory Research in Health: Issues and Experiences*, edited by K. de Koning and M. Martin. London: Zed Books.

Cornwall, A. and R. Jewkes. 1995. 'What is Participatory Research?' *Social Science and Medicine* 41(2): 1667–76.

Correll, S. 1995. 'The Ethnography of an Electronic Bar: The Lesbian Café'. *Journal of Contemporary Ethnography* 24: 270–98.

Corti, L. 1993. 'Using Diaries in Social Research'. Social Research Update, 2. Available at: http://www.soc.surrey.ac.uk/sru/sru2.html (Accessed 8/6/2005).

Corti, L., A. Day and G. Backhouse. 2000. 'Confidentiality and Informed Consent: Issues for Consideration in the Preservation of and Provision of Access to Qualitative Data Archives'. *Forum: Qualitative Social Research* 1(3). Available at: http://www.qualitative-research.net/fqs-texte/3-00/3-00cortietal-e.htm/ (Accessed 15/10/2005).

Cosgrove, L. and M.C. McHugh. 2000. 'Speaking for Ourselves: Feminist Methods and Community Psychology'. *American Journal of Community Psychology* 28(6): 815–38.

Costley, D. 2000. 'Collecting the Views of Young People With Moderate Learning Difficulties'. Pp. 163–72. In *Researching Children's Perspectives*, edited by A. Lewis and G. Lindsay. Buckingham: Open University Press.

Cotterill, P. 1992. 'Interviewing Women: Issues of Friendship, Vulnerability and Power'. *Women's Studies International Forum* 15(5/6): 593–606.

Cotterill, P. and G. Letherby. 1993. 'Weaving Stories: Personal Auto/Biographies in Feminist Research'. *Sociology* 27(1): 67–80.

Cowles, K.V. 1988. 'Issues in Qualitative Research on Sensitive Topics'. *Western Journal of Nursing Research* 10(2): 163–79.

Coyle, A. and C. Wright. 1996. 'Using the Counselling Interview to Collect Research Data on Sensitive Topics'. *Journal of Health Psychology* 1(4): 431–40.

Craig, G., A. Corden and P. Thornton. 2000. 'Safety in Social Research'. *Social Research Update* 20: 1–7. Available at: http://www.soc.surrey.ac.uk/sru/SRU33.html (Accessed 29/11/2005).

Craig, G., A. Corden and P. Thornton. 2001. A Guide of Safety for Social Researchers. London: SRA.

Crawford, J., S. Kippax and C. Waldby. 1994. 'Women's Sex Talk and Men's Sex Talk: Different Worlds'. *Feminist and Psychology* 4: 571–88.

Crawley, S.L. and K.L. Broad. 2004. ' "Be Your(Real Lesbian) Self": Mobilizing Sexual Formula Stories Through Personal (and Political) Storytelling'. *Journal of Contemporary Ethnography* 33: 39–71.

Crigger, N.J., L. Holcomb and J. Weiss. 2001. 'Fundamentalism, Multiculturalism, and Problems Conducting Research with Populations in Developing Nations'. *Nursing Ethics* 8(5): 459–69.

Crockett, B. and S.M. Gifford. 2004. ' "Eyes Wide Shut": Narratives of Women Living With Hepatitis C in Australia'. *Women & Health* 39(4): 117–37.

Crossmaker, M. 1991. 'Behind Locked Doors – Institutional Sexual Abuse'. *Sexuality & Disability* 9(3): 201–19.

Cutcliffe, J.R. 2002. 'Ethics Committee, Vulnerable Groups and Paternalism: The Case for Considering the Benefits of Participating in Qualitative Interviews'. Pp. 204–19. In *Empowerment and Participation: Power, influence and Control in Health Care*, edited by J. Dooher and R. Byrt. London: Quay Books.

Cutcliffe, J.R. and P. Ramcharan. 2002. 'Leveling the Playing Field? Exploring the Merits of the Ethics-As-Process Approach for Judging Qualitative Research Proposals'. *Qualitative Health Research* 12(7): 1000–10.

Dalrymple, L. and E.M. Preston-Whyte. 1992. 'A Drama Approach to AIDS Education: An Experiment in "Action Research" '. *AIDS Bulletin* 1(1): 9–11.

Daly, K. 1992. 'The Fit between Qualitative Research and Characteristics of Families'. Pp. 3–11. In *Qualitative Methods in Family Research*, edited by J.F. Gilgun, K. Daly and G. Handel. Newbury Park, CA: Sage Publications.

Dane, B. 2000. 'Child Welfare Workers: An Innovative Approach for Interacting With Secondary Trauma'. *Journal of Social Work Education* 36(1): 27–38.

Danforth, S. 1997. 'On What Basis Hope? Modern Progress and Postmodern Possibilities'. *Mental Retardation* 35: 93–106.

Darlington, Y. and D. Scott. 2002. *Qualitative Research in Practice: Stories from the Field.* Sydney: Allen and Unwin.

Davey, S.J., S. Dziurawiec and A. O'Brien-Malone. 2006. Men's Voices: Postnatal Depression From the Perspective of Male Partners'. *Qualitative Health Research* 16(2): 206–20.

Davidson, L., D.A. Stayner, S. Lambert, P. Smith and W.H. Sledge. 2001. 'Phenomenological and Participatory Research on Schizophrenia: Recovering the Person in Theory and Practice'. Pp. 163–79. In *From Subjects to Subjectivities: A Handbook of Interpretive and Participatory Methods*, edited by D.L. Tolmin and M. Brydon-Miller. New York: New York University Press.

Davis, R.E. 2002. ' "The Strongest Women": Exploration of the Inner Resources of Abused Women'. *Qualitative Health Research* 12(9): 1248–63.

Dawson, M.T. and Gifford, S.M., 2003, 'Social Change, Migration and Sexual Health: Chilean Women in Chile and Australia', *Women & Health*, 38(4): 39–56.

D'Cruz, P. 2004. 'The Family Context of Care in HIV/AIDS: A Study from Mumbai, India'. *The Qualitative Report* 9(3): 413–34.

Deatrick, J.A. and S.W. Ledlie. 2000. 'Qualitative Research Interview With Children and Their Families'. *Journal of Child and Family Nursing* 3(2): 152–58.

dé Ishtar, Z. 2005a. 'Living On the Ground: The "Culture Woman" and the "Missus" '. *Women's Studies International Forum* 28: 369–80.

dé Ishtar, Z. 2005b. 'Striving for a Common Language: A White Feminist Parallel to Indigenous Ways of Knowing and Researching'. *Women's Studies International Forum* 28: 357–68.

dé Ishtar, Z. 2005c. *Holding Yawulyu: White Culture and Black Women's Law.* North Melbourne: Spinifex Press.

De Laine, M. 2000. *Fieldwork, Participation and Practice: Ethics and Dilemmas in Qualitative Research.* London: Sage Publications.

Demi, A.S. and N.A. Warren. 1995. 'Issues in Conducting Research with Vulnerable Families'. *Western Journal of Nursing Research* 17(2): 188–202.

Denner, J., C. Cooper, E. Lopez and N. Dunbar. 1999, 'Beyond "Giving Science Away": How University-Community Partnerships Inform Youth Programs, Research, and Policy'. *Social Policy Report: Society for Research in Child Development* 13(1): 1–17.

Denzin, N.K. 1968. 'On the Ethics of Disguised Observation'. *Social Problems* 115: 502–04.

Denzin, N.K. 1978. *The Research Act.* New York: Aldine.

Denzin, N.K. 1989. *Interpretive Interactionalism.* Newbury Park, CA: Sage Publications.

Denzin, N.K. 1996. 'Pushing Poets'. *Qualitative Inquiry* 19(4): 525–28.

Denzin, N.K. 1997. *Interpretive Ethnography: Ethnographic Practices for the 21ˢᵗ Century.* Thousand Oaks, CA: Sage Publications.

Denzin, N.K. 1999a. 'Performing Montana'. Pp. 147–58. In *Qualitative Sociology as Everyday Life*, edited by B. Glassner and R. Hertz. Thousand Oaks, CA: Sage Publications.

Denzin, N.K. 1999b. 'Performing Montana, Part II'. Presented at the annual symposium of the Couch-Stone Society for the Study of Symbolic Interaction, February 5–7, Las Vegas.

Denzin, N.K. 1999c. 'Two-Stepping in the 90s'. *Qualitative Inquiry* 5: 568–72.

Denzin, N.K. 2000. 'Aesthetics and the Practices of Qualitative Inquiry'. *Qualitative Inquiry* 6: 256–65.

Denzin, N.K. 2002. 'The Cinematic Society and the Reflective Interview'. Pp. 833–47.

Denzin, N.K. 2003a. *Performance Ethnography: Critical Pedagogy and the Politics of Culture.* Thousand Oaks, CA: Sage Publications.

Denzin, N.K. 2003b. 'The Call to Performance'. *Symbolic Interaction* 26: 187–208.

Denzin, N.K. 2005. 'Emancipatory Discourses and the Ethics and Politics of Interpretation'. Pp. 933–58. In *The Sage Handbook of Qualitative Research,* 3rd edition, edited by N.K. Denzin and Y.S. Lincoln. Thousand Oaks, CA: Sage Publications.

Denzin, N.K. and Y.S. Lincoln. 1998. *The Landscape of Qualitative Research: Theories and Issues.* Thousand Oaks, CA: Sage Publications.

Department of Health. 2001. *Research Governance Framework for Health and Social Care.* London: The Stationery Office.

De Reave, L. 1994. 'Ethical Issues in Palliative Care Research'. *Palliative Medicine* 8: 298–305.

Detheridge, T. 2000. 'Research Involving Children With Severe Learning Difficulties'. Pp. 112–34. In *Researching Children's Perspectives*, edited by A. Lewis and G. Lindsay. Buckingham: Open University Press.

Detzner, D.F. 1992. 'Life Histories: Conflict in Southeast Asian Refugee Families'. Pp. 85–102. In *Qualitative Methods in Family Research*, edited by J.F. Gilgun, K. Daly and G. Handel. Newbury Park, CA: Sage Publications.

DeVault, M.L. 1999. *Liberating Method: Feminism and Social Research*. Philadelphia, PA: Temple University Press.

Devine, F. and S. Heath. 1999. *Sociological Research Methods in Context*. Houndmills, Basingstoke: Macmillan.

Dickson, G. 2000. 'Aboriginal Grandmothers' Experience with Health Promotion and Participatory Action Research'. *Qualitative Health Research* 10(2): 188–213.

Dickson-Swift, V. 2005. *Undertaking Sensitive Health Research: The Experiences of Researchers*. Unpublished doctoral thesis, Department of Public Health, School of Health and Environment, La Trobe University, Bendigo, Australia.

Diversi, M. 1998. 'Glimpses of Street Life: Representing Lived Experience Through Short Stories'. *Qualitative Inquiry* 4(2): 131–47.

Douglas, J. 1985. *Creative Interviewing*. Beverly Hills, CA: Sage Publications.

Douglas, K.B. 1998. 'Impressions: African American First-Year Students Perceptions of Predominantly White University'. *Journal of Negro Education* 67(4): 416–31.

Dowling, R. 2005. 'Power, Subjectivity, and Ethics in Qualitative Research'. Pp. 19–29. In *Qualitative Research Methods in Human Geography,* 2nd edition, edited by I. Hay. Melbourne: Oxford University Press.

Downe, P. 1997. 'Constructing a Complex of Contagion: The Perceptions of AIDS Among Working Prostitutes in South America'. *Social Science & Medicine* 44(10): 1575–83.

Draucker, C.B. 1999. 'The Emotional Impact of Sexual Violence Research on Participants'. *Archives of Psychiatric Nursing* 13(4): 161–69.

Driscoll, T.R., B.P. Hill, J.A. Mandryk, R.A. Mitchell and A.S. Howland. 1997. 'Minimizing the Personal Cost of Involvement in Research into Traumatic Death'. *Safety Science* 25(3): 45–53.

Dunbar, C., D. Rodriquez and L. Parker. 2002. 'Race, Subjectivity, and the Interview Process'. Pp. 279–98. In *Handbook of Interview Research*, edited by J.F. Gubrium and J.A. Holstein. Thousand Oaks, CA: Sage Publications.

Dunlap, E., B. Johnson, H. Sanabria, E. Holliday, V. Lipsey, M. Barnett, W. Hopkins, I. Sobel, D. Randolph and K-L. Chin. 1990. 'Studying Crack Users and Their Criminal Careers: The Scientific and Artistic Aspects of Locating Hard-To-Reach Subjects and Interviewing Them About Sensitive Topics'. *Contemporary Drug Problems* 17(Spring): 121–44.

Dunn, L. 1991. 'Research Alert!: Qualitative Research may be Hazardous to Your Health!'. *Qualitative Health Research* 1(3): 388–92.

Dunne, G.A. 1999. *The Different Dimensions of Gay Fatherhood: Exploding the Myths.* Report to the Economic and Social Research Council, London School of Economics, London.

Dunne, G.A. 2000. 'Opting into Motherhood: Lesbians Blurring the Boundaries and Re-Defining the Meaning of Parenting and Kinship'. *Gender & Society* 14: 11–35.

Dunne, G.A., S. Prendergast and D. Telford. 2002. 'Young, Gay, Homeless and Invisible: A Growing Populations?'. *Culture, Health & Sexuality* 4(1): 103–15.

Dworkin, R.J. 1992. *Researching Persons With Mental Illness.* Newbury Park, CA: Sage Publications.

Dwyer, K. 1982. *Moroccan Dialogues: Anthropology in Question.* Baltimore: Johns Hopkins University Press.

Dyregrov, K. 2004. 'Bereaved Parents' Experience of Research Participation'. *Social Science and Medicine* 58(2): 391–400.

Ebata, A. 1996. 'Making University-Community Collaborations Work: Challenges for Institution and Individuals'. *Journal of Research on Adolescence* 6(1): 71–79.

Eco, U. 1984. *Postscripts to the Name of the Rose.* (Translated by W. Weaver). San Diego, CA: Harcourt Brace Jovanovich.

Eder, D. and L. Fingerson. 2002. 'Interviewing Children and Adolescents'. Pp. 181–201. In *Handbook of Interview Research: Context & Method,* edited by J.F. Gubrium and J.A. Holstein. Thousand Oaks, CA: Sage Publications.

Edwards, R. 1990. 'Connecting Method and Epistemology: A White Woman Interviewing Black Women', *Women's Studies International Forum* 13: 477–90.

Edwards, R. 1993. 'An Education in Interviewing: Placing the Researcher and the Research'. Pp. 181–96. In *Researching Sensitive Topics,* edited by C.M. Renzetti and R.M. Lee. Newbury Park: Sage Publications.

Einhorn, L.J. 2000. *The Native American Oral Tradition: Voices of the Spirit and Soul.* Westport, CT: Praeger.

Eisner, E. 1995. 'What Artistically Crafted Research can Help us to Understand about Schools'. *Educational Theory* 45(1): 1–13.

Eisner, E.W. 1998. *The Enlightened Eye: Qualitative Inquiry and the Enhancement of Educational Practice.* Upper Saddle River, NJ: Prentice Hall.

Ellingson, L.L. 2005. *Communicating in the Clinic: Negotiating Frontstage and Backstage Teamwork.* Cresskill, NJ: Hampton.

Ellingson, L.L. 2006. 'Embodied Knowledge: Writing Researchers' Bodies Into Qualitative Health Research'. *Qualitative Health Research* 16(2): 298–310.

Elliott, H. 1997. 'The Use of Diaries in Sociological Research on Health Experience'. *Sociological Research Online* 2(2). Available at: http://www.socresonline.org.ul/socresonline/2/2/7.html (Accessed 2/3/2005).

Ellis, C. 1991. 'Emotional Sociology'. Pp. 123–45. In *Studies in Symbolic Interaction,* vol 12, edited by N.K. Denzin. Greenwich, Conn: JAI Press.

Ellis, C. 1993. 'There Are Survivors: Telling a Story of Sudden Death'. *Sociological Quarterly* 34: 711–30.

Ellis, C. 1995a. *Final Negotiations: A Story of Love, Loss and Chronic Illness*. Philadelphia, PA: Temple University Press.

Ellis, C. 1995b. 'Speaking of Dying: An Ethnographic Short Story'. *Symbolic Interaction* 18 (1): 73–81.

Ellis, C. 1997. What Counts as Scholarship in Communication? An Autoethnographic Response'. Paper presented at a National Communication Association Research Board Session entitled What Counts as Scholarship in Communication? Evaluating Trends in Performance Studies, Autoethnography, and Communication Research. November, Chicago, IL. Available at: http://acjournal.org/holdings/vol1/Iss2/special/ellis.htm (Accessed 12/7/2005).

Ellis, C. 1998. ' "I Hate My Voice": Coming to Terms with Minor Bodily Stigmas'. *Sociological Quarterly* 39: 517–37.

Ellis, C. 2001. 'With Mother/With Child: A True Story', *Qualitative Inquiry* 7(5): 598.

Ellis, C. 2002. 'Shattered Lives: Making Sense of September 11th and its Aftermath'. *Journal of Contemporary Ethnography* 31: 375–410.

Ellis, C. 2004. *The Ethnographic I: A Methodological Novel About Teaching and Doing Autoethnography*. Walnut Creek, CA: AltaMira.

Ellis, C. and A.P. Bochner. 1992. 'Telling and Performing Personal Stories: The Constraints of Choice in Abortion'. Pp. 79–101. In *Investigating Subjectivity*, edited by C. Ellis and M.G. Flaherty. Newbury Park, CA: Sage Publications.

Ellis, C. and A.P. Bochner. (eds). 1996. *Composing Ethnography: Alternative Forms of Qualitative Writing*. Walnut Creek, CA: AltaMira.

Ellis, C. and A.P. Bochner. 2000. 'Autoethnography, Personal Narrative, Reflexivity: Researcher as Subject'. Pp. 733–68. In *Handbook of Qualitative Research*, 2nd edition, edited by N. Denzin and Y. Lincoln. Thousand Oaks, CA: Sage Publications.

Ellis, C. and L. Ellingson. 2000. 'Qualitative Methods'. Pp. 2287–96. In *Encyclopedia of Sociology*, 2nd edition, edited by E. Borgatta and R. Montgomery. New York: Macmillan.

Ellis, C. and L. Berger. 2002. 'Their Story/My Story/Our Story: Including the Researcher's Experience in Interview Research'. Pp. 849–75. In *Handbook of Interview Research: Context & Method*, edited by J.F. Gubrium and J.A. Holstein. Thousand Oaks, CA: Sage Publications.

Ellsberg, M., L. Heise, R. Peña, S. Agurto and A. Winkvist. 2001. 'Researching Domestic Violence Against Women: Methodological and Ethical Considerations'. *Studies in Family Planning* 32(1): 1–16.

Ely, M., R. Vinz, M. Downing and M. Anzul. 1997. *On Writing Qualitative Research: Living by Words*. London: Falmer Press.

Emanuel, E.J., D. Wendler and C. Grady. 2000. 'What Makes Clinical Research Ethical?' *Journal of the American Medical Association* 283(20): 2701–11.

Emerson, R.M. (ed.). 2001. *Contemporary Field Research: Perspectives and Formulations*, 2nd edition. Prospect Heights, IL: Waveland Press.

Epstein, Y.M., H.S. Rosenberg, T.V. Grant and B.A.N. Hemenway. 2002. 'Use of the Internet as the Only Outlet for Talking about Infertility'. *Fertility and Sterility* 78(3): 507–14.

Erikson, K.T. 1967. 'Disguised Observation in Sociology'. *Social Problems* 14: 366–72.

Errante, A. 2004. 'But Sometimes You're Not Part of the Story: Oral Histories and Ways of Remembering and Telling'. Pp. 411–34. In *Feminist Perspectives on Social Research*, edited by S.N. Hesse-Biber and M.L. Yaiser. New York: Oxford University Press.

Espin, O.M. 1995. ' "Race", Racism, and Sexuality in the Life Narratives of Immigrant Women'. *Feminist and Psychology* 5: 223–38.

Espiritu, Y.L. 1997. *Asian Women and Men: Labor, Laws, and Love.* Thousand Oaks, CA: Sage Publications.

Esposito, L. and J.W. Murphy. 2000. Another Step in the Study of Race Relations'. *Sociological Quarterly* 41(2): 171–87.

Esposito, N. 2005. 'Manifestations of Enduring During Interviews With Sexual Assault Victims'. *Qualitative Health Research* 15(7): 912–27.

Etherington, K. 1996. 'The Counsellor as Researcher: Boundary Issues and Critical Dilemmas'. *British Journal of Guidance and Counselling* 24(3): 339–46.

Ezzy, D. 2002. *Qualitative Analysis: Practice and Innovation.* Sydney: Allen & Unwin.

Falk, G. 2001. *Stigma: How We Treat Outsiders.* New York: Prometheus.

Fals-Borda, O. 1991. 'Remaking Knowledge'. Pp. 349–56. In *Action and Knowledge: Breaking the Monopoly with Participatory Action Research*, edited by O. Fals-Borda and M.A. Rahman. London: Intermediate Technology Publications.

Farquhar, S.A. and S. Wing. 2003. 'Methodological and Ethical Considerations in Community-Driven Environmental Justice Research'. Pp. 221–41. In *Community-Based Participatory Research for Health*, edited by M. Minkler and N. Wallestein. San Francisco: Jossey-Bass.

Faugier, J. and M. Sargeant. 1997. 'Sampling Hard-to-reach Populations'. *Journal of Advanced Nursing* 26: 790–97.

Ferrell, J. and M.S. Hamm. (eds). 1998. *Ethnography at the Edge: Crime, Deviance, and Field Research.* Boston: Northeastern University Press.

Ferri, B. 2000. 'The Hidden Cost of Difference: Women with Learning Disabilities'. *Learning Disabilties: A Multidisciplinary Journal*, 10(3): 129–38.

Fife, W. 2005. *Doing Fieldwork: Ethnographic Methods for Research in Developing Countries and Beyond.* New York: Palgrave Macmillan.

Fine, C. 1994. 'Working the Hyphens: Reinventing Self and Other in Qualitative Research'. Pp. 70–82. In *Handbook of Qualitative Research*, edited by N.K. Denzin and Y.S., Lincoln. Thousand Oaks, CA: Sage Publications.

Finley, S. 2005. 'Arts-Based Inquiry: Performing Revolutionary Pedagogy'. Pp. 681–94. In *The Sage Handbook of Qualitative Research,* 3rd edition, edited by N.K. Denzin and Y.S. Lincoln. Thousand Oaks, CA: Sage Publications.

Finn, J. 1999. 'An Exploration of Helping Processes in an Online Self-Help Group Focusing On Issues of Disability'. *Health & Social Work* 24: 220–31.

Fisher, C.B. and K. Ragsdale. 2005. 'Goodness-of-Fit Ethics for Multicultural Research'. Pp. 3–25. In *Handbook of Ethical Research with Ethnocultural Populations and Communities*, edited by J.E. Trimble and C.B. Fisher. Thousand Oaks, CA: Sage Publications.

Fisk, M. and V. Wigley. 2000. 'Accessing and Interviewing the Oldest Old in Care Homes'. *Quality in Ageing* 1(1): 27–33.

Flaskerud, J.H. and B.J. Winslow. 1998. 'Conceptualising Vulnerable Populations in Health-Related Research'. *Nursing Research* 47(2): 69–78.

Fluehr-Lobban, C. (ed). 2003. *Ethics and the Profession of Anthropology*, 2nd edition. Walnut Creek, CA: AltaMira.

Foley, D. and A. Valenzuela. 2005. 'Critical Ethnography: The Politics of Collaboration'. Pp. 217–34. In *The Sage Handbook of Qualitative Research,* 3rd edition, edited by N.K. Denzin and Y.S. Lincoln. Thousand Oaks, CA: Sage Publications.

Fonow, M.M. and J.A. Cook. 1991. 'Back to the Future: A Look at the Second Wave of Feminist Epistemology and Methodology'. Pp. 1–15. In *Beyond Methodology: Feminist Scholarship as Lived Research*, edited by M.M. Fonow and J.A. Cook. Bloomington: Indiana University Press.

Fontana, A. 2002. 'Postmodern Trends in Interviewing'. Pp. 161–75. In *Handbook of Interview Research: Context & Method*, edited by J.F. Gubrium and J.A. Holstein. Thousand Oaks, CA: Sage Publications.

Fontana, A. and J.H. Frey. 2005. 'The Interview: From Neutral Stance to Political Involvement'. Pp. 695–727. In *The Sage Handbook of Qualitative Research, 3rd edition*, edited by N.K. Denzin and Y.S. Lincoln. Thousand Oaks, CA: Sage Publications.

Fontana, A. and R. Schmidt (with Jennifer O'Brian). 1998. 'The Fluid Self'. Presented at the Society for the Study of Symbolic Interaction, August 22–23, San Francisco.

Fontana, A. and R. Schmidt. 1999. 'Castrato: Predetermined to Fluid Self or a Dialogue/Performance Script Intended to Inform Garfinkel About the Possibilities of Gendering'. Pp. 81–90. In *Studies in Symbolic Interaction: A Research Annual, Vol. 23*, edited by N.K. Denzin. Greenwich, CT: JAI.

France, A., G. Bendelow and S. Williams. 'A "Risky" business: Researching the Health Beliefs of Children and Young People'. Pp. 150–62. In *Researching Children's Perspectives*, edited by A. Lewis and G. Lindsay. Buckingham: Open University Press.

Frank, G. 2000. *Venus on Wheels: Two Decades of Dialogue on Disability, Biography, and Being Female in America*. Berkeley: University of California Press.

Freire, P. 1982. 'Creating Alternative Research Methods and Learning to Do It by Doing It'. Pp. 29–37. In *Creating Knowledge: A Monopoly? Participatory Research in Development*, edited by B. Hall, A. Gillette and R. Tandon. *Participatory Research Network Series, No. 1*. New Delhi: Society for Participatory Research in Asia.

Freire, P. 1997. 'Foreword'. Pp. xi–xiii. In *Nurtured by Knowledge: Learning to Do Participatory Action-Research*, edited by S.E. Smith, D.G. Williams and N.A. Johnson. New York: Apex Press.

Frey, J.H. and A. Fontana. 1993. 'The Group Interview in Social Research'. Pp. 20–34. In *Successful Focus Groups: Advancing the State of the Art*, edited by D.L. Morgan. Newbury Park, CA: Sage Publications.

Frijda, N.H. 1986. *The Emotions*. London: Cambridge University Press.

Gaglio, B., C.C. Nelson and D. King. 2006. 'The Role of Rapport: Lessons Learned from Conducting Research in a Primary Care Setting'. *Qualitative Health Research* 16(5): 723–34.

Gagné, P. 1996. 'Identity, Strategy, and Feminist Politics: Clemency for Battered Women who Kill'. *Social Problems* 43: 77–93.

Gair, S. 2002. 'In the Thick of It: A Reflective Tale From an Australian Social Worker/Qualitative Researcher'. *Qualitative Health Research* 12(1): 130–39.

Galvin, R.D. 2005. 'Researching the Disabled Identity: Contextualising the Identity Transformations which Accompany the Onset of Impairment'. *Sociology of Health and Illness* 27(3): 393–413.

Gamson, W.A. 2002. 'How Storytelling can be Empowering'. Pp. 187–98. In *Culture in Mind: Toward a Sociology of Culture and Cognition*, edited by K.A. Cerulo. New York: Routledge.

Garfinkel, H. 1996. 'An Overview of Ethnomethodology's Program', *Social Psychology Quarterly* 59: 5–21.

Gianotten, V. and T. de Wit. 1991. 'Action and Participatory Research: A Case of Peasant Organization'. Pp. 64–83. In *Action and Knowledge: Breaking the Monopoly with Participatory Action Research*, edited by O. Fals-Borda and M.A. Rahman. London: Intermediate Technology Publications.

Gibson, B.E. 2005. 'Co-producing Video Diaries: The Presence of the "Absent" Researcher'. *International Journal of Qualitative Methods* 4(4). Available at: http://www.ualberta.ca/~iiqm/backissues/4_4/html/gibson.htm (Accessed 14/4/2006).

Gilbert, K.R. 2001a. 'Introduction'. Pp. 3–15. In *The Emotional Nature of Qualitative Research*, edited by K.R. Gilbert. London: CRC.

Gilbert, K.R. 2001b. 'Collateral Damage? Indirect Exposure of Staff Members to the Emotions of Qualitative Research'. Pp. 147–61. In *The Emotional Nature of Qualitative Research*, edited by K.R. Gilbert. London: CRC.

Gilhooly, M. 2002. 'Ethical Issues in Researching Later Life'. Pp. 211–25. In *Researching Ageing and Later Life*, edited by A. Jamieson and C.R. Victor. Buckingham: Open University Press.

Gilmore, S., J. DeLamater and D. Wagstaff. 1996. 'Sexual Decision-Making by Inner-City Black Adolescent Males: A Focus Group Study'. *Journal of Sex Research* 33: 363–71.

Gimlin, D. 2000. 'Cosmetic Surgery: Beauty as Commodity'. *Qualitative Sociology* 23(1): 77–98.

Glantz, N.M., D.C. Halperin and L.M. Hunt. 1998. 'Studying Domestic Violence in Chiapas, Mexico'. *Qualitative Health Research* 8(3): 377–92.

Glesne, C.E. 1997. 'That Rare Feeling: Re-Presenting Research Through Poetic Transcription'. *Qualitative Inquiry* 3(2): 202–21.

Glesne, C. and A. Peshkin. 1992. *Becoming Qualitative Researchers: An Introduction.* London: Longman.

Gluck, S.B. 1984. 'What's so Special About Women: Women's Oral History'. Pp. 221–37. In *Oral History: An Interdisciplinary Anthology*, edited by D. Dunaway and W.K. Baum. Nashville, TH: American Association for State and Local History.

Gluck, S.B. and D. Patai. (eds). 1991. *Women's Words: The Feminist Practice of Oral History.* New York: Routledge.

Goffman, E. 1959. *The presentation of Self in Everyday Life.* Doubleday, New York.

Goffman, E. 1961. *Asylums: Essays on the Social Situation of Mental Patients and Other Inmates.* Garden City, NY: Doubleday.

Goffman, E. 1963. *Stigma: Notes on the Management of Spoiled Identity.* Englewood Cliffs, NJ: Prentice Hall.

Goffman, E. 1973. 'The Mortification of Self'. Pp. 175–88. In *Conformity, Resistance and Self-Determination*, edited by R. Flacks. Boston, MA: Little, Brown.

Goldstein, D.M. 2003. *Laughter Out of Place: Race, Class, Violence, and Sexuality in a Rio Shantytown.* Berkeley, CA: University of California Press.

Goode, E. 2002. 'Sexual Involvement and Social Research in a Fat Civil Rights Organization'. *Qualitative Sociology* 25: 501–34.

Goodman, J.H. 2004. 'Coping with Trauma and Hardship Among Unaccompanied Refugee Youths from Sudan'. *Qualitative Health Research* 14(9): 1177–96.

Goodwin, D., C. Pope, M. Mort and A. Smith. 2003. 'Ethics and Ethnography: An Experiential Account'. *Qualitative Health Research* 13(4): 567–77.

Graham, H. 1983. 'Do Her Answers Fit His Questions? Women and the Survey Method'. Pp. 132–46. In *The Public and the Private*, edited by E. Gamarnikow, D.H.J. Morgan, J. Purvis and D. Taylorson. London: Heinemann.

Gray, R. and C. Sinding. 2002. *Standing Ovation: Performing Social Science Research About Cancer.* Walnut Creek, CA: AltaMira.

Grbich, C. 2004. *New Approaches in Social Research.* London: Sage Publications.

Greenfield, T.K., L.T. Midanik and J.D. Rogers. 2000. 'Effects of Telephone Versus Face-to-Face Interview Modes on Reports of Alcohol Consumption'. *Addiction* 95: 277–84.

Gregory, D., C.K. Russell and L.R. Phillips. 1997. 'Beyond Textual Perfection: Transcribers as Vulnerable Persons'. *Qualitative Health Research* 7(2): 294–300.

Gregory, S. and L. McKie. 1996. 'Reflecting on the Process and Methods of Researching Women's Health'. Pp. 251–65. In *Researching Women's Health: Methods and Process*, edited by L. McKie. Dinton: Quay Books.

Griffiths, P., M. Gossop, B. Powis and J. Strang. 1993. 'Reaching Hidden Populations of Drug Users by Privileged Access Interviewers: Methodological and Practical Issues'. *Addiction* 88: 1617–26.

Grinyer, A. 2004. 'The Narrative Correspondence Method: What a Follow-Up Study Can Tell Us About the Longer Term Effect on Participants in Emotionally Demanding Research'. *Qualitative Health Research* 14(10): 1326–41.

Grinyer, A. 2005. 'Personal Agenda in Emotionally Demanding Research'. *Social Research Update* 46. Available at: http://www.soc.surrey.ac.uk/sru/ (Accessed 3/3/2006).

Groger, L., P. Mayberry and J. Straker. 1999. 'What We Didn't Learn Because of Who Would Not Talk to Us'. *Qualitative Health Research* 9(6): 829–35.

Gueldner, S.H. and M.B. Hanner. 1989. 'Methodological Issues Related to Gerontological Nursing Research'. *Nursing Research* 38: 183–85.

Guillemin, M. 1999. ' "Mauve-That's an Old Woman's Colour": Women's Visual Representation of Menopause'. Pp. 56–69. In *Older Women in Australia*, edited by S. Feldman and M. Poole. Sydney: Allen & Unwin.

Guillemin, M. 2004a. 'Understanding Illness: Using Drawings as a Research Method'. *Qualitative Health Research* 14(2): 272–89.

Guillemin, M. 2004b. 'Embodying Heart Disease Through Drawings'. *Health: An Interdisciplinary Journal for the Social Study of Health, Illness and Medicine* 8(2): 223–39.

Gunsalus, C.K. 2002. 'Rethinking Protections for Human Subjects'. *Chronicle of Higher Education* November 15: B24.

Gurevitch, Z. 2000. 'The Serious Play of Writing'. *Qualitative Inquiry* 6(1): 3–8.

Gysels, M., R. Pool and B. Nnalusiba. 2002. 'Women who Sell Sex in a Ugandan Trading Town: Life Histories, Survival Strategies and Risk'. *Social Science and Medicine* 54: 179–92.

Hagedorn, M. 1994. 'Hermeneutic Photography: An Innovative Aesthetic Technique for Generating Data in Nursing Research'. *Advances in Nursing Science* 17(1): 44–50.

Haglund, K. 2003. 'Sexually Abstinent African American Adolescent Female's Descriptions of Abstinence'. *Journal of Nursing Scholarship* 35(3): 231–36.

Haglund, K. 2004. 'Conducting Life History Research With Adolescents'. *Qualitative Health Research* 14(9): 1309–19.

Hall, B.L. 1981. 'Participatory Research, Popular Knowledge and Power: A Personal Reflection'. *Convergence* XIV(3): 6–17.

Hall, B.L. 1997. 'Preface'. Pp. xiii–xv. In *Nurtured by Knowledge: Learning to Do Participatory Action-Research*, edited by S.E. Smith, D.G. Williams and N.A. Johnson. New York: Apex Press.

Hall, B.L. and J.C. Kulig. 2004. 'Kanadier Mennonites: A Case Study Examining Research Challenges Among Religious Groups'. *Qualitative Health Research* 14(3): 359–68.

Hallowell, L. 1985. 'The Outcome of the Brajuha Case: Legal Implications for Sociologists'. *Footnotes* 13: 13.

Hallowell, N., J. Lawton and S. Gregory. 2005. *Reflections on Research: The Realities of Doing Research in the Social Sciences*. Berkshire: Open University Press.

Hammersley, M. and P. Atkinson. 1995. *Ethnography: Principles in Practice*, 2nd edition, Routledge, London.

Harden, J., S. Scott, K. Backett-Milburn and S. Jackson. 2000. 'Can't Talk, Won't Talk?: Methodological Issues in Researching Children'. *Sociological Research Online* 5(2). Available at: http://www.socresonline.org.uk/5/2/harden.html (Accessed 13/10/2005).

Harding, S. 1987. 'Conclusion: Epistemological Questions'. Pp. 181–90. In *Feminism and Methodology*, edited by S. Harding. Bloomington, IN: Indiana University Press.

Harding, S. 1991. *Whose Science, Whose Knowledge? Thinking From Women's Lives*. Ithaca: Cornell University Press.

Harding, S. 1992. 'After the Neutrality Ideal: Science, Politics, and "Strong Objectivity"'. *Social Research* 59(3): 567–88.

Harper, D. 2001. *Changing Works: Visions of a Lost Agriculture*. Chicago: University of Chicago Press.

Harper, D. 2002. 'Talking About Pictures: A Case for Photo Elicitation'. *Visual Studies* 17(1): 13–26.

Harper, D. 2005. 'What's New Visually?'. Pp. 747–62. In *The Sage Handbook of Qualitative Research*, 3rd edition, edited by N.K. Denzin and Y.S. Lincoln. Thousand Oaks, CA: Sage Publications.

Harper, D. and P. Faccioli. 2000. 'Small Silly Insults', Mutual Seduction and Misogyny: The Interpretation of Italian Advertising Signs'. *Visual Sociology* 15(1/2): 23–49.

Harris, J. 2000. 'Self-Harm: Cutting the Bad Out of Me'. *Qualitative Health Research* 10(2): 164–73.

Harris, J. 2002. 'The Correspondence Method as a Data-Gathering Technique in Qualitative Enquiry'. *International Journal of Qualitative Methods* 1(4), Article 1. Available at: http://www.ualberta.ca/~ijqm/ (Accessed 6/12/2005).

Harris, J. and A. Huntington. 2001. 'Emotions as Analytic Tools: Qualitative Research, Feelings, and Psychotherapeutic Insight'. Pp. 129–45. In *The Emotional Nature of Qualitative Research*, edited by K.R. Gilbert. London: CRC.

Harrison, B. 2002. 'Seeing Health and Illness Worlds – Using Visual Methodologies in a Sociology of Health and Illness: A Methodological Review'. *Sociology of Health and Illness* 24(6): 856–72.

Hart, N. and A. Crawford-Wright. 1999. 'Research as Therapy, Therapy as Research: Ethical Dilemmas in New-Paradigm Research'. *British Journal of Guidance and Counselling* 27: 205–14.

Heary, C. and E. Hennessy. 2002. 'The Use of Focus Group Interviews in Pediatric Health Care Research'. *Journal of Pediatric Psychology* 27: 47–57.

Heckathorn, D. 1997. 'Respondent-Driven Sampling: A New Approach to the Study of Hidden Populations'. *Social Problems* 44: 174–99.

Heintzelman, C. 1996. 'Human Subjects and Informed Consent: The Legacy of the Tuskegee Syphilis Study'. *Scholars: Research, Teaching and Public Service* Fall: 23–29.

Hennessy, E. and C. Heary. 2005. 'Exploring Children's Views Through Focus Groups'. Pp. 236–52. In *Researching Children's Experiences*, edited by S. Greene and D. Hogan. London: Sage Publications.

Henslin, J.M. 2001. 'Studying Deviance in Four Settings: Research Experiences With Cabbies, Suicides, Drug Users, and Abortionees'. Pp. 3–34. In *Ethnography Volume II*, edited by A. Bryman. London: Sage Publications.

Herth, K. 1998. 'Hope as Seen Through the Eyes of Homeless Children'. *Journal of Advanced Nursing* 28(5): 1053–62.

Hertz, R. 1997. *Reflexivity and Voice*. Thousand Oaks, CA: Sage Publications.

Herzog, H. 2005. 'On Home Turf: Interview Location and Its Social Meaning'. *Qualitative Sociology* 28(1): 25–47.

Hess, R.F. 2006. 'Postabortion Research: Methodological and Ethical Issues'. *Qualitative Health Research* 16(4): 580–87.

Hesse-Biber, S.N. and D. Leckenby. 2004. 'How Feminists Practice Social Research'. Pp. 209–26. In *Feminist Perspectives on Social Research*, edited by S.N. Hesse-Biber and M.L. Yaiser. New York: Oxford University Press.

Hesse-Biber, S.N. and L.P. Leavy. 2005. *The Practice of Qualitative Research*. Thousand Oaks, CA: Sage Publications.

Hesse-Biber, S.N., P. Leavy and M.L. Yaiser. 2004. 'Feminist Approaches to Research as a Process: Reconceptualizing Epistemology, Methodology, and Method'. Pp. 3–26. In *Feminist Perspectives on Social Research*, edited by S.N. Hesse-Biber and M.L. Yaiser. New York: Oxford University Press.

Hessler, R. 2006. 'The Methodology of Internet Research: Some Lessons Learned'. Pp. 105–20. *Health Research in Cyberspace: Methodological, Practical and Personal Issues*, edited by P. Liamputtong. New York: Nova Science Publishers.

Hessler, R.M., J. Downing, C. Beltz, A. Pelliccio, M. Powell. M. and W. Vale. 2003. 'Qualitative Research on Adolescent Risk Using E-Mail: A Methodological Assessment'. *Qualitative Sociology* 26(1): 111–24.

Hessler, R.M., S. Hollis and C. Crowe. 1998. 'Peer Mediation: A Qualitative Study of Youthful Frames of Power and Influence'. *Mediation Quarterly* 15(3): 187–98.

Hewitt, R. and S. Stevens. 2006. 'Cross-Cultural Research: Ethics, Methods, and Relationships'. Pp. 30–50. In *Qualitative Research Methods in Human Geography*, 2nd edition, edited by I. Hay. Melbourne: Oxford University Press.

Hill, M. 1997. 'Participatory Research With Children: Research Review'. *Child and Family Social Work* 2: 171–83.

Hirst, J. 2004. 'Researching Young Peoples' Sexuality and Learning about Sex: Experience, Need, and Sex and Relationship Education'. *Culture, Health and Sexuality* 6(2): 115–29.

Hobbs, D. 2001. 'Ethnography and the Study of Deviance'. Pp. 204–19. In *Handbook of Ethnography*, edited by P. Atkinson, A. Coffey, S. Delamont, J. Lofland and L. Lofland. London: Sage Publications.

Hoeyer, K., L. Dahlager and N. Lynöe. 2005. 'Conflicting Notions of Research Ethics: The Mutually Challenging Traditions of Social Scientists and Medical Researchers'. *Social Science and Medicine* 61: 1741–49.

Hoffman, D. and T. Novak. 1998. 'Bridging the Racial Divide on the Internet'. *Science* 280: 390–91.

Holge-Hazelton, B. 2006. Youth and Chronic Illness: Developing Insight into the Lives of Young People with Diabetes by Using Internet Based Interviews'. Pp. 159–70. In *Health Research in Cyberspace: Methodological, Practical and Personal Issues*, edited by P. Liamputtong. New York: Nova Science Publishers.

Holkup, P.A., T. Tripp-Reimer, E.M. Salois and C. Weinert. 2004. 'Community-Based Participatory Research: An Approach to Intervention Research with a Native American Community'. *Advances in Nursing Science* 27(3): 162–75.

Hollander, J.A. 2001. 'Vulnerability and Dangerousness: The Construction of Gender through Conversation about Violence'. *Gender & Society* 15(1): 83–109.

Hollway, W. and T. Jefferson. 2000. *Doing Qualitative Research Differently: Free Association, Narrative and the Interview Method*. London: Sage Publications.

Holman Jones, S. 2005. 'Autoethnography: Making the Personal Political'. Pp. 763–91. In *The Sage Handbook of Qualitative Research,* 3rd edition, edited by N.K. Denzin and Y.S. Lincoln. Thousand Oaks, CA: Sage Publications.

Holstein, J.A. and J.F. Gubrium. 2004. 'The Active Interview'. Pp. 140–61. In *Qualitative Research: Theory, Method and Practice*, edited by D. Silverman. London: Sage Publications.

Holt, C.L. and S.M. McClure. 2006. 'Perceptions of the Religion-Health Connection Among African American Church Members'. *Qualitative Health Research* 16(2): 268–81.

Honey, A. and C. Halse. 2006. 'The Specifics of Coping: Parents of Daughters With Anorexia Nervosa'. *Qualitative Health Research* 16(5): 611–29.

Hopper, C.B. and J. Moore. 2001. 'Women in Outlaw Motorcycle Gangs'. Pp. 138–54. In *Extreme Methods: Innovative Approaches to Social Science Research*, edited by J.M. Miller and R. Tewksbury. Boston: Allyn and Bacon.

Hubbard, G., K. Backett-Milburn and D. Kemmer. 2001. 'Working with Emotions: Issues for the Researcher in Fieldwork and Teamwork'. *International Journal of Social Research Methodology* 4(2): 119–37.

Huber, J. and D. Clandinin. 2002. 'Ethical Dilemmas in Relational Narrative Inquiry with Children'. *Qualitative Inquiry* 8(6): 785–803.

Huby, G. 1997. 'Interpreting Silence, Documenting Experience: An Anthropological Approach to the Study of Health Service Users' Experience with HIV/AIDS Care in Lothian, Scotland'. *Social Science & Medicine* 44(8): 1149–60.

Huff, J.K. 1997. 'The Sexual Harassment of Researchers by Research Subjects: Lessons from the Field'. Pp. 115–27. In *Researching Sexual Violence Against Women: Methodological and Personal Perspectives*, edited by M.D. Schwartz. Thousand Oaks, CA: Sage Publications.

Huisman, K.A. 1997. 'Studying Violence Against Women of Color: Problems Faced by a White Woman'. Pp. 179–92. In *Researching Sexual Violence Against Women: Methodological and Personal Perspectives*, edited by M.D. Schwartz. Thousand Oaks, CA: Sage Publications.

Humphreys, L. 1970. *Tearoom Trade: Impersonal Sex in Public Places*. Chicago: Aldine.

Humphreys, L. 1975. *Tearoom Trade: Impersonal Sex in Public Places,* 2nd edition. Chicago: Aldine.

Humphries, B. and M. Martin. 2000. 'Disrupting Ethics in Social Research'. Pp. 69–85. In *Research in Social Care and Social Welfare*, edited by B. Humphries. London: Jessica Kingsley.

Hurworth, R. 2003. 'Photo-Interviewing For Research'. *Social Research Update* 40. Available at: http://www.soc.surrey.ac.uk/sru/SRU40.html (Accessed 14/4/2006).

Husaini, B.A., D.E. Sherkat, R. Bragg, R. Levine, J.S. Emerson, C.M. Mentes and V.A. Cain. 2001. 'Predictors of Breast Cancer Screening in a Panel Study of African American Women'. *Women & Health* 34(3): 35–51.

Huss, E. and J. Cwikel. 2005. 'Researching Creations: Applying Arts-Based Research to Bedouin Women's Drawings'. International Journal of Qualitative Methods 4(4). Available at: http://www.ualberta.ca/~ijqm/backissues/4_4/pdf/huss.pdf (Accessed 12/4/2006).

Hutchinson, S.A., M.E. Wilson and H.S. Wilson. 1994. 'Benefits of Participating in Research Interviews'. *IMAGE: Journal of Nursing Scholarship* 26(2): 161–64.

Hutchinson, S., W. Marsiglio and M. Cohan. 2002. 'Interviewing Young Men About Sex and Procreation: Methodological Issues'. *Qualitative Health Research* 12(1): 42–60.

Hyde, A., E. Howlett, D. Brady and J. Drennan. 2005. 'The Focus Group Method: Insights From Focus Group Interviews on Sexual Health With Adolescents'. *Social Science and Medicine* 61: 2588–99.

Hyers, L.L., J.K. Swim and R.M. Mallett. 2006. 'The Personal is Political: Using Daily Diaries to Examine Everyday Gender-Related Experiences'. Pp. 313–35. In *Emergent Methods in Social Research*, edited by S.N. Hesse-Biber and P. Leavy. Thousand Oaks, CA: Sage Publications.

Illingworth, N. 2001. 'The Internet Matters: Exploring the Use of the Internet as a Research Tool'. *Sociological Research Online* 6(2). Available at: www.socresonline. org.uk/6/2/illingworth.html (Accessed date 18/6/2003).

Im, E-O. and W. Chee. 2003. 'Feminist Issues in E-Mail Group Discussion among Cancer Patients'. *Advances in Nursing Science* 26(4): 287–98.

Im, E-O. and W. Chee 2006. 'Email Group Discussion among Cancer Patients: Feminist Issues'. Pp. 147–58. In *Health Research in Cyberspace: Methodological, Practical and Personal Issues*, edited by P. Liamputtong. New York: Nova Sciences Publishers.

Irwin, L.G. and J. Johnson. 2005. 'Interviewing Young Children: Explicating Our Practices and Dilemmas'. *Qualitative Health Research* 15(6): 821–31.

Jacelon, C.S. and K. Imperio. 2005. 'Participant Diaries as a Source of Data in Research with Older Adults'. *Qualitative Health Research* 15(7): 991–97.

James, T. and H. Platzer. 1999. 'Ethical Consideration in Qualitative Research with Vulnerable Groups: Exploring Lesbians' and Gay Men's Experiences of Health Care – A Personal Perspective'. *Nursing Ethics* 6(1): 73–81.

Jamieson, J. 2000. 'Negotiating Danger in Fieldwork on Crime: A Researcher's Tale'. Pp. 61–71. In *Danger in the Field: Risk and Ethics in Social Research*, edited by G. Lee-Treweek and S. Linkogle. London: Routledge.

Jarrett, R.L. 1993. 'Focus Group Interviewing with Low-Income Minority Populations: A Research Experience'. Pp. 184–201. In *Successful Focus Groups: Advancing the State of the Art*, edited by D.L. Morgan. Newbury Park, CA: Sage Publications.

Jarrett, R.L. 1994. 'Living Poor: Family Life among Single Parent, African-American Women'. *Social Problems* 41(1): 30–49.

Jewkes, R., L. Penn-Kenana and H. Rose-Junius. 2005. ' "If They Rape me, I Can't Blame Them": Reflections on Gender in the Social Context of Child Rape in South Africa and Namibia'. *Social Science & Medicine* 61: 1809–20.

Johnson, B. and J.M. Clarke. 2003. 'Collecting Sensitive Data: The Impact on Researchers', *Qualitative Health Research* 13(3): 421–34.

Johnson, J.M. 2002. 'In-Depth Interviewing' Pp. 103–119. In *Handbook of Interview Research: Context & Method*, edited by J.F. Gubrium and J.A. Holstein. Thousand Oaks, CA: Sage Publications.

Johnson, V., E. Ivan-Smith, G. Gordon, P. Pridmore and P. Scott. (eds). 1998. *Stepping Forward: Children and Young People's Participation in the Development Process*. London: Intermediate Technology Publications.

Jokinen, E. 2004. 'The Makings of Mother in Dairy Narratives'. *Qualitative Inquiry* 10(3): 339–59.

Jones, C. and J. Tannock. 2000. 'A Matter of Life and Death: A Reflective Account of Two Examples of Practitioner Research Into Children's Understanding and Experience of Death and Bereavement'. Pp. 86–97. In *Researching Children's Perspectives*, edited by A. Lewis and G. Lindsay. Buckingham: Open University Press.

Jones, J.H. 1993. *Bad Blood: The Tuskegee Syphilis Experiment*. New York: Free Press.

Jones, R.K. 2000. 'The Unsolicited Diary as a Qualitative Research Tool for Advanced Research Capacity in the Field of Health and Illness'. *Qualitative Health Research* 10(4): 555–67.

Kamberelis, G. and G. Dimitriadis. 2005. 'Focus Groups: Strategic Articulations of Pedagogy, Politics; and Inquiry'. Pp. 887–907. In The Sage Handbook of Qualitative Research, third edition, edited by N.K. Denzin and V.S. Lincoln. Thousand Oaks, CA: Sage Publications.

Kaufman, S.R. 1994. 'In-Depth Interviewing'. Pp. 123–36. In *Qualitative Methods in Aging Research*, edited by J.F. Gubrium and A. Sankar. Thousand Oaks, CA: Sage Publications.

Kavanaugh, K. and L. Ayres. 1998. 'Not as Bad as it Could Have Been: Assessing and Mitigating Harm during Research Interviews on Sensitive Topics'. *Research in Nursing & Health* 21: 91–97.

Keleher, H.M. and G.K. Verrinder. 2003. 'Health Diaries in a Rural Australian Study'. *Qualitative Health Research* 13(3): 435–43.

Kelly, J.A., Y.A. Amirkhanian, E. Kabakchieve, P. Csepe, D.W. Seal, R. Antonova, A. Mihaylov and G. Gyukits. 2004. 'Gender Roles and HIV Sexual Risk Vulnerability of Roma (Gypsies) Men and Women in Bulgaria and Hungary: An Ethnographic Study'. *AIDS Care* 16(2): 231–46.

Kemmis, S. and R. McTaggart. 2000. 'Participatory Action Research'. Pp. 567–605. In *Handbook of Qualitative Research*, edited by N.K. Denzin and Y.S. Lincoln. Thousand Oaks, CA: Sage Publications.

Kemmis, S. and R. McTaggart. 2005. 'Participatory Action Research: Communitative Action and the Public Sphere'. Pp. 559–604. In *The Sage Handbook of Qualitative Research,* 3rd edition, edited by N.K. Denzin and Y.S. Lincoln. Thousand Oaks, CA: Sage Publications.

Kenyon, E. and S. Hawker. 2000. ' "Once Would Be Enough": Some Reflections on the Issue of Safety for Lone Researcher'. *International Journal of Social Research Methodology* 2(4): 313–27.

Kerr, D. 2003. 'We Know What the Problem Is: Using Oral History to Develop a Collaborative Analysis of Homelessness from the Bottom Up'. *The Oral History Review* 30(1): 27–45.

Khanlou, N. and E. Peter. 2005. 'Participatory Action Research: Considerations for Ethical Review'. *Social Science and Medicine* 60: 2333–40.

Kiesinger, C. 1998. 'From Interview to Story: Writing "Abbie's Life" '. *Qualitative Inquiry* 4(1): 71–96.

King, R.D. and E. Wincup. (eds). 2000, *Doing Research on Crime and Justice*, Oxford University Press, New York.

Kirby, R. and J. Corzine. 1981. 'The Contagion of Stigma: Fieldwork among Deviants'. *Qualitative Sociology* 4(1): 3–20.

Kitson, G.C., R.D. Clark, N.B. Rushforth, P.M. Brinich, H.S. Sudak and S.J. Zyzanski. 1996. 'Research on Difficult Family Topics: Helping New and Experienced Researchers Cope with Research on Loss'. *Family Relations* 45(2): 183–88.

Kitzinger, J. 1994a. 'The Methodology of Focus Groups: The Importance of Interaction between Research Participants'. *Sociology of Health and Illness* 16(1): 103–21.

Kitzinger, J. 1994b. 'Focus Groups: Method or Madness? Pp. 159–75. In *Challenge and Innovation: Methodological Advances in Social Research on HIV/AIDS*, edited by M. Boulton. London: Taylor and Francis.

Kitzinger, J. 1995. 'Qualitative Research: Introducing Focus Groups'. *British Medical Journal* 311: 299–302.

Kleinman, S. and M.A. Copp. 1993. *Emotions and Fieldwork*. Newbury Park, CA: Sage Publications.

Knox, M., M. Mok and T.R. Parmenter. 2000. 'Working with the Experts: Collaborative Research with People with Intellectual Disability'. *Disability and Society* 15(1): 49–61.

Kolker, A. 1996. 'Thrown Overboard: The Human Costs of Health Care Rationing'. Pp. 132–59. In *Composing Ethnography: Alternative Forms of Qualitative Writing*, edited by C. Ellis and A.P. Bochner. Walnut Creek, CA: AltaMira.

Kondo, D. 2001. 'How the Problem of 'Crafting Selves' Emerged'. Pp. 188–202. In *Contemporary Field Research: Perspectives and Formulations*, 2nd edition, edited by R.M. Emerson. Prospect Heights, IL: Waveland Press.

Kondora, L.L. 1993. 'A Heideggerian Hermeneutical Analysis of Survivors of Incest'. *IMAGE: Journal of Nursing Scholarship* 25(1): 11–16.

Kong, T.K., D. Mahoney and K. Plummer. 2002. 'Queering the Interview'. Pp. 239–58. In *Handbook of Interview Research: Context & Method*, edited by J.F. Gubrium and J.A. Holstein. Thousand Oaks, CA: Sage Publications.

Koppelman, N.F. and J.N. Bourjolly. 2001. 'Conducting Focus Groups With Women With Severe Psychiatric Disabilities: A Methodological Overview'. *Psychiatric Rehabilitation Journal* 25(2): 142–51.

Körner, H., O. Hendry and S. Kippax. 2005. 'It's Not Just Condoms: Social Contexts of Unsafe Sex in Gay Men's Narratives of Post-Exposure Prophylaxis for HIV'. *Health, Risk & Society* 7(1): 47–62.

Kossak, S.N. 2005. 'Exploring the Elements of Culturally Relevant Service Delivery'. *Families in Society* 86(2): 189–95.

Kralik, D., T. Koch and B.M. Brady. 2000. 'Pen Pals: Correspondence as a Method for Data Generation in Qualitative Research'. *Journal of Advanced Nursing* 31: 909–17.

Krieger, S. 1983. *The Mirror's Dance: Identity in a Women's Community*. Philadelphia, PA: Temple University Press.

Krogh, K. 2001. 'Beyond Four Walls: The Impact of Home Support on Health, Work, and Citizenship for People with Disabilities'. Toronto: School of Disability Studies, Ryerson University. Available at: http://www.Ryerson.ca/~kkrough/report1 (Accessed 1/12/2001).

Kvale, S. 1996. *Interviews: An Introduction to Qualitative Research Interviewing*. London: Sage Publications.

Lambert, E.Y. (ed.). 1990. *The Collection and Interpretation of Data from Hidden Populations*, Rockville, MD: National Institute on Drug Abuse.

Lampon, D. 1995. 'Lesbians and Safer Sex Practices'. *Feminist and Psychology* 5: 170–76.

Landrine, H., E. Klonoff and A. Brown-Collins. 1995. 'Cultural Diversity and Methodology in Feminist Psychology: Critique, Proposal, Empirical Example'. Pp. 55–75. In *Bringing Cultural Diversity to Feminist Psychology*, edited by H. Landrine. Washington, DC: American Psychological Association.

Lange, J.W. 2002. 'Methodological Concerns for Non-Hispanic Investigators Conducting Research with Hispanic Americans'. *Research in Nursing & Health* 25: 411–19.

Langellier, K.M. 2001. 'You're Marked: Breast Cancer, Tattoo, and the Narrative Performance of Identity'. Pp. 145–84. In *Narrative and Identity: Studies in Autobiography, Self, and Culture*, edited by J. Brockmeier and D. Carbaugh. Amsterdam: John Benjamins.

Langford, D.R. 2000. 'Developing a Safely Protocol in Qualitative Research Involving Battered Women'. *Qualitative Health Research* 10(1): 133–42.

Lankshear, G. 2000. 'Bacteria and Babies: A Personal Reflection on Researcher Risk in a Hospital'. Pp. 72–90. In *Danger in the Field: Risk and Ethics in Social Research*, edited by G. Lee-Treweek and S. Linkogle. London: Routledge.

LaRossa, R. and M.M. LaRossa. 1981. *Transition to Parenthood: How Infants Change Families*. Beverly Hills, CA: Sage Publicaitons.

Larson, E. (1994) Exclusion of certain groups from clinical research. *Image: Journal of Nursing Scholarship* 26: 185–90.

Lather, P. 1991. *Getting Smart: Feminist Research and Pedagogy Within the Postmodern*. London: Routledge.

Lather, P. 2001. 'Postbook: Working the Ruins of Feminist Ethnography'. *Signs: Journal of Women in Culture and Society* 27(1): 199–227.

Lather, P. and C Smithies. 1997. *Troubling the Angels: Women Living with HIV/AIDS*. Boulder, CO: Westview.

Laureau, A. and F. Schultz. (eds). 1996. *Journey Through Ethnography: Realistic Accounts of Fieldwork*. Boulder, CO: Westview Press.

Lawrinson, S. and J. Harris. 1994. 'Violence in Research Settings – Experiences from the Front Line'. *Applied Community Studies* 2(1): 52–68.

Lawton, J. 2001. 'Gaining and Maintaining Consent: Ethical Concerns Raised in a Study of Dying Patients'. *Qualitative Health Research* 11(5): 693–705.

Leaning, J. 2001. 'Ethics of Research in Refugee Populations'. *Lancet* 357(9266): 1432–33.

Lee, R.M. 1993. *Doing Research on Sensitive Topics*. London: Sage Publications.

Lee, R.M. 1995. *Dangerous Fieldwork*. Thousand Oaks, CA: Sage Publications.

Lee, R.M. 2002. 'The Self, Lucid Dreaming and Postmodern Identity'. Electric Dreams 9(3). Available at: http://dreamgate.com/pomo/lucid_lee.htm (Accessed 12/7/2005).

Lee-Treweek, G. 2000. 'The Insight of Emotional Danger: Research Experiences in Home for Older People'. Pp. 114–31. In *Danger in the Field: Risk and Ethics in Social Research*, edited by G. Lee-Treweek and S. Linkogle. London: Routledge.

Lee-Treweek, G. and S. Linkogle. 2000a. 'Overview'. Pp. 1–7. In *Danger in the Field: Risk and Ethics in Social Research*, edited by G. Lee-Treweek and S. Linkogle. London: Routledge.

Lee-Treweek, G. and S. Linkogle. 2000b. 'Putting Danger in the Frame'. Pp. 8–25. In *Danger in the Field: Risk and Ethics in Social Research*, edited by G. Lee-Treweek and S. Linkogle. London: Routledge.

Leiblich, A. 1996. 'Some Unforseen Outcomes of Conducting Narrative Research with People of One's Own Culture'. Pp. 151–84. In *The Narrative Study of Lives, Vol. 4, Ethics and Process in the Narrative Study of Lives*, edited by R. Josselson. Thousand Oaks, CA: Sage Publications.

Leinen, S. 1993. *Gay Cops*. New Brunswick, NJ: Rutgers University Press.

Leipert, B. and L. Reutter. 2005. 'Developing Resilience: How Women Maintain Their Health in Northern Geographically Isolated Settings'. *Qualitative Health Research* 15(1): 49–65.

Lengua, L., M.W. Roosa, E. Schupak-Neuberg, M.L. Michaels, C.N. Berg and L.F. Weschler. 1992. 'Using Focus Groups To Guide the Development of Parenting Program for Difficult-to-Reach, High Risk Families'. *Family Relations* 4(2): 163–8.

Lester, H. and J.Q. Tritter. 2005. '"Listen to My Madness" Understanding the Experiences of People With Serious Mental Illness'. *Sociology of Health and Illness* 27(5): 649–69.

Letherby, G. 2000. 'Dangerous Liaisons: Auto/Biography in Research and Research Writing'. pp. 91–113. In *Danger in the Field: Risk and Ethics in Social Research*, edited by G Lee-Treweek and S. Linkogle. London: Routledge.

Lewis Fravel, D. and P.G. Boss. 1992. 'An In-Depth Interview with the Parents of Missing Children'. Pp. 126–45. In *Qualitative Methods in Family Research*, edited by J.F. Gilgun, K. Daly and G. Handel. Newbury Park, CA: Sage Publications.

Lewis, J. and E. Maticka-Tyndale. 2000. 'Licensing Sex Work: Public Policy and Women's Lives'. *Canadian Public Policy* 26(4): 437–49.

Liamputtong P. 2000. 'Motherhood and the Challenge of Immigrant Mothers: A Personal Reflection'. *Families in Society: The Journal of Contemporary Human Services* 82(2): 195–201.

Liamputtong, P. (ed.) 2006. *Health Research in Cyberspace: Methodological, Practical and Personal Issue*. New York: Nova Science Publishers.

Liamputtong, P. and D. Ezzy. 2005. *Qualitative Research Methods*, 2nd edition. Melbourne: Oxford University Press.

Liamputtong, P. and J. Dwyer. 2003. 'Women and Health: An Ongoing Agenda'. Pp. 119–40. In *Health, Social Change & Communities*, edited by P. Liamputtong and H. Gardner. Melbourne: Oxford University Press.

Liamputtong Rice, P. 1988. *Health and Sickness: The Influence of Cultural Knowledge and Commonsense Interpretations among Thai School Children*. Unpublished doctoral thesis, Faculty of Education, Monash University, Melbourne.

Liamputtong Rice, P. 1991. 'Concepts of Health and Illness in Thai Children'. *International Journal of Science Education* 13(1): 115–27.

Liamputtong Rice, P. 1993. *My Forty Days: A Cross-Cultural Resource Book for Health Professionals in Birthing Services*. Melbourne: The Vietnamese Ante/Postnatal Support Project.

Liamputtong Rice, P. 1994. 'What is Health?, What is Illness?: Meaning of Health and Illness among Thai Schoolchildren'. *Journal of the Institute of Health Education* 32(1): 19–22.

Liamputtong Rice, P. 1996. 'Health Research and Ethnic Communities: Reflections on Practice'. Pp. 50–61. In *Health Research in Practice, Vol. 2: Personal Experiences, Public Issues*, edited by D. Colquhoun and A. Kellehear. London: Chapman & Hall.

Liamputtong Rice, P. 2000. *Hmong Women and Reproduction*. Westport, CT: Bergin & Garvey.

Liamputtong Rice, P., B. Ly and J. Lumley. 1994. 'Soul Loss and Childbirth: The Case of a Hmong Woman'. *The Medical Journal of Australia* 160: 557–78.

Lichtenstein, B. 2000. 'Secret Encounters: Black Men, Bisexuality, and AIDS in Alabama'. *Medical Anthropology Quarterly* 14(3): 374–93.

Lichtenstein, B. and T. Nansel. 2000. 'Women's Douching Practices and Related Attitudes: Findings from Four Focus Groups'. *Women & Health* 31(2/3): 117–31.

Lim, P.C. and S.C. Tan. 2001. 'Online Discussion Boards for Focus Group Interviews: An Exploratory Study'. *Journal of Educational Enquiry* 2(1). Available at: http://www. literacy.unisa.edu.au/jee/Papers/JEEVol2No1/paper4.pdf (Accessed 6/8/2001).

Lincoln, Y.S. 1995. 'Emerging Criteria for Quality in Qualitative and Interpretive Research'. *Qualitative Inquiry* 1: 275–89.

Lincoln, Y.S. and N.K. Denzin. 2000. 'The Seventh Moment: Out of the Past'. Pp. 1047–65. In *The Sage Handbook of Qualitative Research,* 2nd edition, edited by N.K. Denzin and Y.S. Lincoln. Thousand Oaks, CA: Sage Publications.

Lincoln, Y.S. and N.K. Denzin. 2005. 'Epilogue: The Eighth and Ninth Moments – Qualitative Research In/And The Fractured Future'. Pp. 1115–126. In *The Sage Handbook of Qualitative Research,* 3rd edition, edited by N.K. Denzin and Y.S. Lincoln. Thousand Oaks, CA: Sage Publications.

Linkogle, S. 2000. 'Relajo: Danger in a Crowd'. Pp. 132–46. In *Danger in the Field: Risk and Ethics in Social Research,* edited by G. Lee-Treweek and S. Linkogle. London: Routledge.

Linstead, S. 1998. 'The Dishcloth of Minerva: Absence, Presence, and Metatheory in the Everyday Practice of Research'. Pp. 235–43. In *Fiction and Social Research: By Ice or Fire,* edited by A. Banks and S.P. Banks. Walnut Creek: AltaMira Press.

Lipson, J. and A. Meleis. 1989. 'Methodological Issues in Research with Immigrants'. *Medical Anthropology* 12(1): 103–15.

Lira, L.R., M.P. Koss and N.F. Russo. 1999. 'Mexican American Women's Definition of Rape and Sexual Abuse'. *Hispanic Journal of Behavioural Sciences* 21: 236–65.

Loff, B. and J. Black. 2000. 'The Declaration of Helsinki and Research with Vulnerable Populations'. *Medical Journal of Australia* 172: 292–95.

Lomawaima, K.T. 2000. 'Tribal Sovereigns: Reframing Research in American Indian Education'. *Harvard Educational Review* 70(1): 1–21. (Online)

Lombardo, A. and J. Gillett. 2006. Online HIV Research: Assessing Three Case Study Methodologies'. Pp. 133–46. In *Health Research in Cyberspace: Methodological, Practical, and Personal,* edited by P. Liamputtong. New York: Nova Science Publishers.

López, E.D.S., E. Eng and N. Robinson. 2005. 'Quality of Life Concerns of African American Breast Cancer Survivors Within Rural North Carolina: Blending the Techniques of Photovoice and Grounded Theory'. *Qualitative Health Research* 15(1): 99–115.

Loseke, D.R. 2001. 'Lived Realities and Formula Stories of "Battered Women" '. Pp. 107–26. In *Institutional Selves: Troubled Identities in a Postmodern World,* edited by J.F. Gubrium and J.A. Holstein. New York: Oxford University Press.

Lovering, K.M. 1995. 'The Bleeding Body: Adolescents Talk About Menstruation'. Pp. 10–31. In *Feminism and Discourse: Psychological Perspectives,* edited by S. Wilkinson and C. Kitzinger. London: Sage Publications.

Lowe, P. 2005. 'Contraception and Heterosex: An Intimate Relationship'. *Sexualities* 8(1): 75–92.

Lu, Y., S.K. Trout, K. Lu and J.W. Creswell. 2005. 'The Needs of AIDS-Infected Individuals in Rural China'. *Qualitative Health Research* 15(9): 1149–63.

Luginaah I.N. and C. Dakubo. 2003. 'Consumption and Impacts of Local Brewed Alcohol (Akpeteshie) in the Upper West Region of Ghana: A Public Health Tragedy'. *Social Science and Medicine* 57: 1747–60.

Luginaah, I.N., E.K. Yiridoe and M-M. Taabazuing. 2005. 'From Mandatory to Voluntary Testing: Balancing Human Rights, Religious and Cultural Values, and HIV/AIDS Prevention in Ghana'. *Social Science and Medicine* 61: 1689–1700.

Lupton, D. 1998. *The Emotional Self.* London: Sage Publications.

Lykes, M.B. 2001. 'Activist Participatory Research and the Arts with Rural Mayan Women: Interculturality and Situated Meaning Making'. Pp. 183–99. In *From Subjects to Subjectivities: A Handbook of Interpretive and Participatory Methods,* edited by D.L. Tolman and M. Brydon-Miller. New York: New York University Press.

Lyotard, J. 1979. *The Postmodern Condition: A Report on Knowledge*. (Translated by G. Bennington and B. Massumi). Manchester, NH: Manchester University Press.

McCall, M.M. and H.S. Becker. 1990. 'Performance Science'. *Social Problems* 37: 117–32.

McCann, L.L. and L.A. Pearlman. 1994. *Therapists and Vicarious Traumatization*. New York: Guildford Press.

McCarroll, J.E., A.S, Blan and K. Hill. 1995. 'Working with Traumatic Material: Effects on Holocaust Memorial Museum Staff'. *American Orthopsychiatric Association* 65(1): 66–75.

McCarthy, M. 1996. 'Sexual Experiences and Sexual Abuse of Women with Learning Disabilities'. Pp. 199–129. In *Women, Violence and Male Power: Feminist Activism, Research and Practice*, edited by M. Hester, L. Kelly and J. Radford. Buckingham: Open University Press.

McCarthy, M. 1998. 'Interviewing People with Learning Disabilities about Sensitive Topics: A Discussion of Ethical Issues'. *British Journal of Learning Disabilities* 26: 140–45.

McCosker, H., A. Bernard and G. Rod. 2001. 'Undertaking Sensitive Research: Issues and Strategies for Meeting the Safety Needs of all Participants'. *Forum: Qualitative Social Research* 2(1). Available at: http://qualitative-research.net/fqs/fqs-eng.htm (Accessed 14/4/2006).

MacDougall, C. and E. Fudge. 2001. 'Planning and Recruiting the Sample for Focus Groups and In-Depth Interviews'. *Qualitative Health Research* 11(1): 117–26.

McGinnis, T. 1999. 'The Art of Leaving'. Presented at the annual symposium of the Couch-Stone Society for the Study of Symbolic Interaction, February 5–7, Las Vegas.

Macklin, R. 2000. 'Informed Consent for Research: International Perspectives'. *Journal of the American Medical Women's Association* 55: 290–93.

Macklin, R. 2004. *Double Standards in Medical Research in Developing Countries*. New York, Cambridge: University Press.

McNeely, E.A. and S.D. Clements. 1994. 'Recruitment and Retention of the Older Adult into Research Studies', *Journal of Neuroscience Nursing*, vol. 26, Pp. 57–61.

Madge, C. and H. O'Connor. 2002. 'On-Line with E-Mums: Exploring the Internet as a Medium for Research'. *Area* 34(1): 92–102.

Madriz, E. 2000. 'Focus Groups in Feminist Research'. Pp. 835–50. In *The Sage Handbook of Qualitative Research,* 2nd edition, edited by N.K. Denzin and Y.S. Lincoln. Thousand Oaks, CA: Sage Publications.

Madriz, E.L. 1998. 'Using Focus Groups with Lower Socioeconomic Status Latina Women'. *Qualitative Inquiry* 4(1): 114–29.

Maguire, P. 1987. *Doing Participatory Research: A Feminist Approach*. Amherst, MA: Centre for International Education, School of Education, University of Massachusetts.

Maguire, P. 1996. 'Proposing a More Feminist Participatory Research: Knowing and Being Embraced Openly'. Pp. 27–39. In *Participatory Research in Health: Issues and Experiences*, edited by K. de Koning and M. Martin. London: Zed Books

Manderson, L., M. Markovic and M. Quinn. 2005. ' "Like Roulette": Australian Women's Explanations of Gynecological Cancers'. *Social Science and Medicine* 61: 323–32.

Mann, C. and F. Stewart. 2000. *Internet Communication and Qualitative Research: A Handbook for Researching Online*. London: Sage Publications.

Manning, P. 2002. 'Fat Ethics: Response to Erich Goode'. *Qualitative Sociology* 25: 541–47.

Mao, L., J. McCormick and P. van de Ven. 2002. 'Ethnic and Gay Identification: Gay Asian Men Dealing With the Divide'. *Culture, Health & Sexuality* 4(4): 419–30.

Marcus, G. 1992. *Cultural Anthopology at Rice since the 1980s*. Provost Lecture, 17 February. Available at: http://www.ruf.rice.edu/~anth/provost.html (Accessed 12/7/2005).

Marcus, G.E. and M.M.J. Fischer. 1986. *Anthropology as Cultural Critique: An Experimental Moment in the Human Science*. Chicago, IL: University of Chicago Press.

Marindo-Ranganai, R. 1996. 'A Zimbabwean Case'. Pp. 177–90. In *Participatory Research in Health: Issues and Experiences*, edited by K. de Koning and M. Martin. London: Zed Books.

Marino, R., V. Minichiello and J. Browne. 1999. 'Reporting of Events Using Diaries'. Pp. 381–93. In *Handbook for Research Methods in Health Sciences*, edited by V. Minichiello, G. Sullivan, K. Greenwood and R. Axford. Sydney: Prentice Hall.

Markham, A.N. 2005. 'The Methods, Politics, and Ethics of Representation in Online Ethnography'. Pp. 793–820. In *The Sage Handbook of Qualitative Research,* 3rd edition, edited by N.K. Denzin and Y.S. Lincoln. Thousand Oaks, CA: Sage Publications.

Markovic, M., V. Kesic, L. Topic and B. Matejic. 2005. 'Barriers to Cervical Cancer Screening: A Qualitative Study With Women in Serbia'. *Social Science and Medicine* 61: 2528–35.

Marquart, J.W. 2001. 'Doing Research in Prison: The Strengths and Weaknesses of Full Participation as a Guard'. Pp. 35–47. In *Extreme Methods: Innovative Approaches to Social Science Research*, edited by J.M. Miller and R. Tewksbury. Boston: Allyn and Bacon.

Marshall, A. and S. Batten. 2004. 'Researching Across Cultures: Issues of Ethics and Power'. *Forum: Qualitative Social Research*, 5(3), Art, 39. Available at: http://www.qual-itative-research.net/fqs-texte/3–04/04–3–39-e.htm (Accessed 14/10/2005).

Marsiglio, W., S. Hutchinson and M. Cohan. 2000. 'Envisioning Fatherhood: A Social Psychological Perspective on Young Men Without Kids'. *Family Relations* 49: 133–42.

Marsiglio, W., S. Hutchinson and M. Cohan. 2001. 'Young Men's Procreative Identity: Becoming Aware, Being Aware, and Being Responsible'. *Journal of Marriage and the Family* 63: 123–35.

Marston, C. 2005. 'What is Heterosexual Coercion? Interpreting Narratives from Young People in Mexico City'. *Sociology of Health and Illness* 27(1): 68–91.

Martin, E. 1995. *Flexible Bodies: Tracking Immunity in American Culture—From the Days of Polio to the Age of AIDS*. Boston, MA: Beacon.

Martin, J.L. and L. Dean. 1993. 'Developing a Community Sample of Gay Men for an Epidemiological Study of AIDS'. Pp. 82–99. In *Researching Sensitive Topics*, edited by C.M. Renzetti and R.M. Lee. Newbury Park: Sage Publications.

Martinez, R.G. 2005. ' "What's Wrong With Me?": Cervical Cancer in Venezuela—Living in the Borderlands of Health, Disease, and Illness'. *Social Science and Medicine* 61: 797–808.

Martinez-Ebers, V. 1997. 'Using monetary incentives with hard-to-reach populations in panel surveys'. *International Journal of Public Opinion Research* 9(1): 77–87.

Marvasti, A.B. 2004. A *Qualitative Research in Sociology*. London: Sage Publications.

Matocha, L.K. 1992. 'Case Study Interviews: Caring for Persons with AIDS'. Pp. 66–84. In *Qualitative Methods in Family Research*, edited by J.F. Gilgun, K. Daly and G. Handel. Newbury Park, CA: Sage Publications.

Mattley, C. 1997. 'Field Research With Phone Sex Workers: Managing the Researcher's Emotions'. Pp. 101–14. In *Researching Sexual Violence Against Women: Methodological and Personal Perspectives*, edited by M.D. Schwartz. Thousand Oaks, CA: Sage Publications.

Mauthner, M. 1997. 'Methodological Aspects of Collecting Data From Children: Lessons From Three Research Projects'. *Children and Society* 11: 16–28.

Mauthner, M., M. Birch, J. Jessop and T. Miller. (eds). 2002. *Ethics in Qualitative Research*. Thousand Oaks, CA: Sage Publications.

Mayall, B. 1999 'Children and Childhood'. Pp. 10–24. In *Critical Issues in Social Research: Power and Prejudice*, edited by S. Hood, B. Mayall and S. Oliver. Philadelphia, PA: Open University Press.

Maynard, M. 1994. 'Methods, Practice and Epistemology: The Debate about Feminism and Research'. Pp. 10–26. In *Researching Women's Lives from a Feminist Perspective*, edited by M. Maynard and J. Purvis. London: Taylor and Francis.

Maynard-Tucker, G. 2000. 'Conducting Focus Groups in Developing Countries: Skill Training for Local Bilingual Facilitators'. *Qualitative Health Research* 10(3): 396–410.

Mays, V.M., S.D. Cochran, G. Bellinger, R.G. Smith, N. Henley, M. Daniels, T. Tibbits. G.D. Victorianne, O.K. Osei and D.K. Birt. 1992. 'The Language of Black Gay Men's Sexual Behavior: Implications for AIDS Risk Reduction'. *Journal of Sex Research* 29: 425–34.

Meadows, L.M., L.E. Lagendyk, W.E. Thurston and A.C. Eisener. 2003. 'Balancing Culture, Ethics, and Methods in Qualitative Health Research with Aboriginal Peoples'. *International Journal of Qualitative Methods* 2(4). Article 1. Available at: http://www.ualberta.ca/~iiqm/backissues/2_4/pdf/meadows.pdf (Accessed 9/10/2005).

Melrose, M. 2002. 'Labour Pains: Some Considerations on the Difficulties of Researching Juvenile Prostitution'. *International Journal of Social Research Methodology* 5(4): 333–51.

Merkes, M. 2006. 'A Longer Working Life for Australian Women? – The BabyBoomWomen@Work2020 Website' Pp. 193–208. In *Health Research in Cyberspace: Methodological, Practical and Personal Issue*, edited by P. Liamputtong. New York: Nova Sciences Publishers.

Meth, P. 2003. 'Entries and Omissions: Using Solicited Diaries in Geographical Research'. *Area* 35(2): 195–205.

Mienczakowski, J. 1992. *Syncing Out Loud: A Journey into Illness*. Brisbane: Griffith University Reprographics.

Mienczakowski, J. 1996. 'An Ethnographic Act: The Construction of Consensual Theatre'. Pp. 244–63. In *Composing Ethnography: Alternative Forms of Qualitative Writing*, edited by C. Ellis and A. Bochner. Thousand Oaks, CA: Sage Publications.

Mienczakowski, J. 1997. 'Theatre for Change'. *Research in Drama Education* 2(2): 159–72.

Mienczakowski, J. 1998. 'Reaching Wide Audiences: Reflexive Research and Performance'. *NADIE Journal* 22(1): 75–82.

Mienczakowski, J. 2001. 'Ethnodrama: Performed Research'. Pp. 468–76. In *Handbook of Ethnography*, edited by P. Atkinson, A. Coffey, S. Delamont, J. Lofland and L. Lofland. London: Sage Publications.

Mienczakowski, J. 2003. 'The Theater of Ethnography: The Reconstruction of Ethnography into Theater with Emancipatory Potential'. Pp. 415–32. In *Turning Points in Qualitative Research: Tying Knots in a Handkerchief*, edited by Y.S. Lincoln and N.K. Denzin. Walnut Creek, CA: AltaMira.

Mienczakowski, J. and S. Morgan. 1993. *Busting: The Challenge of the Drought Spirit*. Brisbane: Griffith University Reprographics.

Mienczakowski, J. and S. Morgan. 2001. 'Ethnodrama: Constructing Participatory, Experiential and Compelling Action Research through Performance'. Pp. 219–27. In *Handbook of Action Research: Participative Inquiry and Practice*, edited by P. Reason and H. Brabury. London: Sage Publications.

Mienczakowski, J., L. Smith and S. Morgan. 2002. 'Seeing Words—Hearing Feelings: Ethnodrama and the Performance of Data'. Pp. 34–52. In *Dancing the Data*, edited by C. Bagley and M.B. Cancienne. New York: Peter Lang.

Mienczakowski, J., R. Smith and M. Sinclair. 1996. 'On the Road to Catharsis: A Theoretical Framework for Change'. *Qualitative Inquiry* 2(4): 439–63.

Miller, J. 1997. 'Researching Violence Against Street Prostitutes: Issues of Epistemology, Methodology and Ethics'. Pp. 144–56. In *Researching Sexual Violence Against Women: Methodological and Personal Perspectives*, edited by M.D. Schwartz. Thousand Oaks, CA: Sage Publications.

Miller, J. and D. Timson. 2004. 'Exploring the Experiences of Partners who Live with a Chronic Back Pain Sufferer'. *Health and Social Care in the Community* 12(1): 34–42.

Miller, J.M. 2001. 'Covert Participant Observation: Reconsidering the Least Used Method'. Pp. 13–20. In *Extreme Methods: Innovative Approaches to Social Science Research*, edited by J.M. Miller and R. Tewksbury. Boston, MA: Allyn and Bacon.

Miller, J.M. and L. Selva. 1994. 'Drug Enforcement's Double-Edged Sword: An Assessment of Asset Forfeiture Programs'. *Justice Quarterly* 11: 313–35.

Miller, J.M. and R. Tewksbury. (eds). 2001. *Extreme Methods: Innovative Approaches to Social Science Research*. Boston, MA: Allyn and Bacon.

Miller, K.I., J.B. Stiff and B.H. Ellis. 1988. 'Communication and Empathy as Precursors to Burnout among Human Service Workers'. *Communication Monographs* 55(9): 250–56.

Miller, L.C., J. Taylor and M.H. Carver. 2003. *Voices Made Flesh: Performing Women's Autobiography*. Madison, WI: The University of Wisconsin Press.

Miller, T. and L. Bell. 2002. 'Consenting to What? Issues of Access, Gate-Keeping and "Informed" Consent'. Pp. 53–69. In *Ethics in Qualitative Research*, edited by M. Mauthner, M. Birch, J. Jessop and T. Miller. London: Sage Publication.

Milligan, C., A. Bingley and A. Gatrell. 2005. 'Digging Deep: Using Diary Techniques to Explore the Place of Health and Well-Being Amongst Older People'. *Social Science & Medicine* 61: 1882–92.

Milling-Kinard, E. 1996. 'Conducting Research on Child Maltreatment: Effects on Researchers'. *Violence and Victims* 11(1): 65–69.

Mills, C.W. 1959. *The Sociological Imagination*. New York: Oxford University Press.

Mills, C.W. 2000. *The Sociological Imagination*. New York: Oxford University Press.

Minkler, M. and N. Wallestein. 2003. *Community-Based Participatory Research for Health*. San Francisco, CA: Jossey-Bass.

Mirza, M. 1995. 'Some Ethical Dilemmas in Field Work: Feminist and Antiracist Methodologies'. Pp. 163–81. In *Antiracism, Culture and Social Justice in Education*, edited by M. Griffiths and B. Troyna. Stoke-on-Trent: Trentham.

Moloney, M.A., A.S. Dietrich, O.L. Strickland and S. Myerburg. 2003. 'Using Internet Discussion Boards as Virtual Focus Groups'. *Advances in Nursing Science* 26(4): 274–86.

Molyneux, C.S., N. Peshu and K. Marsh. 2004. 'Understanding of Informed Consent in a Low-Income Setting: Three Case Studies from the Kenyan Coast'. *Social Science and Medicine* 59(12): 2547–59.

Molyneux, C.S., D.R. Wassenaar, N. Peshu and K. Marsh. 2005. ' "Even if They Ask You to Stand by a Tree All Day, You Will Have to Do it (Laughter)...!": Community Voices on the Notion and Practice of Informed Consent for Biomedical Research in Developing Countries'. *Social Science and Medicine* 61: 443–54.

Montell, F. 1999. 'Focus Group Interviews: A New Feminist Method'. *NWSA Journal* 11(1): 44–70. (Online)

Moore, L.W. 2002. 'Conducting Research With Visually Impaired Older Adults'. *Qualitative Health Research* 12(4): 559–65.

Moore, L.W. and M. Miller. 1999. 'Initiating Research with Doubly Vulnerable Populations'. *Journal of Advanced Nursing* 30(5): 1034–40.

Moran-Ellis, J. 1996. 'Close to Home: The Experience of Researching Child Sexual Abuse'. Pp. 176–87. In *Women, Violence and Male Power: Feminist Activism, Research and Practice*, edited by M. Hester, L. Kelly and J. Radford, Buckingham: Open University Press.

Moreno, E. 1995. 'Rape in the Field: Reflections from a Survivor'. Pp. 219–51. In *Taboo: Sex, Identity, and Erotic Subjectivity in Anthropological Fieldwork*, edited by D. Kulick and M. Wilson. London: Routledge.

Morgan, D.L. 1988. *Focus Group as Qualitative Research*. Newbury Park, CA: Sage Publications.

Morgan, S., J. Mienczakowski and G. King. 1999. *The Dramatic Representation of Suicide: Issues, Concerns and Guidelines*. Paper presented at Suicide Prevention Australia, Melbourne Convention Centre, Melbourne, 25 March.

Morris, S.M. 2001. 'Joint and Individual Interviewing in the Context of Cancer'. *Qualitative Health Research* 11(4): 553–67.

Morrow, E. 1997. 'Attitudes of Women from Vulnerable Populations to Physician and Assisted Death'. *Journal of Clinical Ethics* 8: 279–89.

Morrow, V. and M. Richards. 1996. 'The Ethics of Social Research With Children: An Overview'. *Children and Society* 10(2): 90–105.

Morse, J.M. 2000. 'Researching Illness and Injury: Methodological Considerations'. *Qualitative Health Research* 10(4): 538–46.

Morse, J.M. 2001. 'Are there Risks in Qualitative Research?'. *Qualitative Health Research* 11(1): 3–4.

Morse, J.M. 2002. 'Interviewing the Ill'. Pp. 317–28. In *Handbook of Interview Research: Context & Method*, edited by J.F. Gubrium and J.A. Holstein. Thousand Oaks, CA: Sage Publications.

Morse, J.M. and C. Mitcham. 1997. 'Compathy: The Contagion of Physical Distress'. *Journal of Advanced Nursing* 26: 649–57.

Morse, J.M. and P.A. Field. 1995. *Qualitative Research Methods for Healthcare Professionals*, 2nd edition. London: Sage Publication.

Morse, J.M., C. Mitcham and V. van der Steen. 1998. 'Compathy or Physical Empathy: Implications for the Caregiver Relationship'. *Journal of Medical Humanities* 19(1): 51–65.

Mosack, K.E., M. Abbott, M. Singer, M.R. Weeks and L. Rohena. 2005. 'If I Didn't Have HIV, I'd Be Dead Now: Illness Narratives of Drug Users Living With HIV/AIDS'. *Qualitative Health Research* 15(5): 586–605.

Mosavel, M., C. Simon, D. van Stage and M. Buchbinder. 2005. 'Community-Based Participatory Research (CBPR) in South Africa: Engaging Multiple Constituents to Shape the Research Question'. *Social Science and Medicine* 61: 2577–87.

Muncey, T. 2005. 'Doing Autoethnography'. *International Journal of Qualitative Methods* 4(1): 1–12. Avalilable at: http://www.ualberta.ca/~iiqm/backissues/4_1/pdf/muncey.pdf (Accessed 14/4/2006).

Munhall, P.L. 1991. 'Institutional Review of Qualitative Research Proposals: A Task of No Small Consequence. Pp. 258–71. In *Qualitative Nursing Research*, edited by J.M. Morse. Newbury Park, CA: Sage Publication.

Murray, E.E. 1995. *Knowledge Machines: Language and Information in a Technological Society*. London: Longman.

Murray, S.A., J. Tapson, L. Turnbull, J. McCallum and A. Little. 1994. 'Listening to Local Voices: Adapting Rapid Appraisal to Assess Health and Social Needs in General Practice'. *British Medical Journal* 308: 698–700.

Mykhalovskiy, E. 1996. 'Reconsidering Table Talk: Critical Thoughts on the Relationship between Sociology, Autobiography and Self-Indulgence'. *Qualitative Sociology* 19(1): 131–52.

Naples, N.A. 2004. 'The Outsider Phenomenon'. Pp. 373–81. In *Feminist Perspectives on Social Research*, edited by S.N. Hesse-Biber and M.L. Yaiser. New York: Oxford University Press.

Ngamvithayapong-Yanai, J., A. Winkvist, S. Luangjina and V. Diwan. 2005. ' "If We Have to Die, We Just Die": Challenges and Opportunities for Tuberculosis and HIV/AIDS Prevention and Care in Northern Thailand'. *Qualitative Health Research* 15(9): 1164–79.

Nicholson, P. and J. Burr. 2003. 'What is "Normal" About Women's (Hetero)Sexual Desire and Orgasm?: A Report of An In-Depth Interview Study'. *Social Science and Medicine* 57: 1735–45.

Nielsen, J.M. 1990. 'Introduction'. Pp. 1–37. In *Feminist Research Methods*, edited by J.M. Nielsen. Boulder, CO: Westview.

Norris, J. 1991. 'Mothers' Involvement in Their Adolescent Daughters' Abortions'. Pp. 201–36. In *The Illness Experience: Dimensions of Suffering*, edited by J.M. Morse and J.L. Johnson. London: Sage Publication.

Norris, J., P.S. Nurius and L.A. Dimeff. 1996. 'Through Her Eyes: Factors Affecting Women's Perception of and Resistance to Acquaintances Sexual Aggression Threat'. *Psychology of Women Quarterly* 20: 123–45.

Nyamathi, A. 1998. 'Vulnerable Populations: A Continuing Nursing Focus'. *Nursing Research* 47(2): 65–66.

Oakley, A., G. Bendelow, J. Barnes, M. Buchanan and O.A. Nasseem Husain. 1995. 'Health and Cancer Prevention: Knowledge and Beliefs of Children and Young People'. *British Medical Journal* 310(6986): 1029–33.

O'Connor, H. and C. Madge. 2001. 'Cyber-Mothers: Online Synchronous Interviewing Using Conferencing Software'. Available at: http://www.socresonline.org.uk/5/4/o'connor.html (Accessed 4/3/2005).

O' Dochartaigh, N. 2002. *The Internet Research Handbook: A Practical Guide for Students and Researchers in the Social Sciences*. London: Sage Publications.

O'Kane, C. 2000. 'The Development of Participatory Techniques: Facilitating Children's Views About Decisions Which Affect Them'. Pp. 136–59. In *Research With Children*, edited by P. Christensen and A. James. London: Farmer Press.

Olesen, V.L. 2000. 'Feminisms and Qualitative Research At and Into the Millennium. Pp. 215–56. In *Handbook of Qualitative Research*, 2nd edition, edited by N.K. Denzin and Y.S. Lincoln. Thousand Oaks, CA: Sage Publications.

Olesen, V. 2005. 'Early Millennial Feminist Qualitative Research: Challenges and Contours'. Pp. 235–78. In *The Sage Handbook of Qualitative Research,* 3rd edition, edited by N.K. Denzin and Y.S. Lincoln. Thousand Oaks, CA: Sage Publications.

O'Neill, M. 1996. 'Researching Prostitution and Violence: Towards a Feminist Praxis'. Pp. 130–47. In *Women, Violence and Male Power: Feminist Activism, Research and Practice*, edited by M. Hester, L. Kelly and J. Radford, Buckingham: Open University Press.

Oringderff, J. 2004. ' "My Way": Piloting an Online Focus Group'. *International Journal of Qualitative Methods* 3(3). Available at: http://www.ualberta.ca/~ijqm/backissues/3_3/html/oringderff.html (Accessed 3/3/2005).

Ortiz Cofer, J. 1997. 'An Interview with Judith Ortiz Cofer'. Pp. 57–74. In *Speaking of the Short Story: Interviews with Contemporary Writers*, edited by F. Iftekharuddin, M. Rohrberger and M.L. Jackson. Jackson, MS: University of Mississippi Press.

Owen, S. 2001. 'The Practical, Methodological and Ethical Dilemmas of Conducting Focus Groups With Vulnerable Clients'. *Journal of Advanced Nursing* 36: 652–58.

Owens, D. 1996. 'Men, Emotions and the Research process: The Role of Interviews in Sensitive Areas'. Pp. 56–65. In *Qualitative Research: The Emotional Dimensions*, edited by K. Carter and S. Delamount. Aldershot: Averbury.

Padfield, M. and I. Procter. 1996. 'The Effect of Interviewer's Gender on the Interviewing Process: A Comparative Enquiry'. *Sociology* 30(2): 355–66.

Paradis, E.K. 2000. 'Feminist and Community Psychology Ethics in Research With Homeless Women'. *American Journal of Community Psychology* 28(6): 839–58.

Park, P., M. Brydon-Miller, H. Budd and T. Jackson. (eds). 2003. *Voices of Change: Participatory Research in the United States and Canada*. Westport, CT: Bergin & Garvey.

Parker, B. and Y. Ulrich. 1990. 'A Protocol of Safety: Research on Abuse of Women'. *Nursing Research* 28: 248–50.

Parker, L. 1992. 'Collecting Data the E-Mail Way'. *Training & Development* 46(7): 52–55.

Parnis, D., J. Du Mont and B. Gombay. 2005. 'Cooperation or Co-Optation?: Assessing the Methodological Benefits and Barriers Involved in Conducting Qualitative Research Through Medical Institutional Settings'. *Qualitative Health Research* 15(5): 686–97.

Paterson, B., D. Gregory and S. Thorne. 1999. 'A Protocol for Researcher Safety'. *Qualitative Health Research* 9(2): 259–69.

Pauw, I. and L. Brener. 2003. ' "You are Just Whores-You Can't be Raped": Barriers to Safer Sex Practices among Women Street Sex Workers in Cape Town'. *Culture, Health & Sexuality* 5(6): 465–81.

Payne, S. 1994. 'Issues for Researchers Using Qualitative Methods'. *Health Psychology Update* 16: 7–9.

Peritore, P. 1990. 'Reflections on Dangerous Fieldwork'. *The American Sociologist* 21(4): 359–72.

Perlis, T.E., D.C. Des Jarlais, S.R. Friedman, K. Arasteh and C.F. Turner. 2004. 'Audio-Computerised Self-Interviewing for Research Data Collection at Drug Abuse Treatment Programs'. *Addiction* 99: 885–96.

Perry, C., M. Thurston and K. Green. 2004. 'Involvement and Detachment in Researching Sexuality: Reflections on the Process of Semistructured Interviewing'. *Qualitative Health Research* 14(1): 135–48.

Petersen, R., K.E. Moracco, K.M. Goldstein and K.A. Clark. 2004. 'Moving Beyond Disclosure: Women's Perspectives on Barriers and Motivators to Seeking Assistance for Intimate Partner Violence'. *Women & Health* 40(3): 63–76.

Phoenix, A. 1994. 'Practicing Feminist Research: The Intersection of Gender and "Race" in the Research Process'. Pp. 49–71. In *Researching Women's Lives from a Feminist Perspective*, edited by M. Maynard and J. Purvis. London: Taylor and Francis.

Pini, B. 2002. 'Focus Groups, Feminist Research and Farm Women: Opportunities for Empowerment in Rural Social Research'. *Journal of Rural Studies* 18: 339–51.

Plant, R. 2004. 'Online communities'. *Technology in Society* 26(1): 51–65.

Poindexter, C.C. 1998. 'Poetry as Data Analysis: Honoring the Words of Research Participants'. *Reflections* Summer: 22–25.

Polit, D.F. and B.P. Hungler. 1995. *Nursing Research: Principles and Methods*, 5th edition, Philadelphia, PA: Lippincott.

Polkinghorne, D. 1997. 'Reporting Qualitative Research as Practice'. Pp. 3–21. In *Representation and the Text: Reframing the Narrative Voice*, edited by W. Tierney and Y.S. Lincoln. New York: State University of New York Press.

Potts, A., V.M. Grace, T. Vares and N. Gavey. 2006. '"Sex for Life"? Men's Counter-Stories on Erectile Dysfunction, Male Sexuality and Ageing'. *Sociology of Health and Illness* 28(3): 306–29.

Prager, E. 1995. 'The Older Volunteer as Research colleague: Toward "Generative Participation" for Older Adults'. *Educational Gerontology* 21: 209–18.

Press, A.L. 1991. 'Working-Class Women in a Middle-Class World: The Impact of Television on Modes of Reasoning About Abortion'. *Critical Studies in Mass Communication* 8: 421–41.

Preston-Whyte, E. and L. Dalrymple. 1996. 'Participation and Action: Reflections on Community-Based AIDS'. Pp. 108–18. In *Participatory Research in Health: Issues and Experiences*, edited by K. de Koning and M. Martin. London: Zed Books.

Pridemore, W.A., K.R. Damphousse and R.K. Moore. 2005. 'Obtaining Sensitive Information from a Wary Population: A Comparison of Telephone and Face-to-Face Surveys of Welfare Recipients in the United States'. *Social Science and Medicine* 61: 976–84.

Pridmore, P. and G. Bendelow. 1995. 'Images of Health: Exploring Beliefs of Children Using the "Draw and Write" Technique'. *Health Education Journal* 54: 473–88.

Punathambekar, A. and T. Fraley. 2000. 'Virtual Focus Groups: A Methodological Assessment'. Paper presented at the Conference of the Midwest Association of Public Opinion Research, November.

Punch, S. 2002. 'Research With Children: The Same or Different from Research With Adults'. *Childhood* 9(3): 321–41.

Pyett, P. 2001. 'Innovation and Compromise: Responsibility and Reflexivity in Research with Vulnerable Groups'. Pp. 105–19. In *Technologies and Health: Critical Compromises*, edited by J. Daly, M. Guillemin and S. Hill. Melbourne: Oxford University Press.

Pyett, P. 2002. 'Working Together to Reduce Inequalities: Reflections on a Collaborative Participatory Approach to Health Research'. *Australian and New Zealand Journal of Public Health* 26(4): 332–36.

Quest, T. and C.A. Marco. 2003. Ethics Seminars: Vulnerable Populations in Emergency Medicine Research'. *Academic Emergency Medicine* 10(11): 1294–98.

Quine, S. and I. Cameron. 1995. 'The Use of Focus Groups With the Disabled Elderly'. *Qualitative Health Research* 5(4): 454–62.

Radley, A. and D. Taylor. 2003a. 'Remembering One's Stay in Hospital: A Study in Photography, Recovery and Forgetting'. *Health: An Interdisciplinary Journal for the Social Study of Health, Illness and Medicine* 7(2): 129–59.

Radley, A. and D. Taylor. 2003b. 'Images of Recovery: A Photo-Elicitation Study on the Hospital Ward'. *Qualitative Health Research* 13(1): 77–99.

Radley, A., D. Hodgetts and A. Cullen. 2005. 'Visualizing Homelessness: A Study in Photography and Estrangement'. *Journal of Community & Applied Social Psychology* 15: 273–95.

Ramcharan, P. and J.R. Cutcliffe. 2001. 'Judging the Ethics of Qualitative Research: The "Ethics-As-Process" Model'. *Health and Social Care* 9(6): 358–67.

Rank, M.R. 1992. 'The Blending of Qualitative and Quantitative Methods in Understanding Childbearing among Welfare Recipients. Pp. 281–300. In *Qualitative*

Methods in Family Research, edited by J.F. Gilgun, K. Daly and G. Handel. Newbury Park, CA: Sage Publications.

Raynes, N.V., J.M. Leach, B. Rawlings and R.J. Bryson. 2000. 'Using Focus Groups to Seek the Views of Patients Dying from Cancer About the Care They Receive'. *Health Expectation* 3: 169–75.

Reavey, P. 1997. 'What Do You Do for a Living Then?: The Political Ramifications of Research Interest Within Everyday Interpersonal Contexts'. *Feminism and Psychology* 7: 553–58.

Rehman, L., J. Gahagan, A.M. DiCenso and G. Dias. 2004. 'Harm Reduction and Women in the Canadian National Prison System: Policy or Practice?' *Women & Health* 40(4): 57–73.

Reid, G., B. Speed, P. Miller, F. Cooke and N. Crofts. 1998. 'A Methodology for Sampling and Accessing Homeless Individuals in Melbourne, 1995–96'. *Australian and New Zealand Journal of Public Health* 22(5): 568–72.

Reinharz, S. 1983. 'Experiential Analysis: A Contribution to Feminist Research'. Pp. 162–91. In *Theories of Women's Studies*, edited by G. Bowles and R.D. Klein. London: Routledge and Kegan Paul.

Reinharz, S. 1992. *Feminist Methods in Social Research*. New York: Oxford University Press.

Reinharz, S. and S.E. Chase. 2002. 'Interviewing Women', Pp. 221–38. In *Handbook of Interview Research: Context & Method*, edited by J.F. Gubrium and J.A. Holstein. Thousand Oaks, CA: Sage Publications.

Renzetti, C.M. 1997. 'Confessions of Reformed Positivist: Feminist Participatory Research as Good Social Science'. Pp. 131–43. In *Researching Sexual Violence Against Women: Methodological and Personal Perspectives*, edited by M.D. Schwartz. Thousand Oaks, CA: Sage Publications.

Renzetti, C.M. and R.M. Lee. (eds). 1993. *Researching Sensitive Topics*. Newbury Park, CA: Sage Publications.

Rhode, K.V., D.S. Lauderdale, T. He, D.S. Howes and W. Levinson. 2002. ' "Between Me and the Computer": Increased Detection of Intimate Partner Violence Using a Computor Questionnaire'. *Annals of Emergency Medicine* 40: 476–84.

Ribbens, S.J. 1989. 'Interviewing Women-An Unnatural Situation?'. *Women's Studies International Forum*, 12: 529–97.

Rich, M. and R. Chalfen. 1998. 'Showing and Telling Asthma: Children Teaching Physicians with Visual Narrative'. *Visual Sociology* 14: 51–71.

Richardson, L. 1990. *Writing Strategies: Reaching Diverse Audiences*. Thousand Oaks, CA: Sage Publications.

Richardson, L. 1992. 'The Consequences of Poetic Representation'. Pp. 125–37. In *Investigating Subjectivity: Research on Lived Experience*, edited by C. Ellis and M.G. Flaherty. Newbury Park, CA: Sage Publications.

Richardson, L. 1994a. 'Nine Poems'. *Journal of Contemporary Ethnography* 23(1): 3–13.

Richardson, L. 1994b. 'Writing: A Method of Inquiry'. Pp. 516–29. In *Handbook of Qualitative Research*, edited by N.K. Denzin and Y.S. Lincoln. Thousand Oaks, CA: Sage Publications.

Richardson, L. 1996a. 'Educational Birds'. *Journal of Contemporary Ethnography* 25(1): 6–15.

Richardson, L. 1996b. 'A Sociology of Responsibility'. *Qualitative Sociology* 19(4): 519–24.

Richardson, L. 1997. *Field of Play: Constructing an Academic Life*. New Brunswick, NJ: Rutgers University Press.

Richardson, L. 1999. 'Jeopardy'. Presented at the Forum Lecture Series, February 4, University of Nevada, Las Vegas.

Richardson, L. 2000. 'Writing: A Method of Inquiry'. Pp. 923–48. In *Handbook of Qualitative Research*, 2nd edition, edited by N.K. Denzin and Y.S. Lincoln. Thousand Oaks, CA: Sage Publications.

Richardson, L. 2002. 'Poetic Representation of Interviews'. Pp. 877–91. In *Handbook of Interview Research: Context & Method*, edited by J.F. Gubrium and J.A. Holstein. Thousand Oaks, CA: Sage Publications.

Richardson, L. and E.A. St. Pierre. 2005. 'Writing: A Method of Inquiry'. Pp. 959–78. In *The Sage Handbook of Qualitative Research,* 3rd edition, edited by N.K. Denzin and Y.S. Lincoln. Thousand Oaks, CA: Sage Publications.

Richardson, M. 2000. 'How We Live: Participatory Research with Six People with Learning Difficulties'. *Journal of Advanced Nursing* 32: 1383–95.

Rickard, W. 2003. 'Collaborative With Sex Workers in Oral History'. *The Oral History Review* 30(1): 47–59.

Ridge, D., A. Hee and R. Aroni. 1999. 'Being "Real" in Suicide Prevention Evaluation: The Role of the Ethnographers Emotions under Traumatic Conditions'. *Australian Journal of Primary Health-Interchange* 5(3): 21–31.

Riessman, C.K. 1990. *Divorce Talk: Women and Men Make Sense of Personal Relationships.* New Brunswick, NJ: Rutgers University Press.

Ringheim, K. 1995. 'Ethical Issues in Social Science Research with Special Reference to Sexual Behaviour Research'. *Social Science and Medicine* 40(12): 1691–97.

Roberts, S.J., C.A. Patsdaughter, C.G. Grindel and M.S. Tarmina. 2004. 'Health Related Behaviors and Cancer Screening of Lesbians: Results of the Boston Lesbian Health Project II'. *Women & Health* 39(4): 41–55.

Robertson, J. 2000. 'Ethical Issues and Researching Sensitive Topics: Mature Women and :"Bulimia" '. *Feminism & Psychology* 10(4): 531–37.

Robinson, N. 1999. 'The Use of Focus Group Methodology – With Selected Examples From Sexual Health Research'. *Journal of Advanced Nursing* 29(4): 905–13.

Romero-Daza, N., M. Weeks and M. Singer. 2003. ' "Nobody Gives a Damn if I Live or Die": Violence, Drugs, and Street-Level Prostitution in Inner-City Hartford, Connecticut'. *Medical Anthropology* 22: 233–59.

Ronai, C.R. 1995. 'Multiple Reflections of Child Abuse: An Argument for a Layered Account'. *Journal of Contemporary Ethnography* 23(4): 395–426.

Ronai, C.R. 1996. 'My Mother is Mentally Retarded'. Pp. 109–31. In *Composing Ethnography: Alternative Forms of Qualitative Writing*, edited by C. Ellis and A.P. Bochner. Walnut Creek, CA: AltaMira.

Ronai, C.R. 1998. 'Sketching with Derrida: An Ethnography of a Researcher/Erotic Dancer'. *Qualitative Inquiry* 4(3): 405–20.

Ronai, C.R. and C. Ellis. 2001. 'Turn-ons for Money: Interactional Strategies of the Table Dancer'. Pp. 168–82. In *Extreme Methods: Innovative Approaches to Social Science Research*, edited by J.M. Miller and R. Tewksbury. Boston, MA: Allyn and Bacon.

Rosenblatt, P.C. 2001. 'Qualitative Research as a Spiritual Experience'. Pp. 111–28. In *The Emotional Nature of Qualitative Research*, edited by K.R. Gilbert. London: CRC.

Rosenblatt, P.C. 2002. 'Interviewing at the Border of Fact and Fiction'. Pp. 893–909. In *Handbook of Interview Research: Context & Method*, edited by J.F. Gubrium and J.A. Holstein. Thousand Oaks, CA: Sage Publications.

Rosenblatt, P.C. and L.R. Fischer. 1993. 'Qualitative Family Research'. Pp. 167–77. In *Sourcebook of Family Theories and Methods: A Contextual Approach*, edited by

P.G. Boss, W.J. Doherty, R. LaRossa, W.R. Schumn and S.K. Steinmetz. New York: Plenum.

Rosenthal, R. 1991. 'Straighter from the Source: Alternative Methods for Researching Homelessness'. *Urban Anthropology* 20(2): 109–26.

Ross, M., E. Rideout and M. Carson. 1994. 'The Use of the Diary as a Data Collection Technique'. *Western Journal of Nursing Research* 16(4): 27–40.

Rothman, B.K. 1986. 'Reflections: On Hard Work'. *Qualitative Sociology* 9: 48–53.

Rowling, L. 1999. 'Being In, Being Out, Being With: Affect and the Role of the Qualitative Researcher in Loss and Grief Research'. *Mortality* 4(2): 167–81.

Rubin, H.J. and I.S. Rubin. 1995. *Qualitative Interviewing: The Art of Hearing Data*. Thousand Oaks, CA: Sage Publications.

Rubin, L.R., M.L. Fitts and A.E. Becker. 2003. ' "Whatever Feels Good in My Soul": Body Ethics and Aesthetics Among African American and Latina Women'. *Culture, Medicine and Psychiatry* 27: 49–75.

Russell, C. 1999. 'Interviewing Vulnerable Old People: Ethical and Methodological Implications of Imagining Our Subjects'. *Journal of Aging Studies* 13(4): 403–17.

Russell, D. 1990. *Rape in Marriage*, New York: Macmillan.

Russon, C. 1995. 'The Influence of Culture on Evaluation'. *Evaluation Journal of Australasia* 7(1): 44–49.

Sachs, G. 1998. 'Informed Consent for Research on Human Subjects With Dementia'. *Journal of the American Geriatrics Society* 46: 8602–14.

Sagui, A. 2002. 'Sex, Inequality and Ethnography: Response to Erich Goode'. *Qualitative Sociology* 25: 549–56.

Salazar, M.C. 1991. 'Young Laborers in Bogota: Breaking Authoritarian Ramparts'. Pp. 54–63. In *Action and Knowledge: Breaking the Monopoly with Participatory Action-Research*, edited by O. Fals-Borda and M.A. Rahman. New York: Apex Press.

Saldaña, J. 1999. 'Playing Writing With Data: Ethnographic Performance Texts'. *Youth Theatre Journal* 13: 60–71.

Saldaña, J. (ed.). 2005. *Ethnodrama: An Anthology of Reality Theatre*. Walnut Creek, CA: AltaMira Press.

Salmon, K. 2001. 'Remembering and Reporting by Children: The Influence of Cues and Props'. *Clinical Psychology Review* 21(2): 267–300.

Sandeloski, M., D. Holditch-Davis and B.G. Harris. 1992. 'Using Qualitative and Quantitative Methods: The Transition to Parenthood of Infertile Couples'. Pp. 301–22. In *Qualitative Methods in Family Research*, edited by J.F. Gilgun, K. Daly and G. Handel. Newbury Park, CA: Sage Publications.

Sandoval, C. 2000. *Methodology of the Oppressed*. Minneapolis, MN: University of Minnesota Press.

Saukko, P. 2000. 'Between Voice and Discourse: Quilting Interviews on Anorexia'. *Qualitative Inquiry* 6: 299–317.

Scambler, G. and A. Scambler. 1997. *Rethinking Prostitution: Purchasing Sex in the 1990s*. London: Routledge.

Scarce, R. 1994. '(No) Trial (But) Tribulations: When Courts and Ethnography Conflict'. *Journal of Contemporary Ethnography* 23(2): 123–49.

Scarce, R. 2001. 'Scholarly Ethics and Courtroom Antics: Where Researchers Stand in the Eyes of the Law'. Pp. 258–72. In *Extreme Methods: Innovative Approaches to Social Science Research*, edited by J.M. Miller and R. Tewksbury. Boston, MA: Allyn and Bacon.

Schneider, B., H. Scissons, L. Arney, G. Benson, J. Derry, K. Lucas, M. Misurelli, D. Nickerson and M. Sunderland. 2004. 'Communication Between People With

Schizophrenia and Their Medical Professionals: A Participatory Research Project'. *Qualitative Health Research* 14(4): 562–77.

Schoenberg, N.E., C. Hopenhayn, A. Christian, E.A. Knight and A. Rubio. 2005. 'An In-Depth and Updated Perspective on Determinants of Cervical Cancer Screening Among Central Appalachian Women'. *Woman & Health* 42(2): 89–105.

Schulze, B. and M.C. Angermeyer. 2003. 'Subjective Experiences of Stigma. A Focus Group Study of Schizophrenia Patients, Their Relatives and Mental Health Professionals'. *Social Science and Medicine* 56: 299–12.

Schwartz, M.D. (ed.). 1997. *Researching Sexual Violence against Women: Methodological and Personal Perspectives.* Thousand Oaks, CA: Sage Publications.

Seal, D.W., F.R. Bloom and A.M. Somlai. 2000. 'Dilemmas in Conducting Qualitative Sex Research in Applied Field Settings'. *Health Education & Behavior* 27(1): 10–23.

Seals, B.F., R.L. Sowell, A.S. Demi, L. Moneyham, L. Cohen and J. Guillory. 1995. 'Falling Through the Cracks: Social Service Concerns of Women Infected with HIV'. *Qualitative Health Research* 5(4): 496–515.

Selwyn, N. and K. Robson. 1998. 'Using E-Mail as a Research Tool', *Social Research Update 21.* Available at: http://www.soc.surrey.ac.uk/sru/SRU21.html (Accessed 14/4/2006)

Seymour, J., G. Bellamy, M. Gott, S.H. Ahmedzai and D. Clark. 2002. 'Using Focus Groups to Explore Older People's Attitudes to End of Life Care'. *Ageing & Society* 22: 517–26.

Seymour, J., G. Bellamy, M. Gott, S.H. Ahmedzai and D. Clark. 2004. 'Planning for the End of Life: The Views of Older People About Advance Care Statement'. *Social Science and Medicine* 59: 57–68.

Seymour, J., G. Dix and T. Eardley. 1995. *Joint Accounts: Methodology and Practice in Research Interviews With Couples.* York, UK: Social Policy Research Unit.

Seymour, J.E. and C. Ingleton. 1999. 'Ethical Issue in Qualitative Research at the End of Life'. *International Journal of Palliative Nursing* 5(2): 65–73.

Seymour, W. 2001. 'Putting Myself in the Picture: Researching Disability and Technology'. Pp. 120–33. In *Technologies and Health: Critical Compromises*, edited by J. Daly, M. Guillemin, S. Hill. Melbourne: Oxford University Press.

Seymour, W. and D. Lupton. 2004. 'Holding the Line Online: Exploring Wired Relationships for People with Disabilities'. *Disability & Society*, 19(4): 291–305.

Shaffir, W.B. and R.A. Stebbins. (eds). 1991. *Experiencing Fieldwork: An Inside View of Qualitative Research.* Newbury Park, CA: Sage Publications.

Shahidian, H. 2001.' "To Be Recorded in History": Researching Iranian Underground Political Activists in Exile'. *Qualitative Sociology* 24(1): 55–81.

Shalhoub-Kevorkian, N. 2003. 'Liberating Voices: The Political Implications of Palestinian Mothers Narrating their Loss'. *Women's Studies International Forum* 26(5): 391–407.

Sharpe, P.A., H.M. Brandt and D.H. McCree. 2005. 'Knowledge and Beliefs About Abnormal Pap Test Results and HPV Among Women With High-Risk HPV: Results from In-Depth Interviews'. *Woman & Health* 42(2): 107–33.

Shelton, A. 1995. 'The Man at the End of the Machine'. *Symbolic Interaction* 18: 505–18.

Shelton, A.J. and N.J. Rianon. 2004. 'Recruiting Participants for a Community of Bangladeshi Immigrants for a Study of Spousal Abuse: An Appropriate Cultural Approach'. *Qualitative Health Research* 14(3): 369–80.

Shostak, M. 2000. *Return to Nisa.* Cambridge, MA: Harvard University Press.

Shuy, R.W. 2002. 'In-Person Versus Telephone Interviewing'. Pp. 537–55. In *Handbook of Interview Research: Context & Method*, edited by in J.F. Gubrium and J.A. Holstein. Thousand Oaks, CA: Sage Publications.

Sieber, J.E. 1992. *Planning Ethically Responsible Research: A Guide for Students and Internal Review Boards*. Newbury Park: Sage Publications.

Sieber, J.E. and B. Stanley. 1988. 'Ethical and Professional Dimensions of Socially Sensitive Research'. *American Psychologist* 43: 49–55.

Silva, M.C. 1995. *Ethical Guidelines in the Conduct, Dissemination, and Implementation of Nursing Research*. Washington, DC: American Nurses Publishing.

Silverman, D. 1993. *Interpreting Text and Data: Methods for Analysing Talk, Text and Interaction*. London: Sage Publications.

Silverman, D. (ed.). 2004. *Qualitative Research: Theory, Method and Practice*, 2nd edition. London: Sage Publications.

Sin, C.H. 2004. 'Sampling Minority Ethnic Older People in Britain'. *Ageing & Society* 24: 257–77.

Sin, C.H. 2005. 'Seeking Informed Consent: Reflections on Research Practice'. *Sociology* 39(2): 277–94.

Slater, R. 2000. 'Using Life Histories to Explore Change: Women's Urban Struggles in Cape Town, South Africa'. *Gender and Development* 8(2): 38–46.

Sluka, J.A.1995. 'Reflections on Managing Danger in Fieldwork'. Pp. 276–94. In *Fieldwork Under Fire: Contemporary Studies of Violence and Survival*, edited by C. Nordstrom and A.C.C.M. Robben. Berkeley, CA: University of California Press.

Small, S. 1996. 'Collaborative, Community-Based Research on Adolescents: Using Research for Community Change'. *Journal of Research on Adolescence* 6(1): 9–22.

Smith, C.Z. and A-M. Woodward. 1999. 'Photo-Elicitation Method Gives Voices and Reactions of Subjects'. *Journalism-and-Mass-Communication-Educator* 53(4): 31–41.

Smith, D.E. 1987. *The Everyday World as Problematic: A Feminist Sociology*. Boston, MA: Northeastern University Press.

Smith, G.H. 1992. *Research Issues Related to Māori Education*. Auckland: Research Unit for Māori Education, the University of Auckland.

Smith, L.T. 1999. *Decolonising Methodologies: Research and Indigenous Peoples*. London and Dunedin: Zed Books and University of Otago Press.

Smith, L.T. 2000. 'Kaupapa Māori Research'. Pp. 225–47. In *Reclaiming Indigenous Voice and Vision*, edited by M. Battiste. Vancouver, WA: University of British Columbia Press.

Smith, L.T. 2005. 'On Tricky Ground: Researching the Native in the Age of Uncertainty'. Pp. 85–108. In *The Sage Handbook of Qualitative Research*, 3rd edition, edited by N.K. Denzin and Y.S. Lincoln. Thousand Oaks, CA: Sage Publications.

Smith, P. 1999. 'Food Truck's Party Hat'. *Qualitative Inquiry* 5: 244–61.

Smith, S.E., D.G. Willms and N.A. Johnson. (eds). 1997. *Nurtured by Knowledge: Learning to Do Participatory Action-Research*. New York: Apex Press.

Smithson, J. 2000. 'Using and Analysing Focus Groups: Limitations and Possibilities'. *International Journal of Social Research Methodology* 3: 103–19.

Socolar, R., D.K. Runyan and L. Amata-Jackson. 1995. 'Methodological and Ethical Issues Related to Studying Child Maltreatment'. *Journal of Family Issues* 16: 565–86.

Solomon, M. 2006. 'Narrative Resources and Identity in an Online Support Group for Multiple Sclerosis'. Pp. 209–28. In *Health Research in Cyberspace: Methodological, Practical and Personal Issues*, edited by P. Liamputtong. New York: Nova Science Publishers.

Sommer, R. 1999. 'Action Research: From Mental Hospital Reform in Saskatchewan to Community Building in California'. *Canadian Psychology* 40(1): 47–55.

Song, M. 1998. 'Hearing Competing Voices: Sibling Research'. Pp. 103–12. In *Feminist Dilemmas in Qualitative Research*, edited by J. Ribbons and R. Edwards. London: Sage Publications.

Soskolne, C.L. 1997. 'Ethical, social, and legal issues surrounding studies of susceptible populations and individuals'. *Environmental Health Perspectives* 105(4): 837–41.

Sparkes, A. 1994. 'Self, Silence, and Invisibility as a Beginning Teacher: A Life History of Lesbian Experience'. *British Journal of Sociology of Education* 15(1): 93–119.

Sparkes, A. 1996. 'The Fatal Flaw: A Narrative of the Fragile Body-Self'. *Qualitative Inquiry* 2(4): 463–94.

Spender, D. 1995. *Nattering on the Net: Women, Power and Cyberspace.* Melbourne: Spinifex.

Spradley, J.P. 1979. 'The Ethnographic Interview'. New York: Holt, Rinehart and Winston.

Spry, T. 1997. 'Skins: A Daughter's (Re)Construction of Cancer: A Performative Autobiography'. *Text and Performance Quarterly* 17: 361–65.

Spry, T. 2001. 'Performing Autoethnography: An Embodied Methodological Praxis'. *Qualitative Inquiry* 7: 706–32.

Sque, M. 2000. 'Researching the Bereaved: An Investigator's Experience'. *Nursing Ethics* 7(1): 23–34.

Stacey, J. 1988. 'Can there be a Feminist Ethnography?'. *Women's Studies International Forum* 11: 21–27.

Stalker, K. 1998. 'Some Ethical and Methodological Issues in Research With People With Learning Difficulties'. *Disability and Society* 13(1): 5–19.

Stanko, E.A. 1997. ' "I Second That Emotion": Reflections on Feminism, Emotionality, and Research on Sexual Violence'. Pp. 74–85. In *Researching Sexual Violence Against Women: Methodological and Personal Perspectives*, edited by M.D. Schwartz. Thousand Oaks, CA: Sage Publications.

Stanley, B., M. Stanley, A. Lautin, J. Kane and N. Schwartz. 1981. 'Preliminary Findings on Psychiatric Patients as Research Participants: A Population at Risk?'. *American Journal of Psychiatry* 138: 669–71.

Stanley, L. 1990. Feminist Praxis and the Academic Mode of Production'. Pp. 3–19. In *Feminist Praxis*, edited by L. Stanley. London: Routledge.

Stanley, L. 1992. *The Auto/Biography I: Theory and Practice of Feminist Auto/Biography.* Manchester, NH: Manchester University Press.

Stanley, L. and S. Wise. 1993. 'Method, Methodology, and Epistemology in Feminist Research Process'. Pp. 20–60. In *Feminist Praxis: Research, Theory and Epistemology in Feminist Sociology*, edited by L. Stanley. New York: Routledge.

Stebbins, R.A. 1991. 'Do We Ever Leave the Field?' Pp. 248–55. In *Experiencing Fieldwork: An Inside View of Qualitative Research*, edited by W.B. Shaffir and R.A. Stebbins. Newbury Park, CA: Sage Publications.

Steinberg, A.M., R.S. Pynoos, A.K. Goenjaan, H. Sossanabadi and L. Sherr. 1999. 'Are Researchers Bound by Child Abuse Reporting Laws?'. *Violence and Victims* 5(1): 67–71.

Steinhauser, K.E., E.C. Clipp, M. McNeilly, N.A. Christakis, L.M. McIntyre and J.A. Tulsky. 2000. 'In Search of a Good Death: Observations of Patients, Families and Providers'. *Annals of Internal Medicine* 132: 825–32.

Stephens, C., J. Carryer and C. Budge. 2004. 'To Have or To Take: Discourse, Positioning, and Narrative Identity in Women's Account of HRT'. *Health: An Interdisciplinary Journal for the Social Study of Health, Illness and Medicine* 8(3): 329–50.

Stephenson, N. 1992. *Snow Crash*. New York: Bantam.

Sterk, C.E., H. Klein and K.W. Elifson. 2004. 'Self-Esteem and "At Risk" women: Determinants and Relevance to Sexual and HIV-Related Risk Behaviors'. *Women & Health* 40(4): 75–92.

Stevens, J.W. and J.A. Capitman. 2005. 'Disaster and Loss: Drug Research in an Urban Community'. *Families in Society* 86(2): 279–86.

Stewart, F., E. Eckerman and K. Zhou. 1998. 'Using the Internet in Qualitative Public Health Research: A Comparison of Chinese and Australian Young Women's Perceptions of Tobacco Use'. *Internet Journal of Health Promotion*, December 29. Available at: http://www.monash.edu.au/health/IJHP/1998/12 (Accessed 5/1/1999).

Stewart, R. and A. Bhangwanjee. 1999. 'Promoting Group Empowerment and Self-Reliance Through Participatory Research: A Case Study of People with Physical Disability'. *Disability & Rehabilitation* 21: 338–45.

Stoller, L.R. 2002. 'Researching Childhood Sexual Abuse: Anticipating Effects on the Researcher'. *Feminism and Psychology* 12(2): 269–74.

Stoller, P. 1989. *The Taste of the Field: On Writing Ethnography*. Chicago, IL: University of Chicago Press.

Stone, T.H. 2003. 'The Invisible Vulnerable: The Economically and Educationally Disadvantaged Subjects of Clinical Research'. *The Journal of Law, Medicine and Ethics* 31(1): 149–53.

Stones, A. and D. Perry. 1998. Preliminary Evaluation of the World Wide Web as a Tool for Data Collection in the Area of Panic Research. Paper presented at the Computers in Psychology Conference, April, University of York.

Strickland, O.L., M.F. Moloney, A.S. Dietrich, S. Myerburg, G.A. Cotsonis and R.V. Johnson. 2003. 'Measurement Issues Related to Data Collection on the World Wide Web'. *Advances in Nursing Science* 26(4): 246–56.

Stringer, E. and W.J. Genat. 2004. *Action Research in Health*. Upper Saddle River, NJ: Pearson Education Inc.

Struthers, R. 2000. 'The Lived Experience of Ojibwa and Cree Women Healers'. *Journal of Holistic Nursing* 18(3): 261–79.

Struthers, R. 2001. 'Conducting Sacred Research: An Indigenous Experience'. *Wicazo Sa Review* 16(1): 125–33.

Struthers, R. and C. Peden-McAlpine. 2005. 'Phenomenological Research Among Canadian and United States Indigenous Populations: Oral Tradition Quintessence of Time'. *Qualitative Health Research* 15(9): 1264–76.

Struthers, R. and V.S. Eschiti. 2005. 'Being Healed by an Indigenous Traditional Healer: Sacred Healing Stories of Native Americans, Part II. *Complementary Therapies in Clinical Practice* 11: 78–86.

Stuttaford, M., C. Bryanston, G.L. Hundt, M. Connor, M. Thorogood and S. Tollman. 2006. 'Use of Applied Theatre in Health Research Dissemination and Data Validation: A Pilot Study from South Africa. *Health: An Interdisciplinary Journal for the Social Study of Health, Illness and Medicine* 10(1): 31–45.

Sullivan, K. 1998. 'Managing the "Sensitive" Interview: A Personal Account'. *Nurse Researcher* 6(2): 72–85.

Sustik, A. 1999. *An Auto-Photographic, Naturalistic Investigation of the Adjustment of Refugees from the Former Soviet Union to Life in the United States*. Unpublished doctoral thesis, Loyola University.

Swain, J., B. Heyman and M. Gillman. 1998. 'Public Research, Private Concerns: Ethical Issues in the Use of Open-Ended Interviews With People Who Have Learning Difficulties'. *Disability and Society* 13: 21–36.

Swantz, M-L., E. Ndedya and M.S. Masaiganah. 2001. 'Participatory Action Research in Southern Tanzania, with Special Reference to Women'. Pp. 386–95. In *Handbook of Action Research: Participative Inquiry and Practice*, edited by P. Reason and H. Bradbury. London: Sage Publications.

Swart, J. 1990. *Malunde: The Street Children of Hillbrow*. Johannesburg: Witwatersrand University Press.

Takahashi, M. and I. Kai. 2005. 'Sexuality After Breast Cancer Treatment: Changes and Coping Strategies Among Japanese Survivors'. *Social Science and Medicine* 61: 1278–90.

Tandon, S.D., J.G. Keyy and L.O. Mock. 2001. 'Participatory Action Research as a Resource for Developing African American Community Leadership. Pp. 200–17. In *From Subjects to Subjectivities: A Handbook of Interpretive and Participatory Methods*, edited by D.L. Tolman and M. Brydon-Miller. New York: New York University Press.

Taylor, W.K., L. Magnussen and M.J. Amundson. 2001. 'The Lived Experience of Battered Women'. *Violence Against Women* 7(5): 563–85.

Tedlock, B. 2005. 'The Observation of Participant and the Emergence of Public Ethnography'. Pp. 467–81. In *The Sage Handbook of Qualitative Research,* 3rd edition, edited by N.K. Denzin and Y.S. Lincoln. Thousand Oaks, CA: Sage Publications.

Temple, B. 1997. 'Watch Your Tongue: Issues in Translation and Cross-Cultural Research'. *Sociology* 31(3): 607–18.

Tewksbury, R. 1994. ' "Speaking of Someone with AIDS" ': Identity Construction of Persons with HIV Disease'. *Deviant Behavior* 15: 337–55.

Tewksbury, R. 2001. 'Acting Like an Insider: Studying Hidden Environments as a Potential Participant'. Pp. 4–12. In *Extreme Methods: Innovative Approaches to Social Science Research*, edited by J.M. Miller and R. Tewksbury. Boston, MA: Allyn and Bacon.

Tewksbury, R. and P. Gagné. 2001. 'Assumed and Presumed Identities: Problems of Self-Presentation in Field Research'. Pp. 72–93. In *Extreme Methods: Innovative Approaches to Social Science Research*, edited by J.M. Miller and R. Tewksbury. Boston, MA: Allyn and Bacon.

Thomas, B., L.L. Stamler, K. Lafreniere, J. Out and T.D. Delahunt. 2002. 'Using the Internet to Identify Women's Sources of Breast Health Education and Screening'. *Women & Health* 36(1): 33–48.

Thomas, G. 1990. *Afro-Caribbean Elderly People: Coping with Ageing*. Coventry, West Midlands: Social Care Practice Centre, Department of Applied Social Studies, University of Warwick.

Thompson, S. 1995. *Going All the Way: Teenage Girls' Tales of Sex, Romance, and Pregnancy*, New York: Hill & Wang.

Thoutenhoofd, E. 1998. 'Method in Photographic Enquiry of Being Deaf'. *Sociological Research Online* 3(2). Available at: http://wwwsocresonline.org.uk/socresonline /3/2/2/html (Accessed 12/8/2005).

Tierney, W.G. 2000. 'Undaunted Courage: Life History and the Postmodern Challenge'. Pp. 537–53. In *Handbook of Qualitative Research*, 2nd edition, edited by N.K. Denzin and Y.S. Lincoln. Thousand Oaks, CA: Sage Publications.

Tierney, W.G. 2002. 'Get Real: Representing Reality'. *Qualitative Studies in Education* 15: 385–98.

Tierney, W.G. and Y.S. Lincoln. (eds). 1997. *Representation and the Text: Re-Framing the Narrative Voice*. Albany, NY: State University of New York Press.

Tilman-Healy, L. 1996. 'A Secret Life in a Culture of Thinness: Reflections on Body, Food, and Bulimia. Pp. 77–109. In *Composing Ethnography6: Alternative Forms of*

Qualitative Writing, edited by C. Ellis and A. Bochner. Walnut Creek, CA: AltaMira Press.

Todorova, I.L.G. and T. Kotzeva. 2003. 'Social Discourses, Women's Resistive Voices: Facing Involuntary Childlessness in Bulgaria'. *Women's Studies International Forum* 26(2): 139–51.

Tourangeau, R. and T.W. Smith. 1996. 'Asking Sensitive Questions: The Impact of Data Collection Mode, Question Format, and Question Context'. *The Public Opinion Quarterly* 60: 275–304.

Treloar, C. and S. Fraser. 2004. 'Hepatitis C, Blood and Models of the Body: New Directions for Public Health'. *Critical Public Health* 14(4): 377–89.

Tsey, K. and A. Every. 2000. 'Evaluating Aboriginal Empowerment Programs – The Case of Family Wellbeing'. *Australian and New Zealand Journal of Public Health* 24: 509–14.

Tsey, K., D. Patterson, M. Whiteside, L. Baird and B. Baird. 2002. 'Indigenous Men Taking Their Rightful Place in Society? A Preliminary Analysis of a Participatory Action Research Process with Yarrabah Men's Health Group'. *Australian Journal of Rural Health* 10(6): 278–83.

Tsey, K., D. Patterson, M. Whiteside, L. Baird, B. Baird and K. Tsey. 2004. 'A Microanalysis of a Participatory Action Research Process with a Rural Aboriginal Men's Health Group'. *Australian Journal of Primary Health* 10(1): 64–71.

Turney, L. and C. Pocknee. 2005. 'Virtual Focus Groups: New Frontiers in Research'. International Journal of Qualitative Methods 4(2). Available at: http://www. ualberta.ca/~ijqm/backissues/4_2/pdf/turney.pdf (Accessed 9/10/2005).

Twinn, S. 1998. 'An Analysis of the Effectiveness of Focus Groups as a Method of Qualitative Data Collection with Chinese Populations in Nursing Research'. *Journal of Advanced Nursing* 28(3): 654–61.

Umaña-Taylor, A.J. and M.Y. Bámaca. 2004. 'Conducting Focus Groups with Latino Populations: Lessons from the Field'. *Family Relations* 53: 261–72.

Usher, K. and C. Holmes. 1997. 'Ethical Aspects of Phenomenological Research with Mentally Ill People'. *Nursing Ethics* 4(1): 49–56.

Valenzuela, A. 1999. *Subtractive Schooling: U.S.-Mexican Youth and the Politics of Caring*. Albany, NY: State University of New York Press.

Van Den Hoonaard, W.C. (ed.). 2002. *Walking the Tightrope: Ethical Issues for Qualitative Researchers*. Toronto: University of Toronto Press.

van Kesteren, N.M.C., H. J. Hospers, G. Kok and P. van Empelen. 2005. 'Sexuality and Sexual Risk Behavior in HIV-Positive Men Who Have Sex With Men'. *Qualitative Health Research* 15(2): 145–68.

Van Maanen, J. 1982. 'Fieldwork on the Beat'. Pp. 103–51. In *Varieties of Qualitative Research*, edited by J. Van Maanen, J. Dabvbsa, Jr and R.R. Faulkner. Beverly Hills, CA: Sage Publications.

Van Maanen, J. 1995. 'An End to Innocence: The Ethnography of Ethnography'. Pp. 245–72. In *Representation in Ethnography*, edited by J. Van Mannen. Thousand Oaks, CA: Sage Publications.

Van Manen, M. 2006. 'Writing Qualitatively, Or the Demands of Writing'. *Qualitative Health Research* 16(5): 713–22.

Vance, D. 1995. 'Barriers and Aids in Conducting Research with Older Homeless Individuals'. *Psychological Reports* 76: 783–86.

Varas-Diaz, N., I. Serrano-Garcia and J. Toro-Alfonso. 2005. 'AIDS-Related Stigma and Social Interaction: Puerto Ricans Living With HIV/AIDS'. *Qualitative Health Research* 15(2): 169–87.

Verbrugge, L. 1980. 'Health Diaries'. *Medical Care* 18: 73–95.

Victoria, G.C. and D. Knauth. 2001. 'Images of the Body and the Reproductive System among Men and Women Living in Shantytown in Porto Alegre, Brazil'. *Reproductive Health Matters* 9: 22–33.

Vissandjée, B., S.N. Abdool and S. Dupéré. 2002. 'Focus Groups in Rural Gujarat, India: A Modified Approach'. *Qualitative Health Research* 12(6): 826–43.

Volker, D.L. 2004. 'Methodological Issues Associated With Studying An Illegal Act: Assisted Dying'. *Advances in Nursing Science* 27(2): 117–128.

Wadsworth, Y. 1984. *Do it Yourself Social Research*. Melbourne: Victorian Council of Social Services.

Wahab, S. 2003. 'Creating Knowledge Collaboratively with Female Sex Workers: Insights from a Qualitative, Feminist and Participatory Study'. *Qualitative Inquiry* 9: 625–42.

Wakefield, H. and R. Underwager. 1998. 'The Application of Images in Child Abuse Investigations. Pp. 176–94. In *Image-Based Research: A Sourcebook for Qualitative Researchers*, edited by J. Prosser. London: Falmer Press.

Waldby, C., M. Rosengarten, C. Treloar and S. Fraser. 2004. 'Blood and Bioidentity: Ideas About Self, Boundaries and Risk Among Blood Donors and People Living With Hepatitis C'. *Social Science and Medicine* 59: 1461–71.

Wallerstein, N. and B. Duran . 2003. 'The Conceptual, Historial, and Practice Roots of Community Based Participatory Research and Related Participatory Traditions'. Pp. 27–52. In *Community-Based Participatory Research for Health*, edited by M. Minkler and N. Wallestein. San Francisco, CA: Jessey-Bass.

Wallestein, N. and M. Minkler. 2003. 'The Conceptual, Historical, and Practice Roots of Community Based Participatory Research and Related Participatory Traditions'. Pp. 27–52. In *Community-Based Participatory Research for Health*, edited by M. Minkler, and N. Wallestein. San Francisco, CA: Jessey-Bass.

Wang, C.C. 1999. 'Photovoice: A Participatory Action Research Strategy Applied to Women's Health'. *Journal of Women's Health* 8(2): 185–92.

Wang, C.C. 2003. 'Using Photovoice as a Participatory Assessment and Issue Selection Tool: A Case Study with the Homeless in Ann Arbor. Pp. 179–96. In *Community-Based Participatory Research for Health*, edited by M. Minkler and N. Wallestein. San Francisco: Jossey-Bass.

Wang, C.C., S. Morrel-Samuels and P. Hutchison. 2004. 'Flint Photovoice: Community Building among Youth, Adults, and Policy Makers'. *American Journal of Public Health* 94(6): 911–13.

Ware, N., M.A. Wyatt and T. Tugenberg. 2005. 'Adherence, Stereotyping and Unequal HIV Treatment for Active Users of Illegal Drugs'. *Social Science and Medicine* 61: 565–76.

Warkentin, R. 2002. 'Writing Competitions as a New Research Method'. *International Journal of Qualitative Methods* 1(4), Article 1. Available at: http://www.ualberta. ca/~ijqm/ (Accessed 6/12/2005).

Warr, D.J. 2004. 'Stories in the Flesh and Voices in the Head: Reflections on the Context and Impact of Research with Disadvantaged Populations'. *Qualitative Health Research* 14(4): 578–87.

Warr, D.J. 2005. ' "It Was Fun ... But We Don't Usually Talk About These Things": Analyzing Sociable Interaction in Focus Groups'. *Qualitative Inquiry* 11(2): 200–25.

Warr, D.J. and P.M. Pyett. 1999. 'Difficult Relations: Sex Work, Love and Intimacy'. *Sociology of Health & Illness* 21(3): 290–309.

Warren, C.A.B. 2002. 'Qualitative Interviewing'. Pp. 83–101. In *Handbook of Interview Research: Context & Method*, edited by J.F. Gubrium and J.A. Holstein. Thousand Oaks, CA: Sage Publications.

Wasserfall, R.R. 1997. 'Reflexivity, Feminism, and Difference'. Pp. 150–68. In *Reflexivity and Voice*, edited by R. Hertz. Thousand Oaks, CA: Sage Publications.

Watson, L., J. Irwin and S. Michalske. 1991. 'Researcher as Friend: Methods of the Interviewer in a Longitudinal Study'. *Qualitative Health Research* 1(4): 497–514.

Weaver, K., J. Wuest and D. Ciliska. 2005. 'Understanding Women's Journey of Recovering from Anorexia Nervosa'. *Qualitative Health Research* 15(2): 188–206.

Weiniger, S. 1998. 'Children Living in Poverty: Their Perception of Career Opportunities'. *Families in Society* May-June: 320–30.

Welbourn, A. 1992. 'Rapid Rural Appraisal, Gender and Health: Alternative Ways of Listening to Needs'. *Institute of Development Studies Bulletin* 23(1): 8–18.

Wellings, K., P. Branigan and K. Mitchell. 2000. 'Discomfort, Discord and Discontinuity as Data: Using Focus Groups to Research Sensitive Topics. *Culture, Health & Sexuality* 2(3): 255–67.

Wenger, G.C. 2002. 'Interviewing Older People'. Pp. 259–78. In *Handbook of Interview Research: Context & Method*, edited by J.F. Gubrium and J.A. Holstein. Thousand Oaks, CA: Sage Publications.

West, M., E. Bondy and S. Hutchinson. 1991. 'Interviewing Institutionalized Elders: Threats to Validity'. *Image: Journal of Nursing Scholarship* 23: 171–76.

Weston, K. 2004. 'Fieldwork in Lesbian and Gay Communities'. Pp. 198–205. In *Feminist Perspectives on Social Research*, edited by S.N. Hesse-Biber and M.L. Yaiser. New York: Oxford University Press.

Wetton, N.M. 1992. 'Primary School Children and the World of Drugs. Pp. 27–39. In *Drug Use and Misuse*, edited by R. Evans and L. O'Connor. London: David Fulton.

Wetton, N.M. and J. McWhirter. 1998. 'Images and Curriculum Development in Health Education. Pp. 263–83. In *Image-Based Research: A Sourcebook for Qualitative Researchers*, edited by J. Prosser. London: Falmer Press.

Whittell, B. and P. Ramcharan. 1999. 'The Trouble with Kids: An Account of Problems Experienced with Local Children by People with Learning Disabilities'. *British Journal of Learning Disabilities* 28(1): 21–24.

Whittier, D. and D.K. Melendez. 2004. 'Intersubjectivity in the Intrapsychic Sexual Scripting of Gay Men'. *Culture, Health, & Sexuality* 6(2): 131–43.

Whyte, W.F. 1996. 'On the Evolution of Street Corner Society'. Pp. 9–74. In *Journey Through Ethnography: Realistic Accounts of Fieldwork*, edited by A. Laureau and F. Schultz. Boulder, CO: Westview Press.

Wiebel, W.W. 1990. 'Identifying and Gaining Access to Hidden Populations'. Pp. 4–11. In *The Collection and Interpretation of Data from Hidden Populations*, edited by E.Y. Lambert. Rockville, MD: National Institute on Drug Abuse.

Wight, D. 1994. 'Boys Thoughts and Talks About Sex in a Working Class Locality of Glasgow'. *The Sociological Review* 42: 703–37.

Wilkins, R. 1993. 'Talking it Personally: A Note on Emotions and Autobiography', *Sociology* 27(1): 93–100.

Wilkinson, S. 2004. 'Focus Groups: A Feminist Method'. Pp. 271–95. In *Feminist Perspectives on Social Research*, edited by S.N. Hesse-Biber and M.L. Yaiser. New York: Oxford University Press.

Williams, C. 2002. 'To Know Me is to Love Me?: Response to Erich Goode'. *Qualitative Sociology* 25: 557–60.

Williams, D., N. Wetton and A. Moon. 1989. *A Picture of Health: What do You do that Makes You Healthy and Keeps You Healthy?* London: Health Education Authority.

Williams, T. 1996. 'Exploring the Cocaine Culture'. Pp. 27–32. In *In the Field: Readings on the Field Research Experience*, 2nd edition, edited by C.D. Smith and W. Kornblum. Westport, CT: Praeger.

Williams, T., E. Dunlop, B. Johnson and A. Hamid. 1992. 'Personal Safety in Dangerous Places'. *Journal of Contemporary Ethnography* 21(3): 343–74.

Williams, T., E. Dunlap, B.D. Johnson and A. Hamid. 2001. 'Personal Safety in Dangerous Places'. Pp. 216–38. In *Extreme Methods: Innovative Approaches to Social Science Research*, edited by J.M. Miller and R. Tewksbury. Boston, MA: Allyn and Bacon.

Williamson, G.R. and S. Prosser. 2002. 'Action Research: Politics, Ethics and Participation'. *Journal of Advanced Nursing* 40(5): 587–93.

Willot, S. 1998. 'An Outsider Within: A Feminist Doing Research with Men'. Pp. 174–90. In *Standpoints and Differences: Essays in the Practice of Feminist Psychology*, edited by K. Henwood, C. Griffith and A. Phoenix. London: Sage Publications.

Willott, S. and C. Griffin. 1997. 'Wham Bam, Am I a Man? Unemployed Men Talk About Masculinities'. *Feminism and Psychology* 7: 107–28.

Winslow, W., W. Honein and M.A. Elzubeir. 2002. 'Seeking Emirati Women's Voices: The Use of Focus Groups with an Arab Population'. *Qualitative Health Research* 12(4): 566–75.

Wojcicki, J.M. and J. Malala. 2001. 'Condom Use, Power and HIV/AIDS Risks: Sex-Workers Bargain for Survival in Hillbrow/Jubert Park/Berea, Johannesburg'. *Social Science and Medicine* 53: 99–121.

Wolcott, H.F. 1995. *The Art of Fieldwork*. Walnut Creek, CA: AltaMira Press.

Wolf, D.R. 1991, 'High-Risk Methodology: Reflections on Leaving an Outlaw Society', In Experiencing Fieldwork, edited by W.B. Shffir and R.A. Stebbins. Newbury Park, CA: Sage Publications.

Wong, G.C., V.C. Li, M.A. Burris and Y. Xiang. 1995. 'Seeking Women's Voices: Setting the Context for Women's Health Interventions in Two Rural Counties in Yunnan, China'. *Social Science and Medicine* 41: 1147–57.

Worth, S. and J. Adair. 1972. *Through Navaho Eyes: An Exploration in Film Communication and Anthropology*. Bloomington, IN: Indiana University Press.

Wright, R., S.H. Decker, A.K. Redfern and D.L. Smith. 2001. 'A Snowball's Chance in Hell: Doing Fieldwork with Active Residential Burglars'. Pp. 94–102 in *Extreme Methods: Innovative Approaches to Social Science Research*, edited by J.M. Miller and R. Tewksbury. Boston, MA: Allyn and Bacon.

Wuest, J., M. Ford-Gilboe, M. Merritt-Gray and H. Berman. 2003. 'Intrusion: The Central Problem for Family Health Promotion Among Children and Single Mothers After Leaving an Abusive Partner'. *Qualitative Health Research* 13(5): 597–622.

Young, D. 2005. 'Will Exercising Informed Consent Stop "Unfortunate Experiments"?'. *Birth* 32(1): 1–3.

Zeller, R.A. 1993. 'Focus Group Research on Sensitive Topics: Setting the Agenda Without Setting the Agenda'. Pp. 167–83. In *Successful Focus Groups: Advancing the State of Art*, edited by D.L. Morgan. Newbury Park, CA: Sage Publications.

Ziller, R. 1990. *Photographing the Self: Methods for Observing Personal Orientations*. Newbury Park, CA: Sage Publications.

Index

Aboriginal grandmothers 181
Aboriginal people 64, 119
Aboriginal women 28, 65
Abortion 5, 6, 41, 67, 75, 81, 97, 108, 173,
    174, 179
Abuse 5, 6, 8, 9, 81, 82, 87, 142
Academic arrogance 185
Accidental fiction 171
Accuracy 32, 61, 99
An active collaborator 130
Activist theatre 172
Acts of colonization 132
African-Americans 63, 65, 75, 125
The AIDS activism 172
Alternative forms of representation/writing 165,
    166, 169, 170, 179, 182, 184, 186
Alternative methods 16, 18, 153
Alternative research approaches 165, 140–62,
    189, 192
Anorexia Nervosa 53, 97
Appalachian women 49
Applied theatre 178
Audio-diary 153, 154
Auto-photography 144

Back regions 2
The Belmont Report 24
Benefits in participating in research 10, 25, 32,
    33, 43, 45, 51, 104, 154, 191, 192
Bi-sexual/bi-sexuality 31, 74, 90, 149
Black humour 170, 171
Black South African women 114
Bouncers 3, 128
Breast cancer 52, 65, 86, 178
Breastfeeding 75
Bulimia 5
Burglaries/burglars 3, 50, 53, 62, 80, 92

Cancer 28, 30, 49, 85, 97, 103, 104, 126, 148, 168
Cancer patients 103

CAP ethnography 166
Catharsis 88, 172, 177, 183
Cervical cancer 49, 126
Child abuse 29, 42, 67, 79, 87, 149
Child death 84, 86, 88, 133, 171
Child prostitution 6, 8, 9, 83
Child rape 29, 42, 67, 90
Children 3, 4, 5, 6, 15, 27, 28, 29, 30, 34, 35,
    39, 40, 42, 52, 58, 60, 61, 67, 69, 77,
    86, 87, 88, 91, 98, 107, 108, 119,
    130, 133, 137, 145, 146, 147,
    148, 149, 152, 155, 156, 158, 159,
    162, 170, 183
The Chin-ups story 89
The civil right movement 172
Coercion 6, 62, 81, 157
Compensation for time 63, 64
Complete-member researcher 127
Confidentiality 23, 28, 29, 32, 33, 35–37, 42, 44,
    50, 51, 64, 66, 80, 89, 98, 191
Conventional forms of representation/writing
    165, 169, 170, 171, 181, 182, 183, 187
Conventional research approaches/methods 72,
    105, 106, 130, 132, 133, 141, 143, 157,
    159, 161, 192
The Council for International Organization of
    Medical Sciences 24
Counselling support 30, 42, 59, 67
Courtesy stigma 81
Covert methodology 128
Crack users 30, 41, 53
Creative interviewing 72
Crime 5, 49, 50, 53, 68, 78
Criminal acts 30, 45
Crisis of representation 165, 187, 189
Critical consciousness 131
Critically ill persons 6, 15, 31, 33, 34, 88, 168
Cross-cultural research 64, 74, 102, 110, 132,
    135, 136
A culture of silence 133

Dangerous fieldwork 91
Dangers in the field 77, 78, 79
Deaf people 144
Death 5, 6, 30, 43, 82, 84, 85, 88, 89, 103, 108,
    133, 148, 167
Death and dying 85, 108
Debriefing 42, 90, 91, 93, 109
Decentered position of researchers 19, 113,
    143, 191
Deception 32, 127
Democratization of exchange 157
Deviance/deviant 4, 6, 8, 12, 38, 49, 57, 59, 81,
    121, 127
A dialogue approach 19
Dialogues 73, 115, 131, 157, 160, 170, 172, 176,
    177, 193
Difficult-to-access people 4, 47, 69, 71, 76, 138
Difficult-to-reach people 48, 52, 77, 108, 122,
    156, 192
Disability and identity 73, 101
Disadvantaged people 1, 3, 24, 58, 60, 66,
    78, 89, 106
Discrimination 2, 27, 32, 45, 152
Disempowerment 25, 33, 177
Disenfranchised groups 2, 31, 47, 60
Domestic servants 112
Domestic violence 4, 28, 30, 38, 41, 64,
    73, 75, 79, 89, 94, 97, 100, 107, 108,
    116, 124
Domination 6, 18
Doubly vulnerable persons 4, 20, 68
Drama 20, 133, 141, 155, 171, 184, 189
Drug injectors 44, 50
Drug users 3, 4, 35, 37, 44, 50, 59, 62, 63, 64,
    94, 121
Dying people 35, 102

Electronic communication 157, 160
Emancipatory 130, 176, 177
Emotional contagion 71, 82
Emotionally laden research 6
Emotions in research 5, 12, 17
Empowerment 10, 11, 13, 17, 21, 29, 88, 100,
    106, 113, 115, 130, 135, 138, 143, 150,
    155, 156, 172, 174, 187
End of life care 28
Ethical issues 23, 24, 28, 32–44, 128, 138, 191
Ethics Committees 24
Ethics-as-process 42, 44
Ethnic community/minority 3, 4, 34, 36, 39,
    63, 88
Ethnicity 14, 57, 99, 162, 172, 194
Ethnographers 121, 167, 174, 182, 191
The experience of caring for a dying
    person 168
The experience of sexual abstinence 114

Experimental forms of writing 165, 166, 182,
    183, 185, 186, 189
Exploitation in research 6, 13, 26, 52, 58, 74
Exploited groups/people 129, 132

Face-to-face research methods 157, 158, 159
Family research 8, 27, 34, 62, 73, 75, 103
Fatherhood 97
Feminism 1, 9–14, 105
Feminism and commitments to social change
    10–14
Feminist ethic of care 13, 62, 136
A feminist Kartiya (White) 137
Feminist methodology 10, 11, 12, 13, 14, 61, 99,
    112, 113, 123, 141, 192
The feminist movement 172
Feminist praxis 11
Feminist research 1, 9–14, 17, 61, 97, 99, 106,
    123, 166, 185, 192
Feminist researchers 14, 17, 61, 62, 63,
    111, 180
Feminist standpoint 43, 75, 185
Flexible and collaborative research methods 13,
    118–38
    Covert participant observation 127–29, 153
    Ethnography 13, 118, 119–29, 138, 153,
        182, 191
    Participant observation 31, 118–25, 136, 153,
        174, 175, 191
    Participatory Action Research (PAR) 13, 16,
        64, 118, 119, 129–37, 138, 154, 160, 174,
        181, 191, 193
Former Soviet immigrants 64
The fourth revolution in the production of
    knowledge 157
Fractured world 1
A fractured world 187

Gang members 3
Gay and lesbian movement 76
Gay fathers 157, 159
Gay identity 108, 118
Gay men and lesbians 3, 4, 5, 31, 36, 73, 74, 76,
    90, 98, 99, 108, 141, 149, 157, 158,
    159, 187
Gender 11, 14, 61, 65, 71, 74–76, 82, 99, 108,
    110, 121, 141, 148, 149, 157, 162, 194
Gender differences between researchers and
    participants 75–76
Gender inequality 14
Grand narratives 15, 16, 192, 193
Ground level guerrilla warfare against oppression
    141, 156

Hard-to-reach people/population 3, 48, 49, 53,
    56, 63, 76, 86, 121, 152

Harm 2, 6, 9, 23, 24, 26, 27, 33, 35, 36, 37–41, 44, 45, 47, 62, 67, 71, 76–82, 85, 93, 94, 127, 181
Health needs of rural people 152–53
Health problems 4, 5, 79, 153, 159
Hidden population 3, 4, 49, 50, 55
The hidden world 59, 121
Hispanic Americans 48, 66, 175, 176
A hit and run approach 44, 57, 98
HIV/AIDS 4, 5, 32, 50, 57, 60, 64, 65, 70, 78, 81, 83, 84, 85, 89, 104, 107, 108, 110, 121, 124, 133, 152, 159, 167, 172
Hmong community 61, 120
Homeless people 3, 4, 25, 37, 49, 62, 63, 115, 147, 149, 150, 178
Homeless women 26, 27
Homosexuality 31, 39, 81
Hospital experience 146

Illegal activities 3, 5, 36, 45, 79, 81
Illness 5, 6, 7, 71, 87, 101, 104, 105, 126, 130, 147, 148, 150, 152, 169, 194
Illness experience 71, 147, 148
Immersion 120, 122
Immigrants 3, 4, 54, 64, 120, 129, 148, 178
Incest 29, 108
Indigenous people 113, 129, 132, 135, 137, 172, 187
The Indigenous Self-determination 131, 136, 137
Infertility 84, 88, 103, 159
Informed consent 23, 32, 33–35, 37, 39, 43, 44, 45, 127, 129, 192
  And disclosure of information 33, 34, 35
  Signing of 33, 34, 35
  Verbal/oral consent 42, 44
Injured workers 64, 133, 134
Innovative interviewing methods 95, 100–05
  Conjoint interviews 102–04
  Flexibilities in doing sensitive research 104–05
  Interview proxies 101–02
  Telephone interviewing 100–01
Innovative research methods 12, 13, 112, 133, 100, 140–62
  Arts-based research 18, 140, 155–56, 191
  Diary as a research method 140, 141, 151–54
  Drawing method 133, 140, 145, 148–51
  Online research 20, 140, 156–61, 189, 192
  Photo elicitation 140, 143–44
  Photoethnography 140, 141–43
  Photographic method 140, 141–48
  Reflexive photography 140, 144–47
  Video diaries 140, 147–48
  Visual imagery methods 133, 141, 142, 145, 147

Institutional Review Boards 24
Intensive biography interview 112
Intolerance 2
Involvement of local people 131, 132, 133

Juvenile prostitutes 28, 36, 42

Kanadier Mennonites 28
The Kapululangu Women's Law and Culture Centre 131, 136, 137
Kaupapa Māori research methodology 132
Key informants 49, 51, 58, 82, 102, 125

The labour movement 172
Latinos 49, 52, 63, 64, 75, 99
Legal authorities and research 38, 44
Legal responsibilities 29, 55, 62, 79
Level playing field 72
Lived experiences 9, 10, 15, 17, 27, 36, 57, 73, 74, 97, 100, 105, 112, 121, 128, 130, 138, 141, 147, 168, 170, 175, 176, 182, 187
Living on the ground method 136, 137
Living with dementia 8
Living with mental illness 102, 107, 108
Location of data collection 66–67
The London poor 121

The Māori 132, 136
Marginalisation 4, 99, 100, 121, 170
Marginalised groups 2, 132, 157, 158, 162
Masculine interpretation 111
Men who have sex with men 4, 50, 51, 64
Menopause and heart disease research 150, 151
Mental illness 4, 25, 39, 102, 107, 108, 130, 135, 174, 192
Mini-narratives 15, 192
Minority groups 3, 12, 33, 36, 73, 108, 192
Miscarriage 5, 6, 67, 84, 88
A moral discourse 176
Moral issues 23, 25–32, 192
Moral project 167
Moral territory 76
Mortification of self 26
Mothers 28, 29, 30, 35, 52, 75, 158, 166
Multicultural framework 113
Multicultural societies 120
Multi-faceted vulnerability 4
Multiple methods 16, 137
Multiple sclerosis 159
A multivocal text 125, 172
Multivoices 19, 105, 175
The mundane messiness of research 190
Mystory 155

Narrative discourse 166
Narrative inquiry 112

Native filmmakers 144
Native photographers 145
Navaho people 144
The Negev Bedouin Arabs 110
New forms of writing 20, 164–87
Nonscience voice 179
The Nuremberg Code 24

Older people 3, 4, 15, 25, 28, 33, 58, 68, 69, 73,
    75, 76, 100, 102, 108, 112, 154, 158, 159
Online research 20, 140, 156–61, 189, 192
  Accessing potential participants 158, 159
  Email as research tool 20, 157, 158, 160, 192
  The internet 20, 133, 141, 156, 157, 159,
    160, 192
  Virtual focus groups 157, 158, 159
Opportunistic research 127
Oppression/oppressed people 1, 11, 12, 17, 115,
    129, 132, 133, 170, 172, 181
Organ donors 26, 39, 87
The Others 165, 187
The Ouch! Factor 72
Overlapping marginality 4

Paintings 19, 60, 61, 133, 140, 145, 155,
    156, 189
Panic attacks 159
Parents of missing children 27, 29
Parents with drug problems 5, 39–41
Parents with learning difficulties 29, 30, 31,
    97–98, 104
Partnered interviewers 92, 93
A pedagogy of freedom 172
Peer group support 105
People living with disabilities 4, 130, 148, 154,
    157, 158, 159, 160, 161, 162
People suffering chronic illness 3, 78, 145, 154,
    159, 187
People undergoing detoxification 177, 178
People with learning disabilities 34, 142, 143
People with mental illness 3, 4, 15, 25, 33, 63
People with traumatic brain injury 177
People with visual impairments 69
People's knowledge 131
Perception of pain 141, 142
Person with developmental disability 180
Personal experiences 6, 11, 36, 75, 82, 85, 87,
    112, 155, 158, 165, 166, 167, 173
Personal narratives 147, 167, 184
Personal problems 111, 185
Personal troubles 62, 166
Persons living with AIDS 4, 57, 64, 70, 83, 89,
    104, 108, 121, 124
Photobiography 145
Photovoice 133, 161, 193
Physical harm 24, 33, 37–41

Plastic surgery 115, 116
Poetry 20, 141, 155, 166, 178, 179, 181, 182,
    183, 193
Political actions 135, 161
Political overtone 130
Political struggle 155, 165
Political violence 78
Polyphony 19
Poor people living in slums 119
Position of the researcher 11, 18, 143
Positivist science 8, 10, 13, 15, 27, 100, 192, 193
Postmodern sensibilities 16, 20
Postmodernism and research 1, 9, 11, 14–20,
    105, 143, 154, 165, 166, 185, 189,
    191, 193
Postmodernist researchers 16, 17, 18, 105
Poverty, impoverished 2, 3, 4, 66, 138, 155, 170,
    171, 172
Power relationships between researchers and
    participants 3, 13, 14, 17, 18, 19, 25, 27,
    33, 34, 58, 60, 66, 80, 105, 106, 143, 179
Prison inmates/prisoners 38, 120, 178
A prison methodology 122
Prison research 38, 80, 97, 122
Privacy issues 27, 32, 35, 66, 77, 127, 169, 191
Private lives 6, 26, 59
Private lives/affairs 2, 4, 6, 8, 26, 36, 39, 45, 59,
    64, 68, 76, 88, 103, 107, 141, 186, 194
Professional danger 169
Prostitution 7, 8, 9, 60, 64, 66, 76, 83

Qualitative inquiry 10, 57, 96, 164, 184,
    186, 192
Qualitative research 1, 7–9, 13, 15, 16, 18, 24,
    27, 28, 31, 34, 36, 37, 47, 66, 72, 76, 86,
    88, 89, 100, 104, 116, 119, 128, 134, 141,
    165, 177, 190
Qualitative researchers 8, 37, 96, 122, 156, 165,
    182, 183, 189, 193
Queer participants 74, 154

Race 54, 58, 75, 154, 157, 172
Rape 4, 8, 54, 57, 70, 79, 85, 87, 108, 142, 171,
    177, 182
The rape model of research 57
Reality 10, 15, 62, 86, 92, 112, 120, 134, 137,
    164, 194
Recruitment 48–56
  Advertisements 49, 52, 53, 55, 56, 134
  Bulletin boards 56
  Chain referral method 49
  Community-academic collaborative
    approach 55
  Flyers 52, 53, 54, 134
  Gatekeepers 34, 51, 52
  Hanging out 50, 121

Recruitment, *cont.*
  Mixed methods of recruitment 53–56
  Peer leader researchers 52, 53
  Personal network 52, 53, 56
  Posters 53, 54, 55
  Snowball sampling method 48, 49, 50,
    53, 65, 98
  The word-of-mouth technique 49, 52, 55
Red-light areas 9, 77, 92, 110
Reflexive photography 145
Reflexivity 11, 12, 14, 17, 143, 193
  And feminism 11, 12, 17
  And postmodernism 17, 18
Refugees 4, 5, 38, 57, 144
Re-presentation of research findings 164–87
  Autobiography 168–69
  Autoethnography 18, 164, 166–69, 183, 191
  Ethnodrama 20, 133, 164, 176–78, 184, 191
  Performance and staged play 164, 172–74
  Performance ethnography 164, 174–76
  Performing street vendors 75, 175–76
  Poetic representation 178–82, 193
  Short story and fiction 164, 170–71
  Storytelling and public performance 164,
    173–74
  Theatre presentation 134, 174
  And the vulnerable researcher 164, 182–87
Requests from participants 13, 62
Research assistants as vulnerable researchers
  88–89, 93
Responsible researchers 20, 25, 32, 36, 59, 86,
  136, 154, 191
Rural people 77, 78, 104, 108, 152, 162

Schizophrenia 5, 107, 130, 134, 135, 174, 177
Secrecy/secret 5, 36, 48, 56, 76, 84, 121,
  127, 136
The seeing words – hearing feelings
    approach 177
Self-disclosure
  Of participants 27, 28, 29, 36, 38–39, 42
  Of researchers 13, 17, 27, 71, 72–74, 96, 193
Sensational journalism 185
The sensitive and vulnerable researchers,
  Authoritative voice 105
  Compathy phenomenon 82
  Dangerous situations of researchers 76, 77, 78,
    79, 81, 92, 169
  Difficulty with leaving the research field
    86, 87
  Emotional distress 83, 84, 85, 87, 90, 93
  Emotional experiences 9, 17, 71, 82–88, 89,
    90, 93, 187
  Emotional support 90, 91
  Emotional unprepareness 86–87
  Forming friendship with participants 86

The sensitive and vulnerable researchers, *cont.*
  Guilt feelings 26, 83, 86, 87
  Imprisonment of 79, 80
  Labour pains 9, 71, 82–88
  Legal dangers 79–81
  Managing of emotions 85–88
  Pain by proxy 82
  Personal safety 76, 77
  Physical dangers 78, 79, 85, 93
  Professional danger 169
  Risk and harm 71, 76–82, 85, 91, 92
  Safeguard the vulnerable researcher 71,
    91–93
  Safety issues 71, 76–82, 85, 91, 92
  Safety procedures 92–93
  Self-disclosure 13, 17, 27, 71, 72–74, 96, 193
  Self-indulgence 169, 183, 185
  Social locations and gendered experiences 71,
    74–76
  Support 71, 90–91
  Training in doing sensitive research 91
  And writing/reporting 18, 32, 36–37, 180,
    182–187
Sensitive research 1, 2, 5, 6, 7, 18, 20, 25, 26, 32,
    33, 36, 41, 45, 49, 56, 57, 64, 66, 67, 70,
    71, 72, 73, 74, 75, 79, 81, 83, 84, 85, 86,
    87, 89, 91, 93, 95, 97, 104, 108, 114, 118,
    122, 123, 128, 133, 159, 189, 190, 194
Sensitive researcher 1, 2, 6, 12, 18, 20, 21, 24, 25,
    26, 27, 31, 32, 33, 34, 35, 36, 37, 38, 44,
    45, 48, 60, 62, 64, 69, 72, 79, 82, 83, 87,
    96, 97, 102, 105, 116, 119, 129, 130, 131,
    133, 135, 138, 141, 151, 154, 157, 161,
    166, 171, 172, 173, 177, 178, 179, 180,
    182, 184, 185, 189, 190, 191, 192
The serious play of writing 166
Seriously injured people 104
Sex trade 4, 55, 56
Sex workers 3, 4, 5, 9, 10, 15, 55, 56, 58, 59,
    60, 64, 65, 68, 77, 81, 87, 89, 94, 110,
    121, 123
Sexual abuse 11, 28, 34, 40, 54, 57, 65, 73, 94,
    108, 142, 168
Sexual assault against women 57
Sexual encounters 31, 99
Sexual lives 98, 99
Sexual relations 31, 32, 39, 51
Sexual violence 11, 57, 142
Sexuality 31, 60, 74, 90, 97, 101, 107, 108, 116,
    124, 151, 157
Silenced 7, 12, 37, 113, 133, 143, 177,
    181, 183
Silent voices 4, 66, 87, 104, 121, 123, 126, 149,
    187, 190
Single mothers 4, 53, 180
Skepticism about research 4, 58, 73

Social class 14, 54, 74, 112, 126

Social control 6, 122

Social movement scholars 113

Social phenomena 119

Social reality 113, 114

Social science researchers 48, 154, 166, 168, 170, 184, 186, 191

Social stigma 3, 81, 82

Social structures 14, 99, 130, 132, 190

Social vulnerability 3

Socially sensitive research 5, 35, 39

Solicited diary 152, 153

Soul loss and soul calling ceremony 120

The Southern tradition of research 129

Speech with magical force 181

Spousal abuse 54, 65

Stigma/stigmatization 3, 26, 27, 32, 40, 45, 46, 81, 107, 124

Stigma contagion 81

Stigmatised illness 5, 124, 157, 159

Stigmatised people 3, 4, 5, 36, 37, 39, 56, 57, 81, 155, 191

The story of us 156

Storytelling 73, 111, 133, 156, 166

Street children 155, 156, 170

Street criminals 50, 53

Street sex workers 9, 10, 58, 60, 64, 66, 77, 94, 107

Street vendors 175–76

Structural transformation 129

Subjective experiences 7, 16, 72, 83, 107, 115, 169, 193

Subjugated knowledge 96

Subjugated voices 96

Subordination 3, 10

Substance abusers 8, 50

Sudanese refugee 52, 57

Suicide 29, 40, 43, 83, 177

Suspicions of researchers 31, 57, 58, 59, 64, 73, 158

Symbolic interactionist framework 112

Tabooed 4

Tearoom trade 31

Terminally ill people 4, 25, 31, 33, 192

Thai immigrant women 165

Theatre for social change 176

Theatre of the oppressed 172, 176

Thick description 121

Threat 2, 4, 5, 6, 38, 43, 48, 59, 65, 66, 68, 76, 77, 78, 79, 80, 83, 92, 93, 194

Tjilimi (women's camp) 136, 137

Traditional forms of report writing 20, 179

Traditional interviewing methods 95–116

  Focus groups 8, 12, 54, 58, 95, 104, 105–110, 124, 138, 158, 159, 162

Traditional interviewing methods, *cont.*

  In-depth interviews 12, 49, 54, 58, 87, 95, 96–100, 107, 119, 122, 124, 125, 134, 143, 148, 149, 151, 153, 157, 162, 192

  Intensive interview 96

  Oral/life history 12, 95, 111–16, 149, 153, 193

Traditional research 13, 132, 157, 171

Transcribers as vulnerable researchers 71, 88–90

Transgender 36, 81

Trauma 5, 29, 57, 125, 137, 150

Traumatic experiences 29, 30, 67, 82

Truth 15, 16, 85, 165, 170, 192, 193

The Tuskegee Syphilis Study 24

Undocumented immigrants 4, 64, 178

The Unfortunate Experiment 24

Unobtrusive researchers and emotional experiences 87

Unprivileged voices 113

Vicarious traumatization 82

Violence 4, 5, 38, 41, 42, 64, 66, 67, 91, 137, 172

A visual life-line project 149–50

Visualization of experience 176

Voices of marginalised research participants 7, 10, 11, 16, 18, 19, 20, 21, 36, 60, 61, 66, 87, 89, 90, 93, 96, 100, 104, 105, 106, 111, 113, 123, 145, 160, 178, 189, 191

Vulnerable people 1, 2, 4, 6, 7, 9, 12, 15, 17, 20, 21, 23, 24, 25, 26, 27, 29, 30, 31, 32, 33, 34, 35, 36, 37, 42, 45, 47, 48, 51, 52, 57, 61, 68, 71, 82, 83, 86, 87, 90, 91, 93, 95, 96, 101, 102, 104, 105, 108, 113, 116, 118, 119, 120, 127, 130, 135, 137, 138, 140, 141, 143, 150, 151, 156, 159, 161, 162, 165, 170, 176, 182, 183, 185, 187, 189, 190, 191, 192, 194

Vulnerable research participants 7, 23, 25, 32, 34, 47–70, 87, 90, 141, 161, 173

  Anonymity 28, 29, 32, 37, 39, 158, 159, 191

  Compensation and incentives 30, 50, 47, 62–66

  Emotional distressed 5, 29, 32, 39, 40, 42, 45, 67, 68, 82, 88, 89, 91, 103, 104, 105, 142, 148, 159, 168, 173, 174, 177

  Gaining access 47, 48–56, 58, 69, 106, 127

  Procedural sensibilities 47–70

  Reciprocity and respect 13, 47, 48, 59–62, 63, 69, 73, 157

  Referrals to support 42, 60, 62, 65, 67

  Reluctance to participate in research 4, 5, 48, 58, 103, 159

  Rights 2, 24, 33, 39, 43, 44, 60, 132

  Risk and harm 23, 24, 33, 37–41

Vulnerable research participants, *cont.*
  Safety issues 7, 23, 25, 36, 37–41, 42, 44, 69,
      87, 99, 101, 191
  Sensitivity to the needs and lives 47, 48,
      66–69
  Strategies to protect research participants 2,
      23, 41–44
  Therapeutic experience of participating in
      research 29–30, 142, 173
  Trust and rapport 8, 13, 47, 48, 49, 56–59, 69,
      72, 74, 75, 98, 124, 193
  Unintentional danger 37, 38

Western Australia's Great Sandy Desert 131, 136
Wife battering 75

Women in outlaw motorcycle gangs
      122, 123
Women who had received clemency 49,
      51, 81
Women with learning disabilities 11,
      34, 142
Women's Yawulya 137
The World Medical Association Declaration of
      Helsinki Agreement 24

The Yarrahah Men's Group 135
Young Black Americans 182
Young men and crime 53, 68, 78
Young people and risky behaviour 157,
      159, 160